Feminist Thought

———— ■ ————

SECOND EDITION

Feminist Thought

■

A More Comprehensive Introduction

Rosemarie Putnam Tong

Davidson College

Westview Press
A Member of the Perseus Books Group

Copyright © 1998 by Westview Press, A Member of the Perseus Books Group

Published in 1998 in the United States of America by Westview Press, 5500 Central Avenue, Boulder, Colorado 80301-2877, and in the United Kingdom by Westview Press, 12 Hid's Copse Road, Cumnor Hill, Oxford OX2 9JJ

Library of Congress Cataloging-in-Publication Data
Tong, Rosemarie Putnam.
    Feminist thought : a more comprehensive introduction / Rosemarie Putnam Tong.
—2nd ed.
        p.   cm.
    Includes bibliographical references and index.
    ISBN 0-8133-3332-6 (hardcover). — ISBN 0-8133-3295-8 (pbk.)
    1. Feminist theory.   I. Title.
HQ1206.T65   1998
305.42'01—dc21   97-46430
                                                                                                            CIP

The paper used in this publication meets the requirements of the American National Standard for Permanence of Paper for Printed Library Materials Z39.48-1984.

10   9   8   7

Contents

Acknowledgments

As ANYONE WHO HAS EVER WRITTEN a book knows, it is not a solo project. Rather, it is a collaborative effort. My only fear is that I will fail to say a public thank-you to one of the persons who helped bring this book to term.

First, I wish to thank Toni Schossler and Kristin Garris for the long hours they spent researching, editing, and typing drafts of various parts of this book. These two young women are gifted and generous individuals who will make important contributions of their own to society. Toni is entering the Ph.D. program in medical humanities at the Institute for Medical Humanities, University of Texas Medical Branch, Galveston, and Kristin has completed her M.A. in religious studies at the University of Virginia.

Second, I want to thank Frances Alexander for all her help typing this manuscript. Without her assistance this book would never have seen the dawn of day. I also want to thank Jean Newman, my administrative assistant for picking up the slack on this project. Jean helped me through many of the most frantic days.

I also want to thank Catherine Pusateri at Westview Press. She is a one-woman cheering team who always encouraged and supported me. In my estimation, she is the perfect editor for someone like me. I also want to thank my able copy editor, Alice Colwell, and the anonymous reviewers who offered insightful comments and critiques.

Finally, I want to thank Davidson College for its support of this project and my husband, Jerry Putnam, for lending me a helping hand, a sympathetic ear, and a strong shoulder as I worked on this book. He bore the brunt of my bad writing days, and he did so with good humor and constant patience.

Rosemarie Putnam Tong

Introduction:
The Diversity of
Feminist Thinking

SINCE WRITING MY FIRST INTRODUCTION to feminist thought nearly a decade ago, I have become increasingly convinced that much of feminist thought resists categorization, especially categorization based on the "fathers'" labels. Believe me, it would be a tragedy if these labels persuaded readers that liberal feminism is only a variation on John Stuart Mill's thoughts, Marxist-socialist feminism only an improvement on Karl Marx's and Friedrich Engels's writings, psychoanalytic feminism only an addendum to Sigmund Freud's speculations, existentialist feminism only a further articulation of Jean-Paul Sartre's ideas, postmodern feminism only a recapitulation of Jacques Lacan's and Jacques Derrida's musings. It would also be a misfortune if these labels detracted from the efforts of radical feminists or ecofeminists, for example, to do philosophy de novo without relying on any patriarch's thought—a daunting, even perilous task, but one that has much to recommend it.

Yet despite the very real problems that come with categorizing thinkers as "x" or "y" or "z," feminist thought is old enough to have a history complete with its own set of labels: "liberal," "radical (libertarian or cultural)," "Marxist-socialist," "psychoanalytic," "existentialist," "postmodern," "multicultural and global," and "ecological." No doubt feminist thought will eventually shed these labels for others that better express its intellectual and political commitments to women. For now, however, feminist thought's old labels remain useful. They signal to the broader public that feminism is not a monolithic ideology, that all feminists do not think alike, and that, like all other time-honored modes of thinking, feminist thought has a past as well as a present and a future. Feminist thought's old labels also serve as useful teaching tools. They help mark the range of different approaches, perspectives, and frameworks a variety of feminists have

1

used to shape both their explanations for women's oppression and their proposed solutions for its elimination.

Because so much of contemporary feminist theory defines itself in reaction against traditional liberal feminism, liberalism is the obvious place to begin a survey of feminist thought. This perspective received its classic formulation in Mary Wollstonecraft's *Vindication of the Rights of Woman*,[1] John Stuart Mill's "Subjection of Women,"[2] and the nineteenth-century woman's suffrage movement. Its main thrust, an emphasis still felt in contemporary groups such as the National Organization for Women (NOW), is that female subordination is rooted in a set of customary and legal constraints blocking women's entrance to and success in the so-called public world. Because society has the false belief that women are by nature less intellectually and physically capable than men, it excludes women from the academy, the forum, and the marketplace. As a result of this policy of exclusion, the true potential of many women goes unfulfilled. If it should happen that when women and men are given the same educational opportunities and civil rights, few women achieve eminence in the sciences, arts, and professions, then so be it. Gender justice, insist liberal feminists, requires us, first, to make the rules of the game fair and, second, to make certain none of the runners in the race for society's goods and services is systematically disadvantaged; gender justice does not also require us to give prizes to the losers as well as the winners.

But is the liberal feminist program drastic and dramatic enough to completely undo women's oppression? Radical feminists think not. They claim the patriarchal system is characterized by power, dominance, hierarchy, and competition. It cannot be reformed but only ripped out root and branch. It is not just patriarchy's legal and political structures that must be overturned on the way to women's liberation. Its social and cultural institutions (especially the family, the church, and the academy) must also be uprooted.

When I wrote the first edition of this book, I was both impressed and overwhelmed by the diverse range of views within the radical feminist community. Although all radical feminists focus on sex, gender, and reproduction as the locus for the development of feminist thought,[3] some of them favor so-called androgyny, stress the pleasures of all kinds of sex (heterosexual, lesbian, or autoerotic), and view as unmitigated blessings for women not only the old reproduction-controlling technologies but also the new reproduction-assisting technologies. In contrast, other radical feminists reject androgyny; emphasize the dangers of sex, especially heterosexual sex; and regard as harmful to women the new reproduction-assisting technologies and, for the most part, the old reproduction-controlling technologies. Not until I read the works of Linda Alcoff, Ann Ferguson, and Alice Echols[4] more carefully did I realize there were at least two kinds of radical feminists, whom I have respectively labeled in this edition "radical-libertarian feminists" and "radical-cultural feminists."

With respect to gender-related issues, radical-libertarian feminists tend to reason that if, to their own detriment, men are permitted to exhibit masculine characteristics only and if, to their own detriment, women are required to exhibit feminine characteristics only, then the solution to this problem is to *permit* each and every person to be androgynous—to exhibit a full range of masculine *and* feminine qualities. Men should be permitted to explore their feminine dimensions and women their masculine ones. No human being should be forbidden the sense of wholeness that comes from combining his or her masculine and feminine dimensions.

Disagreeing with radical-libertarian feminists that a turn to androgyny is a liberation strategy for women, radical-cultural feminists argue against this move in one of three ways. Some anti-androgynists maintain the problem is not femininity in and of itself but rather the low value patriarchy assigns to feminine qualities such as "gentleness, modesty, humility, supportiveness, empathy, compassionateness, tenderness, nurturance, intuitiveness, sensitivity, unselfishness," and the high value it assigns to masculine qualities such as "assertiveness, aggressiveness, hardiness, rationality or the ability to think logically, abstractly and analytically, ability to control emotion."[5] They claim if society can learn to value the feminine as much as the masculine, women's oppression will be a bad memory. Other anti-androgynists disagree, insisting femininity *is* the problem because it has been constructed by men for patriarchal purposes. In order to be liberated, women must give new gynocentric meanings to femininity. Femininity should no longer be understood as those traits that deviate from masculinity. On the contrary, femininity should be understood as a way of being that needs no reference point external to it. Still other anti-androgynists, reverting to a "nature theory," argue that despite patriarchy's imposition of a false, or unauthentic, *feminine* nature upon women, many women have nonetheless unearthed their true, or authentic, *female* nature. Full personal freedom for a woman consists, then, in her ability to renounce her false feminine self in favor of her true female self.

As difficult as it is fully to reflect the range of radical feminist thought on gender, it is even more difficult to do so with respect to sexuality. Radical-libertarian feminists argue that no specific kind of sexual experience should be prescribed as *the best* kind for a liberated woman.[6] Each and every woman should be encouraged to experiment sexually with herself, other women, and men. As dangerous as heterosexuality is for a woman within a patriarchal society—as difficult as it can be for a woman to know when she truly wants to say yes to a man's sexual advances, for example—she must feel free to follow the lead of her own desires.

Radical-cultural feminists disagree. They stress that through pornography, prostitution, sexual harassment, rape, and woman battering,[7] through foot binding, suttee, purdah, clitoridectomy, witch burning, and gynecology,[8] men have controlled women's sexuality for male pleasure. Thus, in order to be liberated, women must escape the confines of heterosexuality and create an exclusively female sexuality through celibacy, autoeroticism, or lesbianism.[9] Alone or with other women, a woman can discover the true pleasure of sex.

Radical feminist thought is as diverse on issues related to reproduction as it is on matters related to sexuality. Radical-libertarian feminists claim biological motherhood drains women physically and psychologically.[10] Women should be free, they say, to use the old reproduction-controlling technologies and the new reproduction-assisting technologies on their own terms—to prevent or terminate unwanted pregnancies or, alternatively, to enable them to have children when they want them (premenopausally or postmenopausally), how they want them (in their own womb or that of another woman), and with whom they want them (a man, a woman, or alone). Some radical-libertarian feminists go farther than this, however. They look forward to the day when ectogenesis (extracorporeal gestation in an artificial placenta) entirely replaces the natural process of pregnancy. In contrast to radical-libertarian feminists, radical-cultural feminists claim biological motherhood is the ultimate source of woman's power.[11] It is women who determine whether the human species continues—whether there is life or no life. Women must guard and celebrate this life-giving power, for without it men will have even less respect and use for women than they have now.[12]

Somewhat unconvinced by the liberal and radical feminist agendas for women's liberation, Marxist and socialist feminists claim it is impossible for anyone, especially women, to achieve true freedom in a class-based society, where the wealth produced by the powerless many ends up in the hands of the powerful few. With Friedrich Engels,[13] Marxist and socialist feminists insist women's oppression originated in the introduction of private property, an institution that obliterated whatever equality of community humans had previously enjoyed. Private ownership of the means of production by relatively few persons, originally all male, inaugurated a class system whose contemporary manifestations are corporate capitalism and imperialism. Reflection on this state of affairs suggests that capitalism itself, not just the larger social rules that privilege men over women, is the cause of women's oppression. If all women—rather than the "exceptional" ones alone—are ever to be liberated, the capitalist system must be replaced by a socialist system in which the means of production will belong to one and all. No longer economically dependent on men, women will be just as free as men are.

Socialist feminists agree with Marxist feminists that *capitalism* is the source of women's oppression, and with radical feminists that *patriarchy* is the source of women's oppression. As they see it, therefore, the way to end women's oppression is to kill the two-headed beast of capitalist patriarchy or patriarchal capitalism (take your pick). Following this outlook, Juliet Mitchell claimed in *Woman's Estate* that women's condition is overdetermined by the structures of production (as Marxist feminists think), reproduction and sexuality (as radical feminists believe), and the socialization of children (as liberal feminists argue).[14] Woman's status and function in all of these structures must change if she is to achieve anything approximating full liberation.

Another powerful attempt to achieve a synthesis between Marxist and radical feminist thought has been made by Alison Jaggar. Conceding that all feminist perspectives recognize the conflicting demands made on women as wives, mothers, daughters, lovers, and workers,[15] Jaggar insisted that socialist feminism is unique because of its concerted effort to interrelate the myriad forms of women's oppression. Jaggar used the unifying concept of alienation to explain how, under capitalism, everything (work, sex, play) and everyone (family, friend) that could be a source of woman's integration as a person instead becomes a cause of her disintegration. Like Mitchell, Jaggar insisted that there are only complex explanations for female subordination. Once again, the emphasis of socialist feminism is on unity and integration both in the sense of interrelating all aspects of women's lives and in the sense of producing a unified feminist theory.

To the degree that liberal, radical, and Marxist-socialist feminists focus on the macrocosm (patriarchy or capitalism) in their respective explanations of women's oppression, psychoanalytic and gender feminists retreat to the microcosm of the individual, claiming the roots of women's oppression are embedded deep in her psyche. For psychoanalytic feminists, a focus on sexuality's role in the oppression of women arises out of Freudian theory. Originally, in the so-called pre-Oedipal stage, all infants are symbiotically attached to their mothers, whom they perceive as omnipotent. The mother-infant relationship is an ambivalent one, however, because the mother at times gives too much—her presence overwhelms— and at other times gives too little—her absence disappoints. The pre-Oedipal stage ends with the so-called Oedipus complex, the process by which the boy gives up his first love object, his mother, in order to escape castration at the hands of the father. As a result of submitting his id (desires) to the superego (collective social conscience), the boy is fully integrated into culture. Together with his father, he will rule over nature and woman, both of whom supposedly contain a similarly irrational power. In contrast to the boy, the girl, who has no penis to lose, separates slowly from her first love object, her mother. As a result, the girl's integration into culture is incomplete. She exists at the periphery of culture as the one who does not rule but is ruled, largely because, as Dorothy Dinnerstein suggested, she fears her own power.[16]

Because the Oedipus complex is the root of male rule, or patriarchy, some psychoanalytic feminists speculate it is nothing more than the product of men's imagination—a psychic trap that everyone, especially women, should try to escape. Others object that unless we are prepared for reentry into a chaotic state of nature, we must accept some version of the Oedipus complex as the experience that integrates the individual into society. In accepting *some* version of the Oedipus complex, Sherry Ortner noted, we need not accept the *Freudian* version, according to which authority, autonomy, and universalism are labeled "male," whereas love, dependence, and particularism are labeled "female."[17] These labels, meant to privilege that which is male over that which is female, are not essential to the Oedipus complex. Rather, they are simply the consequences of a child's actual experience with men and women. As Ortner saw it, dual parenting (as recommended also by Dorothy Dinnerstein and Nancy Chodorow) and dual participation in the workforce would change the gender valences of the Oedipus complex.[18] Authority, autonomy, and universalism would no longer be the exclusive property of men; love, dependence, and particularism would no longer be the exclusive property of women.

In the first edition of this book, I did not make a distinction I stress in this edition. There are, I believe, important differences between psychoanalytic feminists who focus on pre-Oedipal and Oedipal themes on the one hand and so-called gender feminists who focus on the virtues and values associated with femininity on the other hand. Although gender feminists as well as psychoanalytic feminists probe women's psyches, gender feminists like Carol Gilligan and Nel Noddings also pursue the relationship between women's psychology and morality. They ask whether feminine caring or masculine justice is the true path to human goodness and whether the key to all human beings' liberation is to embrace the values and virtues traditionally associated with women. For Gilligan and Noddings, femininity is women's blessing, not women's burden.

Looking into women's psyches more deeply than even the psychoanalytic and gender feminists, Simone de Beauvoir provided an ontological-existential explanation for women's oppression. In *The Second Sex*, one of the key theoretical texts of twentieth-century feminism,[19] she argued that woman is oppressed by virtue of her otherness. Woman is the other because she is not-man. Man is the free, self-determining being who defines the meaning of his existence; woman is the other, the object whose meaning is determined for her. If woman is to become a self, a subject, she must, like man, transcend the definitions, labels, and essences limiting her existence. She must make herself be whatever she wants to be.

Postmodern feminists take de Beauvoir's understanding of otherness and turn it on its head. Woman is still the other, but rather than interpreting this condition as something to be rejected, postmodern feminists embrace it. They claim woman's otherness enables individual women to stand back and criticize the norms, values, and practices that the dominant male culture (patriarchy) seeks to impose on everyone, particularly those who live on its periphery. Thus, otherness, for all of its associations with being excluded, shunned, rejected, unwanted, abandoned, and marginalized, has its advantages. It is a way of existing that allows for change and difference. Women are not unitary selves, essences to be defined and then ossified. On the contrary, women are free spirits.

Multicultural and global feminists agree with postmodern feminists that the so-called self is fragmented, or at least divided. However, for multicultural and global feminists, the roots of this fragmentation are cultural and national rather than sexual and literary. Within the United States, for example, a Hispanic woman is likely to experience herself as a *self* within her own family and friendship circles but as the *other* outside of her home boundaries. Writing from the vantage point of an Argentinean woman who has lived in the United States for several years, philosopher Maria Lugones gave voice to what she means by "we" (namely, other Hispanic women) and "you" (namely, white/Anglo women). She wrote that although Hispanics have to participate in the Anglo world, Anglos do not have to participate in the Hispanic world. An Anglo woman can go to a Hispanic neighborhood for a church festival, for example, and if she finds the rituals and music overwhelming, she can simply get in her car, drive home, and forget the evening. There is no way, however, that a Hispanic woman can escape Anglo culture so easily, for the dominant culture sets the basic parameters for her survival as one of its minority members.

Global feminists also have a schizophrenic sense of self. In their estimation, European and North American colonizers robbed the people of many developing nations not only of their land and resources but also of their self-identities. Prior to being overrun by white imperialists, for example, the peoples of Africa did not think of themselves first and foremost as "black." On the contrary, they thought of themselves as linguistically and culturally unique groups of people whose skin color, by no means identical throughout continental Africa, played only a small role in their self-definition. It was the colonizers who bestowed a "black" identity on their subjects, instructing them that to be black was "bad," whereas to be white was "good."

To the extent that the peoples of Africa internalized the colonists' view of them as uncivilized barbarians, to that same degree did this artificially constructed and systematically imposed "self-conception" do violence to their original, positive self-conceptions. To make matters worse, the longer the colonists remained in power, the more difficult it became for their subjects not to aspire to "whiteness." Realizing that such an aspiration threatened their people's souls, many indigenous African leaders rallied their kith and kin to rebel against white colonizers' ideas and armies. But even when such rebellions were successful politically, they were not always successful culturally. Once a mind is "colonized," it is very difficult to liberate it.

Although most schools of feminist thought favor a relational view of the self, ecofeminists offer the broadest and also the most demanding conception of the self's relationship to the other. According to ecofeminists, we are connected not only to each other but also to the nonhuman world: animal and even vegetative. Unfortunately, we do not always acknowledge our responsibilities to each other, let alone to the nonhuman world. As a result, we deplete the world's natural resources with our machines, pollute the environment with our toxic fumes, and stockpile weapons of total destruction. In so doing, we delude ourselves that we are controlling nature and enhancing ourselves. In point of fact, said ecofeminist Ynestra King, nature is already rebelling, and each day the human self is impoverished as yet another forest is "detreed" and yet another animal species is extinguished.[20] The only way not to destroy ourselves, insist ecofeminists, is to strengthen our relationships to each other and the nonhuman world.

Clearly, it is a major challenge to contemporary feminism to reconcile the pressures for diversity and difference with those for integration and commonality. Fortunately, contemporary feminists do not shrink from this challenge. I am particularly encouraged and delighted by developments in multicultural, global, and ecofeminism. It seems we are on the verge of truly understanding the sources of women's oppression, how sexism is *and* is not related to all the other isms that plague human beings (racism, classism, ageism, ethnocentrism, ableism, heterosexism, and naturism).

I have tried as much as possible to discuss the weaknesses as well as the strengths of each of the feminist perspectives presented here. In so doing, I have aimed not so much at *neutrality* as I have at *respect*, since each feminist approach has made a rich and lasting contribution to feminist thought. Readers looking for one winning view at the end of this book, a champion left standing after an intellectual free-for-all, will be disappointed. Although all of these perspectives cannot be equally correct, and my own views and preferences will show along the way, there is no need here for a definitive final say. There is always, and there will be here, room for growth, improvement, reconsideration, expansion—for all those intellectual processes that free us from the authoritarian trap of having to know it all.

Even though throughout this book I aim to speak on behalf of women, in so doing I remain painfully aware that I do not speak for "woman," for feminists, or for anybody besides myself. I speak out of a specific background of experience, as do we all, and I have tried very hard to avoid either accepting or rejecting an analysis simply because it resonates or fails to resonate with my own ideas and experiences. Whether I have largely succeeded or mostly failed in this attempt is something I must leave up to my readers, however.

Finally, although this introduction to feminist thought is more comprehensive than my introduction of ten years ago, it is still partial, provisional, and suggestive in nature. Anyone steeped in feminist theory and practice will immediately recognize this fact. Limitations of time and space often forced me to sacrifice depth and/or breadth, and my own scholarly background and interests undoubtedly imposed other limitations. I hope that my shortcomings will spur others to do the job better someday. But my overriding hope is that this book will prompt its readers to think themselves into the fullness of being feminism intends.

CHAPTER ONE

—————————— ■ ——————————

Liberal Feminism

LIBERALISM, THE SCHOOL OF POLITICAL thought from which liberal feminism has evolved, is in the process of reconceptualizing, reconsidering, and restructuring itself,[1] which makes it difficult to determine the status of liberal feminist thought. If we wish to gauge the accuracy of Susan Wendell's provocative claim that liberal feminism has largely outgrown its original base,[2] then we must survey the state of contemporary liberal thought and decide for ourselves whether liberal rhetoric does in fact resonate with feminist oratory.

The Eighteenth- and Nineteenth-Century Roots of Liberal Feminism

Alison Jaggar, in *Feminist Politics and Human Nature*,[3] observed that liberal political thought holds a conception of human nature that locates our uniqueness as human persons in our capacity for rationality. The belief that reason distinguishes us from other creatures is relatively uninformative, so liberals have attempted to define reason in various ways, stressing either its *moral* aspects or its *prudential* aspects. When reason is defined as the ability to comprehend the rational principles of morality, then the value of individual autonomy is stressed. In contrast, when reason is defined as the ability to determine the best means to achieve some desired end, then the value of self-fulfillment is stressed.[4]

Whether liberals define reason largely in moral or prudential terms, they nevertheless concur that a just society allows individuals to exercise their autonomy and to fulfill themselves. The "right," liberals assert, must be given priority over the "good."[5] In other words, our whole system of individual rights is justified because these rights constitute a framework within which we can all choose our own separate goods, provided we do

10

not deprive others of theirs. Such a priority defends religious freedom, for example, neither on the grounds that it will increase the general welfare nor on the grounds that a godly life is inherently worthier than a godless one, but simply on the grounds that people have a right to practice their own brand of spirituality. The same holds for all those rights we generally identify as fundamental.

The proviso that the right takes priority over the good complicates construction of the just society. For if it is true, as most liberals claim, that resources are limited and each individual, even when restrained by altruism,[6] has an interest in securing as many available resources as possible, then it will be a challenge to create political, economic, and social institutions that maximize the individual's freedom without jeopardizing the community's welfare.

When it comes to state interventions in the private sphere (family or domestic society),[7] liberals agree the less we see of Big Brother in our bedrooms, bathrooms, kitchens, recreation rooms, and nurseries, the better. We all need places where we can, among family and friends, shed our public personae and become our "real" selves. When it comes to state intervention in the public sphere (civil or political society),[8] however, a difference of opinion emerges between so-called classical, or libertarian, liberals on the one hand, and so-called welfare, or egalitarian, liberals on the other.[9]

For classical liberals, the ideal state protects civil liberties (for example, property rights, voting rights, freedom of speech, freedom of religion, freedom of association) and, instead of interfering with the free market, simply provides all individuals with an equal opportunity to determine their own accumulations within that market. For welfare liberals, in contrast, the ideal state focuses on economic justice rather than on civil liberties. As this latter group of liberals sees it, individuals enter the market with differences based on initial advantage, inherent talent, and sheer luck. At times these differences are so great that some individuals cannot take their fair share of what the market has to offer unless some adjustments are made to offset their liabilities. Because of this perceived state of affairs, welfare liberals call for government interventions in the economy such as legal services, school loans, food stamps, low-cost housing, Medicaid, Medicare, Social Security, and Aid to Families with Dependent Children so that the market does not perpetuate or otherwise solidify huge inequalities.

Although both classical-liberal and welfare-liberal streams of thought appear in liberal feminist thought, contemporary liberal feminists seem to favor welfare liberalism. In fact, when Susan Wendell (not a liberal feminist) described contemporary liberal feminist thought, she stressed it is "committed to major economic re-organization and considerable redistribution of wealth, since one of the modern political goals most closely associated with liberal feminism is equality of opportunity, which would undoubtedly require and lead to both."[10] I leave it to readers to decide for themselves whether Wendell's understanding of contemporary liberal feminist thought is as sound as I believe it to be.

Since it is nearly impossible to discuss all liberal feminist thinkers, movements, and organizations in an introductory book, I have decided to focus only on Mary Wollstonecraft, John Stuart Mill, Harriet Taylor (Mill), the woman's suffrage movement in the United States, Betty Friedan, and the National Organization for Women. My aim is to convince readers that, for all its shortcomings, the overall goal of liberal feminism is to create "a just and compassionate society in which freedom flourishes."[11] Only in such a society can women as well as men thrive.

Liberal Feminist Thought in the Eighteenth Century: Equal Education

Mary Wollstonecraft wrote at a time (1759–1799) when the economic and social position of European women was in decline. Up until the eighteenth century, productive work (work that generated an income from which a family could live) had been done in and around the family home by women as well as men. But then the forces of industrial capitalism began to draw labor out of the private home and into the public workplace. At first this process of industrialization moved slowly and unevenly, leaving its strongest impact on married, bourgeois women. These women were the first to find themselves left at home with little productive work to do. Married to relatively wealthy professional and entrepreneurial men, these women had no incentive to work productively outside the home or, in those cases where they had several servants, even "nonproductively" inside it.[12]

In reading A Vindication of the Rights of Woman,[13] we see how affluence indeed worked against these eighteenth-century, married, bourgeois women. Wollstonecraft compared such "privileged" women (whom she hoped to inspire to a fully human mode of existence) to members of "the feathered race," birds confined to cages who have nothing to do but plume themselves and "stalk with mock majesty from perch to perch."[14] Middle-class ladies were, in Wollstonecraft's estimation, "kept" women who sacrificed health, liberty, and virtue for whatever prestige, pleasure, and power their husbands could provide. Because these women were not allowed to exercise outdoors lest they tan their lily-white skin, they lacked healthy bodies. Because they were not permitted to make their own decisions, they lacked liberty. And because they were discouraged from developing their powers of reason—given that a great premium was placed on indulging self and gratifying others, especially men and children—they lacked virtue.

Although Wollstonecraft did not use terms such as "socially constructed gender roles," she denied that women are, by nature, more pleasure seeking and pleasure giving than men. She reasoned that if men were confined to the same cages that women find themselves locked in, they would develop the same characters.[15] Denied the chance to develop their rational powers, to become moral persons with concerns, causes, and commitments beyond personal pleasure, men, like women, would become overly "emotional," a term Wollstonecraft tended to associate with hypersensitivity, extreme narcissism, and excessive self-indulgence.

Given her generally negative assessment of emotion and the extraordinarily high premium she placed on reason as the capacity distinguishing human beings from animals, it is no wonder Wollstonecraft abhorred Jean-Jacques Rousseau's *Emile*.[16] In this classic of educational philosophy, Rousseau portrayed the development of rationality as the most important educational goal for boys but not for girls. Rousseau was committed to sexual dimorphism, the view that "rational man" is the perfect complement for "emotional woman," and vice versa.[17] As he saw it, men should be educated in virtues such as courage, temperance, justice, and fortitude, whereas women should be educated in virtues such as patience, docility, good humor, and flexibility. Thus, Rousseau's ideal male student, Emile, studies the humanities, the social sciences, and the natural sciences, whereas Rousseau's ideal female student, Sophie, dabbles in music, art, fiction, and poetry while refining her homemaking skills. Rousseau hoped sharpening Emile's mental capacities and limiting Sophie's would make Emile a self-governing citizen and a dutiful paterfamilias and Sophie an understanding, responsive wife and a caring, loving mother.

Wollstonecraft agreed with Rousseau's projections for Emile but not with his projections for Sophie. Drawing upon her familiarity with middle-class ladies, she predicted that fed a steady diet of "novels, music, poetry, and gallantry," Sophie would become a detriment rather than a complement to her husband, a creature of bad sensibility rather than good sense.[18] Her hormones surging, her passions erupting, her emotions churning, Sophie would show no sense in performing her wifely and, especially, motherly duties.

Wollstonecraft's cure for Sophie was to let her, like Emile, be provided with the kind of education that permits people to develop their rational and moral capacities, their full human potential. Sometimes Wollstonecraft phrased her argument in favor of educational parity in utilitarian terms. She claimed that unlike emotional and dependent women, who routinely shirk their domestic duties and indulge their carnal desires, rational and independent women will tend to be "observant daughters," "affectionate sisters," "faithful wives," and "reasonable mothers."[19] The truly educated woman will be a major contributor to society's welfare. Rather than wasting her time and energy on idle entertainments, she will manage her household—especially her children—"properly."[20]

Not all of Wollstonecraft's arguments on behalf of educational parity were utilitarian, however. In fact, the view she usually took in *A Vindication of the Rights of Woman* was remarkably akin to Immanuel Kant's view in the *Groundwork of the Metaphysic of Morals*—namely, that unless a person acts autonomously, he or she is acting as less than a fully human person.[21] Wollstonecraft insisted if rationality is the capacity distinguishing human beings from animals, then unless females are brute animals (a description most men refuse to apply to their own mothers, wives, and daughters), women as well as men have this capacity. Thus, society owes girls the same education as boys simply because all human beings deserve an equal chance to develop their rational and moral capacities so they can achieve full personhood.

Again and again, Wollstonecraft celebrated reason, usually at the expense of emotion. As Jane Roland Martin said, "In making her case for the rights of women . . . [Wollstonecraft] presents us with an ideal of female education that gives pride of place to traits traditionally associated with males at the expense of others traditionally associated with females."[22] It did not occur to Wollstonecraft to question the value of these traditional male traits. Nor did it occur to her to blame children's lack of virtue on their absentee fathers who should be summoned, in her view, only when "chastisement" is necessary.[23] On the contrary, she simply assumed traditional male traits were "good," and women—not men—were the ones who were rationally and morally deficient.

Throughout the pages of *A Vindication of the Rights of Woman*, Wollstonecraft urged women to become autonomous decisionmakers; but over and beyond insisting that the path to autonomy goes through the academy, she provided women with little in the way of concrete guidance.[24] Although Wollstonecraft considered women's autonomy might depend on women's economic and political independence from men, she decided *well-educated* women did not need to be economically self-sufficient or politically active in order to be autonomous. In fact, Wollstonecraft dismissed the woman's suffrage movement as a waste of time, since in her estimation the whole system of legal representation was merely a "convenient handle for despotism."[25]

Despite the limitations of her analysis, Wollstonecraft did present a vision of a woman strong in mind and body, who is not a slave to her passions, her husband, or her children. For Wollstonecraft, the ideal woman is less interested in fulfilling herself—if by self-fulfillment is meant any sort of pandering to duty-distracting desires—than in exercising self-control.[26] In order to liberate herself from the oppressive roles of emotional cripple, petty shrew, and narcissistic sex object, a woman must obey the commands of reason and discharge her wifely and motherly duties faithfully.

What Wollstonecraft most wanted for woman is personhood. Woman is not, she asserted, the "toy of man, his rattle," which "must jingle in his ears whenever, dismissing reason, he chooses to be amused."[27] In other words, woman is not a "mere means," or instrument, to someone else's happiness or perfection. Rather, woman is an "end," a rational agent whose dignity consists in having the capacity for self-determination.[28] To treat someone as a mere means is to treat her as less than a person, as someone who exists not for herself but as an appendage to someone else. So, for example, if a husband treats his wife as no more than a pretty indoor plant, he treats her as an object that he nurtures merely as a means to his own delight. Similarly, if a woman lets herself so be treated, she lets herself be treated in ways that do not accord with her status as a full human person. Rather than assuming responsibility for her own development and growing into a mighty redwood, she forsakes her freedom and lets others shape her into a stunted bonsai tree. No woman, insisted Wollstonecraft, should permit such violence to be done to her.

Liberal Feminist Thought in the Nineteenth Century:
Equal Political Rights and Economic Opportunities

Writing approximately one hundred years later, John Stuart Mill and Harriet Taylor (Mill) joined Wollstonecraft in celebrating rationality. But they conceived of rationality not only morally, as autonomous decisionmaking, but also prudentially, as self-fulfillment or using your head to get what you want. That their understanding of rationality should differ from the beliefs of Wollstonecraft is not surprising. Unlike Wollstonecraft, both Mill and Taylor claimed the ordinary way to maximize aggregate utility (happiness/pleasure) is to permit individuals to pursue whatever they desire, provided they do not hinder or obstruct each other in the process. Mill and Taylor also departed from Wollstonecraft in insisting if society is to achieve sexual equality, or gender justice, then it must provide women with the same political rights and economic opportunities as well as the same education that men enjoy.

Like Mary Wollstonecraft, who twice attempted suicide, refused marriage until late in life, and had a child out of wedlock, John Stuart Mill and Harriet Taylor led fairly unconventional lives. They met in 1830 when Harriet Taylor was already married to John Taylor and was the mother of two sons (a third child, Helen, would be born later). Harriet Taylor and Mill were immediately attracted to each other, both intellectually and emotionally, and they carried on a close, arguably platonic relationship for twenty years, until the death of John Taylor, whereupon they married. During the years before her husband died, Harriet Taylor and Mill routinely saw each other for dinner and frequently spent weekends together along the English coast. John Taylor agreed to this arrangement in return for the "external formality" of Harriet residing "as his wife in his house."[29]

Due to their unorthodox bargain with John Taylor, Harriet Taylor and Mill found the time to author, separately and conjointly, several essays on sexual equality. Scholarly debate concerning who deserves credit for which specific ideas in the essays they authored and coauthored continues. However, it is generally agreed that Taylor and Mill coauthored "Early Essays on Marriage and Divorce" (1832), that Taylor wrote the "Enfranchisement of Women" (1851), and that Mill wrote "The Subjection of Women" (1869). As we shall see, the question of these works' authorship is significant because Taylor's views frequently diverged from Mill's.

Given their personal situation, Mill and Taylor's focus on subjects such as marriage and divorce is not surprising. Far from subscribing to a common train of thought, however, Mill and Taylor often disagreed about how to serve women's and children's best interests. Because she accepted the traditional view that maternal ties are stronger than paternal ties, Taylor simply assumed the mother would be the one to rear the children to adulthood in the event of divorce. Thus, she cautioned women to have few children. In contrast, Mill urged couples to marry late, have children late, and live in extended families or communelike situations so as to minimize divorce's disrupting effects on children's lives.[30] Apparently, Mill envisioned divorced men as well as divorced women playing a role in their children's lives.

Although Taylor, unlike Mill, did not contest society's assumptions about male and female child-rearing roles, she did contest society's assumptions about women's supposed preference for marriage and motherhood over a career or occupation. Mill contended that even after women were fully educated and totally enfranchised, most of them would *choose* to remain in the private realm where their primary function would be to "adorn and beautify" rather than to "support" life.[31] In contrast, Taylor argued in the "Enfranchisement of Women," that women's as well as men's first duty is to "support" life. Women, she insisted, should not simply seek the opportunity to read books and to cast ballots; they should also seek the opportunity to be *partners* with men "in the labors and gains, risks and remunerations of productive industry."[32] Thus, Taylor predicted if society gave women a bona fide choice between devoting their lives "to one *animal* function and its consequence"[33] on the one hand, and writing great books, discovering new worlds, and building mighty empires on the other, few women would be satisfied with what home, sweet home has to offer them.

Whereas the foregoing passages from the "Enfranchisement" suggest Taylor believed a woman had to choose between housewifing and mothering on the one hand and working outside the home on the other, other passages indicate she believed a woman had a third option: namely, adding a career or occupation to her domestic and maternal roles and responsibilities. In fact, Taylor asserted a married woman cannot be her husband's true equal unless she has the confidence and sense of entitlement that come from contributing "materially to the support of the family."[34] Decidedly unimpressed by Mill's 1832 argument that women's economic equality would depress the economy and subsequently lower wages,[35] Taylor insisted it is psychologically vital for every woman to work, regardless of whether her doing so maximizes utility. Taylor wrote: "Even if every woman, as matters now stand, had a claim on some man for support, how infinitely preferable is it that part of the income should be of the woman's earning, even if the aggregate sum were but little increased by it, rather than that she should be compelled to stand aside in order that men may be the sole earners, and the sole dispensers of what is earned."[36] In short, in order to be partners rather than servants of their husbands, wives must earn an income outside of the home.

In further explaining her view that married as well as single women should work, Taylor betrayed her class bias. Realizing that no woman can without considerable help be both an excellent wife and mother *and* an excellent worker, Taylor noted that working wives with children would need a "panoply of domestic servants" to help ease their burdens.[37] In critic Zillah Eisenstein's estimation, Taylor's words revealed just how privileged a woman she was. By 1850 or so, only upper-middle-class women like Taylor were rich enough to hire the many servants needed to do *all* their housework for them.[38] Thus, Taylor, a product of class privilege, suggested ways for rich women to "have it all" without suggesting ways for poor women to lead equally full lives.

Like Wollstonecraft, then, Taylor wrote not so much to *all* women as to a certain class of married women whose privileged status would permit them to work outside the home without in any way jeopardizing the quality of life within it. Nevertheless, Taylor's writings helped smooth many poor women's as well as rich women's entrance into the public world. So, too, did Mill's. He tried to establish in "The Subjection of Women" that if women were recognized as fully rational and worthy of the same civil liberties and economic opportunities as men, society would reap benefits: public-spirited citizens for itself, intellectually stimulating spouses for husbands, a doubling of the "mass of mental faculties available for the higher service of humanity," and a multitude of very happy women.[39] Although Mill's arguments against the subjugation of women did not, according to political theorist Susan Okin, strictly require he

prove women are men's exact equals—indeed most of the projected benefits of women's liberation could accrue even if women were somewhat
less capable than men—he felt obliged to make a strong case for sexual
equality.[40] Unlike Wollstonecraft, who tended to downplay the exceptional woman by putting no "great stress on the example of a few women
who, from having received a masculine education, have acquired courage
and resolution,"[41] Mill used the so-called exceptional woman to
strengthen his case that all the differences claimed to exist between men
and women are differences of average. No one who knows anything
about human history, said Mill, can argue that *all* men are stronger and
smarter than *all* women. Because the average woman cannot do something the average man can do does not justify a law or taboo barring all
women from attempting that thing.[42]

According to Mill, even *if* all women are worse than all men at something, this still does not justify forbidding women from trying to do that
thing, for "what women by nature cannot do, it is quite superfluous to
forbid them from doing. What they can do, but not so well as the men
who are their competitors, competition suffices to exclude them from."[43]
Although Mill believed women would fare quite well in any and all com-
petitions with men, he conceded that occasionally a biological sex difference might tip the scales in favor of male competitors. Like Wollstonecraft, however, he denied there are general intellectual or moral
differences between men and women. He stated: "I do not know a more
signal instance of the blindness with which the world, including the herd
of studious men, ignore and pass over all the influences of social circumstances, than their silly depreciation of the intellectual, and silly pane-
gyrics on the moral, nature of women."[44]

Mill, like Wollstonecraft earlier, claimed society's *ethical* double standard hurts women. Most of the "virtues" extolled in women are, in fact,
negative character traits impeding women's progress toward personhood. This is as true for an ostensibly negative trait (helplessness) as for
an ostensibly positive trait (unselfishness). Mill suggested that because
women's concerns were confined to the private realm, the typical woman
was preoccupied with her own interests and those of her immediate family, overvaluing her family's wants and needs and undervaluing those of
society in general. As a result, her unselfishness took the form of what is
best described as an extended egoism. She spared no effort to further *her*
husband's career and to situate *her* children in good schools and comfortable marriages; the charity of the typical wife and mother thus began and
ended at home. This is not the kind of unselfishness utilitarians such as
Mill value. They value the unselfishness that motivates people to take
into account the good of the whole society as well as the good of the individual person or small family unit. Mill believed were a woman given the

same education and legal rights as a man—were she taught to pay attention to the universals as well as the particulars, to the collective good as well as the individual's good—then she would develop genuine unselfishness. This belief explains Mill's passionate pleas for women's suffrage. Realizing that when it comes to forging public policy, the good of the collectivity is paramount, voters understand that "charity" to others must not end at home even if it begins there.[45]

Mill went further than Wollstonecraft in challenging men's alleged intellectual superiority. Stressing that men's and women's intellectual abilities are of the same *kind*, Wollstonecraft nonetheless entertained the thought women might not be able to attain the same *degree* of knowledge as men.[46] Mill expressed no such reservation. He insisted intellectual achievement gaps between men and women were simply the result of men's more thorough education and privileged position. In fact, Mill was so eager to establish that men are not intellectually superior to women that he tended to err in the opposite direction, by valorizing women's attention to details, use of concrete examples, and intuitiveness as a superior form of knowledge not often found in men.[47]

Despite his high regard for women's intellectual abilities, Mill unlike Taylor, assumed most women would continue to choose family over career even under ideal circumstances—with marriage a free contract between real equals, legal separation and divorce easily available to wives, and jobs open to women living outside the husband-wife relationship. He also assumed that in choosing family over career, these women tacitly agreed to sacrifice their other interests until their families were grown. Mill wrote, "Like a man when he chooses a profession, so, when a woman marries, it may in general be understood that she makes choice of the management of a household, and the bringing up of a family, as the first call upon her exertions, during as many years of her life as may be required for the purpose; and that she renounces not all other objects and occupations, but all which are not consistent with the requirements of this."[48] Mill's words attested to his apparent belief that women, more than men, are ultimately responsible not only for creating a family but also for maintaining it. However enlightened his other ideas about women were, Mill could not overcome the view that she who bears the children is the person most accountable for rearing them.

Although, as noted above, Taylor doubted that *liberated* wives and mothers would be willing to stay at home, she, like Mill, was a reformist, not a revolutionary. To be sure, by inviting married women with children as well as single women to work outside the home, Taylor did challenge the traditional division of labor within the family, where the man earns the money and the woman manages its use. But Taylor's challenge to this aspect of the status quo did not go far enough. For example, it did not occur to her that were husbands to parent alongside their wives and were domestic duties equally divided, then husbands and wives *alike* could work outside the home on a full-time basis, and working wives with children would not have to work a "double day" or hire a "panoply" of female servants to do *their* housework and childcare.

Nineteenth-Century Liberal Feminist Action

Both John Stuart Mill and Harriet Taylor Mill believed women needed suffrage in order to become men's equals. To be able to vote, they said, is to be in a position not only to express one's personal political views but also to change those systems, structures, and attitudes that contribute to one's own or others' oppression. Thus, as Angela Davis observed in her book *Women, Race and Class*, it is no accident that in the United States the entire nineteenth-century women's rights movement, including the woman suffrage movement, was intimately tied to the abolitionist movement.[49]

When white men and women began to work in earnest for the abolition of slavery, it soon became clear to the female abolitionists that male abolitionists were reluctant to link the women's rights movement with the slaves' rights movement. Observing it was difficult for whites (or was it simply white *men*?) to view women (or was it simply *white* women?) as an oppressed group, male abolitionists persuaded female abolitionists to disassociate women's liberty struggles from blacks' liberty struggles. For this very reason, abolitionist Lucy Stone, for example, agreed to lecture on abolition on the weekends and on women's rights during the week.[50]

Convinced their male colleagues would reward them for their cooperation, the U.S. women who attended the 1840 World Anti-Slavery Convention in London believed they would play a major role at the meeting. Nothing could have proved less true. No woman, not even Lucretia Mott or Elizabeth Cady Stanton, two of the most prominent leaders of the U.S. women's rights movement, was even allowed to speak at the meeting. Angered by the way in which the men at the convention had silenced women, Mott and Stanton vowed to hold a women's rights convention upon their return to the United States. Eight years later, in 1848, 300 women and men met in Seneca Falls, New York, and produced a Declaration of Sentiments and twelve resolutions. Modeled on the Declaration of Independence, the Declaration of Sentiments stressed the issues Mill and Taylor had emphasized in England, particularly the need for reforms in marriage, divorce, property, and child custody laws. The twelve resolutions emphasized women's rights to express themselves in public—to speak out on the burning issues of the day, especially "in regard to the great subjects of morals and religion," which women were supposedly more qualified to address than men.[51] The only one of these resolutions

the Seneca Falls convention did not unanimous'
Anthony's Woman's Suffrage Resolution: "Resol
the women of this country to secure to themselves the
franchise."[52] The majority of the convention delegates w
press such an "extreme" demand for fear that all of their dema
be rejected.

Angela Davis pointed out that the Seneca Falls convention, like the en
tire nineteenth-century women's rights movement, was really a white,
middle-class, educated women's affair. With the exception of Lucretia
Mott's hastily added resolution to secure for women "an equal participation with men in the various trades, professions, and commerce,"[53] the
convention did not address the concerns of overworked, underpaid,
white, female mill and factory workers who were too tired to worry about
voting, let alone about lecturing on morals and religion. Moreover, the
convention rendered black women invisible. In the same way that the
abolitionist movement had focused on the rights of black *men*, the
women's rights movement focused on the rights of *white* women. No one
seemed to care about black women.

Yet many black women became particularly effective spokespersons for
women's rights, even though white women tended to ignore or minimize
their contributions. At an 1851 women's rights convention in Akron,
Ohio, black abolitionist-feminist Sojourner Truth delivered an extraordinarily powerful speech on behalf of women. Responding to a group of
male hecklers, who taunted that it was ludicrous for women to desire the
vote since they could not even step over a puddle or get into a horse car-
riage without male assistance, Sojourner Truth pointed out no man had
ever extended such help to her. Demanding the audience look at her
body, Sojourner Truth proclaimed that her "womanhood," her "female
nature" had never prevented her from working, acting, and yes, speaking
like a man: "I have ploughed, and planted, and gathered into barns and
no man could head me! And ain't I a woman? I could work as much and
eat as much as a man—when I could get it—and bear the lash as well!
And ain't I a woman? I have borne thirteen children and seen them most
all sold off to slavery, and when I cried out with my mother's grief, none
but Jesus heard me! And ain't I a woman?"[54]

Just when the women's rights movement had gained considerable mo-
mentum, however, the Civil War began. Seeing in this tragic war the opportunity at last to free the slaves, male abolitionists again asked feminists to put the women's cause on the back burner, which they reluctantly
did. But the end of the Civil War did not bring women's liberation with it,
and feminists increasingly found themselves at odds with recently emancipated black men. Concerned that women's rights would once again be
lost in the struggle to secure black (men's) rights, the male as well as fe-

e delegates to an 1866 national women's rights convention decided to
tablish an Equal Rights Association. Cochaired by Frederick Douglass
nd Elizabeth Cady Stanton, the association had as its announced purpose the unification of the black (men's) and woman suffrage struggles.
There is considerable evidence, however, that Stanton and some of her
coworkers actually "perceived the organization as a means to ensure that
Black men would not receive the franchise unless and until white women
were also its recipients."[55] Unmoved by Frederick Douglass's and Sojourner Truth's observation that on account of their extreme vulnerability
black men needed the vote even more than women did, Anthony and
Stanton were among those who successfully argued for the dissolution of
the Equal Rights Association just when it seemed that the association
might indeed endorse the passage of the Fifteenth Amendment, which
enfranchised black men but not women.

Upon leaving the Equal Rights Association, Anthony and Stanton established the National Woman Suffrage Association. At approximately
the same time, Lucy Stone, who had some serious philosophical disagree-
ments with Stanton and especially Anthony about the role of organized
religion in women's oppression, founded the American Woman Suffrage
Association. Henceforward, the U.S. women's rights movement was split
in two.

In a variety of ways, the National Woman Suffrage Association forwarded a revolutionary and radical feminist agenda for women, whereas
the American Woman Suffrage Association pushed a reformist and liberal
feminist agenda. Most American women gravitated toward the more
moderate American Woman Suffrage Association. By the time these two
associations merged in 1890 to form the National American Woman Suffrage Association, the wide-ranging, vociferous women's rights movement of the early nineteenth century had been transformed into the sin-
gle-issue, relatively tame woman's suffrage movement of the late
nineteenth century. From 1890 until 1920, when the Nineteenth Amendment was passed, the National American Woman Suffrage Association
confined almost all of its activities to gaining the vote for women. Victori-
ous after fifty-two years of concerted struggle, most of the exhausted suffragists chose to believe that simply by gaining the vote women had indeed become men's equals.[56]

Twentieth-Century Liberal Feminist Action

For nearly forty years after the passage of the Nineteenth Amendment,
feminism lay dormant in the United States. Then, around 1960, a new
generation of feminists proclaimed as true fact what the suffragists Stanton and Anthony always suspected: In order to be fully liberated, women

need economic opportunities as well as civil liberties. Like their grandmothers, some of these young women pushed a liberal agenda, whereas others forwarded a more radical program of action.

In the mid-1960s, liberal feminists assembled in one of several so-called women's rights groups (e.g., the National Organization for Women [NOW], the National Women's Political Caucus [NWPC], and the Women's Equity Action League [WEAL]), the general purpose of which was to improve women's status "by applying legal, social, and other pressures upon institutions ranging from the Bell Telephone Company to television networks to the major political parties."[57] In contrast to 1960s liberal feminists, 1960s radical feminists gathered in one of several so-called women's liberation groups. Much smaller and personally focused than the women's rights groups, these women's liberation groups aimed to increase women's consciousness about women's oppression. Their spirit was the spirit of the revolutionary new left, whose goal was not to *reform* what they regarded as an elitist, capitalistic, competitive, individualistic "system" but to *replace* it with egalitarian, socialistic, cooperative, communitarian, sisterhood-is-powerful systems. Among the largest of these women's liberation groups were the Women's International Terrorist Conspiracy from Hell (WITCH), the Redstockings, the Feminists, and the New York Radical Feminists. Although Maren Lockwood Carden correctly noted in her 1974 book, *The New Feminist Movement*, that the ideological contrasts between the women's rights and women's liberation groups of the 1960s had blurred,[58] even in the late 1990s women's rights groups remain less "revolutionary" than women's liberation groups.

Because this chapter is focused on liberal feminists, I try as much as possible to discuss only the history of twentieth-century women's *rights* groups and their activities, most of which have been in the area of legislation. Between the passage of the Nineteenth Amendment and the advent of the second wave of U.S. feminism during the 1960s, only two groups— the National Woman's Party and the National Federation of Business and Professional Women's Clubs (BPW)—promulgated women's rights. Despite their efforts, however, discrimination against women did not end, largely because the importance of women's rights had not yet been impressed on the consciousness (and conscience) of the bulk of the U.S. population. This state of affairs changed with the eruption of the civil rights movement. Sensitized to the myriad ways in which U.S. systems, structures, and laws oppressed blacks, those active in or at least sympathetic toward the civil rights movement were able to see analogies between discrimination against blacks and discrimination against women. In 1961 President John F. Kennedy established the Commission on the Status of Women, which produced much new data about women and resulted in the formation of the Citizens' Advisory Council, various state commissions on the status of women, and the passage of the Equal Pay Act. When Congress passed the 1964 Civil Rights Act—amended with the Title VII provision to prohibit discrimination on the basis of *sex* as well as race, color, religion, or national origin by private employers, employment agencies, and unions—a woman shouted from the congressional gallery: "We made it! God bless America!"[59] Unfortunately, this woman's jubilation and that of women in general was short-lived; the courts were reluctant to enforce Title VII's so-called sex amendment. Feeling betrayed by the "system," women's joy turned to anger, an anger that feminist activists used to mobilize women to fight for their civil rights with the same passion blacks had fought for theirs.

Among these feminist activists was Betty Friedan, one of the founders and first president of the National Organization for Women. Reflecting on how she and some of her associates had reacted to the courts' refusal to take Title VII's "sex amendment" seriously, she wrote: "The absolute necessity for a civil rights movement for women had reached such a point of subterranean explosive urgency by 1966, that it only took a few of us to get together to ignite the spark—and it spread like a nuclear chain reaction."[60]

The "spark" to which Friedan pointed was the formation of NOW, the first explicitly feminist group in the United States in the twentieth century to challenge sex discrimination in all spheres of life: social, political, economic, and personal. After considerable behind-the-scenes maneuvering, Friedan—at the time viewed as a highly controversial figure on account of her 1963 book *The Feminine Mystique* (see the next section for discussion)—was elected as NOW's first president in 1966 by its 300 charter members, male and female.

Although NOW's first members included radical and conservative feminists as well as liberal feminists, within a very short time it became clear NOW's *essential* identity and agenda were liberal. For example, the aim of NOW's 1967 Bill of Rights for Women was to secure for women the same rights men have. NOW demanded the following for women:

I. That the U.S. Congress immediately pass the Equal Rights Amendment to the Constitution to provide that "Equality of rights under the law shall not be denied or abridged by the United States or by any State on account of sex," and that such then be immediately ratified by the several States.

II. That equal employment opportunity be guaranteed to all women, as well as men, by insisting that the Equal Employment Opportunity Commission enforces the prohibitions against racial discrimination.

III. That women be protected by law to ensure their rights to return to their jobs within a reasonable time after childbirth without the loss of seniority or other accrued benefits, and be paid maternity leave as a form of social security and/or employee benefit.

IV. Immediate revision of tax laws to permit the deduction of home and child-care expenses for working parents.

V. That child-care facilities be established by law on the same basis as parks, libraries, and public schools, adequate to the needs of children from the pre-school years through adolescence, as a community resource to be used by all citizens from all income levels.

VI. That the right of women to be educated to their full potential equally with men be secured by Federal and State legislation, eliminating all discrimination and segregation by sex, written and unwritten, at all levels of education, including colleges, graduate and professional schools, loans and fellowships, and Federal and State training programs such as the Job Corps.

VII. The right of women in poverty to secure job training, housing, and family allowances on equal terms with men, but without prejudice to a parent's right to remain at home to care for his or her children; revision of welfare legislation and poverty programs which deny women dignity, privacy, and self-respect.

VIII. The right of women to control their own reproductive lives by removing from the penal code laws limiting access to contraceptive information and devices, and by repealing penal laws governing abortion.[61]

NOW's list of demands pleased NOW's liberal members but made both its conservative and radical members angry, for different reasons. Whereas conservative members objected to NOW's push for permissive contraception and abortion laws, radical members were angered by NOW's failure to support women's sexual rights, particularly the right to choose among heterosexual, bisexual, and lesbian life-styles.

Conceding that "the sex-role debate . . . cannot be avoided if equal opportunity in employment, education and civil rights are ever to mean more than paper rights,"[62] Friedan nonetheless exposed herself as a liberal feminist when she stated "that the gut issues of this revolution involve employment and education and new social institutions and not sexual fantasy."[63] Worried NOW would change its traditional liberal focus to a more radical one, Friedan was among those who most strongly opposed NOW's public support of lesbianism. Allegedly, she termed NOW's lesbian members a "lavender menace,"[64] since, as she saw it, they alienated mainstream society from feminists in general.

Despite NOW's disavowal of homophobia in its 1971 resolution recognizing the double oppression of lesbians, NOW's agenda remained fundamentally liberal. NOW stressed, however, that its aim was to serve not only the women most likely to survive and thrive in the "system" but any woman who believes women's rights should be equal to men's. Beginning with the 1971 presidency of Arlein Hernandez, a Hispanic woman, a wide variety of minority and lesbian women (including Patricia Ireland, president of NOW from 1993 to 2001) assumed leadership as well as membership roles in NOW.[65] The organization's greater attention to women's differences means its members can no longer claim to know what *all* women want but only what *specific groups* of women (e.g., poor, Hispanic, heterosexual women) want. Increasingly, the intellectual energies of NOW as well as other women's rights groups are focused on the so-called sameness-difference debate: Is gender equality best achieved by stressing women's "oneness" as a gender or their "diversity" as individuals, the "samenesses" between women and men or the "differences" between them?

Twentieth-Century Liberal Feminist Thought: Treating Women and Men the Same or Differently?

It is instructive to reflect upon Betty Friedan's career as a writer not only because of her identification with NOW but also because of her own evolution as a thinker. Like most contemporary liberal feminists, Friedan gradually accepted both the *radical* feminist critique that liberal feminists are prone to co-optation by the "male establishment" and the *conservative* feminist critique that liberal feminists are out of touch with the bulk of U.S. women who hold the institutions of marriage, motherhood, and the family in high regard. In *The Feminine Mystique*,[66] Friedan seemed oblivious to any other perspectives than those of white, middle-class, heterosexual, educated women who found the traditional roles of wife and mother unsatisfying. She wrote that in lieu of more meaningful goals these women spent too much time cleaning their already tidy homes, improving their already attractive appearances, and spoiling their already obnoxious children.[67] Focusing on this unappealing picture of family life in affluent U.S. suburbs, Friedan concluded that contemporary women needed to find meaningful work in the full-time, public workforce. Wives' and mothers' partial absence from home would enable husband and children to become more self-sufficient people, capable of cooking their own meals and doing their own laundry.[68]

Although Friedan had little patience for obsequious wives and doting mothers, she did not demand women *sacrifice* marriage and motherhood for a high-powered career. On the contrary, she stated to many groups of women: "The assumption of your own identity, equality, and even political power does not mean you stop needing to love, and be loved by, a man, or that you stop caring for your own kids."[69] In Friedan's estimation, the error in the feminine mystique was not that it *valued* marriage and motherhood but that it *overvalued* these two institutions, seeing in them the answer to *all* of women's human needs and desires. To think, as Mill and even Wollstonecraft did, that a woman who is a wife and mother has no time for a career is to limit her development as a full human person, said Friedan. As soon as a woman sees housework for what it is—something to get out of the way, to be done "quickly and efficiently"—and sees marriage and motherhood for what it is—a part of her life but not all of it—she will find plenty of time and energy to develop her total self in "creative work" outside the home.[70] With just a bit of help, any woman, like any man, can meet all of her personal obligations, leaving her free to assume significant roles and responsibilities in the public world.

Although *The Feminine Mystique* helped explain why marriage and motherhood are not enough for a certain kind of woman, in critics' estimation the book failed to address a host of issues deeper than "the problem that has no name"—Friedan's tag for the dissatisfaction of the suburban, white, educated, middle-class, heterosexual housewife in the United States. In particular, *The Feminine Mystique* misjudged just how difficult it would be for even privileged women to combine a career with marriage and motherhood unless major structural changes were made within as well as outside the family. Like Wollstonecraft, Taylor, and Mill before her, Friedan sent women out into the public realm without summoning men into the private domain.

In *The Second Stage*,[71] written nearly a quarter century after *The Feminine Mystique*, Friedan did consider the difficulty of combining marriage, motherhood, and career. Observing the ways in which some members of her daughter's generation ran themselves ragged in the name of feminism—trying to be full-time career women as well as full-time housewives and mothers—Friedan concluded that 1980s "superwomen" were no less oppressed (albeit for different reasons) than their 1960s "stay-at-home" mothers had been. Thus, Friedan urged 1980s feminists to ask themselves whether women either can or should try to meet not simply one but two standards of perfection: the one set in the workplace by traditional men who had wives to take care of all their nonworkplace needs *and* the one set in the home by traditional women whose whole sense of worth, power, and mastery came from being ideal housewives and mothers.[72]

In Friedan's estimation, 1980s feminists needed to stop trying to "do it all" and "be it all." She insisted, however, the proper cure for the "superwoman" syndrome was not to renounce love in favor of work or vice versa. On the contrary, said Friedan, women who chose *either* work *or* love often told her they regretted their decision. For example, one woman who renounced marriage and motherhood for a full-time career confessed to Friedan: "I was the first woman in management here. I gave everything to the job. It was exciting at first, breaking in where women never were before. Now it's just a job. But it's the devastating loneliness that's the worst. I can't *stand* coming back to this apartment alone every night. I'd like a house, maybe a garden. Maybe I should have a kid, even without a father. At least then I'd have a family. There has to be some better way to live."[73] Another woman who made the opposite choice, forsaking job for family, admitted to Friedan:

> It makes me mad—makes me feel like a child—when I have to ask my husband for money. My mother was always dependent on my father and so fearful of life. She is lost now without him. It frightens me, the thought of being dependent like my mother, though I have a very happy marriage. I get so upset, listening to battered wives on television, women with no options. It improves your sense of self-worth when you don't depend on your husband for everything good in life, when you can get it for yourself. I'm trying so hard to treat my daughter equally with my son. I don't want her to have the fears that paralyzed my mother and that I've always had to fight. I want her to have real options.[74]

Rather than despairing over these and other women's choices, Friedan used them as an argument to convince 1980s feminists to move from what she termed first-stage feminism to what she labeled second-stage feminism. Friedan noted this new form of feminism would require women to work with men in order to escape the excesses of the *feminist* mystique, "which denied the core of women's personhood that is fulfilled through love, nurture, home" as well as the excesses of the *feminine* mystique, "which defined women solely in terms of their relation to men as wives, mothers and homemakers."[75] Together with men, said Friedan, women might be able to develop the kind of social values, leadership styles, and institutional structures that will permit both genders to achieve fulfillment in both the public and private worlds.

Friedan's program for reigniting the women's movement was, as we shall see, vulnerable to several attacks. For example, it did not adequately challenge the assumption that women are "responsible for the private life of their family members."[76] Zillah Eisenstein criticized Friedan's support of so-called flextime (an arrangement that permits employees to set their starting and leaving hours) by stating: "It is never clear whether this arrangement is supposed to ease women's double burden (of family and work) or significantly restructure *who* is responsible for childcare and *how* this responsibility is carried out."[77] Suspecting that women rather than men would use flextime to mesh their workday with their children's school day, Eisenstein worried flextime would give employers yet another reason to devalue female employees as less committed to their work than male employees.

In all fairness to Friedan, however, she did explicitly mention in *The Second Stage* (written after Eisenstein's critique of Friedan) that when an arrangement like flextime is described as a structural change permitting mothers to better care for their children, the wrongheaded idea that home and family are *women's* sole responsibility rather than *women's and men's* joint responsibility is reinforced.[78] Unlike the Friedan of *The Feminine Mystique*, the Friedan of *The Second Stage* seemed quite aware that unless women's assimilation into the public world is coupled with the simultaneous assimilation of men into the private world, women will always have to work harder than men. Although Friedan conceded most men might not be ready, willing, or able to embrace the "househusband" role, she nonetheless insisted it is just as important for men to develop their private and personal selves as it is for women to develop their public and social selves. Men who realize this also realize women's liberation is men's liberation. At last a man does not have to be "just a breadwinner"[79] or just a runner in the rat race. Like his wife, he, too, can be an active participant in the thick web of familial and friendship relationships he and she weave together.

In some ways, the difference between the Friedan of *The Feminine Mystique* and the Friedan of *The Second Stage* is the difference between a feminist who believes women need to be the *same* as men in order to be equal to men and a feminist who believes women can be men's equals provided society values the "feminine" as much as the "masculine." The overall message of *The Feminine Mystique* was that unless women become like men, they would never be liberated. Friedan peppered the pages of *The Feminine Mystique* with comments such as: "If an able American woman does not use her human energy and ability in some meaningful pursuit (which necessarily means competition, for there is competition in every serious pursuit of our society), she will fritter away her energy in neurotic symptoms, or unproductive exercise, or destructive 'love'"[80] and "Perhaps men may live longer in America when women carry more of the burden of the battle with the world instead of being a burden themselves. I think their wasted energy will continue to be destructive to their husbands, to their children, and to themselves until it is used in their own battle with the world."[81] To be a full human being is, in short, to think and act like a man.

Seven years after the publication of *The Feminine Mystique*, Friedan's message to women had substantially changed. In *The Second Stage*, she described as culturally feminine so-called beta styles of thinking and acting, which emphasize "fluidity, flexibility and interpersonal sensitivity," and as culturally masculine so-called alpha styles of thinking and acting, which stress "hierarchical, authoritarian, strictly task-oriented leadership based on instrumental, technological rationality."[82] Rather than offering 1980s women the same advice she had offered 1960s women—namely, minimize your feminine, beta tendencies and maximize your masculine, alpha tendencies—Friedan counseled 1980s women to embrace the feminine, beta style. Having convinced herself that women did not need to deny their differences from men in order to achieve equality with men, Friedan urged 1980s women to stop "aping the accepted dominant Alpha mode of established movements and organizations" and start using their "Beta intuitions" to solve the social, political, and economic problems that threaten humankind.[83] The challenge of the second stage of feminism, insisted Friedan, was for women (and men) to replace the "win-or-lose, do-or-die method of the hunter or the warrior" with the kind of thinking "women developed in the past as they dealt on a day-to-day basis with small problems and relationships in the family, mostly without thinking about it in the abstract."[84] Only then would the world's citizens realize their very survival depends on replacing competitive strategies with cooperative initiatives.

Given the foregoing analysis, it is not surprising that Friedan later claimed gender-specific laws rather than general-neutral laws are better able to secure equality between the sexes. In 1986 she joined a coalition supporting a California law requiring employers to grant as much as four months unpaid leave to women disabled by pregnancy or childbirth. In taking this stand, she alienated those members of the National Organization for Women who believed that to treat men and women equally should mean to treat them in the same way. If men should not receive special treatment on account of their sex, then neither should women. According to Friedan, this line of reasoning, which she herself pressed in the 1960s, is misguided. It asks the law to treat women as "male clones," when in fact "there has to be a concept of equality that takes into account that women are the ones who have the babies."[85]

If the Friedan of the 1980s is right, then the task of liberal feminists is to determine not what liberty and equality are for abstract rational persons but what liberty and equality are for concrete men and women. To be sure, this is a difficult and dangerous task. Among others, Rosalind Rosenberg has cautioned liberal feminists in particular by saying: "If women as a group are allowed special benefits, you open up the group to charges that it is inferior. But, if we deny all differences, as the women's movement has so often done, you deflect attention from the disadvantages women labor under."[86] Rosenberg's cautionary words raise many questions. Is there really a way to treat women and men *differently* yet *equally* without falling into some version of the pernicious "separate but equal" approach that characterized race relations in the United States until the early 1960s? Or should liberal feminists work toward the elimination of "differences" as the first step toward true equality? If so, should women become like men in order to be equal with men? Or should men become like women in order to be equal with women? Or finally, should both men and women become androgynous, each person combining the same "correct" blend of positive masculine and feminine characteristics in order to be equal with every other person?

Whereas *The Feminine Mystique* advised women to become like men, *The Second Stage* urged women to be women. However, it also encouraged both men and women to work toward an androgynous future in which all human beings would mix within themselves mental and behavioral "masculine" and "feminine" traits. In her most recent book, *The Fountain of Age*, Friedan reiterated her support for androgyny. She urged aging alpha men to develop their passive, nurturing, or contemplative "feminine" qualities, and aging beta women to develop their bold, assertive, commanding, or adventurous "masculine" qualities.[87] Convinced it is in the best interests of people over fifty to explore their "other side"— whether "masculine" or "feminine"—Friedan noted, for example, that women over fifty who go back to school or work or who become very actively engaged in the public world, report the fifty-plus years as being the best ones of their lives. Similarly, men over fifty who start focusing on the quality of their personal relationships and interior lives report a similar kind of satisfaction in old age. Unfortunately, added Friedan, the number of men who age well is far smaller than the number of women who age well. In our society, there are simply more opportunities for older women to develop their "masculine" traits than there are for older men to develop their "feminine" traits. If a man has neglected his wife and children for years because he has made work his first priority, by the time he is ready to attend to his personal relationships, these relationships may be extremely troubled or beyond repair. As a result, he may decide to seek a new wife with whom to have a second family—*repeating* the activities of his youth in the hope of "getting it right" this time. Empathizing with the left-behind "old wife" and "first family," Friedan urged these aging men—indeed all aging men and women—to find ways of loving and working in their fifties that *differed* from the ways they loved and worked as twenty-, thirty-, or forty-year-olds.

The overall message of *The Fountain of Age* is that the people most likely to grow, change, and become more fully themselves as they age are precisely those people who are able to move beyond polarized sex roles and creatively develop whichever "side" of themselves they neglected to develop as young men and women. In short, the happiest and most vital old men and women are androgynous persons.

The more she focused on the idea of androgyny, the more Friedan seemed to move toward humanism and away from feminism. She began by describing feminist "sexual politics" as the "no-win battle of women as a whole sex, oppressed victims, against men as a whole sex, the oppressors,"[88] everywhere urging women to join with men "in the new [human] politics that must emerge beyond reaction."[89] Eventually, Friedan claimed that because "human wholeness" is the "promise of feminism," feminists should move beyond a focus on *women's* issues (issues related to women's reproductive and sexual roles, rights, and responsibilities) in order to work with men on "the concrete, practical, everyday problems of living, working and loving as equal persons."[90]

In a shift that appears to be more than mere coincidence, NOW's focus has moved in the "human" direction suggested by Friedan, a trend that has brought NOW as well as its first president under concerted attack by radical feminists in particular. In contrast to Friedan and many liberal members of NOW, radical feminists doubt feminism can move beyond "women's issues" and still remain *feminism*. They claim so long as our culture's understanding of what it means to be a human being remains androcentric (male-centered), it is premature for feminists to become humanists.

To be sure, Friedan is not the first liberal feminist who has found humanism attractive. In their own distinct ways, Wollstonecraft, Taylor, and Mill each wanted *personhood*, full membership in the human community for women. The hypothesis that the ends and aims of feminism may, after all, be identical with those of humanism is a controversial one but worth keeping in mind as we consider recent trends in liberal feminism.

Contemporary Directions in Liberal Feminism

Betty Friedan is just one of thousands of women who may be classified as liberal feminists. As Zillah Eisenstein noted, Elizabeth Holtzman, Bella Abzug, Eleanor Smeal, Pat Schroeder, and Patsy Mink are liberal feminists, as are many other leaders and members of the National Organization for Women and the Women's Equity Action League.[91] Although these women are sometimes divided, they do agree the single most important goal of women's liberation is sexual equality, or, as it is sometimes termed, gender justice.

Liberal feminists wish to free women from oppressive gender roles—that is, from those roles used as excuses or justifications for giving women a lesser place, or no place at all, in the academy, the forum, and the marketplace. They stress that patriarchal society conflates *sex* and *gender*,[92] deeming appropriate for women only those jobs associated with the feminine personality. Thus, in the United States, for example, women are pushed into jobs like nursing, teaching, and childcare; and legislation specifically barring women from such "masculine" jobs as mining and bartending or preventing women from working the night shift or overtime is easily passed. Although such de jure gender discrimination is largely a memory today, de facto gender discrimination lingers. Faced with a choice between a male or female candidate, for example, many voters unreflectively vote "male" on the grounds women are too emotional—jittery, flighty, high-strung—to steer the ship of state. For similar reasons, if a "gut feeling" can be deemed a reason, employers prefer to hire men for certain positions, even when women are at least as qualified.

It is sometimes argued that men, no less than women, are the victims of de facto discrimination—that even if the law has always been kind to men, other vehicles of social control have not. Thus, we hear complaints about the parents who consistently refuse to hire male baby-sitters and about the nursery schools supposedly unable to find "qualified" men to fill their staff positions. Although liberal feminists sympathize with men who have found it difficult to pursue child-centered careers because of de facto discrimination, they nonetheless observe the kind of de facto discrimination men experience is not nearly as systematic as the kind women experience. Society remains structured in ways that favor men and disfavor women in the competitive race for the goods with which our society rewards us: power, prestige, and money.

In their discussions of the structural and attitudinal impediments to women's progress, contemporary liberal feminists often disagree about how to handle these hurdles. Classical liberal feminists believe that after discriminatory laws and policies have been removed from the books, thereby formally enabling women to compete equally with men, not much else can be done about "birds of a feather flocking together"—about male senior professors, for example, being more favorably disposed toward a male candidate than toward an equally qualified female candidate.

In contrast, welfare liberal feminists urge society to break up that "old flock (gang) of mine," especially when failure to make feathers fly results in asymmetrical gender ratios such as the one that characterized Harvard University's senior arts and sciences faculty in the early 1970s: 483 men, zero women.[93] Society should, they say, not only compensate women for past injustices but also eliminate socioeconomic as well as legal impediments to women's progress today. Thus, welfare liberal feminists advocate that female applicants to schools and jobs either be (1) selected over *equally* qualified white male applicants (so-called preferential admissions or hiring) or (2) selected over *more*, as well as equally, qualified white male applicants, provided the female applicants are still able to perform adequately (so-called reverse discrimination).[94] However, welfare liberal feminists believe that policies of preferential hiring and reverse discrimination are compatible with the essential values of liberalism only if they are regarded as transitional measures whose justification ceases when women have de facto as well as de jure equality with men.

We may think the only meaningful liberal feminist approaches to combating gender discrimination are the classical and welfare approaches, both of which rely heavily on legal remedies. But as noted above, liberal feminists like Betty Friedan offered another approach that used the ideal of androgyny to counteract society's traditional tendency to value masculine traits and to devalue feminine traits. If society encouraged everyone to develop both positive masculine and positive feminine traits, then people would have no more reason to devalue their feminine sides than their masculine sides. Discrimination on the bases of gender and biological sex would cease.

Discussions of sex differences, gender roles, and androgyny have indeed helped focus liberal feminists' drive toward liberty, equality, and fairness of all. According to Jane English, terms such as *sex roles* and *gender traits* denote "the patterns of behavior which the two sexes are socialized, encouraged, or coerced into adopting, ranging from 'sex-appropriate' personalities to interests and professions."[95] Boys are instructed to be masculine, girls to be feminine. Psychologists, anthropologists, and sociologists tend to define the "masculine" and "feminine" in terms of prevailing cultural stereotypes, which are influenced by racial, class, and ethnic factors. Thus, to be masculine in middle-class, white, Anglo-Saxon, Protestant United States is, among other things, to be rational, ambitious, and independent; and to be feminine is, among other things, to be emotional, nurturant, and dependent. To be sure, even within this segment of the population, exceptions to the rule will be found. Some biological males will manifest feminine gender traits, and some biological females will manifest masculine gender traits. But these individuals will be "exceptional" or "deviant." No matter what group of people (for example, working-class Italian Catholics) is under scrutiny, then, gender-role stereotyping will limit the individual's possibilities for development as a unique self. The woman who displays characteristics her social group regards as "masculine" will be viewed as less than a *real* woman; the man who shows "feminine" traits will be considered less than a *real* man.[96]

In order to liberate women as well as men from the culturally constructed cages of masculinity and femininity, many liberal feminists besides Betty Friedan advocate the formation of androgynous personalities.[97] Some liberal feminists favor monoandrogyny—the development of an ideal personality type that embodies the best of prevailing masculine and feminine gender traits.[98] According to psychologist Sandra Bem, the monoandrogynous person possesses a full complement of traditional female qualities—nurturance, compassion, tenderness, sensitivity, affiliativeness, cooperativeness—along with a full complement of traditional male qualities—aggressiveness, leadership, initiative, competitiveness.[99] (Recall once again that this list of traditional qualities probably needs to be modified depending on the racial, class, and ethnic characteristics of the group under consideration.) Other liberal feminists resist monoandrogyny and instead advocate polyandrogyny—the development of multiple personality types, some of which are totally masculine, others totally feminine, and still others a mixture.[100] Whether liberal femini monoandrogyny or polyandrogyny, however, they tend to a $_{5}$--- __ ₚ__ son's biological sex should in no way determine his or her psychological and social gender.

Critiques of Liberal Feminism

In recent years nonliberal feminists have faulted liberal feminists for a number of reasons, particularly their tendencies to give political rights priority over economic rights and to emphasize women's and men's sameness.[101] Because many liberal feminists are in the process of criticizing *themselves* for these tendencies, however, it is not certain how devastating these challenges to liberal feminism are. Consider, for example, that NOW's agenda is increasingly a welfare liberal feminist agenda stressing issues such as homelessness, hunger, and the feminization of poverty.[102] Also consider, as noted above, that liberal feminist leaders like Betty Friedan are much more inclined today than they were in the 1960s and 1970s to discuss men's and women's *differences*. Nevertheless, despite some of the changes in NOW's agenda and in certain liberal feminists' ideologies, many liberal feminists remain focused on the political arena, continuing to stress there men's and women's *sameness*. For this reason, it is important to consider carefully the major criticisms registered against liberal feminism.

Critique One: Can Women Become Like Men?
Do Women Want To? Should They Want To?

Jean Bethke Elshtain, a political theorist, is one of liberal feminism's most severe critics. She claimed liberal feminists are wrong to emphasize individual rights over the common good and choice over commitment, since: "There is no way to create real communities out of an aggregate of 'freely' choosing adults."[103] Elshtain also claimed liberal feminists are wrong to put a high premium on so-called male values. She accused the Friedan of the 1960s—and, to a lesser extent, Wollstonecraft, Mill, and Taylor—of equating male being with human being, "manly" virtue with human virtue. In her critique "Why Can't a Woman Be More Like a Man?" Elshtain identified what she considered liberal feminism's three major flaws: (1) its claim women *can* become like men if they set their minds to it; (2) its claim most women *want* to become like men; and (3) its claim all women *should* want to become like men, to aspire to masculine values.

With respect to the first claim, that women *can* become like men, Elshtain pointed to the general liberal feminist belief that male-female differences are the products of culture rather than biology, of nurture rather than nature. Elshtain claimed liberal feminists refuse to entertain the possibility some sex differences are biologically determined, for fear affirmative answers could be used to justify the repression, suppression, and oppression of women. For this reasons, many liberal feminists have, in Elshtain's estimation, become "excessive environmentalists," people who believe that gender identities are the nearly exclusive product of socialization, changeable at society's will.[104]

Although she wanted to avoid both the reactionary position of contemporary sociobiologists—according to whom biology is indeed destiny—and the sentimental speculations of some nineteenth- and twentieth-century feminists—according to whom women are, by nature, morally better than men[105]—Elshtain nonetheless claimed long-standing "male"-"female" differences cannot be erased overnight without doing violence to people. Unless we wish to do what Plato suggested in *The Republic*, namely, banish everyone over the age of twelve and begin an intensive program of centrally controlled and uniform socialization from infancy onward, we cannot hope, said Elshtain, to eliminate gender differences between men and women in just a few generations. In sum, women *cannot* be like men unless they are prepared to commit themselves to the kind of social engineering and behavior modification that is incompatible with the spirit, if not also the letter, of liberal law.[106]

Liberal feminism also has a tendency, claimed Elshtain, to overestimate the number of women who *want* to be like men. She dismissed the claim that any woman who wants more than anything else to be a wife and mother is a benighted and befuddled victim of patriarchal "false consciousness." Patriarchy, in Elshtain's estimation, is simply not powerful enough to make mush out of millions of women's minds. If it were, feminists would be unable to provide a cogent explanation for the emergence of feminist "true consciousness" out of pervasive patriarchal socialization. Observing that liberal feminists' attempt to reduce "wifing" and "mothering" to mere "roles" is misguided, Elshtain wrote:

> Mothering is *not* a "role" on par with being a file clerk, a scientist, or a member of the Air Force. Mothering is a complicated, rich, ambivalent, vexing, joyous activity which is biological, natural, social, symbolic, and emotional. It carries profoundly resonant emotional and sexual imperatives. A tendency to downplay the differences that pertain between, say, mothering and holding a job, not only drains our private relations of much of their significance, but also over-simplifies what can and should be done to alter things for women, who are frequently urged to change roles in order to solve their problems.[107]

If after investing years of her blood, sweat, tears, and toil in being a wife and mother, a woman is told she made the wrong choice, that she could have done something "significant" with her life instead, her reaction is not likely to be a positive one. It is one thing to tell a woman she should change her hairstyle; it is quite another to tell her she should get a more meaningful identity.

Finally, as Elshtain saw it, liberal feminists are wrong to sing "a paean of praise to what Americans themselves call the 'rat race,'"[108] to suggest that either women or men *should* absorb traditional masculine values. Articles written for women about dressing for success, making it in a man's world, being careful not to cry in public, avoiding intimate friendships, being assertive, and playing hardball serve only to erode what may, after all, be best about women: their learned ability, according to Elshtain, to create and sustain community through involvement with friends and family. Woman ought not to learn these lessons. Rather than encouraging each other to mimic the traditional behavior of successful men, who spend a minimum of time at home and a maximum of time at the office, women ought to work toward the kind of society in which men as well as women have as much time for friends and family as for business associates and professional colleagues.

Although she came close here to forwarding the problematic thesis that every wife and mother is the Virgin Mary in disguise, Elshtain insisted maternal thinking "need not and must not descend into the sentimentalization that vitiated much Suffragist discourse."[109] Fearing full participation in the public sphere would threaten female virtue, the suffragists reasoned "the vote" alone was a way for women to reform the evil, deceitful, and ugly public realm without ever having to leave the supposed goodness, truth, and beauty of the private realm. As Elshtain saw it, had the suffragists not constructed a false polarity between male vice and female virtue, between the "evil" public world and the "good" private world—had they instead realized the world we live in is one in which virtue and vice coexist and in which the public and private worlds intermingle—then they might have marched into the public world, demanding it absorb the virtues and values of the private world from which they had come.[110]

In assessing Elshtain's critique of liberal feminism, 1990s liberal feminists observed that although Elshtain's 1981 critique of liberal feminism applied to *The Feminine Mystique* (1963), it did not apply to *The Second Stage* (1981) which, in their estimation, was no less *conservative* than Elshtain's 1981 book, *Public Man/Private Woman*. Cautioning women that there is a thin line between, on the one hand, admitting women aren't just like men and, on the other, pushing women back into the private world from which they have only recently emerged, many 1990s liberal feminists rejected *The Second Stage* as a pseudofeminist text. To claim women can't be just like men (because of some of men's traditionally "bad" traits and behavior) is, they noted, also to claim men can't be just like women, often don't want to be just like women, and sometimes shouldn't want to be just like women (because of some of women's traditionally "bad" traits and behavior). Elshtain's tune, echoed by Friedan in *The Second Stage*, is sweet music to the ears of those men who have wanted to hear that, after all, androgyny *is* a misguided goal—men not only can't and don't want to be "feminine"; they shouldn't want to be "feminine."

Critique Two: Woman Does Not Live by Reason and Autonomy Alone

In *Feminist Politics and Human Nature*, Alison Jaggar formulated a second critique of liberal feminism, aimed at those concepts she believed fundamental to it. Like Elshtain, Jaggar criticized liberal feminists for being too eager to adopt "male" values, but she targeted primarily what she perceived as their concept of the self. According to Jaggar, liberal feminists conceive of the self as a rational, autonomous agent, that is, as a "male" self.

Realizing not everyone will understand why rationality or autonomy are "male," Jaggar carefully explained her point. She first noted that because liberal feminists locate human beings' "specialness" in human rationality and autonomy, they are so-called normative dualists—thinkers committed to the view that the functions and activities of the mind are somehow better than those of the body.[111] Eating, drinking, excreting, sleeping, and reproducing are not, according to this view, quintessential human activities because members of most other animal species also engage in them. Instead, what sets human beings apart from the rest of animal creation is their capacity to wonder, imagine, and comprehend.

Jaggar then speculated that because of the original sexual division of labor, mental activities and functions were increasingly emphasized over bodily activities and functions in Western liberal thought. Given his distance from nature, his undemanding reproductive and domestic roles, and the amount of time he was consequently able to spend cultivating the life of the mind, man tended to devalue the body, regarding it as a protective shell whose contours had little to do with his self-definition. In contrast, given her close ties to nature, her heavy reproductive and domestic roles, and the amount of time she consequently had to spend caring for bodies, woman tended to value the body, viewing it as essential to her personal identity. Because men have traditionally been the philosophers, observed Jaggar, their way of seeing themselves has come to dominate Western culture's collective history of ideas. As a result, all liberals, male or female, nonfeminist or feminist, tend to accept as truth the priority of the mental over the bodily, even when their own daily experiences contradict this belief.

Liberal feminism's adherence to normative dualism is problematic, according to Jaggar, not only because it leads to a devaluation of bodily activities and functions but also because it usually leads to both political solipsism and political skepticism. (Political solipsism is the belief that the rational, autonomous person is essentially isolated, with needs and interests separate from, and even in opposition to, those of every other individual. Political skepticism is the belief that the fundamental questions of political philosophy—in what does human well-being and fulfillment consist, and what are the means to attain it?—have no common answer.) Thus, the result of emphasizing mind over body and self over others is the creation of a set of political attitudes and behaviors that puts an extraordinary premium on liberty—on the rational, autonomous, independent, self-determining, isolated, separated, unique person being able to think, do, and be whatever he or she deems worthy.[112]

Jaggar criticized political solipsism on empirical grounds, noting it makes little sense to think of individuals as somehow existing prior to the formation of community through some sort of contract. She observed, for example, that any pregnant woman knows a child is related to others (at least to her) even before it is born. The baby does not—indeed could not—exist as a lonely atom prior to subsequent entrance into the human community. Human infants are born helpless and require great care for many years. Because this care cannot be adequately provided by a single adult, humans live in social groups that cooperatively bring offspring to maturity: "Human interdependence," said Jaggar, "is . . . necessitated by human biology, and the assumption of individual self-sufficiency is plausible only if one ignores human biology."[113] Thus, she insisted, liberal political theorists need to explain not how and why isolated individuals come together but how and why communities dissolve. Competition, not cooperation, is the anomaly.

To add force to her empirical argument, Jaggar observed political solipsism makes no sense conceptually. Here she invoked Naomi Scheman's point that political solipsism requires belief in abstract individualism.[114] The abstract individual is one whose emotions, beliefs, abilities, and interests can supposedly be articulated and understood without any reference whatsoever to social context. Kant's person is this type of abstract individual—a pure reason unaffected/uninfected by either the empirical-psychological ego or the empirical-biological body. However, Kant's philosophy notwithstanding, said Scheman, we are not *abstract* individuals. We are instead *concrete* individuals able to identify certain of our physiological sensations as ones of sorrow, for example, only because we are "embedded in a social web of interpretation that serves to give meaning"[115] to our twitches and twinges, our moans and groans, our squealings and screamings. Apart from this interpretative grid, we are literally *self-less*— that is to say, our very identities are determined by our socially constituted wants and desires. We are, fundamentally, the selves our communities create, a fact that challenges the U.S. myth of the self-sufficient individual.

Political skepticism collapses together with political solipsism according to Jaggar, for it, too, depends on an overly abstract and individualistic conception of the self. In contrast to those liberals/liberal feminists who insist the state should refrain from privileging any one conception of human well-being over another, Jaggar insisted the state should serve as more than a traffic cop who, without commenting on drivers' stated destinations, merely makes sure their cars do not collide. Whether we like it or not, she said, human biology and psychology dictate a set of basic human needs, and societies that treat these basic needs as "optional" cannot expect to survive, let alone to thrive. Thus, said Jaggar, the state must do more than keep traffic moving; it must also block off certain roads even if some individuals want very much to travel down them.

Defenders of liberal feminism challenge Jaggar's and Scheman's critique of liberal feminism on the grounds that the liberalism of liberal *feminists* is not the same as the liberalism of liberal *nonfeminists*. In what she termed a "qualified" defense of liberal feminism, Susan Wendell stressed that liberal feminists are not fundamentally committed either to separating the rational from the emotional or to valuing the former over the latter. On the contrary, they seem fully aware that reason and emotion, mind and body are "equally necessary to human survival and the richness of human experience."[116] Indeed, observed Wendell, if liberal feminists lacked a conception of the self as an *integrated* whole, we would be hard pressed to explain their tendency to view androgyny as a positive state of affairs. For the most part, liberal feminists want their sons to develop a wide range of emotional responses and domestic skills as much as they want their daughters to develop a wide range of rational capacities and professional talents. Complete human beings are *both* rational and emotional. Thus, Wendell urged feminists to read liberal feminist texts sympathetically, as "a philosophically better kind of liberalism"[117] and to overcome the misconception that "[a] commitment to the value of individuals and their self-development, or even to the ethical priority of individuals over groups," is automatically a commitment "to narcissism or egoism or to the belief that one's own most important characteristics are somehow independent of one's relationships with other people."[118] Just because a woman refuses to spend *all* of her time nurturing her family does not mean she is any more selfish than her husband, who probably spends even less of his time taking care of their children than she does. A person is selfish only when he or she takes more than his or her fair share of a resource: money, time, or even something intangible like love.

Critique Three: Liberal Feminism as Racist, Classist, and Heterosexist

Critics frequently claim, as I have mentioned, that liberal feminism serves only or mainly the interests of white, heterosexual, middle-class women.

Although liberal feminists accept this criticism as a just and fair one, they nonetheless note in their partial defense that many minority women, lesbian women, and working-class women allied with liberal feminists in the past and continue to do so today. For example (and as noted above), black women were part of the U.S. woman's suffrage movement from its inception. To be sure (and also as noted above), *white* suffragists often failed to welcome and acknowledge black women's contributions to women's rights movements, but white liberal feminists have come a long way since the nineteenth century when (*white*) women's concerns were set in opposition to black (*men's*) concerns. Nowadays, liberal feminists are particularly attentive to the ways in which a woman's *race* affects what she counts as an instance of gender discrimination. This sort of awareness invites us to consider, for example, white and black women's divergent views on topics such as housework.

Because Friedan addressed a largely white, middle-class, and well-educated group of women in *The Feminist Mystique*, it made sense for her to describe the "housewife" role as oppressive. After all, her audience did suffer from the kind of psychological problems people experience when they are underchallenged and restricted to repeatedly performing the same routine tasks. But as Angela Davis commented, the housewife role tends to be experienced as liberatory rather than oppressive by black, poor, minimally educated women. For these women, housework in their own homes is preferable to domestic work in white women's homes.[119] In fact, stressed Davis, many black women would be only too happy to trade their problems for the "problem that has no name." They would embrace white, middle-class, suburban life enthusiastically, happy to have plenty of time to lavish on their families and themselves.

Liberal feminists' increased stress on issues of race has prompted an increasing number of minority women to join and become active in liberal feminist organizations. For example, largely because NOW has allied itself with minority organizations devoted to welfare reform, civil rights, immigration policy, apartheid, and migrant worker and tribal issues, minority women currently constitute 30 percent of NOW's leadership and 10 percent of its staff.[120] Unlike nineteenth-century liberal feminists, today's liberal feminists no longer mistakenly contrast women's rights with blacks' rights, implying that black women are neither "real women" nor "real blacks" but some sort of hybrid creatures whose rights are of little concern to either white women or black men.

In addition to racism, classism has cropped up within liberal feminism, largely because the women who initially led the women's rights movement were from the upper middle class. Seemingly oblivious to the social and economic privileges of the women whom she addressed in *The Feminine Mystique*, Friedan simply assumed all or most women were supported by men and therefore worked for other than *financial* reasons. Later, when she came into increased contact with single mothers trying to support their families on meager wages or paltry welfare benefits, Friedan realized just how hard life can be for a poor urban woman working in a factory, as opposed to a wealthy suburban woman driving to a PTA meeting. Thus, Friedan made an effort in *The Second Stage* to address some of the economic concerns of working women. Nevertheless, her primary audience remained the daughters of the housewives she had tried to liberate in the 1960s: well-educated, financially comfortable, working mothers whom she wished to rescue from the hardships of the so-called double day. In the final analysis, *The Second Stage* is a book for middle-class professional women (and men) much more than a text for working-class people. It envisions a society in which men and women assume equal burdens and experience equal benefits in both the public and private worlds. But it fails to ask whether a *capitalist* society can afford to develop ideal work and family conditions for *all* of its members or only for the "best" and "brightest"—that is, for those professionals and quasi professionals who are already well enough off to take advantage of joint appointments, parental leaves, the mommy track, flextime, leaves of absence, and so on.

Similarly, Friedan's 1993 book, *The Fountain of Age*, is directed more toward relatively well-to-do and healthy old people than relatively poor and frail old people. Although Friedan's anecdotes about people remaking their lives after the age of sixty are inspiring, they are, as one commentator noted, mostly tales about "life-long achievers with uncommon financial resources"[121] who are continuing to do in their "golden years" what they did in their younger years. The experience of this group of people is to be contrasted with those U.S. citizens whose work years have worn them out physically and psychologically and who find it extremely difficult to survive let alone thrive on a small fixed income. As such people age, especially if they are infirm, their main enemy is not "self-image." On the contrary, it is "unsafe neighborhoods, unmanageable stairs, tight budgets and isolation."[122] To be sure, Friedan noted the plight of aging, infirm U.S. citizens in *The Fountain of Age* and recommended a variety of concrete ways (e.g., home care and community support) to ameliorate their situation. Yet she failed to address society's *general unwillingness* to allocate time, money, and love to old people who act old and need more than what some consider their fair share of society's resources. Indeed, by emphasizing the importance of remaining "vital" in old age, Friedan may have inadvertently helped widen the gap between advantaged and disadvantaged old people.

Finally, in addition to racism and classism, heterosexism has posed problems for liberal feminists. When lesbians working within the women's rights movement decided publicly to avow their sexual identity, the leadership and membership of organizations such as NOW disagreed about how actively and officially they should support gay rights. As noted above, Friedan was among the feminists who feared a vocal and visible lesbian constituency might further alienate the general public from "women's rights" causes. The woman who succeeded Friedan in office, Arlein Hernandez, was embarrassed by her predecessor's lukewarm support for lesbians. Upon accepting the presidency of NOW in 1970, Hernandez issued a strong statement in support of lesbians: "[NOW does] not prescribe a sexual preference test for applicants. We ask only that those who join NOW commit themselves to work for full equality for women and that they do so in the context that the struggle in which we are engaged is part of the total struggle to free all persons to develop their full humanity."[123] Even more significant, as Judith Hole and Ellen Levine observed, Hernandez accused the media in particular of employing a kind of "sexual McCarthyism" in its eagerness to discredit the women's movement by labeling it a "lesbian" movement: "[The media] attempts to turn us away from the real business of the movement and towards endless and fruitless discussions on matters which are *not* at issue. . . . We need to free *all* our sisters from the shackles of a society which insists on viewing us in terms of sex."[124] Lesbians no less than heterosexual women, insisted Hernandez, have sexual rights.

To be sure, Hernandez's statements did not win her NOW's universal approval. Conservative members of NOW complained "gay rights" was not a bona fide woman's issue. Radical members of NOW countered that if anyone knew what a real *woman's* issue was, it was the lesbian: she who puts women, not men, at the center of her private as well as public life. The battle between these two groups in NOW escalated to such a degree it threatened NOW's existence for a year or so before NOW officially identified lesbian rights as a feminist issue and a NOW issue. In 1990 NOW manifested its support of lesbians in a particularly visible way: It elected Patricia Ireland, an open bisexual, as its president. It is important to stress, however, that even today NOW supports lesbianism as a *personal* sexual preference—as a life-style or partner choice some women make—rather than as a *political* statement about the *best* way to achieve women's liberation. Liberal feminists do not claim that women must orient all of their sexual desires toward women and away from men or that all women must love women more than they love men. They instead claim that men as well as women must treat each other as equals, as persons equally worthy of love.

Conclusion

One way to react to the limitations of liberal feminism is to dismiss it as a bourgeois, white movement. In essence, this is precisely what Ellen Willis did in her 1975 article "The Conservatism of *Ms.*," which faulted *Ms.* magazine, one of the chief organs of liberal feminism, for imposing a pseudofeminist "party line." After enumerating several points in this "line," Willis noted their cumulative emphasis is a denial of women's pressing need to overthrow patriarchy and capitalism and an affirmation of women's supposed ability to make it in the "system." Whatever *Ms.* has to offer women, insisted Ellis, it is not feminism: "At best, *Ms.*'s self-improvement, individual-liberation philosophy is relevant only to an elite; basically it is an updated women's magazine fantasy. Instead of the sexy chick or the perfect homemaker, we now have a new image to live up to: the liberated woman. This fantasy, misrepresented as feminism, misleads some women, convinces others that 'women's lib' has nothing to do with them, and plays into the hands of those who oppose any real change in women's condition."[125]

Willis's criticism may have been on target at the time, but *Ms.* has changed since the mid-1970s. Its editors have featured articles that show, for example, how classism, racism, and heterosexism intersect with sexism, thereby doubling, tripling, and even quadrupling the oppression of some women. Moreover, liberal feminists have with few exceptions[126] moved away from their traditional belief that any woman who wants to can liberate herself "individually" by "throwing off" her conditioning and "unilaterally" rejecting "femininity."[127] They now believe that achieving even a modest goal such as "creating equal employment opportunity for women" calls for much more than the effort of individual women; it will require the effort of a whole society committed to "giving girls and boys the same early education and ending sex prejudice, which in turn will require major redistribution of resources and vast changes in consciousness."[128] Sexual equality cannot be achieved through individual women's willpower alone. Also necessary are major alterations in the deepest social and psychological structures.

Liberal feminism is by no means passé; it may even have the "radical future" Eisenstein predicted. For all its limitations, its strengths are undeniable. We owe to liberal feminists many of the educational and legal reforms that have improved the quality of life for women. It is doubtful that without liberal feminists' efforts, so many women could have attained their newfound professional and occupational stature. To be sure, there is more to feminism than educational and legal reforms aimed primarily at increasing women's professional and occupational status. But such reforms are to be neither trivialized nor memorialized as *past* accomplishments. Liberal feminists still have much work to do before *all* women's educational, legal, and professional/occupational gains are entirely secure.

◼

CHAPTER TWO

Radical Feminism: Libertarian and Cultural Perspectives

AFTER THE RATIFICATION OF THE NINETEENTH AMENDMENT in 1920, U.S. feminists were relatively quiescent until the mid-1960s, when they became increasingly active either in so-called women's rights groups or women's liberation groups.[1] Although it is somewhat simplistic to tag the former groups "liberal feminist" and the latter groups "radical feminist," it is not entirely inaccurate. Most of the 1960s and 1970s women (and men) who belonged to women's rights groups such as the National Organization for Women believed they could achieve gender equality by reforming the "system"—by working to eliminate discriminatory educational, legal, and economic policies. Achieving equal rights for women was the paramount goal of these reformers, and the fundamental tenets of liberal political philosophy were a comfortable fit for them. In contrast, most of the women who formed groups such as the Redstockings, the Feminists, and the New York Radical Feminists and who later kept the spirit of these groups alive in thousands of small consciousness-raising groups throughout the United States perceived themselves as revolutionaries rather than reformers. Unlike the feminists who joined the women's rights groups, these feminists did not become interested in women's issues as a result of working for government agencies, being appointed to commissions on the status of women, or joining women's business or professional groups. Instead, their desire to improve women's condition emerged in the context of their participation in one or more of the radical social movements that swept across the United States in the early 1960s: the civil rights movement, new left politics, and the peace movement.[2] None of these feminists wanted to preserve the status quo, especially the sex/gender system that they identified as the primary cause of women's oppression.

In drawing the contrast between women's rights and women's liberation groups and associating the former with liberal feminism and the latter with radical feminism, I realize a large number of feminists fall between the cracks of these two feminisms. For example, in Chapter One I classified Elizabeth Cady Stanton as a liberal feminist, largely because of the role she played in securing *legal* rights for women and because of her conviction women must have the vote. I did this even though she expressed many radical feminist thoughts in her writings, particularly in those related to her critique of Christianity. Indeed, in *The Woman's Bible* Stanton proclaimed in no uncertain terms that "creeds, codes, scriptures and statutes, are all based" on the patriarchal ideal "that woman was made after man, of man, and for man, an inferior being, subject to man."[3] Stanton was quite aware of the ways in which the sex/gender system oppressed women, but because most of her contemporaries, including most of the women active in the women's rights movement, were either unwilling or unable to see what Stanton saw so clearly, Stanton devoted herself mainly to liberal-reformist, not radical-revolutionary programs of action. She contented herself with winning a few battles, leaving it to future generations of feminists to win the war. If there were feminists like Stanton in the nineteenth century, it stands to reason there are feminists like Stanton in the twentieth century: radical women who espouse liberal programs for pragmatic, as opposed to theoretical, reasons. Nevertheless, it is also true many feminists were then and are now radical "women's liberation" feminists unwilling to yield philosophical theory to the exigencies of political practice.

As hard as it is to draw a boundary line between "liberal" women's rights groups and "radical" women's liberation groups, it is even more difficult to articulate the differences existing within the radical feminist community. To be sure, in order to qualify as a radical feminist, a feminist must insist the sex/gender system is the fundamental cause of women's oppression. According to Alison Jaggar and Paula Rothenberg, this claim can be interpreted to mean:

1. That women were, historically, the first oppressed group.
2. That women's oppression is the most widespread, existing in virtually every known society.
3. That women's oppression is the deepest in that it is the hardest form of oppression to eradicate and cannot be removed by other social changes such as the abolition of class society.
4. That women's oppression causes the most suffering to its victims, qualitatively as well as quantitatively, although the suffering may

often go unrecognized because of the sexist prejudices of both the oppressors and the victims.

5. That women's oppression . . . provides a conceptual model for understanding all other forms of oppression.[4]

In recent years it has become clear that just because a group of feminists agree in principle that sexism is the first, most widespread, or deepest form of human oppression does not mean they also agree about the nature and function of this pernicious ism or the best way to eliminate it. On the contrary, with the emergence of so-called essentialism in feminist thought, the radical feminist community has divided into two camps: radical-libertarian feminists and radical-cultural feminists.

Today's radical-libertarian feminists generally espouse the ideas of those 1960s and 1970s radical feminists in Boston and New York who first drew attention to the ways in which the very concept of femininity as well as women's reproductive and sexual roles and responsibilities often serve to limit women's development as full human persons. These were the radical feminists who, among other things, longed for androgyny. For example, Joreen J. wrote: "What is disturbing about a Bitch is that she is androgynous. She incorporates within herself qualities defined as 'masculine' as well as 'feminine.' A Bitch is blatant, direct, arrogant, at times egoistic. She has no liking for the indirect, subtle, mysterious ways of the 'eternal feminine.' She disdains the vicarious life deemed natural to women because she wants to live a life of her own."[5]

Reflecting upon the words of Joreen, commentator Alice Echols observed that however "skewed" in the direction of masculinity Joreen's concept of androgyny might have been, it nonetheless expressed radical feminists' original desire to transcend the limits of the sex/gender system by daring to be masculine as well as feminine.[6] Later, however, a number of radical feminists began to question whether they wanted to be masculine at all. As they saw it, a "bitch" was not a full human person but instead a woman who had embraced some of the worst features of masculinity. According to Echols, this group of radical feminists rejected the idea of androgyny as a desirable goal for feminists, replacing it with a proposal to affirm women's essential "femaleness."[7] Far from believing the liberated woman must exhibit both masculine and feminine traits and behaviors, these radical-cultural feminists expressed the view that it is better to be female/feminine than it is to be male/masculine. Thus, women should not try to be like men. On the contrary, they should try to be more like women, emphasizing the values and virtues culturally associated with women ("interdependence, community, connection, sharing, emotion, body, trust, absence of hierarchy, nature, immanence, process, joy, peace and life") and deemphasizing the values and virtues culturally associated with men ("independence, autonomy, intellect, will, wariness, hierarchy, domination, culture, transcendence, product, asceticism, war and death").[8]

Although I agree with Echols and other feminists such as Linda Alcoff concerning the important differences between today's radical-libertarian and radical-cultural feminists, I do think these differences can be overstated. In fact, Echols and Alcoff themselves conceded that not all radical-cultural feminists believe male-female differences are rooted in nature. Some of them, noted Echols, think sex/gender differences flow not so much (if at all) from biology as from "socialization" or "from the total history of existing as a woman in a patriarchal society."[9] Nevertheless, stressed Alcoff, these variations on essentialism do not seem to make that much difference in the end. Whether men's behavior toward women is the result of their nature or their culture, radical-cultural feminists will still condemn it as bad. "Masculinity" is just as big a problem for women as "maleness" is. Thus, radical-cultural feminists, unlike radical-libertarian feminists, instruct women to keep their feminine characters free of poisonous masculine additives.[10]

To be certain, like any classification of radical feminists, the libertarian-cultural distinction is subject to criticism. Yet even if I, for one, am not always certain whether a radical feminist is more "libertarian" than "cultural" or vice versa, I think the libertarian-cultural feminist distinction helps explain why some radical feminists find sex "dangerous" and why others find it "pleasurable." I also think this same distinction helps explain why some feminists view natural reproduction as the primary cause of women's oppression and why others view it as the ultimate source of women's power. I leave it up to readers to decide for themselves, however, whether they find the libertarian-cultural feminist distinction as helpful as I do.

Radical-Libertarian and Radical-Cultural Feminists: Interpreting the Sex/Gender System

Analyzing the Oppressive Features of Gender ("Masculinity" and "Femininity")

In order fully to understand radical-libertarian and radical-cultural feminist views on androgyny, it is necessary first to define the sex/gender system. According to radical-libertarian feminist Gayle Rubin, the sex/gender system is a "set of arrangements by which a society transforms biological sexuality into products of human activity."[11] So, for example, patriarchal society uses certain facts about male and female physiology (chromosomes, anatomy, hormones) as the basis for constructing a set of

"masculine" and "feminine" identities and behaviors that serve to empower men and disempower women. In the process of accomplishing this
ideological task, patriarchal society manages to convince itself its cultural
constructions are somehow "natural" and therefore that one's "normal-
ity" depends on one's ability to display the *gender* identities and behaviors society culturally links with one's biological *sex*.

Among others, radical-libertarian feminists rejected the assumption
there is or should be a necessary connection between one's sex (male or
female) and one's gender (masculine or feminine). Instead, they claimed
that gender is separable from sex and that patriarchal society uses rigid
gender roles to keep women passive ("affectionate, obedient, responsive
to sympathy and approval, cheerful, kind and friendly") and men active
("tenacious, aggressive, curious, ambitious, planful, responsible, original
and competitive").[12] Thus, the way for women to dispel men's unjustified
power over women is for both sexes first to recognize women are no more
destined to be passive than men are destined to be active, and then to develop whatever combination of feminine and masculine traits best reflects
their individually unique personalities.

Some Radical-Libertarian Feminist Views: Millett and Firestone

Millett's *Sexual Politics*.   One of the first radical-libertarian feminists to
insist the roots of women's oppression are buried deep in patriarchy's
sex/gender system was Kate Millett. In her *Sexual Politics* (1970), Millett
argued that sex is political primarily because the male-female relationship is the paradigm for all *power* relationships: "Social caste supersedes
all other forms of inegalitarianism: racial, political, or economic, and unless the clinging to male supremacy as a birthright is finally forgone, all
systems of oppression will continue to function simply by virtue of their
logical and emotional mandate in the primary human situation."[13] Because male control of the public and private worlds constitutes patriarchy, male control must be eliminated if women are to be liberated. But
this is no easy task. To eliminate male control, men and women have to
eliminate gender—specifically, sexual status, role, and temperament—as
it has been constructed under patriarchy.

Patriarchal ideology, according to Millett, exaggerates biological differences between men and women, making certain that men always have
the dominant, or masculine, roles and women always have the subordinate, or feminine, ones. This ideology is so powerful that men are usually
able to secure the apparent consent of the very women they oppress. They
do this through institutions such as the academy, the church, and the family, each of which justifies and reinforces women's subordination to men,

resulting in most women's internalization of a sense of inferiority to men. Should a woman refuse to accept patriarchal ideology and should she manifest her mistrust by casting off her femininity—that is, her submissiveness/subordination—men will use coercion to accomplish what conditioning has failed to achieve. Intimidation, observed Millett, is everywhere in patriarchy. The streetwise woman realizes if she wants to survive in patriarchy, she had better act "feminine," or else she may be subjected to "a variety of cruelties and barbarities."[14]

Millett stressed that despite men's continual attempts to condition and coerce all women, many women have proved uncontrollable. During the 1800s, for example, U.S. women's resistance to men's power took several forms, including the women's movement inaugurated in 1848 at Seneca Falls, New York. As noted in Chapter One, this spirited movement helped women gain many important legal, political, and economic liberties and equalities. Nevertheless, the women's movement of the 1800s failed fully to liberate women because it failed to challenge the sex/gender system at its deepest roots. As a result, twentieth-century patriarchal forces were able to regain the ground they had lost from nineteenth-century feminist activists.

Millett singled out authors D. H. Lawrence, Henry Miller, and Norman Mailer as some of the most articulate leaders of patriarchy's 1930–1960 assault on feminist ideas. She claimed that because readers took Lawrence's, Miller's, and Mailer's *descriptions* of relationships in which women are sexually humiliated and abused by men as *prescriptions* for ideal sexual conduct, they tended to regard themselves as sexual failures, unable to emulate the sexual behavior of the characters in Miller's *Sexus*, for example:

> "You never wear any undies do you? You're a slut, do you know it?"
> I pulled her dress up and made her sit that way while I finished my coffee.
> "Play with it a bit while I finish this."
> "You're filthy," she said, but she did as I told her.
> "Take your two fingers and open it up. I like the color of it."
> . . . With this I reached for a candle on the dresser at my side and I handed it to her.
> "Let's see if you can get it in all the way. . . . "
> "You can make me do anything, you dirty devil."
> "You like it, don't you?"[15]

To the objection that readers of *Sexus* can tell the difference between fiction and reality, Millett replied pornography often functions in much the same way advertising does. The perfectly slim bodies of the models who grace the covers of *Vogue* become standards for the whole of womankind. Nobody has to articulate an explicit law, "Thou shalt mold thine lumpen body in the image of Cindy Crawford." Every woman simply knows what is expected of her, what it means to be a beautiful woman. In the same way, every reader of *Sexus* simply knows what is expected of him or her, what it means to be a sexually vital person.

In addition to these literate pornographers, Millett identified two other patriarchal groups—neo-Freudian psychologists and Parsonian sociologists—as leading the assault on feminists. Although Sigmund Freud's openness about sexuality, his willingness to talk about what people do or do not do in the bedroom, initially appeared as a progressive step toward better, more various, and more liberating sexual relations, Millett claimed Freud's disciples used his writings to "rationalize the invidious relationship between the sexes, to ratify traditional roles, and to validate temperamental differences."[16] In a similar vein, the followers of Talcott Parsons, an eminent sociologist, used his writings to argue that distinctions between masculine and feminine traits are biological/natural rather than cultural/artificial, and that without rigid gender dimorphism, society could not function as well as it does now. Convinced gender identities and behaviors are not "an arbitrary imposition on an infinitely plastic biological base" but rather "an adjustment to the real biological differences between the sexes," Parsons's disciples confidently asserted that women's subordination to men is natural.[17]

Rather than concluding her discussion of patriarchal reactionaries on a despairing note, however, Millett chose to end it on an optimistic note. In the late 1970s women were, she believed, regrouping their forces. Aware of their nineteenth-century predecessors' mistakes, these twentieth-century feminists were determined not to repeat history. Millett observed in contemporary feminism a determined effort to destroy the sex/gender system—the basic source of women's oppression—and to create a new society in which men and women are equals at every level of existence.[18]

Although in 1970 Millett looked forward to an androgynous future, to an integration of separate masculine and feminine subcultures, she insisted this integration must proceed cautiously with a thorough evaluation of all masculine and feminine traits. "Obedience," as it has been traditionally exhibited by women, for example, should not be unreflectively celebrated as a desirable human trait, that is, as a trait an androgynous person should recognize as positive and therefore seek to possess. Nor is "aggressiveness," as it has been traditionally exhibited by men, to be incorporated into the psyche of the androgynous person as a desirable human trait. Androgyny, speculated Millett, is a worthy ideal only if the feminine and masculine qualities integrated in the androgynous person are separately worthy.[19] After all, if we are told the ideal human combines in herself or himself masculine arrogance and feminine servility, we will be less favorably impressed than if we are told the ideal human combines

the strength traditionally associated with men and the compassion traditionally associated with women. Not only is it undesirable to combine in
one person the two vices of arrogance and servility—the excess and defect, respectively, of the virtue of self-respect—it is also impossible, since
these two vices are polar opposites. In contrast, it is both possible and desirable to combine in one person the qualities of strength and compassion, since these two virtues are complementary and likely to help a person live well in his or her community.

Firestone's *Dialectic of Sex.*   Like Millett, Shulamith Firestone, another
radical-libertarian feminist, claimed the material basis for the sexual/po-
litical ideology of female submission and male domination was rooted in
the reproductive roles of men and women. However, Firestone believed
Millett's solution to this problem—the elimination of the so-called sexual
double standard that had permitted men but not women to experiment
with sex and the inauguration of a dual-parenting system that would give
fathers and mothers equal child-rearing responsibilities—was inadequate. It would, in her estimation, take far more than such modest reforms in the sex/gender system to free women's (and men's) sexuality
from the biological imperatives of procreation and to liberate women's
(and men's) personalities from socially constructed, Procrustean prisons
of "femininity" and "masculinity." In fact, said Firestone, it would take a
major biological and social revolution to effect this kind of human liberation: artificial (ex utero) reproduction would have to replace natural (in
utero) reproduction and so-called intentional families, whose members
chose each other for reasons of friendship or even simple convenience,
would have to replace the traditional biological family constituted in and
through its members' genetic connections to each other.

Firestone maintained that with the end of the biological family would
come the breakup of the Oedipal family situation that prohibits, among
other things, parent-child incest. No longer would there be concerns
about so-called inbreeding, said Firestone, as humanity reverted to its
natural "polymorphous perversity"[20] and once again delighted in all
types of sexual behavior. Genital sex, so important for the purposes of biological sex, would become just one kind of sexual experience, and a relatively unimportant one, as people rediscovered the erotic pleasures of
their oral and anal cavities and engaged in sexual relations with members
of the same as well as the opposite sex.

Firestone claimed that as soon as men and women were truly free to engage in polymorphous, perverse sex, it would no longer be necessary for
men to display only "masculine" identities and behaviors and for women
to display only "feminine" ones. Freed from their gender roles at the level
of biology (that is, reproduction), women would no longer have to be pas-

sive, receptive, and vulnerable, sending out "signals" to men to dominate, possess, and penetrate them in order to keep the wheels of human procreation spinning. Instead, men and women would be encouraged to mix and match feminine and masculine traits and behaviors in whatever combination they wished. As a result, not only would human beings evolve into androgynous persons; all of culture would become androgynous. As Firestone saw it, the biological division of the sexes for the purpose of procreation had created not only a false dichotomy between masculinity and femininity but also an invidious cultural split between the sciences and the arts.

Firestone believed our culture associates science and technology with men and the humanities and the arts with women. Thus, the "masculine response" to reality is the "technological response"—"objective, logical, extroverted, realistic, concerned with the conscious mind (the ego), rational, mechanical, pragmatic and down-to-earth, stable."[21] In contrast, the "feminine response" to reality is the "aesthetic response"—"subjective, intuitive, introverted, wishful, dreamy or fantastic, concerned with the subconscious (the *id*), emotional, even temperamental (hysterical)."[22] Only when the biological revolution described above eliminates the need for maintaining rigid lines between "male" and "female," "masculine" and "feminine," will it be possible for our culture to bridge the gap between the sciences and the arts. Androgynous persons will find themselves living in an androgynous culture in which the categories of "the technological" and "the aesthetic," together with the categories of "the masculine" and "the feminine," will have disappeared through what Firestone termed "a mutual cancellation—a matter-antimatter explosion, ending with a poof!"[23] At last, claimed Firestone, the male Technological Mode would be able to "produce in actuality what the female Aesthetic Mode had envisioned"[24]—namely, a world in which we use our knowledge to create not hell but heaven on earth—a world in which men no longer have to toil by the sweat of their brow to live and in which women no longer have to bear children in pain and travail.[25]

Clearly, Firestone's version of androgyny is quite different from Millett's. Indeed, one wonders whether it is androgyny in the strict sense of the term, for in the world envisioned by Firestone "men" and "women" as defined by current gender traits and role responsibilities no longer exist. Nevertheless, because the ideal person in Firestone's utopia is permitted to combine within "himself"/"herself" a range of those qualities we currently term "masculine" and "feminine," Firestone's version of androgyny might, after all, be situated on the same continuum with Millett's. However, it is important to emphasize that, for Millett, the ideal androgynous person combines a balance of the *best* masculine and feminine characteristics, whereas, for Firestone, there is no *one* way to be androgynous.

Some Radical-Cultural Feminist Views: French and Daly

Marilyn French. Because Marilyn French attributes male-female differences more to biology (nature) than to socialization (nurture), I view her as more of a radical-cultural feminist than a radical-libertarian feminist and, therefore, as a theorist whose androgynous person seems to incorporate far more feminine than masculine traits. In fact, in French's book *Beyond Power*, a form of androgyny emerges that suggests women's traditional traits are somehow better than men's traditional traits. Like Millett and Firestone fifteen years earlier, French claimed men's oppression of women leads logically to other systems of human domination. If it is possible to justify men's domination of women, it is possible to justify any and all forms of domination. "Stratification of men above women," wrote French, "leads in time to stratification of classes: an elite rules over people perceived as 'closer to nature,' savage, bestial, animalistic."[26] Because French believed sexism is the model for all other isms, including racism and classism, she sought to explain the ideology of "power-over" that sustains it and the liberating ideology of "pleasure-with" that could undo it.

After inquiring into the origins of patriarchy, French concluded early humans lived in harmony with nature. They saw themselves as small parts of a larger whole into which they had to fit if they wanted to live. Based on evidence from primates and the world's remaining "simple societies," French speculated the first human societies were probably matricentric (mother centered), for it was the mother who more than likely played the primary role in the group's survival-oriented activities of bonding, sharing, and harmonious participation in nature. Nature was friend; and as sustainer of nature and reproducer of life, woman was also friend.[27] French also speculated that as the human population grew, food inevitably became scarce. No longer experiencing nature as a generous mother, humans decided to take matters into their own hands. They developed techniques to free themselves from the whims of nature. They drilled, dug, and plowed nature for the bounty "she" had decided to hold back from them. The more control humans gained over nature, however, the more they separated themselves from it physically and psychologically. French commented that because a "distance had opened up between humans and their environment as a result of increasing controls exercised over nature," humans became alienated from nature.[28] Alienation, defined by French as a profound sense of separation, aroused "hostility," which in turn led to "fear" and finally to "enmity." It is not surprising, then, that these negative feelings intensified man's desire to control not only nature but also woman, whom they had associated with nature on account of her role in reproduction.[29]

With man's desire to control the dyad "woman/nature" was born patriarchy, a hierarchical system that values so-called power-over. Originally developed to ensure the human community's survival, power-over rapidly became, under patriarchy, a value cultivated simply for the experience of being the person in charge, the lawgiver, the boss, number one in the pecking order. French speculated that untempered by cooperation, patriarchal competition would inevitably lead to unbridled human conflict.[30]

Intent on sparing the world conflict—particularly as it could, in these times, escalate into a nuclear holocaust—French claimed feminine values must be reintegrated into the masculine society patriarchal ideology has created. If we want to see the twenty-first century, said French, we must treasure in our lives and actions "love and compassion and sharing and nutritiveness [sic] equally with control and structure, possessiveness and status."[31] Were we to take this last assertion at face value, we could easily infer that, for French, the best society is an androgynous one in which individual men and women embrace the historically feminine values of love, compassion, sharing, and nurturance just as eagerly as they embrace the historically masculine values of control, structure, possessiveness, and status. Yet a closer reading of French suggests she actually esteemed feminine values *more* than masculine values and that any time she affirmed a masculine value, she had previously subjected it to what Joyce Trebilcot termed a "feminist reconceiving"[32]—that is, a linguistic reinterpretation of a concept that involves a change in the descriptive meaning of a term, the evaluative meaning of a term, or both.[33] According to French, most of her reinterpretations of masculine values involved a change in their descriptive rather than evaluative meaning. For example, she did not argue the masculine value of so-called structure is bad. Instead, she argued that structure, understood as a system or an organization, is good so long as it serves to connect rather than disconnect people.[34]

That French's androgyny involved a substantial reinterpretation of male/masculine traits but not of female/feminine traits became increasingly clear throughout *Beyond Power*. Because "humanness" had been deleteriously identified with a destructive, power-mongering masculine world in the past, French suggested it should be identified with a creative, power-sharing feminine world now and in the future. Based as it is on the value of power-over, the masculine world can accommodate only those ways of being and doing which keep a small group of people in power. It has room for "true grit," "doing what you have to do," and "the end justifying the means" but no room for "knowing when to stop," savoring the "best things in life" (which, we are told, are "for free"), or reflecting on process as well as product. Thus, to be a total man, or patriarch, is not to be a full human being but apparently to be what psychoanalytic feminist Dorothy Dinnerstein termed a minotaur—"[the] gigantic and eternally infantile offspring of a mother's unnatural lust, [the] male representative of mindless, greedy power, [who] insatiably devours live human flesh."[35]

In contrast, the feminine world, based as it is on the value of pleasure—by which French meant the ability of one group or person to affirm all others—can accommodate many ways of being and doing, including those derived from what we generally view as opposite sources. Pleasure, she insisted, can be derived from self as well as others, from the mind as well as the body, from the simple and bucolic as well as the complex and urbane. French saw pleasure as a very broad and deep concept, encompassing all of the enriching experiences we believe a full human person should have.[36]

Because of her obvious dislike for the masculine value of power-over, French claimed the androgynous person must strike a balance not between pleasure-with and power-over but between pleasure-with and a *feminized* version of power-over she labeled "power-to." French emphasized it is good for people to have power as well as pleasure in their lives, provided the power appears not as the desire to destroy (power-over) but as the desire to create (power-to). Conceding human beings will probably never be able to completely eliminate their desire to be top dog, French nonetheless insisted it is possible for people to curb their competitive drives and to cultivate instead their cooperative capacities. By exposing, as best we can, the pain inherent in power-over, we can open the way for the pleasure inherent in power-to.

Mary Daly. More than Millett, Firestone, and even French, radical-cultural feminist Mary Daly denigrated traditional masculine traits. Although Daly began her intellectual journey in *Beyond God the Father* with a plea for androgyny, she ultimately rejected the terms "masculine" and "feminine" as hopelessly befuddled products of patriarchy. Her term-transforming travels through *Gyn/Ecology* ended in *Pure Lust*, a spirited defense of "wild," "lusty," and "wandering" women—women who no longer desire to be androgynous and who prefer to identify themselves as radical lesbian feminist separatists.

In her first major work, *Beyond God the Father: Toward a Philosophy of Women's Liberation*, Daly focused on God as the paradigm for all patriarchs, arguing that unless he is dethroned from both men's and women's consciousness, women will never be empowered as full persons.[37] An oft-repeated idea in *Beyond God the Father* suggests that if anyone ever had a power-over complex, it is the transcendent God we meet in Judaism, Islam, and especially Christianity. This God is so remote and aloof that he dwells in a place beyond earth, suggesting that "power-over" inevitably leads to "separation-from." A transcendent God, observed Daly, is a God who thinks in terms of I-it, subject-object, or self-other relationships. Furthermore, what is most alien to this transcendent God, this total being, is the natural world he called into existence out of total nothingness. Thus, woman, who is associated with nature on account of her reproductive powers, plays the roles of object and other against both God's and man's roles of subject and self.

Because the old transcendent God rejected women, Daly wished to replace him with a new, immanent God. Dwelling within the universe as opposed to outside of it, an immanent God thinks in terms of I-thou, subject-subject, or self-self relationships, and the natural world is as much a part of this God as he/she/it is of the natural world. Thus, women are equal to men before this God, whom Daly described as Be-ing.[38]

One of the main ways in which I-it thinking is reflected in patriarchal society, said Daly, is through the institution of rigid masculine and feminine gender roles, polarizing the human community into two groups. Because men collectively perceive and define women as the second sex, each man becomes an I, or self, and each woman becomes an it, or other. One way, then, to overcome I-it thinking, and the transcendent God who thinks I-it thoughts, is to break down gender dimorphism by constructing an androgynous person who is neither "I" nor "it" but beyond both forms.

Despite her apparent openness to androgyny in *Beyond God the Father*, Daly's concept of androgyny was actually more akin to French's than Millett's or Firestone's. She rejected the "pluralist" model of androgyny, according to which men and women have separate but supposedly equal and complementary traits, and the "assimilation" model of androgyny, according to which both women and men must incorporate both masculine and feminine traits into themselves in order to achieve full personhood.[39] As she saw it, both of these models of androgyny were deficient because neither of them asked whether "masculinity" and "femininity" are concepts worth preserving.

Although Daly's concerns about using the terms "masculinity" and "femininity" were similar to those previously raised by French, she proposed to handle these terms in a different way than French had. Whereas French seemed interested in reinterpreting traditional *masculine* traits, Daly seemed intent on reinterpreting traditional *feminine* traits. Daly insisted that positive feminine traits such as love, compassion, sharing, and nurturance must be carefully distinguished from their pathological excesses, the sort of masochistic feminine "virtues" for which they are frequently mistaken. For example, to love is good, but under patriarchy loving can become, for women, a form of total self-sacrifice or martyrdom. Thus, Daly argued that the construction of the truly androgynous person cannot and must not begin until women say no to the values of the "morality of victimization." Out of this no, said Daly, will come a yes to the values of the "ethics of personhood."[40] By refusing to be the other, by becoming a self with needs, wants, and interests of her own, woman will end the game of man as master and woman as slave.

In *Beyond God the Father*, Daly observed what she described as the Unholy Trinity of Rape, Genocide, and War combining in their one patriarchal person the legions of sexism, racism, and classism. In *Gyn/Ecology: The Metaethics of Radical Feminism*, she articulated this claim more fully, arguing that this Unholy Trinity, this single patriarchal person, has but one essential message: necrophilia, defined as "obsession with and usually erotic attraction toward and stimulation by corpses, typically evidenced by overt acts (as copulation with a corpse)."[41] Whereas Daly emphasized in *Beyond God the Father* that a woman cannot *thrive* so long as she subscribes to the morality of victimization, she stressed in *Gyn/Ecology* that a woman cannot even *survive* so long as she remains in patriarchy. Not only are men out to twist women's minds, they are out to destroy women's bodies through such practices as Hindu suttee, Chinese foot binding, African female circumcision, European witch burning, and Western gynecology.[42]

In *Gyn/Ecology* Daly rejected three terms she had used in *Beyond God the Father: God, homosexuality,* and *androgyny.* She rejected the term *God* because for her it signals death to woman and blocks her "life-loving being." She rejected the term *homosexuality* because for her it erases lesbians and suggests same-sexed love is the same for women as for men. Finally, she rejected the term *androgyny* because for her it twists words and conveys something like "John Travolta and Farrah Fawcett-Majors Scotch-taped together."[43]

Reflecting on the concept of femininity, Daly became convinced there is nothing good in this notion for women to pursue. She asserted patriarchy has constructed Mary as well as Eve, the Madonna as well as the whore, the positive feminine qualities of nurturance, compassion, and gentleness as well as the negative feminine qualities of pettiness, jealousy, and vanity. Thus, she concluded women should reject the seemingly "good" aspects of femininity together with the obviously "bad" ones on the grounds they are all "man-made constructs" shaped for the purposes of trapping women deep in the prison of patriarchy.[44]

Stripped of their *femininity*, women would be revealed in their original (prepatriarchal) *female* power and beauty, insisted Daly. Daly used Jerzy Kosinski's image of a painted bird to detail the differences between false femininity and true femaleness. Kosinski tells the tale of a keeper who imprisons a natural, plain-looking bird simply by painting its feathers with a glittering color. Eventually, the bird is destroyed by her unpainted "friends," the victim of their jealousy. Reversing Kosinski's image, Daly claimed when it comes to women, it is not the artificial, painted "birds" (whom Daly looks upon as tamed, domesticated, feminized females), but the natural, plain-looking "birds" (whom Daly calls "wild females") who suffer. For Daly, painted birds are those women who permit "Daddy" to deck them out in splendor, to "cosmetize" and perfume them, to girdle and corset them. They are the women whom "Daddy" dispatches to destroy real, natural women: that is, the women who refuse to be what the patriarchs want them to be, who insist on being themselves no matter what, and who peel patriarchal paint off their minds and bodies.[45] In Daly's words, the "painted bird functions in the anti-process of double-crossing her sisters, polluting them with poisonous paint."[46] The real, natural woman, in contrast, is "attacked by the mutants of her own kind, the man-made women."[47]

For Daly, flying is the antidote to being painted. The real, natural woman does not take off patriarchal paint only to become vulnerable. Rather, she "takes off"; she "sends the paint flying back into the eyes of the soul-slayers"; she "soars . . . out of the circle of Father Time" and flies "off the clock into other dimensions."[48] She flies free of "mutant fembirds," those women who have permitted themselves to be constructed by patriarchy. She also flies free of the power of patriarchal language and therefore patriarchal values.

In many ways Daly's adamant rejection of androgyny in *Gyn/Ecology* led her to where Friedrich Nietzsche's transvaluation of values led him: to a redefinition of what is good and what is bad, counter to prevailing notions of good and bad. In *On the Genealogy of Morals*, Nietzsche contended there are two basic kinds of moralities: master and slave. In the master morality, good and bad are equivalent to noble and despicable, respectively. To be good is to be on top of the world. To be bad is to be repressed, oppressed, suppressed, or otherwise downtrodden. The criteria for goodness articulated in the slave morality are the polar opposites of the criteria for goodness articulated in the master morality: Those who espouse a slave morality extol qualities such as kindness, humility, and sympathy as virtues and denigrate qualities such as assertiveness, aloofness, and pridefulness as vices. Whereas weak and dependent individuals are regarded as saints, strong and independent individuals are regarded as sinners. By the standards of slave morality, then, the good man of the master morality is evil and the bad man is good.

Motivated by the all-consuming resentment (*resentiment*) of the masters, the slaves gradually develop a negative attitude toward what Nietzsche believed is the most natural drive of a human being: the will to power. As Nietzsche saw it, not only do the slaves have no desire for power; they have no desire for life. Fearful of conflict, of challenge, of charting the course of their destinies, the slaves wish to be complacent in their mediocrity. Nietzsche found them profoundly boring. He also found them incredibly dangerous, for they seemed intent on clogging Western civilization's arteries with sugarplums, placebos, and the milk of human kindness. Nietzsche wrote:

For this is how things are: the diminution and leveling of European man constitutes *our* greatest danger, for the sight of him makes us weary.—We can see nothing today that wants to grow greater, we suspect that things will continue to go down, down, to become thinner, more good-natured, more prudent, more comfortable, more mediocre, more indifferent, more Chinese, more Christian—there is no doubt that man is getting "better" all the time.

Here precisely is what has become a fatality for Europe—together with the fear of man we have also lost our love of him, our reverence for him, our hopes for him, even the will to him. The sight of man now makes us weary.[49]

In order to stop this will to impotence, mediocrity, and death, Nietzsche mandated a transvaluation of all values. By this, he did not intend the creation of a new set of moral values. Rather, he meant to declare war upon the accepted slave values of his time, which he identified as the values of Judaism, Christianity, democracy, and socialism—any philosophy or theology that asks the individual to sacrifice himself or herself for the greater good of the community. Because slave morality is, according to Nietzsche, a perversion of the original, natural morality/psychology of the masters, transvaluation must consist in rejecting the slave morality/psychology. Transvaluation implies that all the stronger, or master, values still exist but now go unrecognized under false names such as "cruelty," "injury," "appropriation," "suppression," "exploitation." These names are false because, having been distorted by the slaves, they do not connote what the masters originally meant, which had nothing to do with embracing death.

Daly is Nietzschean because she insists that when it comes to women, she whom the patriarch calls evil is in fact good, whereas she whom the patriarch calls good is in fact bad. Providing a dictionary of new language in the last section of *Gyn/Ecology*, Daly invited "hags," "spinsters," and "haggard heretics" to "unspook" traditional language and their old feminine selves by *"spinning"* for themselves a new, unconventional language and new female selves. Daly insisted that *women* decide who women want to be. For example, it is good for a woman to be a hag. Daly explained:

> *Hag* is from an Old English word meaning harpy, witch. Webster's gives as the first and "archaic" meaning of *hag*: "a female demon: FURY, HARPY." It also formerly meant: "an evil or frightening spirit." (Lest this sound too negative, we should ask the relevant questions: "Evil" by whose definition? "Frightening" to whom?) A third archaic definition of *hag* is "nightmare." (The important question is: Whose nightmare?) *Hag* is also defined as "an ugly or evil-looking old woman." But this, considering the source, may be considered a compliment. For the beauty of strong, creative women is "ugly" by misogynistic standards of "beauty." The look of female-identified women is "evil" to those who fear us. As for "old," ageism is a feature of phallic society. For women who have transvalued this, a Crone is one who should be an example of strength, courage, and wisdom.[50]

By the time she wrote *Gyn/Ecology*, Daly had clearly rejected the ideal of the androgynous person and put in its place the ideal of the "wild female" who dwells beyond masculinity and femininity. To become whole, a woman needs to strip away the false identity—femininity—patriarchy has constructed for her. Then and only then will she experience herself as the self she would have been had she lived her life in a matriarchy rather than a patriarchy.

In *Pure Lust: Elemental Feminist Philosophy*, Daly continued her transvaluation of values. In this book about woman's power, Daly extended French's analysis of power-to. It is this power men have fed on, making women grow thin, weak, frail, even anorexic. In order to grow strong, women must resist the trap of androgyny. Utterly dependent upon their God-given helpmates, patriarchs offer women androgyny in a last-ditch effort to keep women by their sides: "Come, join forces with us. Masculinity and femininity together!" Women should not, said Daly, be deceived by these inviting words. They are simply a ploy on the part of men to appropriate for themselves whatever is best about women. Men have gradually realized it is in their own (but not women's) best interests to become androgynous persons, since their maleness has so little to offer them. For example, at the end of the film *Tootsie*, after the lead character's male identity has been disclosed (he had been posing as a female television star named Dorothy), he tells Julie, a woman he had befriended in his incarnation as Dorothy, that he actually *is* Dorothy. "The message clearly is one of cannibalistic androgynous maleness. Little Dustin, whom Julie had loved but rejected because she believed he was a woman, incorporates the best of womanhood—like Dionysus and Jesus before him."[51] Men want to be androgynous so that they can subsume or even consume all that is female, draining women's energies into their bodies and minds. Instead of submitting to the gynocidal process of androgyny, women must, said Daly, spin new, powerful self-understandings, remaining radically apart from men, reserving their energies for their own pursuits.

What is most impressive about *Pure Lust* is Daly's ability to provide new meanings, simultaneously prescriptive and descriptive, for terms. The term *lust* is a case in point. Daly wrote, "The usual meaning of *lust* within the lecherous state of patriarchy is well known. It means 'sexual desire, especially of a violent self-indulgent character: LECHERY, LASCIVIOUSNESS.'"[52] Lust, then, is evil, conceded Daly, but only because we live in a patriarchy with its slave morality, which resents women. If we lived instead in a nonpatriarchal society, continued Daly, lust would have good meanings such as "vigor," "fertility," "craving," "eagerness," and "enthusiasm."[53] Thus, the lusty women of *Pure Lust* are the wild females of *Gyn/Ecology*, the women who refuse to be domesticated by men and confined to the cruel rigors of a "sadosociety," which is "formed/framed by statutes of studs, degrees of drones, canons of cocks, fixations of fixers, precepts of prickers, regulations of rakes and rippers . . . bore-ocracy."[54]

The Daly of *Pure Lust* had no use for what she regarded as the petrified language of patriarchy, referring to it only with the aim of redefining, reinterpreting, or reclaiming its terms. *Pure Lust* transvaluated what counts as moral virtue and moral vice for women. In particular, it showed how patriarchal forces deprived natural women of bona fide passions, substituting for them all sorts of what Daly called "plastic" and "potted" passions—inauthentic, counterfeit passions created for artificial women.

According to Daly, such plastic passions as guilt, anxiety, depression, hostility, bitterness, resentment, frustration, boredom, resignation, and fulfillment are no substitute for such genuine passions as love, desire, joy, hate, aversion, sorrow, hope, despair, fear, and anger. Whereas the latter genuine passions spur women to meaningful action, the former plastic passions enervate women. In Daly's estimation, the plastic passion of fulfillment, for example, is not to be confused with the genuine passion of joy. Fulfillment is simply the "therapeutized perversion" of joy. A fulfilled woman is "filled full," "finished," "fixed" just the way patriarchy likes her. Because she is so "totaled," she cannot live the "e-motion of joy." She lacks the energy to move/act purposely.[55] Fulfillment, said Daly, is just another term for Betty Friedan's "problem that has no name"[56]—having a comfortable home, a successful husband, a wonderful child, but no joy.

Like plastic passions, potted passions are also a poor substitute for genuine passions, in Daly's estimation. Although potted passions are in many ways more real than plastic passions, they are not nearly as grand as genuine passions. To appreciate Daly's point, simply compare a real orange tree with one of those miniature versions people are prone to purchase for their homes come January. Love, for example, may be a "many-splendored thing," but when it is potted, packaged, and sold as "romance," women are duped into settling for love's illusion rather than its reality.[57] There is, of course, something tragic about settling for so little when there is so much to be had. Nietzsche hoped the advent of the *übermensch* (overman) would unleash people's potential for greatness. Similarly, Daly hoped to use the words in *Pure Lust* to inspire women to release themselves from the pots and plastic molds blocking their passions. Once woman's passions are released, no patriarchal morality will be able to restrain her volcanic and tidal forces. She will be pure, positive spinster.

Analyzing the Oppressive Features of Sexuality ("Male Domination" and "Female Subordination")

Radical-libertarian and radical-cultural feminists have very different ideas not only about gender but also about sexuality.[58] Among the feminists who have written insightfully on this difference is Ann Ferguson. Unfortunately for my purposes, whereas we agree on certain concepts, we use different labels. In order to avoid as much confusion as possible in my discussion of Ferguson's work, I have taken the liberty of substituting in her work my terms *radical-libertarian* and *radical-cultural* for her terms *libertarian* and *radical*.

According to Ferguson, radical-libertarian feminists are usually heterosexual feminists or lesbian feminists whose views on sexuality include the following:

1. Heterosexual as well as other sexual practices are characterized by repression. The norms of patriarchal bourgeois sexuality repress the sexual desires and pleasures of everyone by stigmatizing sexual minorities, thereby keeping the majority "pure" and under control.
2. Feminists should repudiate any theoretical analyses, legal restrictions, or moral judgements that stigmatize sexual minorities and thus restrict the freedom of all.
3. As feminists we should reclaim control over female sexuality by demanding the right to practice whatever gives us pleasure and satisfaction.
4. The ideal sexual relationship is between fully consenting, equal partners who negotiate to maximize one another's sexual pleasure and satisfaction by any means they choose.[59]

In contrast, also according to Ferguson, radical-cultural feminists' views on sexuality include the following:

1. Heterosexual sexual relations generally are characterized by an ideology of sexual objectification (men as subjects/masters; women as objects/slaves) that supports male sexual violence against women.
2. Feminists should repudiate any sexual practice that supports or normalizes male sexual violence.
3. As feminists we should reclaim control over female sexuality by developing a concern with our own sexual priorities, which differ from men's—that is, more concern with intimacy and less with performance.
4. The ideal sexual relationship is between fully consenting, equal partners who are emotionally involved and do not participate in polarized roles.[60]

After reflecting on the differences between radical-libertarian and radical-cultural views on sexuality, Ferguson concluded that their respective assumptions about the nature and function of sexuality, the ways in which society constructs and controls sexuality, and the necessary and sufficient conditions of sexual freedom were diametrically opposed. She claimed that for radical-libertarian feminists sexuality is "the exchange of physical erotic and genital sexual pleasure,"[61] a powerful force that society aims to control by separating so-called good, normal, legitimate, healthy sexual practices from so-called bad, abnormal, illegitimate, unhealthy sexual practices. In order to be maximally free from society's attempts to limit sexual freedom in the name of law and order, individuals must destroy all existing sexual taboos, taking care not to substitute for them their own view of "politically correct sexuality."[62]

In Ferguson's estimation, Gayle Rubin is among the most articulate spokespersons for radical-libertarian feminist ideology. In the 1960s and 1970s, Rubin argued that one of the keys to human liberation, including women's liberation, is to end the kind of sexual repression that flows from those ideologies describing sex in terms "of sin, disease, neurosis, pathology, decadence, pollution or the decline and fall of empires."[63] She stressed the repression of sex is built on the doctrine of sexual essentialism: the belief that sex is a natural force that existed prior to social life and must be controlled lest it threaten the structures civilization imposes on human beings.[64]

In discussing modern Western societies' views on sex, Rubin noted that although these societies tend to view *all* sex as *generally* bad, dangerous, destructive, and negative, they view some types of sex as *particularly* so.[65] Typically, the average person in a modern Western society places "marital reproductive heterosexuals . . . at the top of the erotic pyramid" and "transsexuals, transvestites, fetishists, sadomasochists, sex workers such as prostitutes and porn models, and the lowliest of all, those whose eroticism transgresses generational boundaries"[66] at the bottom of the erotic pyramid. In Rubin's estimation, the more thickly a culture draws the boundary line between tolerable and intolerable sex, the more likely it is to insist this line must be guarded vigilantly, lest sexual chaos replace sexual order.

Convinced sexual repression is one of the cruelest and most irrational ways for the forces of so-called civilization to control human behavior, Rubin claimed sexual permissiveness is in women's as well as men's best interests. Thus, Rubin insisted it is just as misguided for *radical-cultural feminists* to tell women to engage only in "monogamous lesbianism that occurs within long-term, intimate relationships and which does not involve playing with polarized roles"[67] as it is for *antifeminists* to tell women their sexual role is to meet men's sexual desires and needs first and foremost. It matters not who makes the rules about what counts as "good sex" and what counts as "bad sex." Sexual repression is sexual repression, according to Rubin.

In contrast to Rubin, most radical-cultural feminists cautioned women to reject male sexuality as intrinsically flawed. They claimed male sexuality is "driven, irresponsible, genitally-oriented and potentially lethal," whereas female sexuality is inherently "muted, diffuse, interpersonally-oriented, and benign."[68] Insisting men want "power and orgasm" in sex and women want "reciprocity and intimacy" in sex,[69] radical-cultural feminists concluded heterosexual relations as we know them within patriarchy are a misadventure for women. Heterosexuality is about male domination and female subordination setting the stage for pornography, prostitution, sexual harassment, rape, and woman-battering. Thus, according to radical-cultural feminists, the key to women's liberation is to eliminate "all patriarchal institutions (e.g., the pornography industry, family, prostitution, and compulsory heterosexuality) and sexual practices (sadomasochism, cruising, and adult/child and butch/femme relationships) in which sexual objectification occurs."[70]

Pornography: Symptom and Symbol of Male-Controlled Female Sexuality or Opportunity for Female-Controlled Female Sexuality?

Among the issues that account for the split between radical-libertarian and radical-cultural feminists is pornography. Radical-libertarian feminists stressed that because our society provides so "few images of healthy, assertive sexuality,"[71] it is not surprising people, but especially women, are inclined to have some fairly negative ideas about sex. Our sexphobic culture, said radical-libertarian feminists, bombards women with images of man, the sexual predator, the animal on the prowl for his female "kill." It also repeatedly offers men pictures of woman, the manipulative sexual temptress who uses her physical charms to gain control over an unsuspecting man's heart and, of course, wallet. Believing feminists should take the lead in rejecting such a negative view of human sexuality, radical-libertarian feminists shook their heads in dismay when radical-cultural feminists adopted what they regarded as repressive "Christian" or "Victorian" ideas about sex according to which a good person (especially a good woman) does not have sex with someone unless she loves or is otherwise emotionally committed to that person. As radical-libertarian feminists saw it, the view that sex must be linked with love in order to be "good" was precisely the idea women needed to challenge.

Convinced women could and should use pornography to arouse long-repressed sexual passions and to generate pleasure-giving sexual fantasies, radical-libertarian feminists encouraged women to view as many forms of sexually explicit material designed to arouse prurient human interests as they desired. Nothing, including so-called violent pornography, was to be considered taboo. Radical-libertarian feminists stressed there was nothing wrong about a woman fantasizing about a man so passionate about her he cannot wait to get her into bed and have "his way" with her. To be sure, conceded radical-libertarian feminists, the line separating such a fantasy from a real-life *rape* can and has been crossed. The same woman who derives sexual pleasure from playing Scarlett O'Hara–Rhett Butler "sex games" with her husband would protest loudly were she *really* raped by her husband. In other words, just because a woman wants to explore whether playing with power is part of what makes sex "sexy" does not mean she wants to volunteer as an object for male violence in real life. Rather than stubbornly insisting that visual *representations* of men "sexually dominating" women somehow violate women in real life, said radical-libertarian feminists, feminists should engage in an entirely open-minded and nondefensive examination of pornography, saving their venom for real rapists.[72]

Ironically, the radical-libertarian feminists' defense of pornography served to increase, not decrease, the radical-cultural feminists' opposition to it. Radical-cultural feminists stressed that sexuality and gender *are* the products of the same oppressive social forces. There is no difference between gender discrimination against women in the boardroom and the sexual objectification of women in the bedroom, they said. In both instances the harm done to women is about men's power over women. Pornography is nothing more than patriarchal propaganda about women's "proper" role as man's servant, helpmate, caretaker, plaything. Whereas men exist for themselves, women exist for men. Men are subjects; women are objects.

Insisting virtually all forms of pornography fail to express the kind of intimacy that creates love between people who care about each other, radical-cultural feminists claimed pornography harms women in one or more of three ways: (1) by encouraging men to behave in sexually harmful ways toward women (e.g., sexual harassment, rape, woman battering); (2) by defaming women as persons who have so little regard for themselves they actively seek or passively accept sexual abuse; and (3) by leading men not only to think less of women as human beings but also to treat them as second-class citizens unworthy of the same due process and equal treatment to which men are accustomed.

Not able to *prove* that exposure to pornographic representations *directly causes* men either to harm women's bodies or defame women's characters, radical-cultural feminists sought protection for women in antidiscrimination laws. They followed the lead of Andrea Dworkin and Catharine MacKinnon, who defined pornography as

> the graphic sexually explicit subordination of women through pictures or words that also includes women dehumanized as sexual objects, things, or commodities; enjoying pain or humiliation or rape; being tied up, cut up, mutilated, bruised, or physically hurt; in postures of sexual submission or servility or display; reduced to body parts, penetrated by objects or animals, or presented in scenarios of degradation, injury, torture; shown as filthy or inferior; bleeding, bruised, or hurt in a context that makes these conditions sexual.[73]

Claiming sexuality is *the* locus of male power in which gender and gender relations are constructed,[74] radical-cultural feminists argued that pornography, as defined above, encourages men to treat women as second-class persons not only in the private world of the bedroom but also in the public world of the boardroom. Thus, radical-cultural feminists reasoned that because pornography creates a frame of reference in which women are viewed as less human and therefore less deserving of respect and good treatment than men, pornographers can and ought to be viewed as agents of sexual discrimination, guilty of violating women's civil rights. For this reason, any woman—or man, child, or transsexual used in the place of a woman—should be granted a legal cause of action against a particular pornographer or pornographic business if she is coerced into a pornographic performance, has pornography forced on her, or has been assaulted or attacked because of a particular piece of pornography. Further, any woman should be able to bring civil suit against traffickers in pornography on behalf of all women.[75] Emptying the pockets of pornographers is the best way for feminists to fight the misogynistic ideology pornographers so willingly spread.

Although radical-cultural feminists, under the leadership of MacKinnon and Dworkin, were initially successful in their attempt to have antipornography ordinances passed in Minneapolis and Indianapolis, a coalition of radical-libertarian and liberal feminists called the Feminist Anti-Censorship Taskforce (FACT) joined nonfeminist free speech advocates to work against MacKinnon and Dworkin's legislation. Partially because of FACT's efforts, the Supreme Court eventually declared the Minneapolis and Indianapolis antipornography ordinances unconstitutional.[76] During the period of time in which FACT worked to defeat MacKinnon and Dworkin's legislation, its membership insisted phrases such as "sexually explicit subordination of women" have no context-free, fixed meaning.[77] FACT referred to the film *Swept Away* to show just how difficult it is to decide whether or not a particular scene or set of scenes depicts the sexually explicit subordination of women.

In essence, *Swept Away* is a story of human domination and human submission. An attractive, upper-class woman and a brawny, working-class man are shown, during the first half of the film, as *class* antagonists and then, during the second half of the film, as *sexual* antagonists when they are stranded on an island and the man exacts his revenge on his "boss" by repeatedly raping her. Initially, she resists him, but gradually she falls in love with him and, eventually, he with her. Because scenes in *Swept Away* clearly present the woman character as enjoying her own sexual humiliation, the film falls under a radical-cultural feminist definition of pornography and could have been suppressed pending the outcome of a civil suit brought against its creators, manufacturers, and distributors.

According to FACT, however, such suppression would have represented censorship of the worst sort because the film challenged viewers to think seriously about precisely what does and does not constitute the sexually explicit subordination of women. Critical and popular opinion of the film varied, ranging from admiration to repulsion. Whereas the reviewer for *Ms.* wrote that "'Swept Away' comes to grips with the 'war' between the sexes better than anything" she had ever read or seen, the reviewer for the *Progressive* stated he did not know what was "more distasteful about the film—its slavish adherence to the barroom credo that what all women really want is to be beaten, to be shown who's boss, or the readiness with which it has been accepted by the critics."[78] FACT emphasized if two film critics can see the images and hear the words of *Swept Away* so differently, contextual factors, such as the critics' own sexual fantasies and erotic impulses, must ultimately explain their divergent interpretations. What *looks* like the sexually explicit subordination of a woman to a radical-cultural feminist may, as far as the woman herself is concerned, be the height of sexual pleasure.

Shocked by radical-libertarian feminists' seeming acceptance of women's sexual abuse, radical-cultural feminists accused radical-libertarian feminists of false consciousness, of buying a "bill of goods" men are only too eager to sell women. Bitter debates about sexuality broke out between radical-libertarian and radical-cultural feminists, reaching fever pitch at the 1982 Barnard College sexuality conference. A coalition of radical-libertarian feminists, including lesbian practitioners of sadomasochism and butch-femme relationships, bisexuals, workers in the sex industry (prostitutes, porn models, exotic dancers), and heterosexual women eager to defend the pleasures of sex between consenting men and women, accused radical-cultural feminists of "prudery." To this charge radical-cultural feminists responded they were not prudes. On the contrary, they were *truly* free women who could tell the difference between *erotica*, where the term denotes sexually explicit depictions and descriptions of women being integrated, constituted, or focused during loving or at least life-affirming sexual encounters, and *thanatica*, where the term denotes sexually explicit depictions and descriptions of women being disintegrated, dismembered, or disoriented during hate-filled or even death-driven sexual encounters.

Radical-libertarian feminists were not impressed by the distinction radical-cultural feminists drew between erotica and thanatica. They claimed this distinction suggests the only good sex is "vanilla" sex—gentle, touchy-feely, side-by-side (no one on the top or the bottom), altogether pretty sex. Why, asked radical-libertarian feminists, should we limit women, or men for that matter, to a particular "flavor" of sex? If women are given free rein, some may choose vanilla sex, but others may prefer "rocky-road" sex—encounters where pain punctuates pleasure, for example. No woman should be told that if she wants to be a *true* feminist, then she must limit herself to only certain sorts of sexual encounters. After all, if women's sexuality is as "absent" as Catharine MacKinnon herself has claimed,[79] then it is premature for anyone, including radical-cultural feminists, to fill the vacuum with only their own ideas. Better that all sorts of women offer all sorts of descriptions of what they find truly pleasurable. To this line of reasoning, radical-cultural feminists retorted once again that radical-libertarian feminists were not *true* feminists but deluded pawns of patriarchy who had willfully shut their eyes and closed their ears to pornography's women-hating message. Before too long, the Barnard conference collapsed, as the gulf between radical-libertarian and radical-cultural feminists widened.

Lesbianism: A Mere Sexual Preference or the Paradigm for Female-Controlled Female Sexuality?

Another topic that divided radical-libertarian feminists from radical-cultural feminists was lesbianism, particularly "separatist" lesbianism. Lesbianism fully surfaced as an issue within the women's movement during the 1970s. At the Second Conference to Unite Women, a group of women wearing T-shirts emblazoned with the label "lavender menace" staged a protest. The organizers of the conference had anticipated "trouble" since virtually the entire feminist community was in the process of assessing Ann Koedt's provocative essay "The Myth of the Vaginal Orgasm." In this essay Koedt claimed many women believe the orgasms they feel during heterosexual intercourse are vaginally caused when in point of fact they are clitorally stimulated. Koedt also claimed that many men fear "becom(ing) sexually expendable if the clitoris is substituted for the vagina as the center of pleasure for women."[80] Viewing men's fear of "sexual expendability" as alarmist, Koedt noted that even if all women recognized they did not *need* men as sexual partners for *physiological* reasons, many women would still select men as sexual partners for *psychological* reasons.[81]

Radical-libertarian feminists interpreted Koedt as providing women with a strong rationale to engage only in so-called noncompulsory heterosexuality. Since a woman does not *need* a male body to achieve sexual pleasure, she should not engage in sexual relations with a man unless *she* wants to. In contrast to radical-libertarian feminists, radical-cultural feminists interpreted Koedt as implying that since there is no physiological reason for a woman to have sex with a man, there is no *feminist* psychological reason for a woman to *want* to have sex with a man. Indeed, there are only *nonfeminist* psychological reasons for a woman to want to have sex with a man, the kind of bad reasons Adrienne Rich discussed in her essay on compulsory heterosexuality.[82] Therefore, if a woman wants to be a *true* feminist, she must become a lesbian—doing what comes "naturally," thereby freeing her own consciousness from the false idea that she is deviant, abnormal, sick, crazy, or bad because she enjoys sex with women not men.

For a time, the radical-cultural feminists' interpretation of Koedt's essay predominated in feminist circles, so much so that many heterosexual feminists felt deviant, abnormal, sick, crazy, or bad if they wanted to have sex with men. Deirdre English, a radical-libertarian feminist, reported she found it "fascinating and almost funny"[83] that so many heterosexual feminists "seemed to accept the idea that heterosexuality meant cooperating in their own oppression and that there was something wrong with being sexually turned on to men. How many times have I heard this? 'Well, unfortunately, I'm not a lesbian but I wish I was, maybe I will be.'"[84] The so-called political lesbian was born: she who did not find herself erotically attracted to women but who tried as hard as possible to reorient her sexual impulses toward women and away from men.

Although radical-libertarian feminists agreed with radical-cultural feminists that heterosexuality had probably been forced upon many women who, left to their own devices, would have been lesbians, they nonetheless insisted it was just as wrong for radical-cultural feminists to impose an idealized version of lesbianism on women as it had been for patriarchy to impose heterosexuality on women.[85] Radical-libertarian feminists noted their dissatisfaction with heterosexual sex had to do not with men having sex with women but men having sex with women in a particular way: "fucking for a minute and a half and pulling out."[86] Women could and would find pleasure in sexual relations with men, they said, provided men made women's sexual satisfaction just as important as their own sexual satisfaction.

Radical-libertarian feminists also stressed that individual men, as bad as they could be, were not women's primary oppressors. On the contrary, women's main enemy was the patriarchal system, the product of centuries of male privilege, priority, and prerogative. Thus, unlike those radical-cultural feminists who urged women to stop relating to men on all levels beginning with the *sexual*, radical-libertarian feminists did not press for a separatist agenda. On the contrary, radical-libertarian feminists urged women to confront individual men about their chauvinistic attitudes and behaviors in an effort to get men freely to renounce the unfair privileges patriarchy had bestowed upon them.[87] These feminists recalled that even WITCH, one of the most militant feminist groups in the 1960s, had not urged women to renounce men or heterosexuality entirely but to relate to men only on gynocentric terms:

Witches have always been women who dared to be: groovy, courageous, aggressive, intelligent, nonconformist, explorative, curious, independent, sexually liberated, revolutionary. (This possibly explains why nine million of them have been burned.) Witches were the first Friendly Heads and Dealers, the first birth-control practitioners and abortionists, the first alchemists (turn dross into gold and you devalue the whole idea of money!). They bowed to no man, being the living remnants of the oldest culture of all—one in which men and women were equal sharers in a truly cooperative society, before the death-dealing sexual, economic, and spiritual repression of the Imperialist Phallic Society took over and began to destroy nature and human society.

WITCH lives and laughs in every women. She is the free part of each of us, beneath the shy smiles, the acquiescence to absurd male domination, the make-up or flesh-suffocating clothing our sick society demands. There is no "joining" WITCH. If you are a women and dare to look within yourself, you are a Witch. You make your own rules. You are free and beautiful. You can be invisible or evident in how you choose to make your witch-self known. You can form your own Coven of sister Witches (thirteen is a cozy number for a group) and do your own actions.

You are pledged to free our brothers from oppression and stereotyped sexual roles (whether they like it or not) as well as ourselves. You are a Witch by saying aloud, "I am a Witch" three times, and *thinking about that*. You are a Witch by being female, untamed, angry, joyous, and immortal.[88]

Thus, women in the 1990s, like women in the 1960s, do not have to live together on the fringes of society or to have sex only with each other in order to be liberated, according to today's radical-libertarian feminists. Freedom comes to women as the result of women giving each other the power of self-definition and the energy continually to rebel against any individual man, group of men, or patriarchal institution seeking to disempower or otherwise weaken women.

Radical-Libertarian and Radical-Cultural Feminists: Is Reproduction Women's Curse or Blessing?

Not only do radical-libertarian and radical-cultural feminists have different views about sex, they also have different ideas about reproduction. Whereas radical-libertarian feminists believe women should substitute artificial for natural modes of reproduction, radical-cultural feminists believe it is in women's best interests to procreate naturally. As we shall see, radical-libertarian feminists are convinced the less women are involved in the reproductive process, the more time and energy they will have to engage in society's productive processes. In contrast, radical-cultural feminists are convinced the ultimate source of women's power rests in their power to gestate new life. To take this power from a woman is to take away her trump card and to leave her with an empty hand, entirely vulnerable to men's power.

Natural Reproduction as the Cause of Women's Oppression

Firestone's *The Dialectic of Sex*. In *The Dialectic of Sex*, Shulamith Firestone claimed that patriarchy, the systematic subordination of women, is rooted in the biological inequality of the sexes. Firestone's reflections on women's reproductive role led her to a feminist revision of the materialist theory of history offered by Karl Marx and Friedrich Engels. Although Marx and Engels correctly focused upon class struggle as the driving forces of history, they paid scant attention to what she termed "sex class." Firestone proposed to make up for this oversight by developing a feminist version of historical materialism in which sex class, rather than economic class, is the central concept.

To appreciate Firestone's co-optation of Marxist method, we have only to contrast her definition of historical materialism with Engels's definition of historical materialism as "that view of the course of history which seeks the ultimate cause and great moving power of all historical events in the economic development of society, in the changes of the modes of production and exchange, in the consequent division of society into distinct classes, and in the struggles of these classes against one another."[89] Firestone reformulated his definition as follows:

> Historical materialism is that view of the course of history which seeks the ultimate cause and the great moving power of all historical events in the dialectic of sex: the division of society into two distinct biological classes for procreative reproduction, and the struggles of these classes with one another; in the changes in the modes of marriage, reproduction and child care created by these struggles; in the connected development of other physically-differentiated classes (castes); and in the first division of labor based on sex which developed into the (economic-cultural) class system.[90]

In other words, for Firestone relations of reproduction rather than of production are the driving forces in history. The original class distinction is rooted in men's and women's differing reproductive roles; it is sex class that furnishes the paradigm for class based on productive differences between human beings and even for class based on racial differences among human beings.

In much the same way that Marx concluded workers' liberation requires an economic revolution, Firestone concluded women's liberation requires a biological revolution.[91] Whereas the proletariat must seize the means of *production* in order to eliminate the economic class system, women must seize control of the means of *reproduction* in order to eliminate the sexual class system. Just as the ultimate goal of the communist revolution is, in a classless society, to obliterate class distinctions, the ultimate goal of the feminist revolution is, in an androgynous society, to obliterate sexual distinctions. As soon as technology overcomes the biological limits of natural reproduction, said Firestone, that some persons have wombs and others have penises will "no longer matter culturally."[92]

No matter how much educational, legal, and political equality women achieve and no matter how many women enter public industry, Firestone insisted nothing fundamental will change for women so long as natural reproduction remains the rule and artificial or assisted reproduction the exception. Natural reproduction is neither in women's best interests nor in those of the children so reproduced. The joy of giving birth—invoked so frequently in this society—is a patriarchal myth. In fact, pregnancy is "barbaric," and natural childbirth is "at best necessary and tolerable" and at worst "like shitting a pumpkin."[93] Moreover, said Firestone, natural reproduction is the root of further evils, especially the vice of possessiveness that generates feelings of hostility and jealousy among human beings. Engels's *Origin of the Family, Private Property, and the State* was incomplete not so much because he failed adequately to explain why men became the producers of surplus value, said Firestone, but because he failed adequately to explain *why* men wish so intensely to pass *their* property on to *their* biological children. The vice of possessiveness—the favoring of one child over another on account of the child's being the product of one's own ovum or sperm—is precisely what must be overcome if we are to put an end to divisive hierarchies.

Piercy's *Woman on the Edge of Time*. This last point was developed by Marge Piercy in her science fiction novel *Woman on the Edge of Time*.[94] Piercy set the story of her utopia within the tale of Connie Ramos's tragic life. Connie is a late-twentieth-century, middle-aged, lower-class Chicana with a history of what society describes as "mental illness" and "violent behavior." Connie has been trying desperately to support herself and her daughter, Angelina, on a pittance. One day, when she is near the point of exhaustion, Connie loses her temper and hits Angelina too hard. As a result of this one outburst, the courts judge Connie an unfit mother and take her beloved daughter away from her. Depressed and despondent, angry and agitated, Connie is committed by her family to a mental hospital, where she is selected as a human research subject for brain-control experiments. Just when things could get no worse, Connie is transported by a woman named Luciente to a future world call Mattapoisett—a world in which women are not defined in terms of reproductive functions and in which both men and women delight in rearing children. In Mattapoisett there are neither men nor women; rather, everyone is a "per" (short for *person*).

What makes Piercy's future world plausible is artificial reproduction. In Mattapoisett babies are born from the "brooder." Female ova, fertilized in vitro with male sperm selected for a full range of racial, ethnic, and personality types, are gestated within an artificial placenta. Unable to comprehend why Mattapoisett women have rejected the experience that meant the most to her—physically gestating, birthing, and nursing an offspring—Connie is initially repelled by the brooder. She sees the embryos "all in a sluggish row . . . like fish in the aquarium."[95] Not only does she regard these embryos as less than human, she pities them because no woman loves them enough to carry them in her own womb and, bleeding and sweating, bring them into the world.

Eventually, Connie learns from Luciente that the women of Mattapoisett did not casually give up natural reproduction for artificial reproduction. They did so only when they realized natural reproduction was the ultimate cause of all isms, including sexism: "It was part of women's long revolution. When we were breaking all the old hierarchies. Finally there was the one thing we had to give up too, the only power we ever had, in return for no power for anyone. The original production: the power to give birth. Cause as long as we were biologically enchained, we'd never be equal. And males never would be humanized to be loving and tender. So we all became mothers. Every child has three. To break the nuclear bonding."[96] Thus, as a result of women's giving up their monopoly on the power to give birth, the original paradigm for power relations was destroyed, and all residents of Mattapoisett found themselves in a position to reconstitute human relationships in ways that defied the hierarchical ideas of better-worse, higher-lower, stronger-weaker, and especially dominant-submissive.

Piercy's utopia is more radical than a Marxist utopia because the family is eliminated as a biological as well as an economic unit. Individuals possess neither private property nor private children. No one has his or her own genetic child. Children are not the possessions of their biological mothers and fathers, to be brought into this world in their parents' image and likeness and reared according to their idiosyncratic values. Rather, children are precious human resources for the entire community, to be treasured on account of their uniqueness. Each child is reared by three co-mothers (one man and two women or two men and one woman) who are assisted by "kidbinders," a group of individuals who excel at mothering Mattapoisett's children. Child-rearing is a communal effort, with each child having access to large-group experiences at childcare centers and small-group experiences in the separate dwellings of each of his or her co-mothers.[97]

Connie initially doubts that Mattapoisett's system for begetting, bearing, and rearing children is all it is touted to be. She wonders whether co-mothers and kidbinders really love the children they rear. But gradually she decides a biological relationship is not essential to good parenting. Indeed, she eventually agrees that artificial reproduction is superior to natural reproduction because it results in a truly nurturing and unselfish mode of mothering, totally separated from ambivalent feelings of resentment and guilt and always freely chosen.

Natural Reproduction as the Source of Women's Liberation

A Critique of Marge Piercy. As beautifully as Piercy expressed and modified some of Firestone's more controversial ideas, radical-cultural feminists challenged her views as well as Firestone's. Empathizing with Connie's disgust at ex utero gestation and her initial bewilderment at Luciente's explanation for why the women of Mattapoisett had to give up the only power they had ever had, radical-cultural feminists claimed Mattapoisett is currently both implausible and unintelligible. Women should not give up biological motherhood for ex utero gestation, not now, not ever.

Radical-cultural feminists insisted Mattapoisett is implausible for today's women because women's oppression is not likely to end if, as Azizah al-Hibri observed, women give up the only source of men's dependence on them: "Technological reproduction does not equalize the natural reproductive power structure—it *inverts* it. It appropriates the reproductive power from women and places it in the hands of men who now control both the sperm and the reproductive technology that could make it indispensable. . . . It 'liberates' them from their 'humiliating dependency' on women in order to propagate."[98] Far from liberating women, reproductive technology further consolidates men's power over women.

In addition to being implausible, Mattapoisett is, in the estimation of radical-cultural feminists, also unintelligible to today's women—at least to women like Connie Ramos. Even though some women use other women's eggs and wombs to procreate and some women adopt other women's children, society continues to define a mother as someone who is genetically, gestationally, and socially related to the children she rears with or without a spouse or partner. For all the exceptions to this rule, most women have a hard time viewing "egg brooders" and "kidbinders" as real mothers. Indeed, most of the women who go to infertility clinics do so because they want Connie's experience of carrying a child nine months "heavy under their hearts," bearing a baby "in blood" and even some pain, and nursing a child.[99] Thus, there is no way for women to decide in the abstract whether they should deprive themselves of a very meaningful present experience for a future experience they might or might not find equally meaningful.

**Critiques of Firestone and Other Wholesale Endorsements of Repro-
ductive Technology.** To the degree radical-cultural feminists criticized
Piercy's utopian vision as implausible and unintelligible, they criticized
Firestone's analysis as a blueprint for woman's further enslavement. They
claimed woman's oppression was caused not by female biology in and of
itself but rather by men's jealousy of women's reproductive abilities and
subsequent desire to seize control of female biology through scientific
and technological means.[100]

Analyzing natural reproduction through the lens of male alienation
from the gestational process and female immersion in it, radical-cultural
feminist Mary O'Brien noted that until the introduction of artificial reproduction, men's "reproductive consciousness" differed from women's "reproductive consciousness" in at least three ways. First, the woman experienced the process of procreation as one continuous movement taking
place *within* her body, whereas the man experienced this same process as
a discontinuous movement taking place *outside* of his body. Subsequent to
the act of sexual intercourse through which he impregnated his wife, the
man had no other procreative function to perform. Second, the woman,
not the man, necessarily performed the fundamental *labor* of reproduction—pregnancy and birthing. At most the man could attend childbirth
classes with his wife and try to imagine what being pregnant and giving
birth feel like. Third, the woman's connection to her child was certain—
she knew, at the moment of birth, the child was flesh of her flesh. In contrast, the man's connection to the child was uncertain; he could never be
absolutely sure, even at the moment of birth, whether the child was in
fact genetically related to him. For all he knew, the child was the genetic
progeny of some other man.[101]

In radical-cultural feminists' estimation, men's alienation from the
process of natural reproduction helps explain why men have played a
smaller role in the life of the "product" of natural reproduction than
women have. It also helps explain why men have sought to limit
women's reproductive powers. In her book *Of Woman Born*, Adrienne
Rich noted men realize patriarchy cannot survive unless men are able to
control women's power to *bring* or *not bring* life into the world. Thus, Rich
concluded, in order to maintain their position of power in society, men
took the "birthing" process into their own hands. Rich described how
male obstetricians replaced female midwives, substituting their "hands of
iron" (obstetrical forceps) for midwives' hands of flesh (female hands sensitive to female anatomy).[102] In addition, Rich catalogued the ways in
which male physicians wrote the rules not only for giving birth but also
for being pregnant. Male experts told women how to act during pregnancy—when to eat, sleep, exercise, have sex, and the like. In some instances, they even dictated to women how to feel during the process of

childbirth—when to feel pain and when to feel pleasure. The overall effect of men's intrusion into the birthing process was to confuse women, since men's "rules" for women's pregnancies often clashed with women's "intuitions" about what was best for their bodies, psyches, and babies. For example, when a woman and physician disagreed about whether she needed a C-section to deliver her baby, a woman did not know whether to trust the *authority* of her physician or the *experience*, the sensations, of her own body.

To the degree they were deprived of control over their pregnancies, said Rich, women experienced pregnancy as a mere event, as something that simply happened to them. Indeed, confessed Rich, she herself felt out of control and alienated during her pregnancy:

> When I try to return to the body of the young woman of twenty-six, pregnant for the first time, who fled from the physical knowledge of her pregnancy and at the same time from her intellect and vocation, I realize that I was effectively alienated from my real body and my real spirit by the institution—not the fact—of motherhood. This institution—the foundation of human society as we know it—allowed me only certain views, certain expectations, whether embodied in the booklet in my obstetrician's waiting room, the novels I had read, my mother-in-law's approval, my memories of my own mother, the Sistine Madonna or she of the Michelangelo Pietà, the floating notion that a woman pregnant is a woman calm in her fulfillment or, simply, a woman waiting.[103]

Reflecting upon her youth, Rich concluded that if women reclaimed their pregnancies from the authorities, they would no longer have to sit passively waiting for their physicians to deliver their babies to them. Instead, women would actually direct the childbirth process, experiencing its pleasures as well as its pains. In Rich's estimation, childbirth does not have to feel like "shitting a pumpkin."[104] On the contrary, it can feel a great deal more exhilarating and certainly far less dehumanizing.

Rich's concerns about the ways in which patriarchal authorities have used medical science to control women's reproductive powers reached new heights in the works of Andrea Dworkin, Margaret Atwood, Genea Corea, and Robyn Rowland. Dworkin claimed infertility experts have joined gynecologists and obstetricians to seize control of women's reproductive powers once and for all. Made possible through sperm and egg donation, in vitro fertilization, sex preselection, and embryo transplantation, artificial reproduction is, she said, patriarchy's most recent attempt to make sure women have the number and kind of children men supposedly want and that women's procreative experience is just as alienating as men's.[105] With the introduction of in vitro fertilization and the use of surrogate mothers, a woman's experience of bringing a child into the world becomes discontinuous, especially if her only contribution to this process is the donation of her egg. Moreover, the woman who relies on artificial reproduction to procreate can be no more certain than her husband that the child born to them is indeed *their* genetic child. For all they know, the embryo transplanted into her womb is not her and her husband's embryo but the embryo of some other couple. Finally, should scientists develop an artificial placenta, women's "labor" would no longer be needed to complete the procreative process. Speculating that patriarchal society would probably view a reproductively useless woman as a body "good" only for sex work or domestic work, Dworkin urged women to resist the further development of reproductive technology.

Concerns such as Dworkin's are one of the inspirations for Margaret Atwood's *Handmaid's Tale*,[106] a work of feminist science fiction in stark contrast to Marge Piercy's *Woman on the Edge of Time*. In the Republic of Gilead, Atwood's antiutopia, women are reduced to one of four functions. There are the Marthas, or domestics; the Wives, or social secretaries and functionaries; the Jezebels, or sex prostitutes; and the Handmaids, or reproductive prostitutes. One of the most degrading Gileadean practices, from a women's perspective, consists in the commander's engaging in ritualistic sexual intercourse with his Wife. The Wife, who is infertile, lies down on a bed with her legs spread open. The Wife's Handmaid, one of the few fertile women in Gilead, puts her head between the spread legs of the Wife, whereupon the commander engages in sexual intercourse not with his Wife but with her Handmaid. Should the Handmaid become pregnant, the Commander and his Wife will proclaim the child she bears theirs. Indeed, on the day the Handmaid gives birth to the child, the Wife will simulate labor pains, and all the other Wives and Handmaids in Gilead will gather round the Wife and her Handmaid in what passes for a moment of female bonding.

After one such birth day, the central character, Offred—whose name literally means "to be of Fred"—recalls better times and speaks in her mind to her mother, who had been a feminist leader: "Can you hear me? You wanted a woman's culture. Well, now there is one. It isn't what you meant, but it exists. Be thankful for small mercies."[107] Of course, they are *very* small mercies, for with the exception of birth days—those rare occasions when a Handmaid manages to produce a child—women have little contact with each other. The Marthas, Wives, Jezebels, and Handmaids are segregated from one another, and the contact women do have—even within an assigned class—is largely silent, for women are permitted to speak to each other only when absolutely necessary.

Like Dworkin and Atwood, Genea Corea was suspicious of what the new reproductive technologies and their concomitant social arrangements promise women. Corea claimed if men control the new reproductive technologies, men will use them not to empower women but to further empower themselves. To reinforce her point, she drew provocative analogies between Count Dracula and Dr. Robert Edwards, one of the codevelopers of in vitro fertilization. In fact, she suggested that just as Dracula never had enough blood to drink, Dr. Edwards never had enough ova upon which to experiment. As a result, he would routinely appear at the hysterectomies his colleagues were performing in order to secure more eggs for his experiments.[108] Fearing male infertility experts like Dr. Edwards do not always have women's best interests at heart, Corea ended her essay "Egg Snatchers" with a series of questions she insisted all women should ask themselves:

> Why are men focusing all this technology on woman's generative organs— the source of her procreative power? Why are they collecting our eggs? Why do they seek to freeze them?
> Why do men want to control the production of human beings? Why do they talk so often about producing "perfect" babies?
> Why are they splitting the functions of motherhood into smaller parts? Does that reduce the power of the mother and her claim to the child? ("I only gave the egg. I am not the real mother." "I only loaned my uterus. I am not the real mother." "I only raised the child. I am not the real mother.")[109]

Agreeing with Dworkin, Atwood, and Corea that the new reproductive technologies will simply increase men's control over women, Robyn Rowland, another radical-cultural feminist, pointed to the work of microbiologist John Postgate as an example of the form this new power over women might take. In an interview with Rowland, Postgate proposed the development of a "manchild pill," able to ensure the conception of large numbers of male children, thereby creating a scarcity of female children and therefore an inevitable decline in birthrates. Conceding a fierce competition might ensue among men for the sexual and reproductive "services" of society's few remaining women, Postgate speculated these women would probably have to be sequestered for their own good while society developed rules for a system of male access to them.[110]

As if a vision of a future world in which the term *trophy wife* denotes an even uglier reality than it does now is not bad enough, Rowland imagined an even worse scenario: a world in which only a few superovulating women are permitted to exist, a world in which eggs are taken from women, frozen, and inseminated in vitro for transfer into artificial placentae. The replacement of women's childbearing capacity by male-controlled technology would, she said, leave women entirely vulnerable, "without a product" with which "to bargain" with men: "For the history of 'mankind' women have been seen in terms of their value as childbearers. We have to ask, if that last power is taken and controlled by men, what role is envisaged for women in the new world?"[111]

Unlike radical-libertarian feminists, radical-cultural feminists urged women not to give up the ultimate female power—the power to reproduce naturally. There is, they said, a difference between the kind of affirming power women exert when they bring new life into the world and the kind of negating power men exert when they seek to control nature/women/life through technology. Only oppressive forms of power need to be forsaken, and, according to radical-cultural feminists, women's reproductive powers are anything but oppressive. If women's power over life is the paradigm for anything, it is for one person's or group's ability to connect with another and to bring what French meant by "pleasure" to another.

Radical-Libertarian and Radical-Cultural Feminists: Is Mothering in Women's Interests or Not?

Although commentators do not always make adequate distinctions between biological and social motherhood, these two dimensions of mothering need to be distinguished. If we accept Alison Jaggar's extension of the term *mothering* to "any relationship in which one individual nurtures and cares for another,"[112] then a person does not need to be a biological mother in order to be a social mother. Nevertheless, patriarchal society teaches its members that the woman who bears a child is best suited to rear him or her. In viewing this tenet as one that often places unreasonable demands upon women's bodies and energies, radical-libertarian feminists have tended to make strong arguments against biological motherhood. Not surprisingly, many radical-cultural feminists have challenged these arguments, insisting no woman should, in an act of unreflective defiance against patriarchy, deprive herself of the satisfaction that comes from not only bearing a child but also playing a major role in his or her personal development. As we shall see, the arguments on both sides of this debate are powerful.

The Case Against Biological Motherhood

There are at least two versions of the radical-libertarian feminist case against biological motherhood: a weaker, more general version offered by Ann Oakley, and a stronger, more specific version offered by Shulamith Firestone. As Oakley saw it, biological motherhood is a myth based on the threefold belief that "all women need to be mothers, all mothers need their children, all children need their mothers."[113]

The first assertion, that all women need to be mothers, gains its credibility, according to Oakley, from the ways in which girls are socialized and from popular psychoanalytic theory that provides "pseudo-scientific backing" for this process of socialization. If parents did not give their daughters dolls; if the schools, the churches, and the media did not stress the wonders of biological motherhood; if psychiatrists, psychologists, and physicians did not do everything in their power to transform "abnormal" girls (i.e., "masculine" girls who do not want to be mothers) into "normal" girls (i.e., "feminine" girls who do want to be mothers), then girls would not grow into women who *need* to mother in order to have a sense of self-worth. As far as Oakley was concerned, women's supposed need to mother "owes nothing" to women's "possession of ovaries and wombs" and everything to the way in which women are socially and culturally conditioned to be mothers.[114]

The second assertion, that mothers need their children, is based on the belief that unless a woman's "maternal instinct" is satisfied, she will become increasingly frustrated. In Oakley's view, there is no such thing as maternal instinct; normal women do not experience a desire to have a biological child, and hormonally based drives that "irresistibly draw the mother to her child in the tropistic fashion of the moth drawn to the flame"[115] do not exist during and subsequent to pregnancy. To support her contention that the "instinct" for mothering is learned, Oakley pointed to a study in which 150 first-time mothers were observed. Few of these women knew how to breast-feed, and those who did had seen either their own mother or some other female relative nursing a baby. Additionally, Oakley noted most women who abuse or neglect their children were themselves abused or neglected as children. Never having seen a woman mothering properly, these women never learned the behavior repertoire society associates with adequate mothering. Mothers, in short, are not born; they are made.[116]

The third assertion, that children need their mothers, is, according to Oakley, the most oppressive feature of the myth of biological motherhood. Oakley noted this assertion contains three assumptions unnecessarily tying women to children: first, that children's mothering needs are best met by their biological mothers; second, that children, especially young children, need the devoted care of their biological mothers much more than the care of anyone else, including their biological fathers; and third, that children need *one* nurturant caretaker (preferably the biological mother), not many.[117]

As Oakley saw it, each of these three assumptions (in support of the assertion children need their mothers) is false. First, social mothers are just as effective as biological mothers. Studies have shown, claimed Oakley, adopted children are at least as well adjusted as nonadopted children.[118] Second, children do not need their biological mothers more than their biological fathers; in fact, not only do children not need to be reared by their biological parents; they do not need to be reared by women. What a child needs, wrote Oakley, are adults with whom to establish intimate relationships—trustworthy and dependable persons who will provide the child with consistent care and discipline, recognize and cherish the child's uniqueness, and be there when the child needs him or her. Men no less than women can play the major role in their children's upbringing. Finally, one-on-one child-rearing is not necessarily better than collective socialization or "multiple mothering." Children reared in Israeli kibbutzim, for example, are just as happy, intelligent, emotionally mature, and socially adept as children reared exclusively by their biological mothers in U.S. suburbs.[119]

In Oakley's estimation, being a biological mother is not a natural need of women anymore than being reared by one's biological mother is a natural need of children. Therefore, she concluded biological motherhood is a cultural construction, a myth with an oppressive purpose. Not wanting to be accused of selfishness and even abnormality, women who would be happier not having children at all reluctantly become mothers; and women who would be happier sharing their child-rearing responsibilities with one or more nurturant adults make of mothering an exclusive and twenty-four-hour-a-day job. No wonder, said Oakley, so many mothers are unhappy—an unhappiness made all the worse because for a woman to admit any serious dissatisfaction with mothering is for her to admit failure as a person.

Although Shulamith Firestone's negative assessment of biological motherhood did not substantively differ from Oakley's, it was harsher in tone. In *The Dialectic of Sex*, Firestone suggested the desire to bear and rear children is less the result of an "authentic liking" for children and more a "displacement" of ego-extension needs. For a man, a child is a way to immortalize his name, property, class, and ethnic identification; for a woman, a child is a way to justify her homebound existence as absolutely necessary. At times, a father's need for immortality or a mother's need for justification becomes pathological. When this happens, said Firestone, the less than "perfect" child inevitably suffers.[120]

Firestone believed if adults, especially women, did not feel they had some sort of obligation to have children, they might discover in themselves an *authentic* desire to live in close association with children. People do not need to be biological parents in order to lead child-centered lives, said Firestone. Ten or more adults could agree, for example, to live with three or four children for a determinate period of time—seven to ten years, or however long the children needed a stable structure. During their years together, the people in this household would relate not as parents and children but as older and younger friends. Firestone did not think adults have a natural desire to be any closer to children than this kind of household arrangement permits. Instead, she believed adults have been socialized to view biological reproduction as life's raison d'être because without this grandiose sense of mission and destiny, the pains of childbearing and the burdens of child-rearing would have proved overwhelming. Now that technology promises to liberate the human species from the burdens of reproductive responsibility, Firestone predicted women will no longer want to bear children in pain and travail or rear children endlessly and self-sacrificially. Rather, women and men will want to spend some, though by no means most, of their time and energy with and on children.[121]

The Case for Biological Motherhood

Although Adrienne Rich agreed with some of Firestone's analysis, she criticized Firestone for condemning biological motherhood "without taking full account of what the experience of biological pregnancy and birth might be in a wholly different political and emotional context."[122] Throughout her book *Of Woman Born*, Rich sharply distinguished between biological motherhood understood as "the *potential relationship* of any woman to her powers of reproduction and to children" and biological motherhood understood as "the *institution*, which aims at ensuring that that potential—and all women—shall remain under male control."[123] As Rich saw it, there is a world of difference between *women's* deciding who, how, when, and where to mother and *men's* making these decisions for women.

Rich agreed with Firestone that biological motherhood, as it has been institutionalized under patriarchy, is definitely something from which women must be liberated. If success is measured in terms of patriarchy's ability to determine not only women's gender behavior but also their gender identity through "force, direct pressure . . . ritual, tradition, law and language, customs, etiquette, education, and the division of labor," then *institutionalized* biological motherhood is one of patriarchy's overwhelming successes.[124] Men, suggested Rich, have convinced women that unless a woman is a mother, she is not really a woman. Indeed, until relatively recently, the forces of patriarchy convinced most women that mothering is their one and only job. This view of women's role is, of course, very restricting. It denies women access to the public realm of culture. It also denies women the right to have and to fulfill their own wants and needs. Good mothers are not supposed to have any personal friends or plans unrelated to those of their families. They are supposed to be on the job twenty-four hours a day and love every minute of it. Ironically, observed Rich, it is just this expectation that causes many women to act in anything but "motherly" ways. The constant needs of a child can tax a mother's patience and, with no relief from her husband or any other adult, ultimately make her feel angry, frustrated, and bitter: "I remember

being uprooted from already meager sleep to answer a childish night-
mare, pull up a blanket, warm a consoling bottle, lead a half-asleep child
to the toilet. I remember going back to bed starkly awake, brittle with
anger, knowing that my broken sleep would make the next day hell, that
there would be more nightmares; more need for consolation, because out
of my weariness I would rage at those children for no reason."[125] Rich's
point was not that women do not love children but that no person can be
expected to remain always cheerful and kind unless the person's own
physical and psychological needs are satisfactorily met.

Rich also argued eloquently that the _institution_ of biological motherhood prevents women from rearing their children as women think they
should be reared. Rich recounted squabbles with her own husband about
the best way to raise their two sons. She also recalled doing it _his_ way
even though she knew full well "father" did not always know best. Under patriarchy, she wrote, most men have demanded sons for the wrong
reasons: "as heirs, field-hands, cannon-fodder, feeders of machinery, images and extensions of themselves; their immortality."[126] What is worse,
most husbands have demanded their wives help them raise their sons to
be "real men"—that is, "macho" or hyperaggressive and supercompeti-
tive men. Rich happily recalled a seashore vacation she spent with her
two boys, but without her husband. While vacationing alone, she and her
children lived spontaneously for several weeks, ignoring most of the established rules of patriarchy. They ate the wrong food at the wrong time.
They stayed up past the proper bedtime. They wore the wrong clothes.
They giggled at silly jokes. Through all of these "trespasses" against the
rules of the father, they were enormously happy. Indeed, suggested Rich,
were fathers told they do _not_ know best, then mothers would find child-
rearing energizing rather than enervating, joyful rather than miserable.

As Rich saw it, if women took control of child-rearing as well as childbearing, more mothers would be able to experience biological motherhood on their own terms. Rich insisted no woman should renounce, in
the name of "liberation," what female biology has to offer:

I have come to believe . . . that female biology—the diffuse, intense sensual-
ity radiating out from clitoris, breasts, uterus, vagina; the lunar cycles of
menstruation; the gestation and fruition of life which can take place in the female body—has far more radical implications than we have yet come to appreciate. Patriarchal thought has limited female biology to its own narrow
specifications. The feminist vision has recoiled from female biology for these
reasons; it will, I believe, come to view our physicality as a resource, rather
than a destiny. In order to live a fully human life we require not only control
of our bodies (though control is a prerequisite); we must touch the unity and
resonance of our physicality, our bond with the natural order, the corporeal
ground of our intelligence.[127]

According to Rich, Firestone was wrong to argue that female biology is necessarily limiting and that the only way to liberate women from this limitation is through reproductive technology. In a patriarchal society, the solution to the pains of childbearing is not reproductive technology but rather for a woman to ride with, not against, her body. A woman must not give up on her body before she has had a chance to use it as she thinks best. Likewise, the solution to the impositions of child-rearing in a patriarchal society is not the renunciation of children; the solution is for each and every woman to rear those children with feminist values.

What Makes a Woman a Mother?
Genetic, Gestational, and/or Rearing Connections

The attention of radical-cultural feminists and radical-libertarian feminists has recently centered on surrogate, or contracted, motherhood—an arrangement where a third party is hired and usually paid to bear a child who will be reared by someone else.[128] The birth mother (the woman whose gestational services have been contracted) is either the full biological mother of the child (both the genetic and the gestational mother) or the gestational but not the genetic mother of the child.

In general, radical-cultural feminists oppose contracted motherhood on the grounds it creates destructive divisions among women. One such division is between economically privileged women and economically disadvantaged women. The former are able to hire the latter in order to meet their reproductive needs, adding gestational services to the child-rearing services economically disadvantaged women traditionally provided to economically privileged women. The second division is one Genea Corea envisioned, namely, among childbegetters, childbearers, and child-rearers. According to Corea, the process of reproduction is currently being segmented and specialized as if it were simply a mode of production. In the future, no one woman will beget, bear, and rear a child. Rather, genetically superior women will beget embryos in vitro; strong-bodied women will bear these test-tube babies to term; and sweet-tempered women will rear these newborns from infancy to adulthood.[129] As a result of this division of labor, a dystopia similar to the one Margaret Atwood described in the *Handmaid's Tale* could come into existence, complete with divisive female-female relationships. No woman was whole in Gilead; all individual women were reduced to parts or aspects of the monolith, Woman.

In addition to lamenting the ways in which contracted motherhood might negatively affect women's relationships to each other and to their children, radical-cultural feminists bemoan its rooting of parental rights either in persons' *genetic* contribution to the procreative process or in persons' professed *intention* to rear children. Basing parental rights exclusively on genetic contribution means if a surrogate mother is genetically unrelated to the embryo in her womb, she has no parental rights to play a role in that embryo's life after it is born. Only if she is the genetic as well as gestational mother of the embryo does she have grounds for claiming parental rights to the child—rights that have to be balanced against those of the child's genetic father. In contrast, basing parental rights exclusively on one or more persons' *professed intention* to rear the embryo implies that because the surrogate mother has *professed* no such intentions, she has no grounds for claiming parental rights to the child even if she is genetically related to the child.

According to radical-cultural feminists, men have reason to root all parental rights in either genetic or intentional grounds. After all, until the time a man takes an active part in the rearing of his child, the only kind of "relationship" he can have with his child is a genetic or intentional one. Unlike his wife or female partner, he cannot experience the kind of relationship a pregnant woman can experience with her child. For this reason, observe radical-cultural feminists, patriarchal society dismisses the gestational relationship as unimportant, as a mere biological event. In its stead, it stresses the psychological value of parents' genetic and/or intentional connections to their children, underscoring the meaning of "living on" in one's progeny and/or keeping one's promises to future generations.

Conceding that like all men, some women might have only a genetic or an intentional connection to a child prior to its birth, radical-cultural feminists claim this is no reason to deny the gestational connection as a source of parental rights. After all, at the moment of a child's birth only the child's gestator has proven through her concrete actions, some of which may have caused her inconvenience and even pain, that she is *actually* committed to the child's well-being. As radical-cultural feminists see it, the kind of *lived commitment* a gestational parent has to a child cannot be fairly compared to the kind of *contemplated commitment* a genetic or intentional parent has to a child.

Radical-libertarian feminists disagree with radical-cultural feminists' assessment of contracted motherhood. They argue contracted motherhood arrangements, if handled properly, can bring women closer together rather than drive them farther apart. They note some contracted mothers and commissioning couples live in close proximity to each other so they can *all* share in the rearing of the child whom they have collaboratively reproduced.[130] Thus, contracted motherhood need not be viewed as the male-directed and male-manipulated specialization and segmentation of the female reproductive process but as women getting together (as in the case of the postmenopausal South African mother who carried her daughter's in vitro fetus to term) to achieve, in unison, something they could not achieve without each other's help.[131] So long as women control collaborative-reproduction arrangements, contracted motherhood increases rather than decreases women's reproductive freedom, in radical-libertarian feminists' estimation.

Believing it is not in women's best interests to overstate the importance of the gestational connection, radical-libertarian feminists object to the radical-cultural feminist position on contracted motherhood for two reasons. In the first place, if women want men to spend as much time caring for children as women now do, then women should not repeatedly remind men of women's *special* connection to infants. Doing so implies that women are more suited to parenting tasks than men are. Second, if women want to protect their bodily integrity from the forces of state coercion, then women should not stress the symbiotic nature of the maternal-fetal connection. Increasingly aware of pregnant women's power to affect the well-being of their fetuses during the gestational process, society is more and more eager to control the pregnancies of "bad gestators." If a pregnant woman negatively affects her fetus by imbibing large quantities of alcohol or using illicit drugs, concerned citizens will urge that she be treated, voluntarily or involuntarily, for her addictions. Should treatment fail, many of these same citizens will become more aggressive in their demands; they will recommend that the state punish the "bad gestator" for negligently, recklessly, or intentionally engaging in life-style behavior resulting in serious, largely irreparable damage to her future child. Society will brand such a woman as a "fetal abuser" or "fetal neglecter." For this reason, if no other, radical-libertarian feminists believe the less women emphasize how "special" the mother-fetus relationship is, the better served will women's interests be.

Critiques of Radical-Libertarian and Radical-Cultural Feminism

In many ways radical-libertarian and radical-cultural feminists are each other's best critics, but they are certainly not each other's only critics. Nonradical feminists have directed some strong criticisms against both the "libertarian" and the "cultural" wings of radical feminist thought. They have faulted radical-libertarian feminists for the same reason they have faulted liberal feminists—namely, for their insistence on making everything a "choice" when in point of fact women's ability to choose is precisely what is in question in a patriarchal context. In contrast, they have faulted radical-cultural feminists for propounding so-called essentialism, the view that men and women are fundamentally and perhaps irrevocably different either by nature or by nurture.

In an effort to avoid redundancy, I direct readers to the critiques of liberal feminism at the end of Chapter One. What is said there about women's limited ability to choose applies almost as well to radical-libertarian feminist thought as to liberal feminist thought. I do, however, want to present here Jean Bethke Elshtain's critique of radical-cultural feminism. Her views on essentialism merit considerable thought. In addition, I want to draw attention to the ways in which both radical-libertarian and radical-cultural feminists unnecessarily polarize issues related to sex, reproduction, and biological motherhood.

Woman's Nature: Is It the Root of Her "Goodness"?

Jean Elshtain claimed radical-cultural feminists are wrong to suggest males and females are, on either the biological or the ontological level, two kinds of creatures: the men corrupt and the women innocent. Such a biology or ontology denies the individuality and history of actual men and women. It implies what is important and real about human beings is some sort of a priori essence.

Falling into the trap of essentialism—the conviction that men are men and women are women and that there is no way to change either's nature—is both an analytic dead end and a political danger, in Elshtain's estimation. Essentialist claims about what makes certain groups of people the way they are (for example, women, blacks, Jews) are the political-philosophical constructs of conservatism. The history of essentialist arguments is one of oppressors telling the oppressed to accept their lot in life because "that's just the way it is." Essentialist arguments were used to justify slavery, to resist the Nineteenth Amendment (which gave women the vote), and to sustain colonialism by arguing "altruistically" that "the natives are unable to run their own governments." By agreeing women are a priori nurturing and life giving and men are a priori corrupt and obsessed with death, said Elshtain, radical-cultural feminists fall into the trap of doing unto others that which they do not want done unto themselves and other oppressed groups.[132]

Elshtain urged radical-cultural feminists to overthrow the categories that entrap women (and men) in rigid roles. Roles, she said, are simplistic definitions that make every man a conscious exploiter and oppressor and every woman an exploited and oppressed victim. The fact of the matter is not every woman is a victim and not every man is a victimizer. Elshtain cited Mary Beard's *Women as a Force in History* (a liberal feminist text charting women's role in shaping preindustrial culture)[133] and Sheila Rowbotham's *Women, Resistance and Revolution* (a Marxist feminist text detailing women's involvement in twentieth-century revolutions)[134] to support her view that women have played strong and active roles in social history. She also pointed to examples of men who have supported women in their liberatory struggles.[135] According to Elshtain, essentialism in any form has no place in the complex world we live in.

Also at issue in Elshtain's critique is the radical-cultural feminist understanding of patriarchy. Elshtain faulted Mary Daly for implying that no matter when and where it appears, patriarchy, be it in the form of Hindu suttee, Chinese foot binding, African female circumcision, or Western gynecology, is about men's *hating* women. To claim all these various practices boil down to the same thing, said Elshtain, is to show little or no awareness of the rich diversity of different societies.[136] As a Western feminist searching for signs of patriarchy in Asia and Africa, Daly was sometimes unaware of her own cultural baggage. As an outsider, she was not always privy to the contextual meaning certain rituals and customs have for their female participants. Female circumcision is a case in point. For Daly, this practice is about men's depriving women of a wide range of sexual experiences; for the women circumcised, it may mean something different—for example, a rite of passage into a much-coveted womanhood or a means of rebelling against civilized, Christian, colonial powers. To Daly's objection that these women are not ready, willing, or able to see the harm men are doing to them, Elshtain responded it might be Daly's vision rather than these women's that is clouded. Indeed, Daly's failure to acknowledge the possibility certain African and Asian rituals have *positive*, non-Western meanings suggests a certain ethnocentrism on her part.[137]

Admitting that Daly and other radical-cultural feminists may have wanted to stress the metaphorical rather than the historical meaning of patriarchy, Elshtain conceded that, as a metaphorical term, *patriarchy* carries a certain emotional force and lends direction to women searching for a point of attack. Nevertheless, Elshtain claimed the concept of patriarchy is troubling, even in its strictly metaphorical capacity. To be sure, she said, the term *patriarchy* is a useful analytical tool for those women who are just beginning to rethink their political and personal experiences of oppression. But beyond this, patriarchy becomes a blunt instrument. If chanted incessantly, the formula "men *over* women; women *for* men" becomes monotonous and even meaningless. In Elshtain's estimation, the tendency of radical-cultural feminists to view all patriarchies as equally evil (women-hating, misogynistic) contributes to the "broken record effect" characterizing some feminist texts.[138]

Elshtain speculated the absolute condemnation of patriarchy by radical feminists might be rooted in their fear that women may have certain things—even ugly things—in common with the men. Unable to accept their own "masculine" qualities, radical-cultural feminists project these rejected qualities onto men in order to shield themselves from the more awful parts of their own personalities. This defensiveness, said Elshtain, then leads radical-cultural feminists toward a utopian vision of an all-women community. Man encompasses evil; woman encompasses good. Because the essence of womanhood is supposedly about the positive force of "power-to" rather than the negative force of "power-over," a world of women will be warm, supportive, nurturing, and full of creativity. It will be a return to the womb. Only men are holding women back.

Elshtain believed if her critique was on target, radical-cultural feminists were in for a grave disappointment. Given that women as well as men are human beings, vice as well as virtue will inevitably appear in an all-women community. Elshtain asked radical-cultural feminists to reconsider the concept of "pure voice"—the idea that the victim, in her status as victim, speaks in a pure voice—"I suffer, therefore I have moral purity."[139] This belief about women's moral purity is exactly what Victorian men used to keep women on high pedestals, away from the world of politics and economics; Elshtain was distressed twentieth-century radical-cultural feminists had not expanded beyond this nineteenth-century male notion.

Dichotomizing: The Stumbling Block That Retards the Development of Radical Feminist Thought?

In the estimation of socialist feminists such as Ann Ferguson, radical-libertarian and radical-cultural feminists need to heal the split between them in order to avoid unnecessary polarization. As emphasized above, Ferguson stressed that despite their reservations about male-female sexual relationships, radical-libertarian feminists nonetheless believed consensual (noncompulsory) heterosexuality could be just as pleasurable for women as for men. In addition to celebrating consensual heterosexuality, radical-libertarian feminists affirmed the "liberated sexuality" of lesbians—a form of sexual expression in which equal partners seemed particularly intent on mutually satisfying each other's sexual needs.

Contrasting radical-libertarian feminists with radical-cultural feminists, Ferguson noted that the latter group not only stressed the dangers of heterosexuality but also implied there is no such thing as consensual heterosexuality—that is, mutually desired sex between men and women who treat each other as equals. Only lesbians are capable of consensual sex in a patriarchal society. Whenever a man and a woman have sex in a patriarchal society, the man will, more or less, use sex as an instrument to control the woman. He will have his "way" with her, even if it means raping her, beating her, or reducing her to a sex object. In contrast, whenever two women have sex, to the extent their psyches have escaped the norms of patriarchal society, they will experience the "erotic" as that which resides not only in women's *physical* desire for each other but also in their emotional bondings and connections to each other. Supposedly, female sexuality is essentially about emotional intimacy, whereas male sexuality is essentially about physical pleasure; it is the kind of love women would have had for each other had not the institution of "compulsory heterosexuality" forced them to redirect their original love for their mothers to men.[140]

According to Ferguson, both the radical-libertarian and the radical-cultural feminist perspectives on sexuality fail on account of their *ahistoricity*. There is, she said, no one universal "function" for human sexuality, whether it is conceived as emotional intimacy or as physical pleasure.[141] Rather, "sexuality is a bodily energy whose objects, meaning and social values are historically constructed."[142] Thus, radical-cultural feminists are wrong to posit an *essential* female sexuality that for all practical purposes amounts to a certain form of lesbian sexuality.

Ferguson used her own sexuality as a case study in the historical construction of human sexuality in general. She observed that her lesbianism is no more based on the fact that her "original," or first, sexual object was her mother than on the fact that her second sexual object was her father. Rather, what explains her current way of loving is "first, the historical and social contexts in my teenage years which allowed me to develop a first physical love relationship with a woman; and, second, the existence of a strong self-identified lesbian-feminist oppositional culture today which allowed me to turn toward women again from an adult life hitherto exclusively heterosexual."[143] Ferguson speculated that had she grown up in a more restricted sexual environment or in a less feminist era, she probably would not have *wanted* to have lesbian lovers. After all, she said, "One's sexual objects are defined by the social contexts in which one's *ongoing* gender identity is constructed in relation to one's peers."[144]

Like radical-cultural feminists, radical-libertarian feminists are guilty of ahistoricism, in Ferguson's estimation, but in a different way. They seem to think, said Ferguson, that women are always able to give free or true consent; they make no distinction between real and apparent consent. Thus, radical-libertarian feminist Gayle Rubin claimed if a woman experiences herself *as* consenting to heterosexual or lesbian sadomasochism or bondage and domination, then she *is* consenting to these practices. No one has a right to criticize her as a "victim of false consciousness" who fails to realize that were she truly a man's equal, she would have nothing to do with any form of sexuality that eroticizes dominance-and-subordination relationships. But in Ferguson's estimation, depending on this woman's "social context," she may in fact be a "victim of false consciousness." The "freedom" of an economically dependent housewife to consent to S/M sex with her husband must be challenged; so, too, must the "freedom" of a teenage prostitute to consent to sex with a person far older and richer than he or she.[145]

Issues of real versus apparent consent arise just as frequently in the reproductive arena as they do in the sexual realm. Radical-libertarian feminists like Firestone and Rubin would probably accept as a *real* choice a woman's decision to rent her womb or sell her gestational services. No doubt they would view such a decision as helping to erode the institution of biological motherhood, which maintains that she who bears a child should rear the child not only because she is best suited for this task but also because she wants to do so. By virtue of the fact a surrogate mother is prepared to walk away from the child she has gestated for the "right price," she debunks the "myth" of biological motherhood. In contrast to radical-libertarian feminists, socialist feminists maintain that depending on a woman's social circumstances, her consent to surrender her biological child to the couple who contracted for it may not be "real." Since most surrogate mothers, like most prostitutes, are much poorer than their clients, they might easily be driven to sell the only thing they have that seems to have any enduring value in a patriarchal society: their bodies. To say women "choose" to do this might simply be to say that when women are forced to choose between being poor and being exploited, they may choose being exploited as the lesser of two evils.

Assuming socialist feminists like Ferguson are correct to stress that women's sexual and reproductive desires, needs, behaviors, and identities are largely the product of the time and place they occupy in history, they are also right to argue that (1) neither heterosexuality nor lesbianism is either inherently pleasurable or inherently dangerous for women; and (2) neither natural reproduction nor artificial reproduction is either inherently empowering or inherently disempowering for women. Socialist feminists urge *all* radical feminists to ask themselves what kind of sexual and reproductive practices people would adopt in a society in which all economic, political, and kinship systems were structured to create equality between men and women and as far as possible between adults and children. In an egalitarian world, would men and women engage in "male breadwinner/female housewife sex prostitution," or would they instead develop forms of heterosexuality seldom imagined let alone practiced in our very unequal, patriarchal world? Would some lesbians continue to engage in S/M and butch-femme relationships, or would all lesbians suddenly find themselves "turned off" by such practices? Would there be "man-boy" love or "parent-child" love (incest)? Would women use more or less in the way of contraceptives? Would couples contract for gestational mothers' services, or would they instead prefer to adopt children? Would there be more or fewer children? Would most people choose to reproduce themselves "artificially," or would they instead choose to reproduce in the "old-fashioned," natural way?

What is common to the kind of questions just posed, said Ferguson, is the answers they yield will be *lived* in the future world feminists imagine and not, for the most part, in the present world feminists experience. For now, feminists should seek to develop an approach to sexuality that permits women to see *both* the pleasures *and* the dangers of sex (and, I would add, *both* the liberatory *and* the enslaving aspects of reproduction). The dead-end approaches of the past have turned out to be part of the problem of human oppression rather than a remedy for it. The sooner these either-or approaches are replaced with both-and approaches, the less time we will have to waste "playing" the destructive games of male domination and female subordination.

∎

CHAPTER THREE

Marxist and Socialist Feminism

ALTHOUGH IT IS POSSIBLE TO DISTINGUISH BETWEEN Marxist and socialist feminist thought, it is quite difficult to do so. Over the years I have
become convinced that the differences between these two schools of
thought are more a matter of emphasis than of substance. Marxist feminists tend to pay their respects directly to Marx, Engels, and other nineteenth-century thinkers; they also tend to identify classism rather than
sexism as the ultimate cause of women's oppression. In contrast, socialist
feminists seem more influenced by twentieth-century thinkers such as
Louis Althusser and Jürgen Habermas. Moreover, they insist the fundamental cause of women's oppression is neither "classism" nor "sexism"
but an intricate interplay between capitalism and patriarchy. In the final
analysis, however, the differences between Marxist and socialist feminists
are not nearly as important as their common conviction. Marxist and socialist feminists alike believe women's oppression is not the result of individuals' intentional actions but is the product of the political, social, and
economic structures within which individuals live.

Some Marxist Concepts and Theories:
Their Feminist Implications

The Marxist Concept of Human Nature

Just as the liberal concept of human nature is present in liberal feminist
thought, the Marxist concept of human nature is present in Marxist feminist thought. As noted in Chapter One, liberals believe what distinguishes
human beings from other animals includes: a specified set of abilities, such
as the capacity for rationality and the use of language; a specified set of
practices, such as religion, art, and science; and a specified set of attitude

and behavior patterns, such as competitiveness and the tendency to put self over other. Marxists reject this liberal conception of human nature, emphasizing that what makes us human is that we produce our means of subsistence. We are what we are because of what we do—specifically, what we do to meet our basic needs through productive activities such as fishing, farming, and building. Unlike bees, beavers, and ants, whose activities are governed by instinct, we create ourselves in the process of intentionally, or consciously, transforming and manipulating nature.[1]

In his *Introduction to Marx and Engels*, Richard Schmitt insisted the statement "Human beings create themselves" is not to be read as "Men and women, *individually*, make themselves what they are" but instead as "Men and women, through production, *collectively* create a society that, in turn, shapes them."[2] This emphasis on the collective accounts for the Marxist view of history.

For the liberal, the ideas, thoughts, and values of individuals account for change over time. For the Marxist, material forces—the production and reproduction of social life—are the prime movers in history. In the course of articulating this doctrine of how change takes place over time, a doctrine usually termed *historical materialism*, Marx stated, "The mode of production of material life conditions the general process of social, political, and intellectual life. It is not the consciousness of men that determines their existence, but their social existence that determines their consciousness."[3] In other words, Marx believed a society's mode of production—that is, its forces of production (the raw materials, tools, and workers that actually produce goods) plus its relations of production (the ways in which the production process is organized)—generates a superstructure (a layer of legal, political, and social ideas) that in turn bolsters the mode of production. So, for example, Americans think in certain characteristic ways about liberty, equality, and freedom *because* their mode of production is capitalist.

Like Marxists in general, Marxist feminists believe social existence determines consciousness. The comment that "women's work is never done" is, for Marxist feminists, more than an aphorism; it is a description of the *nature* of woman's work. Always on call, a woman forms a conception of herself that she would not have if her role in the family and at the workplace did not keep her socially and economically subordinate to men. Thus, Marxist feminists believe in order to understand why women are oppressed in ways men are not, we need to analyze the links between women's work status and women's self-image.[4]

The Marxist Theory of Economics

To the degree Marxist feminists believe women's work shapes women's thoughts and thus "female nature," they also believe capitalism is a system of power relations as well as exchange relations. When capitalism is viewed as a system of exchange relations, it is described as a commodity or market society in which everything, including one's labor power, has a price and all transactions are fundamentally exchange transactions. When capitalism is viewed instead as a system of power relations, it is described as a society in which every kind of transactional relation is fundamentally exploitative. Thus, depending on one's emphasis, the worker-employer relationship can be looked at as either an exchange relationship in which equivalents are freely traded—labor for wages—or as a workplace struggle where the employer, who has superior power, coerces workers to labor ever harder for no discernible increase in wages.

Whereas the liberal views capitalism primarily as a system of voluntary exchange relations, the Marxist views capitalism primarily as a system of exploitative power relations. According to Marx, the value of any commodity produced for sale is determined by the amount of labor, or actual expenditure of human energy and intelligence, necessary to produce it.[5] To be more precise, the value of any commodity is equal to the *direct* labor incorporated in the commodity by the worker, plus the *indirect* labor stored in the worker's artificial appendages—the tools and machines made by the direct labor of his or her predecessors.[6] Because all commodities are worth exactly the labor necessary to produce them and because the worker's labor power (capacity for work) is a commodity that can be bought and sold, the value of the worker's labor power is exactly the cost of whatever it takes (food, clothing, shelter) to maintain him or her throughout the workday. But there is a difference between what the employer pays the worker for his or her capacity to work (labor power) and the value the worker actually creates when he or she puts these capacities to use in producing commodities.[7] Marx termed this difference *surplus value,* and from it employers derive their profits. Thus, capitalism is an exploitative system because employers pay workers only for their labor power, without also paying them for the actual expenditure of human energy and intelligence taken out of them and transferred into the commodities they produce.[8]

At this point, it is natural to ask how the employer can induce workers to labor for more hours than are necessary to produce the value of their subsistence, especially when workers receive no compensation for this extra work. Why do not workers, after supplying the employer with labor value equal to the cost of their own subsistence, quit working? The answer is, as Marx explained in *Capital,* a simple one: Employers have a monopoly on the means of production. Thus, workers must choose between being exploited and having no work at all. It is a liberal fiction that workers freely sign mutually beneficial contractual agreements with their employers. Capitalism is just as much a system of power relations as it is one of exchange relations. A worker is "free" to contract with an employer only in the sense that no one is holding a gun to his or her head as the worker signs on the dotted line. But even this small level of freedom is undermined in that workers do not own the means of production; they must work for those who do. Thus, by virtue of the employers' monopoly over factories, tools, land, means of transportation, and communication, employers are able to force workers to labor under exploitative conditions.

There is another, less-discussed reason why employers are able to exploit workers under capitalism. According to Marx, capitalist ideologies lead workers and employers to focus on capitalism's surface structure of exchange relations.[9] As a result of this ideological ploy, which Marx called the *fetishism of commodities*, workers gradually convince themselves that even though their money is very hard earned, there is nothing inherently wrong with the specific exchange relationships into which they have entered because life, in all its dimensions, is simply one colossal system of exchange relations.

That liberal ideologies defend quasi-contractual relations such as prostitution and surrogate motherhood as exercises of free choice, then, is no accident, insist Marxist feminists. These ideologies claim women become prostitutes and surrogate mothers because they prefer these "jobs" more than other available jobs. But, claim Marxist feminists, when a poor, illiterate, unskilled woman chooses to sell her sexual or reproductive services, chances are her choice is more coerced than free. After all, if one has nothing of value to sell over and beyond one's body, one's leverage in the marketplace is limited indeed.

The Marxist Theory of Society

Like the Marxist analysis of power, the Marxist analysis of class has provided feminists with some of the conceptual tools necessary to understand women's oppression. Marx observed that every political economy—the primitive communal state, the slave epoch, the precapitalist society, and the bourgeois society—contains the seeds of its own destruction. Thus, there are within capitalism enough internal contradictions to generate a class division so severe it will overwhelm the very system that produced it. For example, there exist many poor and propertyless workers. These workers live in squalor, receiving subsistence wages for their exhausting labor while their employers live in luxury. When these two groups of people, the haves and the have-nots, become conscious of themselves *as* classes, class struggle inevitably ensues and ultimately topples the system that produced these classes.[10]

It is important to emphasize the dynamic nature of class. Classes do not simply appear. They are slowly and often painstakingly formed by similarly situated people who share the same wants and needs. According to Marx, these people initially have no more unity than "potatoes in a sack of potatoes";[11] but through a long and complex process of struggling together about issues of local and later national interest to them, they gradually become a unity, a true class. Because class unity is difficult to achieve, its importance cannot be overstated. As soon as a group of people is fully conscious of itself as a class, it has a better chance of achieving its fundamental goals. There is power in numbers.

Class consciousness is clearly the opposite of false consciousness, a state of mind that impedes the creation and maintenance of true class unity. It causes exploited people to believe they are as free to act and speak as their exploiters. The bourgeoisie is especially adept at fooling the proletariat. For this reason, Marxists discredit egalitarian, or welfare, liberalism, for example, as a ruling-class ideology that tricks workers into believing their employers actually care about them. As Marxists see it, however, fringe benefits and the like serve only to impede workers from forming a class dedicated to securing workers' real needs. Overly grateful for small sops, workers minimize their hardships and sufferings. Gradually, they, like the ruling *class*, begin to perceive the status quo as the best possible world for workers and employers alike.

Because Marxist feminists, like most feminists, are eager to view women as a "collectivity," Marxist teachings on class and class consciousness play a large role in Marxist feminist thought. Much debate within the Marxist feminist community has centered on the following question: Do women per se constitute a class? Given that some women are wives, daughters, friends, and lovers of *bourgeois* men, whereas other women are the wives, daughters, friends, and lovers of *proletarian* men, it would appear women do not constitute a single class in the strict Marxist sense. However, bourgeois and proletarian women's domestic experiences bear enough similarities to motivate unifying struggles such as the wages-for-housework campaign (see the section below). Thus, Marxist feminists believe women can gain a consciousness of themselves as a *class* of workers by insisting, for example, that domestic work be recognized as real work. That wives and mothers usually love the people for whom they work does not mean that cooking, cleaning, and childcare are not work. At most it means wives' and mothers' working conditions are better than average.[12]

By keeping the Marxist conceptions of class and class consciousness in mind, we can understand another crucial concept in both Marxist and Marxist feminist social theories: alienation. Like many Marxist terms, *alienation* is difficult to capture in a succinct dictionary definition. In his book *Karl Marx*, Allen Wood suggested we are alienated "if we either experience our lives as meaningless or ourselves as worthless, or else are capable of sustaining a sense of meaning and self-worth only with the help of illusions about ourselves or our condition."[13] Robert Heilbroner added that alienation is a profoundly fragmenting experience. Things and/or persons who are or should be connected in some significant way are instead viewed as separate. As Heilbroner saw it, this sense of fragmentation and meaninglessness is particularly strong under capitalism.

As a result of invidious class distinctions, as well as the highly specialized and highly segmented nature of the work process, human existence loses its unity and wholeness in four basic ways. First, workers are alienated from the *product* of their labor. Not only do workers have no say in what commodities they will or will not produce, but the fruits of their labor are snatched from them. Therefore, the satisfaction of determining when, where, how, and to whom these commodities will be sold is denied them. In short, what should partially express and constitute their being-as-workers confronts them as a thing apart, a thing alien.[14]

Second, workers are alienated from *themselves* because when work is experienced as something unpleasant to be gotten through as quickly as possible, it is deadening. When the potential source of a worker's humanization becomes the actual source of his or her dehumanization, the worker undergoes a major psychological crisis.

Third, workers are alienated from *other human beings* because the structure of the capitalist economy encourages and even forces workers to see each other as competitors for jobs and promotions. When the potential source of the worker's community (the other worker as cooperator, friend, someone to be with) becomes the actual source of his or her isolation (the other worker as competitor, enemy, someone to avoid), the worker is bound to lose identification with those who have, at least in part, constituted his or her identity.

Fourth and finally, workers are alienated from *nature* because the kind of work they do and the conditions under which they do it make them see nature as an obstacle to their survival. This sets up an opposition where in fact a connectedness should exist—the connectedness among all elements in nature. The elimination of alienation, entailing a return to a humane kind of labor, is an important justification for the overthrow of capitalism.[15]

Building on the idea that in a capitalist society human relations take on an alienated nature in which "the individual only feels himself or herself when detached from others,"[16] Ann Foreman argued this state of affairs is worse for women than it is for men. She wrote:

> The man exists in the social world of business and industry as well as in the family and therefore is able to express himself in these different spheres. For the woman, however, her place is within the home. Men's objectification within industry, through the expropriation of the product of their labour, takes the form of alienation. But the effect of alienation on the lives and con-

sciousness of women takes an even more oppressive form. Men seek relief from their alienation through their relations with women; for women there is no relief. For these intimate relations are the very ones that are essential structures of her oppression.[17]

As Foreman saw it, women's alienation is profoundly disturbing because women experience themselves not as selves but as "others." All too often, said Foreman, a woman's sense of self is entirely dependent on her families' and friends' appreciation of her. If they express loving feelings toward her, she will be happy; but if they fail to say even a thank-you to her, she will be sad. Thus, Marxist feminists aim to create a world in which women can experience themselves as whole persons, as integrated rather than fragmented beings, as people who can be happy even when they are unable to "make" their families and friends happy.

The Marxist Theory of Politics

Like those of economics and society, the Marxist theory of politics similarly offers Marxist feminists an analysis of class that promises to liberate women from the forces that oppress them. In fact, much of Marxist thought is devoted to sketching a blueprint to guide workers, be they male or female, as they struggle first to constitute themselves as a class, then to effect the transition from capitalism to socialism, and finally to achieve communism—full community and complete freedom.

As noted previously, class struggle takes a certain form within the workplace because the interests of the employers are not those of the workers. Whereas it is in the employers' interests to use whatever tactics may be necessary (harassment, firing, violence) to get workers to work ever more effectively and efficiently for ever lower wages, it is in the workers' interests to use whatever countertactics may be necessary (sick time, coffee breaks, strikes) to limit the extent to which their labor power is converted into the kind of actual labor that produces profits for their employers.

The relatively small and everyday class conflicts occurring within the capitalist workplace serve as preliminaries to the full-fledged, large-scale class struggles that, according to Marx, undergird the progress of history. Should workers, on account of their common exploitation and alienation, achieve class consciousness, they will be able to fight their employers for control over the means of production (for example, the nation's factories). If workers manage to take over the means of production, then a highly committed, politically savvy, well-trained group of revolutionaries—Marx called them the "vanguard of the revolution"—will be able to marshall a broad-based attack against every political and economic structure of capitalism. If successful, this attack will lead to the replacement of capitalism with socialism, a political economy in which workers are neither exploited nor alienated and through which communism, "the complete and conscious return of man himself as a social, that is, human being,"[18] can come into existence.

Under capitalism, Marx suggested, people are largely free to *do* what they want to do within the confines of the system, but they have little say in determining those confines, which make them behave like self-interested egoists. "Personality," said Marx, "is conditioned and determined by quite definite class relationships."[19] What Marx meant by this epigram, explained Richard Schmitt, is the following:

> In as much as persons do certain jobs in society, they tend to acquire certain character traits, interests, habits, and so on. Without such adaptations to the demands of their particular occupations, they would not be able to do a great job. A capitalist who cannot bear to win in competition, or to outsmart someone, will not be a capitalist for long. A worker who is unwilling to take orders will not work very often. In this way we are shaped by the work environment, and this fact limits personal freedom for it limits what we can choose to be.[20]

In contrast to the persons living under capitalism, persons living under communism are free not only to *do* but also to *be* what they want because they have the power to structure the system shaping them.

If we read between these lines, we can appreciate another of Marxism's major appeals to women: its promise to reconstitute human nature in ways that preclude all the pernicious dichotomies that have made slaves of some and masters of others. Marxism also promises to make people free, a promise women would like to see someone keep. There is, after all, something very liberating about the idea of women and men constructing together the social structures and social roles that will permit both genders to realize their full human potential.

Friedrich Engels: *The Origin of the Family, Private Property, and the State*

Although the fathers of Marxism did not take women's oppression nearly as seriously as workers' oppression, some of them offered explanations for why women are oppressed qua women. With the apparent blessing of Marx, Engels wrote *The Origin of the Family, Private Property, and the State* (1845), in which he showed how changes in the material conditions of people affect the organization of their family relations. He argued that before the family, or structured conjugal relations, there existed a primitive state of "promiscuous intercourse"[21] where every woman was fair game for every man and vice versa. All were essentially married to all. In the process of natural selection, suggested Engels, various kinds of blood relatives were gradually excluded from consideration as eligible marriage partners.[22] As fewer and fewer women in the tribal group became available to any given man, individual men began to put forcible claims on individual women as their possessions. As a result, the pairing family, in which one man is married to one woman, came into existence.

Noting that when a man took a woman, he came to live in *her* household, Engels interpreted this state of affairs not as a sign of women's subordination but as a sign of women's economic power. Because women's work was vital for the tribe's survival[23] and because women produced most of the material goods (for example, bedding, clothing, cookware, tools) that could be passed on to future generations, Engels concluded that early pairing societies were probably matrilineal, with inheritance and lines of descent traced through the mother.

In a digression, Engels speculated pairing societies were probably not only matrilineal but also matriarchal, societies in which women had much political and social as well as economic power.[24] But his main and certainly less debatable point remained that whatever status woman had in times past, it was derived from her position in the household, the primitive center of production.[25] Only if the site of production changed would she lose her superior position.[26] This, claimed Engels, was precisely what happened. The "domestication of animals and the breeding of herds" led to an entirely new source of wealth for the human community.[27] After men gained control of the tribe's animals (Engels did not tell us why or how),[28] the relative power of men and women shifted in favor of men, as men learned to produce more than enough animals to meet the tribe's needs for milk and meat.

This surplus of animals constituted an accumulation of wealth men could use as a means of intergenes exchange. When men possessed more than enough of a valuable socioeconomic good, the issue of inheritance took on major significance for them. Inheritance, directed through the mother's line, was originally a minor matter of the bequest of a "house, clothing, crude ornaments and the tools for obtaining and preparing food—boats, weapons and domestic utensils of the simplest kinds."[29] As production outside the household began to outstrip production within it, the traditional sexual division of labor between men and women, which had supposedly arisen out of the physiological differences between the sexes—specifically, the *sex act*[30]—took on new social meanings. As men's work and production grew in importance, not only did the value of women's work and production decrease, but the status of women within society decreased. Because men now possessed something more valuable than that which women possessed and because men, for some unexplained reason, suddenly wanted *their own* children to get *their* posses-

This went I am →

sions, they exerted enormous pressure to convert society from a matrilineal one into a patrilineal one. As Engels phrased it, mother right had "to be overthrown, and overthrown it was."[31]

Engels regarded this conversion as pivotal in its impact on women's position in society because the "overthrow of mother right" constituted *"the world-historic defeat of the female sex."*[32] Having produced and staked a claim to wealth, man took control of the household, reducing woman to the "slave" of his carnal desire and a "mere instrument for the production of his children."[33] In this new familial order, said Engels, the husband ruled by virtue of his economic power: "He is the bourgeois and the wife represents the proletariat."[34] Engels believed man's control of woman is rooted in the fact that he, not she, controls the property. The oppression of woman will cease only with the dissolution of the institution of private property.

The emergence of private property and the shift to patrilineage also explains, for Engels, the transition to the monogamous family. Because women give birth, the mother of any child is always known. However, the identity of the father is never certain because a woman could have been impregnated by a man other than her husband. To secure their wives' marital fidelity, men supposedly seek to impose an institution of compulsory monogamy on women. Ideally, husbands should be as monogamous as their wives, but patriarchal society does not *require* marital fidelity from its men. Thus, according to Engels, the sole purpose of the institution of monogamy is to serve as a vehicle for the orderly transfer of a father's private property to his children. Male dominance, in the forms of patrilineage and patriarchy, is simply the result of the class division between the propertied man and the propertyless woman. Engels commented monogamy was "the first form of the family to be based not on natural but on economic conditions,"[35] which suggests the monogamous family is the product not of love and commitment but of power plays and economic exigencies. Only the elimination of class society—of women's economic dependence on men—will allow men and women to enter marriages based on love.

Because monogamous marriage is a social institution that has nothing to do with love and everything to do with private property, Engels argued that if wives are to be emancipated from their husbands, women must first become economically independent of men. In fact, the first presupposition for the emancipation of women is "the reintroduction of the entire female sex into public industry"; the second is the socialization of housework and child-rearing.[36]

It is noteworthy that Engels believed proletarian women experience less oppression than do bourgeois women. As he saw it, the bourgeois family consists of a relationship between a husband and a wife in which the husband agrees to support his wife provided that she promises to remain sexually faithful to him and to reproduce only his legitimate heirs. "This marriage of convenience," observed Engels, "often enough turns into the crassest prostitution—sometimes on both sides, but much more generally on the part of the wife, who differs from the ordinary courtesan only in that she does not hire out her body, like a wageworker, on piecework, but sells it into slavery once and for all."[37]

Unlike the bourgeois marriage, the proletarian marriage is not, in Engels's estimation, a mode of prostitution because the material conditions of proletarian family differ substantially from those of the bourgeois family. Not only is the proletariat's lack of private property significant in removing the primary male incentive for monogamy—namely, the reproduction of legitimate heirs for one's property—but the general employment of proletarian women as workers outside the home leads to a measure of equality between husband and wife. This equality, according to Engels, provides the foundation of true "sex-love." In addition to these differences, the household authority of the proletarian husband, unlike that of the bourgeois husband, is not likely to receive the full support of the legal establishment. For all these reasons, Engels concluded that with the exception of "residual brutality" (spouse abuse), all "the material foundations of male dominance had ceased to exist"[38] in the proletarian home.

Although Marxist feminists still refer to Engels's *Origin* positively in their writings, most of them nonetheless point to its failings. For example, Jane Flax faulted Engels for asserting "the ultimate determinants of all history" are "the production *and* reproduction of life,"[39] only to focus solely on the *production* of life, which remained for him the primary means of comprehending class struggle and hence historical movement. For example, Engels explained the overthrow of "mother right" simply as a change in the mode of production; community property is overthrown by private property. But because community property is associated with *women* and private property with *men*, Flax theorized the overthrow of "mother right" (if it ever existed) probably reflected a change in the mode of reproduction at least as much as in the mode of production. She said: "The overthrow of matriarchy was a political as well as economic revolution in which men as men subdued or destroyed the privileged or perhaps equal position of women for a number of historically possible reasons (such as men discovering their role in reproduction and/or asserting control over reproduction)."[40]

Even more worrisome for Flax than Engels's slighting of reproduction-of-life factors was his belief in an *original* sexual division of labor. Without explaining how this division came to be, Engels simply stated that in the tribe women were charged with the care of the household, whereas men provided food and engaged in productive work. As mentioned earlier, the sexual division of labor originated, for Engels as well as for Marx, from the "division of labor in the sexual act."[41] But if the institution of heterosexuality is more responsible for women's oppression than the institution of private property, a program for women's liberation that begins with women's entrance into public industry, continues with women's domestic labor being taken over by service industries, and peaks in class struggle against capitalist exploiters cannot in and of itself end women's oppression. The institution of heterosexuality, as well as the institution of private property, must be challenged.

Contemporary Marxist Feminism

Because Marxist theory has little room for issues dealing *directly* with women's reproductive and sexual concerns (contraception, sterilization, and abortion; pornography, prostitution, sexual harassment, rape, and woman battering), many Marxist feminists initially focused on women's work-related concerns. They elucidated, for example, how the institution of the family is related to capitalism, how women's domestic work is trivialized as not *real* work, and how women are generally given the most boring and low-paying jobs. As we shall see, even if the nature and function of woman's work are not complete explanations for gender oppression, they are very convincing partial ones.

The Family or Household Under Capitalism

Prior to industrial capitalism, the family or household was the site of production. Parents, their children, and assorted relatives all worked together to reproduce themselves generationally as well as transgenerationally. The work women did—cooking, canning, planting, preserving, childbearing, and child-rearing—was as central to the economic activity of this extended family as the work men did. But with industrialization and the transfer of the production of goods from the private household to the public workplace, women, who for the most part did not initially enter the public workplace, were regarded as "nonproductive" in contrast to "productive," wage-earning men.

To view women's work—the production of people—as nonproductive when compared to men's work—the production of things—is, according to Engels's theory, a failure to understand what the term *production* includes:[42]

According to the materialistic conception, the determining factor in history is, in the final instance, the production and reproduction of immediate life. This, again, is of a twofold character: on the one side, the production of the means of existence, of food, clothing and shelter and the tools necessary for that production; on the other side, the production of human beings themselves, the propagation of the species. The social organization under which the people of a particular historical epoch live is determined by both kinds of production.[43]

Engels's words notwithstanding, even in contemporary socialist countries there is a tendency to conceive as unproductive the very large job of *reproducing* the labor force—a job for which women in socialist as well as capitalist countries are primarily responsible. As a result, investment in the socialization of domestic work and childcare is, in Hilda Scott's words, "the Cinderella of every socialist budget."[44] While socialist planners endlessly debate the wisdom of diverting funds from industrial and military development toward socialized housework and childcare, socialist women, she wrote, wait to be freed of the burdens of the double day.

If women's work is the Cinderella of the socialist budget, it is also the neglected stepdaughter of the capitalist budget. As much as it can, capitalism needs to keep women working "for free" in the household, even when it also needs them working for low wages in the workplace. Marx and Engels predicted that under capitalism the whole working class, including women and children above a very low age, would have to enter the public workforce in order to together earn a family wage. With no one left within the household to reproduce the labor power of working-class men, men as well as women and most children "would be exploited *individually* as wage labourers reproducing their own individual means of consumption/reproduction."[45] A proletarian revolution would then be easy to foment because virtually all of the working class would be feeling the direct results of exploitation.

Although Marx and Engels correctly predicted that working-class women and even children would enter the workforce, they failed to realize that as victims of false consciousness, working-class people would react to their increasing exploitation under capitalism not by revolting but by gradually removing their children and then their women from the workforce in an effort to approximate the bourgeois life-style. Liberal reformist laws banned children from the workplace and limited the number of hours women, especially pregnant women, could spend there. At the same time, the unions strove to increase men's wages so they could bring home a "family wage" single-handedly. Although unmarried women were still welcome in the workplace, they were asked to do the equivalent of women's work there: sewing, weaving, ironing, nursing, teaching, cleaning. Married women were also welcome in the workplace from time to time, especially during the world wars, when women were permitted to do men's as well as women's work. For the most part, however, married women stayed at home with their children, while their husbands went to work.

The Socialization of Domestic Labor

What angered many Marxist feminists most about the description of the nature and function of women's work under capitalism was its trivialization of women's work. Women were increasingly regarded as mere consumers, as if the role of men was to earn wages and the role of women was simply to spend them on "the right products of capitalist industry."[46] But, said Margaret Benston, women are primarily producers and only secondarily consumers. In fact, as Benston saw it, women constitute a class—namely, that class of people "responsible for the production of simple use-values in those activities associated with the home and family."[47]

Just because a woman does not sell the products of her labor (e.g., things such as the meals consumed by her family) does not mean her work is any less difficult than the kind of work resulting in marketable products (e.g., things such as frozen entrees). Benston stressed unless a woman is freed from her heavy domestic duties, including childcare, her entrance into the workforce will be a step away from, rather than toward, liberation:

> At all times household work is the responsibility of women. When they are working outside the home they must somehow manage to get both outside job and housework done (or they supervise a substitute for the housework). Women, particularly married women with children, who work outside the home simply do two jobs; their participation in the labor force is only allowed if they continue to fulfill their first responsibility in the home. This is particularly evident in countries like Russia and those in Eastern Europe where expanded opportunities for women in the labor force have not brought about a corresponding expansion in their liberty. Equal access to jobs outside the home, while one of the preconditions for women's liberation, will not in itself be sufficient to give equality for women; as long as work in the home remains a matter of private production and is the responsibility of women, they will simply carry a double work-load.[48]

To introduce a woman into public industry without simultaneously socializing the jobs of cooking, cleaning, and childcare is to make her oppressed condition even worse, claimed Benston. The key to woman's liberation is the socialization of domestic work.

Benston conceded that the socialization of domestic work might lead to a woman's doing the same work outside the home tomorrow as she does inside the home today. A change to communal eating arrangements, for example, might simply mean moving a woman from her small, private, individual kitchen into a large, public, communal one. Benston predicted, however, even this simple change would represent progress for women. The significance of socializing domestic work is not that it will necessarily free women from it but rather that it will enable everyone to recognize how socially necessary such work is. As soon as everyone realizes just how difficult domestic work is, society will no longer have grounds for the oppression of women as parasitic people of inferior value. In sum, for Benston, the socialization of private housekeeping and tending children is the single factor that will end women's oppression as a group and give each and every woman the respect she deserves.

The Wages-for-Housework Campaign

Some Marxist Feminist Arguments for Waged Housework. Although Benston, in contrast to Engels, assigned priority to the socialization of domestic labor rather than to the entrance en masse of women into public industry, she remained within the orthodox Marxist fold. In "Women and the Subversion of the Community," Mariarosa Dalla Costa and Selma James made the unorthodox Marxist claim that women's domestic work is productive not in the colloquial sense of being "useful" but in the strict Marxist sense of "creating surplus value."[49] No woman has to enter the productive workforce because all women are already in it, even if no one recognizes the fact. Women's work is the necessary condition for all other labor, from which, in turn, surplus value is extracted. By providing current (and future) workers not only with food and clothes but also with emotional and domestic comfort, women keep the cogs of the capitalist machine running.

Given their view of women's domestic work as productive work, it is not surprising that Dalla Costa and James's program for women's liberation differed not only from Benston's but also from Engels's. As these two leaders of the wages-for-housework campaign saw it, women who enter public industry work a double day that begins with paid, recognized work on the assembly line and ends with unpaid, unrecognized work at home. The way to end this inequity, said Dalla Costa and James, is for women to demand wages for housework.

Like other advocates of waged housework, Dalla Costa and James proposed the state (the government and employers), not individual men (husbands, fathers, and boyfriends), pay wages to housewives[50] because *capital* ultimately profits from women's exploitation.[51] Required to pay women for housework, the state will not be able to accumulate huge profits while housewives work themselves to the bone for a pittance.

Advocates of waged housework maintained that wages need not take the form of a paycheck. Such wages can be dispensed in the form of payments to welfare mothers for the work they have been doing in the home or in the form of childcare for any mother who is overburdened with work. If the state refuses to pay housewives wages, then housewives should strike. According to advocates of waged housework, some housewives (married or single women who are not paid or not paid enough for providing services to men and/or children) have already gone on strike. When a women divorces her husband, she refuses the work that comes with having a husband around the house. Similarly, when a woman practices contraception or has an abortion, she refuses to accept the extra work a large family would bring. Finally, when a secretary says no to making coffee or a teacher says no to taking her students on extra field trips or a nurse says no to eighteen-hour shifts, she refuses to work "for love"—that is, for free. Such rebellions on the part of women have revolutionary potential, for capitalism needs women to produce labor power in men and children.[52]

Some Marxist Feminist Arguments Against Waged Housework. Despite the power of Dalla Costa and James's line of reasoning, the emerging consensus among Marxist feminists is that, ultimately, paying wages for housework is neither feasible nor desirable as a liberatory strategy for women. It is not entirely feasible because even if the state pays out wages to housewives, it will do so in a way that will preserve itself. Contrary to the dreams of wages-for-housework campaigners, the state has no intention of going under as it pays to housewives a salary that, according to several reliable estimates, would exceed the salary of the average woman in the workforce two or threefold.[53] What the state is likely to do, said Barbara Bergmann, is put a special tax on married men that might be redistributed to their wives by the Internal Revenue Service. Depending on how large the tax bite was on her husband's dollar—and there is reason to believe it would be hefty—the wife's paycheck would, insofar as the family's real income is concerned, represent a mere status gain. Alternatively, the state could pay housewives out of its ordinary revenue. If it took this approach, the state would tax everyone regardless of whether he or she was living in a household serviced by a housewife. The net effect of this scheme would be to overly burden single people and two-earner families who are, on the average, already less well off than single-earner families, where the husband works outside the home and the wife within it. As a result, this scheme would "encourage women to become and remain housewives."[54]

This last point, made by Barbara Bergmann in *The Economic Emergence of Women*, summarizes what many Marxist feminists find undesirable about the wages-for-housework campaign. In the first place, wages for housework would have the effect of keeping a woman isolated in her own home, where she has few opportunities to do anything other than increasingly trivial work. Carol Lopate observed:

The decrease in house size and the mechanization of housework have meant that the housewife is potentially left with much greater leisure time; however, she is often kept busy buying, using, and repairing the devices and their attachments which are theoretically geared toward saving her time. Moreover, the trivial, manufactured tasks which many of these technological aids perform are hardly a source of satisfaction for housewives. Max-Pacs may give "perfect coffee every time," but even a compliment about her coffee can offer little more than fleeting satisfaction to the housewife. Finally, schools, nurseries, day care, and television have taken from mothers much of their responsibility for the socialization of their children.[55]

Second, by demanding wages for housework, the housewife would be contributing to capitalism's tendency to commodify everything, including husband-wife and mother-child relationships. Third, being paid for housework would give a woman little incentive to work outside the household. As a result, just when it looked as if it might weaken, the sexual division of labor would actually be strengthened. Men would feel no pressure to do "women's work," and women would have no incentive to do "men's work."[56]

If breaking down the division of sexual labor is one of the ultimate goals of Marxist feminists, then paying housewives for housework seems at best a distraction and at worst an impediment. It would be far better to take Benston's recommendations and socialize housework and childcare. Even if a woman winds up doing "women's work" outside of the home, it will give her an opportunity to work with other women and to form a class consciousness; if a woman is paid what her work is truly worth, at least some of "women's work" might become appealing to men who can earn a decent wage doing it.

Another argument against the wages-for-housework campaign asserts it undercuts the traditional Marxist emphasis on reintegrating women into social production. According to Nancy Holmstrom, the writings of Benston, Dalla Costa, and James, for example, are flawed for at least two reasons. First, it is simply not true that women constitute a class in the Marxist sense of the term *class*. Women, stressed Holmstrom, are all oppressed *as women*, but they are not all equally oppressed. There are, after all, significant differences between the ways in which working-class women are oppressed and the ways in which middle- and upper-class women are oppressed:

> Working class women are super-exploited in their wage work and exploited in their domestic work. In other ways as well they suffer more from sexism than do middle- and upper-class women. They have less reproductive freedom in that they have less access to abortion, contraception and child care, and are often subject to sterilization abuse. They are also more subject to sexual abuse on the job and in the streets. Hence the interests of working-class

women are more consistently opposed to sexism as well as capitalism than are the interests of middle- and upper-class women.[57]

Second, it is not the case, in Holmstrom's (and others') opinion that "capital" is served only by women who work in the home; it is also served by women who work outside the home. Fewer and fewer women are exclusively housewives. Less restrictive laws and policies have facilitated women's entrance into the workforce; advances in birth control have enabled women to better space their pregnancies; and inventions such as home appliances and convenience foods have eased women's domestic duties. These developments, combined with the emancipatory effects of the 1960s women's liberation movement, the increasing need for two incomes, and the proliferation of service-oriented or "women's work" jobs, have contributed to major changes in the composition of the contemporary workforce. By the early 1980s more than 45 percent of the U.S. workforce was female.[58]

That nearly half of the workforce is female indicates that capital wants and indeed needs women in the workforce. What this bald statistic does not show, however, is that capital wants and needs women in the workforce largely because women's work does not command as much compensation as men's work. Moreover, this statistic does not show capital's unwillingness to make the lives of women workers easier by providing the kinds of services—especially adequate care for the young, the old, and the infirm—that would release women from the pressures of the double day. Because capital is unwilling to reduce its profits in order to pay workers the kind of wage they need to hire domestic help, workers need to do most of their own cooking, cleaning, and people care.[59]

To be sure, the working class could decide not to live in traditional nuclear families, thereby releasing women from the domestic duties associated with this mode of human organization. But for largely ideological and emotional reasons, working-class men and women wish to maintain, at least as an ideal, the nuclear family. When domestic work becomes so burdensome that two fully employed people cannot possibly handle it without costly outside help (imagine, for example, if a working couple becomes the proud parents of triplets, if an aged parent develops Alzheimer's disease, or if an adolescent contracts AIDS), chances are one or the other will drop down to part-time employed or even unemployed status. Although there is no abstract capitalist law mandating that the person who drops out of the workforce should be female rather than male, in most cases the woman rather than the man will be the one to quit work, since on the average her wages will be lower than the man's.[60] In the opinion of many Marxist feminists, women will always be the ones to retreat from the public world back into the private world so long as women's wages remain less than men's and so long as women are viewed as more capable of giving care to the young, the old, and the infirm than men are.

Comparable Worth

In recent years many Marxist feminists have become less interested in how the sexual division of labor operates in the household and more interested in how it functions in the workplace. As these thinkers see it, when a woman enters public industry, she tends to do women's work there: teaching, nursing, clerking, cooking, sewing, and the like. Moreover, as in the household, this work is undervalued.

Angered that women often receive two-thirds of the money men receive for comparable work, many Marxist feminists have become active in the so-called comparable-worth movement. In their estimation, this movement is an opportunity not only to secure better wages for women but also to force society to reconsider why it pays some people so much and others so little.[61] Women in the 1990s earned just sixty-nine cents for every dollar men earned; this situation, though somewhat improved, has not changed much since the 1960s, when women earned about sixty-four cents for every dollar men earned. Even when this wage differential is adjusted for such factors as educational preparation, work experience, or labor force commitment, at least half of the gap between male and female wages goes unexplained. Many social scientists attribute the gender gap in wages to job segregation according to sex. Women in female-dominated occupations typically earn far less than men in male-dominated occupations. For example, nurses, 99 percent of whom are female, earn an average of $12,000 annually, whereas truck drivers, 98 percent of whom are male, earn $16,300; childcare workers, 97 percent of whom are female, earn $7,900 annually, whereas mail carriers, 88 percent of whom are male, earn $21,000 annually.[62] But why should a truck driver earn so much more than a nurse or a mail carrier so much more than a childcare worker? Is it because truck driving and mail carrying are so much more physically, psychologically, and intellectually demanding than nursing and childcaring? Or is it because truck drivers and mail carriers are so much more valuable to their respective employers than nurses and childcare workers are to theirs? Or is it simply because most truck drivers and mail carriers are *men* and most nurses and childcare workers are *women*?

Convinced a person's gender is the best explanation for why that person's salary is either high or low, comparable-worth advocates, be they Marxist or non-Marxist, urge employers to evaluate their employees objectively by focusing on the "worth points" for the four components found in most jobs: (1) "knowledge and skills," or the total amount of information or dexterity needed to perform the job; (2) "mental demands," or the extent to which the job requires decisionmaking; (3) "accountability," or the amount of supervision the job entails; and (4) "working conditions," such as how physically safe the job is.[63] When Norman D. Willis and Associates used this index to establish the worth points for various jobs performed in the state of Washington, they found the following disparities: "A Food Service I, at 93 points, earned an average salary of $472 per month, while a Delivery Truck Driver I, at 94 points, earned $792; a Clerical Supervisor III, at 305 points, earned an average of $794. A Nurse Practitioner II, at 385 points, had average earnings of $832, the same as those of a Boiler Operator with only 144 points. A Homemaker I, with 198 points and an average salary of $462, had the lowest earnings of all evaluated jobs."[64] After reflecting upon the Willis and Associates study, a federal court judge in Tacoma, Washington, ruled that the state was in violation of Title VII of the 1964 Civil Rights Act, which prohibits discrimination by type of employment and level of compensation, and should eliminate pay gaps within its system.[65]

Marxist feminists support comparable worth for two sets of reasons—one having to do with assessing the feminization of poverty, the other with assessing the value of work. Because nearly half of all poor families are headed by single women and because women are the primary recipients of food stamps, legal aid, and Medicaid, if wage-earning women were paid what their jobs are worth, these women might be able to support themselves and their families adequately without being forced, in one way or another, to attach themselves to men as an additional source of income. In reply to the objection that capital will respond to any mandatory hiking of women's wages with "automation, elimination of state programs, and runaway shops to countries in which women still provide a super-exploitation labor force," Marxist feminists like Teresa Amott and Julie Matthaei concede comparable worth must be pursued in conjunction with job security demands, retraining programs, and plant-closing legislation.[66] In reply to the further objection that like wages for housework, comparable worth will have the effect of keeping traditionally female jobs "female," Marxist feminists predict no such result. They claim as traditionally female jobs offer higher wages and as traditionally male jobs offer wages no higher than those offered in traditionally female jobs, more men will be attracted to "women's work," leaving more spaces for women in equally rewarding "men's work."[67] In other words, comparable worth will gradually result in the elimination of the sexual division of labor in the workplace.

In addition to seeing comparable worth as a way to alleviate women's poverty and to eliminate sex segregation in the workplace, Marxist feminists see it as a way to highlight just how arbitrary a society's judgments about what counts as "worthy" work can be. According to Amott and Matthaei, for example, we need to ask ourselves questions such as the following one:

> Why should those whose jobs give them the most opportunity to develop and use their abilities also be paid the most? The traditional argument—that higher pay must be offered as an incentive for workers to gain skills and training—is contradicted by the fact that our highly paid jobs attract many more workers than employers demand. And given unequal access to education and training, a hierarchical pay scheme becomes a mechanism for the intergenerational transmission of wealth privilege, with its historically-linked racism, sexism, and classism.[68]

Whether the value a society assigns to work is this "subjective" is certainly debatable. Nevertheless, many Marxist feminists derive satisfaction from the thought that as a result of the comparable-worth movement, capitalist assumptions about what kind of work counts as valuable could be seriously, even permanently, undermined.

Critiques of Marxist Feminism

Marxist feminists remain committed to the core teaching of Engels's *Origin*. To a greater or lesser degree, they still urge women to enter public industry, and they still press for the full socialization of housework and childcare. What is more, they remain attracted to programs aiming to destroy the family as an *economic* unit—as a structure serving to bolster the capitalist system. Finally, Marxist feminists, more than any other group of feminists, have made women's economic well-being and independence their primary concern and have focused on the intersection between women's experience as workers and their position in the family.

Although non-Marxist feminists have directed several criticisms against the wages-for-housework campaign and the comparable-worth movement, their main criticism of Marxist feminism has been what they perceive as its simplistic conception of the family and preoccupation with the nature and function of women's work as the only or best means of understanding and ending women's oppression. In the following two sections, we see how Jean Bethke Elshtain's communitarian, even traditionalist, critique of Marxist feminists differs from the more sympathetic but no less thoroughgoing critique by socialist feminist Alison Jaggar.

A Communitarian Critique of Marxist Feminism

In *Public Man, Private Woman*, Jean Bethke Elshtain was particularly critical of what some Marxist feminists have had to say about the family under capitalism. As she saw it, the family is not simply and finally a Frankensteinian creation, constructed by capitalism to reproduce labor power at women's expense. Rather, the family is the only place where human beings can still find some love, security, and comfort—indeed, the only place where human beings can still make decisions based on something other than a monetary bottom line.[69]

Elshtain cautioned Marxist feminists that the institution of the family is people's best protection against the tendencies of a totalizing state that cannot tolerate diversity of any sort. Were the state the only socializing mechanism in society, all individuals would be inculcated with the same set of values. As a result, they would find it difficult to gain a critical perspective on the society that produced them. An individual family allows for this critical perspective because its values are somewhat idiosyncratic. For example, pacifist families react to an arms buildup differently than do nonpacifist families; religious families react to prayer in public school differently than do atheist families. To be sure, conceded Elshtain, an individual family's values are not always *better* than those of society as a whole; but if children do not experience their own family's values as somehow "good," then they will have no basis against which to consider the values of children who come from different families.[70]

Elshtain claimed being a member of a small family is particularly important for children. Conceding it is appealing to view children as a group of little people everyone should love, Elshtain nonetheless insisted something very important is lost in depriving a child of the intimacy that comes from daily contact with one or two adults committed to parenting him or her. Although she admitted problems can and do arise in a society where parents regard their biological or adopted children as their special "possessions," Elshtain predicted that even greater problems would arise in a society where children belonged to everyone in general but to no one in particular.[71]

In response to Elshtain's critique, Marxist feminists accused her of accepting the stereotypical image American capitalists have of "communist" women who bear children only to let dispassionate daycare attendants rear them. Marxist feminists advised Elshtain to remember the Marxist condemnation of the family is directed toward the family as an *economic* unit, not as an *emotional* unit. They observed Engels himself spoke eloquently about the future of the family.

> What we can now conjecture about the way in which sexual relations will be ordered after the impending overthrow of capitalist production is mainly of negative character, limited to the most part to what will disappear. But what will there be new? That will be answered when a new generation has grown up: a generation of men who never in their lives have known what it is to buy a woman's surrender with money or any other social instrument of

power; a generation of women who have never known what it is to give themselves to a man from any other considerations than real love or to refuse to give themselves to their lover from fear of the economic consequences. When these people are in the world, they will care precious little what anybody today thinks they ought to do; they will make their own practice . . . and that will be the end of it.[72]

Although Engels's words summoned Marxist feminists to envision radically new forms of relationships, commitments, households, and communities—"families" in which heterosexuals, homosexuals, and/or lesbians might live together—most Marxist feminists nonetheless continued to envision the traditional biological family, minus its gender-oppressive features, as constituting the ideal family. In other words, most Marxist feminists speculated that in the truly or fully socialist society, men will marry women, but these women will be their equals; heterosexual couples will have their own biological children, but these children will be regarded as everyone's social responsibility; and people will set up individual households, even though little in the way of cooking, cleaning, and/or childcare will go on in them. Far from rejecting Elshtain's family, then, many Marxist feminists viewed themselves as actually embracing it as a description of how the family would appear under authentic socialism.

A Socialist Feminist Critique of Marxist Feminism

Alison Jaggar's critique of Marxist feminism is written from the perspective of a socialist feminist who worries Marxist feminists have said too little about women's oppression by *men*. When Marxist feminists speak about women's oppression, they argue capital is the primary oppressor of women as workers, and men are, at most, the secondary oppressors of women as women. Thus, Jaggar asked what is specifically *feminist* about a Marxist feminist analysis and whether it is true men are merely the secondary, or indirect, oppressors of women. She also asked whether there is adequate room in a Marxist feminist analysis to express dissatisfaction about those women's issues unrelated to the nature and function of women's *work*.

It concerned Jaggar that Marxist feminists rarely discuss issues related to sex. When they do, they tend to compare sex to work by equating, for instance, not only the pimp-prostitute relation but also the husband-wife relation to the bourgeois-proletariat relation, as if male-female relations in marriage and prostitution were exploitative and alienating in precisely the same way as those in employer-employee relationships. Marxist feminists draw these analogies, said Jaggar, because they want "to link the Marxist treatment of women's sex-specific oppression with Marxism's main theoretical system, incorporating domination both by class and by gender in the same explanatory framework."[73] As Jaggar saw it, however, Marxist feminists cannot make this important link because, for all the similarities, exploited workers do not suffer in the same way as do oppressed wives and prostitutes.

In order to disassociate class exploitation from gender oppression, Jaggar began with a detailed recapitulation of the Marxist feminist analysis of prostitution and marriage. Because women in a capitalist system do not have sufficient access to the workplace, in order to survive they must connect themselves financially to men. In this respect, Marxist feminists see the difference between a prostitute and a wife as merely a difference of degree, not of kind. Both sell themselves—their sexual services and, in the case of wives, their domestic and nurturing services—for economic livelihood. Whether this takes the form of "hustling" or of a "marriage of convenience" is a secondary issue for Marxists.[74]

In describing bourgeois marriage as a form of prostitution, Marx and Engels implicitly acknowledged that services other than sexual services can be prostituted. Housework, childcare, and emotional support are also services sold by the wife-prostitute. From this, Jaggar pointed out, it is only a short step to describing the sale of a number of services as types or instances of prostitution.[75] In fact, Marx made this exact point in the *Economic and Philosophical Manuscript*: "Prostitution is only a *specific* expression of the *general* prostitution of the laborer, and since it is a relationship in which falls not the prostitute alone, but also the one who prostitutes—and the latter's abomination is still greater—the capitalist, etc., also comes under this head."[76]

This statement certainly gives us insight into the Marxist view of prostitution. First, it points out that prostitution, like wage labor, is a class phenomenon. The economic situation of unemployed or underemployed women explains why they, like laborers, sell themselves to others. Second, it points out the alienation of prostitutes. Just as wage laborers are estranged from their work, from themselves, and from humanity itself, so, too, are prostitutes. Selling oneself, whether as a wife or a prostitute, alienates oneself from one's work because the work is being done for another, not for oneself. This concept is particularly appalling in the case of the prostitute, for what she is selling is what is closest to her: her body, her sexuality. Under capitalism, a woman's sexuality becomes a commodity; this is true for both the wife-prostitute and for the prostitute proper. For both women, an essential human capacity is alienating. Like wage laborers, the wife-prostitute and the prostitute proper become dehumanized, and their value as persons is reduced to their market value.

Inequalities of wealth are the cause of prostitution, just as they are of wage labor. According to traditional Marxist analysis, therefore, the typical prostitute is an unemployed or underemployed female, and the typical patron is an upper- or middle-class male. As long as there are men who have enough money to purchase the sexual services of women[77] and as long as there are women who are in need of money and without other "marketable skills," these women will probably "choose" to sell their bodies to support themselves and, in some instances, their children. Thus, to fight capitalism is also to fight prostitution—whatever form it takes, including marriage—because most women will not have access to meaningful work at a decent wage until the capitalist system that depends upon their exploitation is smashed.

Writing before the collapse of communism in the USSR and Eastern Europe, Jaggar stressed that the supposed elimination of capitalism in socialist nations had not substantially transformed the lives of socialist women. She observed that since socialist women's entrance into the workplace was seldom accompanied by the full socialization of housework and childcare, women in communist countries were as likely to do two jobs—housework *and* outside work—as were women in capitalist countries. What is more, issues of particular concern to women—such as sexual violence against women and reproductive freedom—were likely to rank as low among the Russian government's priorities as they did among the U.S. government's priorities, if not lower.

The usual explanation of why socialist women and men in the former Eastern bloc never became full equals is "residual capitalism." Through the 1980s, defenders of socialism stressed that capitalist ideologues do not die off immediately; it takes time for the ideas of formerly capitalist populations to change. Apparently so, since in the 1990s the Eastern bloc started to revert to capitalism. Only Cuba and the People's Republic of China remain identifiably communist, and even in those two nations only relatively small steps have been made toward the full socialization of housework and childcare. Contemporary Chinese and Cuban women seem to work in the home almost as much as contemporary capitalist women do, and they seem to have far less sexual and reproductive freedom than capitalist women do. If Marxism is to ensure the liberation of women, it must incorporate some understanding not only of capitalism but also of patriarchy as incredibly powerful and tenacious systems. Marxism must recognize, as Jaggar insisted, the possibility that part of what women in the United States, in the People's Republic of China, in Cuba, and in Russia have in common is their oppression *as women*, by men *as men*.

Contemporary Socialist Feminism

Socialist feminism is largely the result of Marxist feminists' dissatisfaction with the essentially gender-blind character of Marxist thought, with the tendency of Marxists to regard women's oppression as far less important than worker's oppression. Marxists assume that what women suffer at the hands of men is small compared to what the proletariat suffers at the hands of the bourgeoisie. Thus, women must wait for their turn to be liberated.

Although many Marxist feminists have waited for women's turn, some have been impatient. Clara Zetkin, one of Lenin's corevolutionaries, provides a case in point. Indeed, Marxist feminists remember Lenin unfavorably largely because he berated Zetkin for encouraging women members of the Communist Party to discuss sexual issues. Lenin stated:

> The record of your sins, Clara, is even worse. I have been told that at the evenings arranged for reading and discussion with working women, sex and marriage problems come first. They are said to be the main objects of interest in your political instruction and educational work. I could not believe my ears when I heard that. The first state of proletarian dictatorship is battling with the counter-revolutionaries of the whole world. The situation in Germany itself calls for the greatest unity of all proletarian revolutionary forces, so that they can repel the counter-revolution which is pushing on. But active Communist women are busy discussing sex problems and the forms of marriage—"past, present and future." They consider it their most important task to enlighten working women on these questions.[78]

From Lenin's point of view, Zetkin focused on trivial matters, catering to women's self-indulgent tendencies, when she should have been working to raise their revolutionary consciousness. But as Zetkin saw it, there was a real need for women to understand the form oppression takes in the "private" as well as "public" domain.

Convinced Zetkin understood the nature of women's oppression better than Lenin, contemporary socialist feminists stress that although Marxist feminists explained how and why capitalism caused the separation of the workplace from the homestead, they failed to explain why capitalism assigned *women* to the homestead and *men* to the workplace in the first place.[79] The categories of Marxist analysis, commented socialist feminist Heidi Hartmann, "give no clues about why particular people fill particular places. They give no clues about why *women* are subordinate to *men* inside and outside the family and why it is not the other way around. *Marxist categories, like capital itself, are sex-blind.* The categories of Marxism cannot tell us who will fill the empty places."[80]

To overcome what they perceive as the limitations of traditional Marxist feminist thought, socialist feminists seek to explain the ways in which capitalism interacts with patriarchy to oppress women more egregiously than men.[81] Although socialist feminists agree with Marxist feminists that women's liberation depends on the overthrow of capitalism, they claim that capitalism cannot be destroyed unless patriarchy is also destroyed and that people's material, or economic, relations cannot change unless their ideologies are also changed. Women must fight two wars, not one, in order to be liberated from the forces of oppression.

Fighting on Two Fronts: Assaulting the Two-Headed Beast of Capitalist Patriarchy

Juliet Mitchell

Juliet Mitchell combined a materialist, or economic, account of capitalism with a largely nonmaterialist, or ideological, account of patriarchy.[82] She said a Marxist revolution aimed at destroying class society must be combined with a specifically feminist revolution aimed at destroying the sex/gender system.[83] In her book *Woman's Estate*, Mitchell abandoned the traditional Marxist feminist position according to which woman's condition is simply a function of her relation to capital, of whether or not she is part of the productive workforce. In place of this monocausal explanation for woman's oppression, she suggested woman's status and function are multiply determined by her role in production, reproduction, the socialization of children, and sexuality: "The error of the old Marxist was to see the other three elements as reducible to the economic; hence the call for the entry into production was accompanied by the purely abstract slogan of the abolition of the family. Economic demands are still primary, but must be accompanied by coherent policies for the other three elements (reproduction, sexuality and socialization), policies which at particular junctures may take over the primary role in immediate action."[84]

In the course of her 1971 attempt to determine which of these elements most oppress contemporary women, Mitchell concluded somewhat pessimistically that women have not made enough progress in the areas of production, reproduction, and the socialization of children.[85] Mitchell noted that even though women are just as physically and psychologically qualified for high-paying, prestigious jobs as men are, employers continue to confine women to low-paying, low-status jobs.[86] What is more, said Mitchell, despite the widespread availability of safe, effective, and inexpensive reproduction-controlling technologies, women fail or refuse to use them. As a result, the causal chain of "maternity—family—absence from production and public life—sexual inequality" continues to bind women to their subordinate status. Furthermore, although women have far fewer children now than they did at the turn of the century, they spend no less time socializing them.[87]

Still, Mitchell thought 1970s women had made significant progress in the area of sexuality, thanks largely to the efforts of radical feminists. Mitchell nevertheless cautioned that, pushed to extremes, women's newly won sexual liberation could mutate into a form of sexual oppression. Whereas traditional society generally condemned sexually promiscuous women as "wanton whores," contemporary society often celebrates them as "sex experimenters." Instead of branding sexually liberated women with scarlet letters, contemporary society offers them up as healthy role models for those women it regards as sexually repressed. If contemporary society views any group of women as unhealthy, implied Mitchell, it is probably virgins. No wonder, then, that women who view sex as a part though certainly not the whole of a meaningful life start to feel abnormal. Commenting on this state of affairs, Mitchell observed that too much sex, like too little sex, can be oppressive.[88]

Mitchell speculated that patriarchal ideology, which views women as lovers, wives, and mothers rather than as workers, is at least as responsible for women's position in society as capitalist economics is. Even if a Marxist revolution manages to destroy the family as an economic unit, it will not make women men's equals. Because of the ways in which patriarchy has constructed men's and women's psyches, women will continue to remain subordinate to men until their minds and men's minds have been liberated from the thought that women are less than men's full equals.

Although Mitchell did not develop her thoughts on the need for a "psychic revolution" in *Woman's Estate*, she did develop them in *Psychoanalysis and Feminism*. Mitchell claimed the psychology of women, produced by the castration and Oedipus complexes, is essentially constant within patriarchal society, the *only* kind of human society there presently is. No matter how rich or poor, black or white, beautiful or ugly a woman is, "in relation to the law of the father" she has approximately the same status and function as any other woman.[89]

Convinced the causes of women's oppression are buried deep in the human psyche, Mitchell rejected the claim of liberal feminists that social reforms aimed at giving women more educational and occupational opportunities will make women men's equals. Women's suffrage, coeducational studies, and affirmative action policies might change the "expression of femininity," but they cannot, in her view, significantly change the overall status of women. Likewise, Mitchell rejected the claim of radical feminists that reproductive technology is the key to women's liberation because, as she saw it, a purely biological solution cannot resolve an essentially psychological problem. Finally, Mitchell rejected the claim of traditional Marxist feminists that an economic revolution aimed at overthrowing the capitalist order will make men and women full partners in action and friends in virtue.[90] Just because women enter the productive workforce to labor side by side with men does not mean women will return home in the evening arm in arm with men. Mitchell observed that even Mao Zedong admitted that "despite collective work, egalitarian legislation, social care of children, etc., it was too soon for the Chinese really, deeply and irrevocably to have changed their *attitudes* towards women."[91] As Mitchell saw it, attitudes toward women will never really change so long as female and male psychology are dominated by the phallic symbol. Thus, patriarchy as well as capitalism must be overthrown in order to truly humanize society.[92]

Iris Young

According to Iris Young, so long as socialist feminists try to use "class" as their central category of analysis, they will not be able to explain why women in socialist countries are no less oppressed than women in capitalist countries. Because class is a gender-blind category, it is not adequate for the analysis of women's specific oppression in Young's estimation. Thus, Young suggested only a gender-sighted category such as "division of labor" has the conceptual power to transform Marxist feminist theory into a socialist feminist theory able to discuss women's entire estate—that is, women's position in the family as well as the workplace, women's reproductive and sexual roles as well as women's productive roles.

The advantage of a division-of-labor analysis, said Young, is that it is far more specific than a standard class analysis. Whereas class analysis aims to scan the system of production as a whole, focusing on the means and relations of production in the most general terms possible, a division-of-labor analysis pays attention to the individual people who do the producing in society. In other words, a class analysis calls for only a general discussion of the respective roles of the bourgeoisie and the proletariat, whereas a division-of-labor analysis requires a detailed discussion of who gives the orders and who takes them, who does the stimulating work and who does the drudge work, who works the desirable shift and who works the undesirable shift, and who gets paid more and who gets paid less. Therefore, as compared to a class analysis, a division-of-labor analysis can better explain why *women* usually take the orders, do the drudge jobs, work the undesirable shifts, and get paid less, whereas *men* usually give the orders, do the stimulating jobs, work the desirable shifts, and get paid more.

Because she believed that capitalism and patriarchy are necessarily linked, Young insisted that a division-of-labor analysis is a total substitute for, not a mere supplement to, class analysis. We do not need one theory (Marxism) to explain *gender-neutral capitalism* and another theory (feminism) to explain *gender-biased patriarchy*. Rather, we need a single theory—a socialist feminist theory—to explain *gender-biased capitalist patriarchy*. Capitalism is, was, and always will be essentially and fundamentally a patriarchy. "*My thesis,*" wrote Young, "*is that marginalization of women and thereby our functioning as a secondary labor force is an essential and fundamental characteristic of capitalism."*[93]

Young's thesis is a controversial one, a major departure from the more traditional Marxist view according to which workers, be they male or female, are interchangeable.[94] As Young saw it, however, capitalism is very much aware of its workers' gender and, I may add, race and ethnicity. Because a large reserve of unemployed workers is necessary to keep wages low and to meet unanticipated demands for increased supplies of goods and services, capitalism has both implicit and explicit criteria for determining who shall constitute its primary, employed workforce and who shall act as its secondary, unemployed workforce. For a variety of reasons, not the least being a well-entrenched gender division of labor, capitalism's criteria identify men as "primary" workforce material and women as "secondary" workforce material. Because women are needed at home in a way men are not—or so *patriarchy* believes—men are more free to work outside the home than women are.

Under capitalism as it exists today, women experience patriarchy as unequal wages for equal work, sexual harassment on the job, uncompensated domestic work, and the pernicious dynamics of the public-private split. Earlier generations of women also experienced patriarchy, but they lived it differently depending on the dynamics of the reigning economic system. As with class society, reasoned Young, patriarchy should not be considered a system *separate* from capitalism just because it existed *first*. In fact, class and gender structures are so intertwined that neither one actually precedes the other. A feudal system of gender relations accompanied a feudal system of class arrangements, and the social relations of class and gender grew up together and evolved over time into the forms we now know (for example, the capitalist nuclear family). To say gender relations are independent of class relations is to ignore how history works.

A look at the formation of our particular type of capitalist patriarchy or patriarchal capitalism will help us appreciate Young's insistence that capitalism and patriarchy are joined at the hip. In her essay "Beyond the Unhappy Marriage: A Critique of the Dual Systems Theory," Young provided a historical analysis of the gender division of labor. She traced the decline in women's relative status as they moved from a precapitalist economy into a capitalist one.

In precapitalist times marriage was, said Young, an "economic partnership"; wives did not expect to be supported by their husbands. They generally retained their own property, labored side by side with their husbands in home-based businesses, and even participated in craft guilds on equal terms with their spouses. The advent of capitalism, however, dissolved the economic partnership between husbands and wives. A new deal was struck for men and women when the forces of capitalism drove a wedge between the workplace and the home, sending men, as a primary workforce, out into the former and confining women, as a secondary workforce, to the latter. Women became the reserve army of labor to which I have already made reference. Thus, when new industries opened, such as the New England textile mills, women were usually recruited to fill the initial need; and when wars had to be fought by men, women quickly took over the factory jobs, only to be sent packing when "Johnny" came marching home. Young cited examples such as these to support her thesis that the "marginalization of women" is essential to capitalism. She also invoked the work of Esther Boserup, who showed how, with their nations' transformation into capitalist economies, Third World women rapidly move from the primary to the secondary workforce.[95] So convinced was Young of her analysis, she challenged her readers to find a single advanced capitalist society in which women's labor is not, at root, marginalized. Only if such an instance is discovered, wrote Young, are we warranted in regarding the marginalization of women's labor as peripheral to capitalism.[96]

Alison Jaggar

Like Young, Alison Jaggar advanced a concept other than class as the quintessential Marxist concept. In her book *Feminist Politics and Human Nature*, Jaggar identified "alienation" as a concept powerful enough to accommodate the main insights of Marxist, radical, and even liberal feminist thought:

> Contemporary feminists are united in their opposition to women's oppression, but they differ not only in their views of how to combat that oppression, but even in their conception of what constitutes women's oppression in contemporary society. Liberal feminists ... believe that women are oppressed insofar as they suffer unjust discrimination; traditional Marxists believe that women are oppressed in their exclusion from public production; radical feminists see women's oppression as consisting primarily in the universal male control of women's sexual and procreative capacities; while socialist feminists characterize women's oppression in terms of a revised version of the Marxist theory of alienation.[97]

Jaggar noted that Marx considered work the humanizing activity par excellence; it is meant to connect human beings to the products of their minds and bodies, nature, and other people. Under capitalism, however, work becomes a dehumanizing activity. Labor is organized in ways that put human beings at odds with everything and everyone, including themselves. Rejecting the traditional Marxist doctrine that a person has to participate directly in the capitalist relations of production in order to be considered truly alienated, Jaggar claimed not only non-wage-earning women can be alienated but also that wage-earning women experience alienation in different ways than wage-earning men do. Alienation, insisted Jaggar, is a gender-mediated experience.[98]

Jaggar organized her discussion of woman's alienation and fragmentation under the rubrics of sexuality, motherhood, and intellectuality. In the same way a wageworker is alienated, or separated, from the product(s) upon which he works, a woman is alienated from the product upon which she works—her body. A woman may insist that she diets, exercises, and dresses to please herself, but in reality she is probably shaping and adorning her flesh for the pleasure of men. A woman has little or no say about when, where, how, or by whom her body will be used because it can be appropriated from her through acts as varied as rape or "standing on the corner, watching all the girls go by." Likewise, to the same degree a wageworker is gradually alienated from himself—his body beginning to feel like a thing, a mere machine from which labor power is extracted—a woman is gradually alienated from herself. As she works away on her body—plucking this eyebrow and shaving that underarm, slimming this thigh and augmenting that breast, painting this nail and corseting that torso—her body becomes an object for men and for herself. Finally, just as a wageworker is in competition with other wageworkers for the "top dollar," a woman is in competition with other women for the "male gaze," for male approbation and approval. Female friendship is often so strong among lesbian women, suggested Jaggar, because lesbian women are not each other's rivals for male attention.[99]

Motherhood, like sexuality, is also an alienating experience for women. A woman, contended Jaggar, is alienated from the *product* of her reproductive labor when not she but someone else decides, for example, how many children she ought to bear. In societies where children's labor power is used nearly as much as adults' labor, a woman is pressured into bearing as many children as physically possible. In societies where children are viewed as an economic burden, a woman is discouraged from having as many children as she wishes. Many a woman has been pressured into an unwanted abortion or sterilization.[100]

Similarly, continued Jaggar, women are alienated from the *process* of their reproductive labor. Obstetricians manage women's deliveries with the most sophisticated technology available. Worse, and for little or even no good cause, obstetricians take total control of the birthing process, sometimes performing medically unnecessary Caesarian sections or anesthetizing a woman against her wishes. In the future, as the new reproductive technologies develop, women are likely to be further alienated from the product and process of childbirth. In vitro fertilization makes possible so-called full surrogacy, in which a woman can have one or more of her eggs surgically removed, fertilized in vitro with her husband's sperm, and then transferred into the womb of another woman for gestation. Likewise, artificial insemination by donor makes possible so-called partial surrogacy, in which a woman agrees to gestate a child to which she is genetically related so that the genetic father of the child and his wife will have the pleasure of rearing the child to adulthood. Although it may be argued a woman's decision to contract a surrogate or to serve as a surrogate represents a free choice on her part, her choice may well be no more voluntary than some of the sterilizations, abortions, or unwanted pregnancies into which women have been bullied.[101]

Child-rearing, like childbearing, is an alienating experience when scientific experts (most of whom are male), not women, take charge of it. As Jaggar saw it, the pressures on mothers are enormous because, with virtually no assistance, they are supposed to execute every edict of the experts. Isolated in her suburban home, each mother labors longer days and even longer nights in order to raise her children the experts' way rather than her way.

Echoing the words of Adrienne Rich in *Of Woman Born* (see Chapter Two), Jaggar explained how contemporary child-rearing practices ultimately alienate, or estrange, mothers from their children:

> The extreme mutual dependence of mother and child encourages the mother to define the child primarily with reference to her own needs for meaning, love and social recognition. She sees the child as her product, as something that should improve her life and that often instead stands against her, as something of supreme value, that is held cheap by society. The social relations of contemporary motherhood make it impossible for her to see the child as a whole person, part of a larger community to which both mother and child belong.[102]

One of the most distressing features of a mother's alienation from her children is that her inability to see her children as persons is equaled only by their inability to see her as a person. Alluding to Dorothy Dinnerstein and some other psychoanalytic feminists, Jaggar described the ways in which children gradually turn on their mothers by viewing them not as persons but as objects who are guilty of doing either too little or too much for them. In addition to separating mothers from their children, the conditions of contemporary motherhood drive wedges between mothers and fathers. All too many arguments begin with a demanding father who lays down the law for the household and a resentful mother who executes its terms. The standards governing "proper" mothering impede the growth of friendships between women, and mothers compete with each other to produce and to process the "perfect child"[103]—what I would describe as the well-mannered, multitalented, physically fit, achievement-oriented boy or girl who wins all the class awards and whose photograph appears on every other page of the yearbook.

Finally, said Jaggar, not only are many women alienated from their own sexuality and from the product and process of motherhood; they are also alienated from their intellectual capacities. A woman is made to feel so unsure of herself she hesitates to express her ideas in public, for fear her thoughts are not worth expressing; she scurries up and down the hallowed halls of academe frequently fearing she will be exposed as a pretender, not possessor, of knowledge. To the extent men set the terms of thought and discourse, suggested Jaggar, women are never at ease.[104]

Women must, stressed Jaggar, understand that within the structures of late-twentieth-century capitalist patriarchy women's oppression takes the form of women's alienation from everything and everyone, especially themselves.[105] Only when women understand the true source of their unhappiness will women be in a position to do battle with it.

Conclusion

Contemporary Marxist-socialist feminists, as typified here by Iris Young and Alison Jaggar, have enabled feminists to stop asking questions such as "Does capitalism cause patriarchy or vice versa?" and instead recognize, as did Nancy Fraser, the similarities and mutual reinforcements between, for example, the U.S. male-headed nuclear family and the U.S. state-regulated official economy. In a provocative analysis of Jürgen Habermas's critical social theory, Fraser claimed Habermas's relative inattention to gender issues weakens his otherwise excellent explanation of how welfare state capitalism *inflates* our role as consumers, transforming us all into passive clients, while it simultaneously *deflates* our role as citizens, reducing us all into mere voters.

Observing that the roles of citizen and worker are masculine roles whereas those of consumer and child-rearer are feminine roles, Fraser noted that although welfare state capitalism oppresses everyone, it oppresses women in different and arguably worse ways than it oppresses men. She claimed the "new client role has a gender,"[106] and this gender is female. What is more, said Fraser, the *logic* of the capitalist welfare system is gendered. For example, in the United States there are two fundamental kinds of welfare programs: "masculine" social insurance programs and "feminine" relief programs. Whereas social insurance programs are tied to primary labor force participation and designed to benefit the principal breadwinner, relief programs are oriented to domestic "failures," that is, to families without a *male* principal breadwinner. In Fraser's estimation, the masculine social insurance programs and the feminine relief programs are "separate and unequal."[107] Fraser commented:

> Clients of feminine programs, virtually exclusively women and their children, are positioned in a distinctive, feminizing fashion as the "negatives of possessive individuals": they are largely excluded from the market both as workers and as consumers and are familiarized, that is, made to claim benefits, not as individuals but as members of "defective" households. They are also stigmatized, denied rights, subjected to surveillance and administrative harassment and generally made into object defendants of state bureaucracies. But this means that the rise of the client role in welfare state capitalism . . . is not only a change in the link between system and lifeworld institutions; it is also a change in the character of male dominance, a shift, in Carol Brown's phase, "from private patriarchy to public patriarchy."[108]

It is ironic that a poor woman who manages to escape economic dependence on an abusive or shiftless husband by going on welfare will probably find herself economically dependent on a new "male" oppressor, a patriarchal and androcentric state bureaucracy.

As useful as Fraser's analysis is, she does not emphasize the role race and age, for example, play in the welfare system. The agents of this system treat African American women, Hispanic women, and white women differently; they treat young and old women differently. The general consensus of these women—all of them "clients" of the welfare system—is that some female clients are asked to jump through extra bureaucratic hoops not because they are women but because they are young *African American* or *Hispanic* women with several children. Although all these women may share the standpoint of "client," they will not all view their oppression in the same way.

Using the term *standpoint* serves as an invitation to address a question that has occupied the attention of a wide variety of feminists: Do women, simply because they are women, see reality differently from men? Although the answer to this question is a qualified yes, the fact remains that even if women see reality differently from men, not all women see reality the same. A woman's race, class, ethnicity, age, sexual preference, physical condition, or psychological condition, for example, will affect what position she occupies on the feminist-standpoint platform. Realizing this, many socialist feminists have begun to consider seriously the "epistemological consequences" of the differences as well as the similarities among women. Rather than fearing this new development, however, socialist feminists like Alison Jaggar have embraced it. Indeed, Jaggar claimed that *only* by working through their myriad differences could women develop "a systematic representation of reality that is not distorted in ways that promote the interests of men above those of women."[109]

The fact many women have not been willing or even able to take part in this process means, of course, that women are still the captives of a distorted representation of reality that promotes men's over women's interests. However, as Jaggar claimed, the bad news—"we women have only begun to fight"—is also the good news. Women's standpoint is not an ossified truth some feminist academicians have chiseled in stone for all women to worship; rather, it is a kaleidoscope of truths, continually shaping and reshaping each other, as more and different women begin to work and think together. The challenge for socialist feminists, therefore, is to draw on the experiences of all women, never falling prey to the temptation to valorize the experiences of one group of women—for example, the most oppressed group of women—as somehow the paradigm for what it means to be a woman.

CHAPTER FOUR

————— ■ —————

Psychoanalytic and
Gender Feminism

So FAR EACH OF THE SCHOOLS OF FEMINIST THOUGHT I have described
has provided explanations and solutions for women's oppression that are
rooted either in society's political and economic structures or in human
beings' sexual and reproductive relationships, roles, and practices. Liberal feminists claimed changes in society's political structures, particularly in its laws, could eliminate or at least reduce gender inequity by ensuring women are provided with the same educational and occupational
opportunities men are provided. Radical feminists—be they radical-libertarian or radical-cultural in emphasis—instead insisted we need to examine men's and women's sexual and reproductive rights and responsibilities in order to understand fully the persistence of the systems that foster
male domination and female subordination. Radical-libertarian feminists
claimed that women need to be liberated not only from the burdens of
natural reproduction and biological motherhood but also from the restrictions of the so-called sexual double standard that permits men but not
women to experiment sexually. Radical-cultural feminists disagreed.
They claimed that the source of women's power is rooted in women's
unique reproductive role. All children are born of women; without
women *no* children would be born. Radical-cultural feminists also
stressed that male sexual behavior is not worthy of women's emulation,
since men frequently use sex as an instrument of control and domination
rather than of love and bonding. Finally, Marxist and socialist feminists
hypothesized that unless capitalist economic structures are destroyed,
people will continue to be divided into two oppositional classes—the
haves and the have-nots—and because of the ways in which capitalism
and patriarchy reinforce each other, more women than men will find
themselves within the ranks of the have-nots.

In contrast to liberal, radical (libertarian and cultural), and Marxist and socialist feminists, psychoanalytic and gender feminists believe the fundamental explanation for women's way of acting is rooted deep in women's psyche, specifically, in women's way of thinking. Relying on Freudian concepts such as the pre-Oedipal stage and the Oedipus complex, they claim that gender inequity is rooted in a series of early childhood experiences that result not only in men's viewing themselves as masculine and women's viewing themselves as feminine but also in patriarchal society's regarding masculinity as somehow better than femininity. Hypothesizing that in a nonpatriarchal society masculinity and femininity would be both differently constructed and equally valued, psychoanalytic feminists recommend that we work toward a more androgynous society in which the full human person is a blend of positive feminine and positive masculine traits.

Unlike psychoanalytic feminists, gender feminists (sometimes referred to as cultural feminists)[1] tend to think there may be biological as well as psychological or cultural explanations for men's masculinity and women's femininity. They also stress that the values traditionally associated with women (gentleness, modesty, humility, supportiveness, empathy, compassion, tenderness, nurturance, intuitiveness, sensitivity, and unselfishness) are morally better virtues than the values traditionally associated with men (strength of will, ambition, courage, independence, assertiveness, hardiness, rationality, and emotional control).[2] Thus, gender feminists conclude that women should hold on to their femininity and that men should forsake at least the most extreme forms of their masculinity. A new feminine ethics of care should, they say, replace the old masculine ethics of justice.

The Roots of Psychoanalytic Feminism: Sigmund Freud

Freud's theories about sexuality disturbed his contemporaries not so much because he publicly addressed formerly taboo topics (e.g., homosexuality, sadism, masochism, oral, and anal sex) but because he publicly proclaimed that all sexual "aberrations," "variations," and "perversions" are simply stages in the development of *normal* human sexuality.[3] According to Freud, children go through distinct psychosexual development stages, and the gender of any given adult is the product of how he or she deals with these stages. Masculinity and femininity are, in other words, the product of sexual maturation. If boys develop "normally" (that is, typically), they will end up as men who display expected masculine traits; if women develop "normally," they will end up as women who display expected feminine traits.

The theoretical basis for Freud's views on the relationship between one's sex and one's gender is found in *Three Contributions to the Theory of Sexuality*. There, Freud discussed the sexual stages of infancy. Because adults in Freud's time equated sexual activity with reproductive genital sexuality (heterosexual intercourse), adults thought children were sexless. Dismissing this view of children as naive, Freud argued that far from being without sexual interests, children engage in all sorts of sexual behavior. He claimed that children's sexuality is "polymorphous perverse"—that insofar as the infant is concerned, her or his entire body, especially its orifices and appendages, is sexual terrain. The infant moves from this type of "perverse" sexuality to "normal" heterosexual genital sexuality by passing through several stages. During the *oral* stage, the infant receives pleasure from sucking her or his mother's breast or her or his own thumb. During the *anal* stage, the two- or three-year-old child particularly enjoys the sensations associated with controlling the expulsion of her or his feces. During the *phallic* stage, the three- or four-year-old child discovers the pleasure potential of the genitals and either resolves or fails to resolve the so-called Oedipus and castration complexes. Around age six, the child ceases to display overt sexuality and begins a period of *latency* that ends around puberty, at which time the young person enters the *genital* stage characterized by a resurgence of sexual impulses. If all goes normally during this stage, the young person's libido (defined by Freud as undifferentiated sexual energy) will be directed outward, away from autoerotic and homoerotic stimulation, and toward a member of the opposite sex.

Freud noted that the critical juncture of the preceding psychosexual drama is the child's resolution of the so-called Oedipus and castration complexes. According to psychoanalytic doctrine, that boys have penises and girls do not fundamentally affects the way in which boys and girls proceed to resolve the complexes of the phallic stage. The boy's Oedipus complex stems from his natural attachment to his mother, for it is she who nurtures him. Because of this, he wants to possess her—to have sexual intercourse with her—and to kill his father, his rival for his mother's attentions. Freud added, however, that the boy's hatred of his father is muted by his simultaneous love for his father. Because the boy wants his father to love him, he situates himself beside his mother, competing with her for his father's affections and experiencing more and more antagonism toward her. Nevertheless, despite his increasing antagonism toward his mother, the boy still wishes to possess her and would attempt to take her from his father were it not for his fear of being punished by his father. Having seen either his mother or some other female naked, the boy speculates that these creatures without penises must have been castrated, by his father no less. Shaken by this thought, the boy fears his father will castrate him, too, should he dare to act upon his desire for his mother. This fear causes the boy to squelch his mother love, a painful process that propels him into a period of sexual latency that will not surface again until the time of puberty.[4]

During the period of sexual latency, the boy begins to develop what Freud called a superego. To the degree the superego is the son's internalization of his father's values, it is a patriarchal, social conscience. The boy who successfully resolves the Oedipus and castration complexes develops a particularly strong superego. In the course of giving up mother love (albeit out of fear of castration), he learns how to defer to the authority of his father. He waits his turn for his own woman, temporarily subordinating his id (instincts) to his superego (the voice of social constraints). Were it not for the trauma of the Oedipus and castration complexes, the boy would fail to mature into a man ready, willing, and able at the appropriate time to claim the torch of civilization from his aging and dying father.

The female experience of the Oedipus and castration complexes is drastically different from the male experience. Like the boy, the girl's first love object is her mother. But unlike the typical boy, whose love object will remain a woman throughout his life, the typical girl has to switch from desiring a woman to desiring a man—at first her father and later other men who take the place of the father. According to Freud, this transition from a female to a male love object begins when the girl realizes she does not have a penis, that she is castrated: "They [girls] notice the penis of a brother or playmate, strikingly visible and of large proportions, at once recognize it as the superior counterpart of their own small and inconspicuous organ (the clitoris), and from that time forward they fall a victim to envy for the penis."[5]

Preoccupied by her lack, the girl notices her mother also lacks a penis. Disgusted by the sight of her mother, the girl turns to her father to make good her lack. However, the girl's turn to her father is a very painful one. She does not reject her mother without feeling an incredible sense of loss. Freud claimed that the girl, like any person who loses a love object, will attempt to handle her loss by trying to become, in some way or other, the abandoned love object. Thus, the girl tries to take her mother's place with her father. As a result, the girl comes to hate her mother not only because of her mother's "inferior" state of being but also because her mother is a rival for the father's affections. At first the girl desires to have her father's penis, but gradually she begins to desire something even more precious— a baby, which for her is the ultimate penis substitute.[6]

Freud theorized that it is much more difficult for girls than for boys to achieve normal adult sexuality. The boy's first love object is a woman, his mother. If he develops "normally," the boy will continue to want women, and the primary source of his boyhood sexual gratification, the penis, will continue to be the primary source of his adult sexual gratification. Like the boy, the girl's first love object is also a woman, her mother. But if she develops "normally," the girl will stop wanting to love women[7] and start wanting to love men, a switch in love objects that requires the girl to derive sexual pleasure from the "feminine" vagina instead of the "masculine" clitoris.[8]

According to Freud, before the phallic stage the girl has active sexual aims. Like the boy, she wants to take sexual possession of her mother, but with her clitoris. If the girl goes through the phallic stage successfully, said Freud, she will enter the stage of latency without this desire; and when genital sensitivity reappears at puberty, she will no longer long to use her clitoris actively. Instead, the girl will be content to use it passively for autoerotic masturbation or as a part of foreplay preparatory to heterosexual intercourse. But because the clitoris is not easy to desensitize, there is always the possibility the girl will either regress into the active clitoral stage or, exhausted from suppressing her clitoris, give up on sexuality altogether.

The long-term negative consequences of penis envy and rejection of the mother go beyond possible frigidity. Freud taught that the girl's passage through the Oedipus and castration complexes scars her with several undesirable gender traits as she grows toward womanhood. First, she becomes *narcissistic* as she switches from active to passive sexual aims. Girls, said Freud, seek not so much to love as to be loved; the more beautiful a girl is, the more she expects and demands to be loved. Second, she becomes *vain*. As a compensation for her original lack of a penis, the girl focuses on her total physical appearance, as if her general "good looks" could somehow make up for her penile deficiency. Finally, the girl becomes a victim of an exaggerated sense of *shame*. It is, said Freud, not uncommon for girls to be so embarrassed by the sight of their "castrated" bodies that they insist on dressing and undressing under their bedsheets.[9]

As bad as female narcissism, vanity, and shame are, Freud suggested these character flaws in women are small in comparison to what really accounts for women's inferiority as a sex. We will recall the boy's fear of losing his penis, of castration, is precisely the fear that enables him to get out of his Oedipus complex, to successfully submit himself to the laws of the father. In contrast, because the girl has no such fear—since she literally lacks anything to lose—her lack, which she experiences as a deprivation, is precisely what drives her into the Oedipus complex, setting her at odds with the father's laws for an indeterminate length of time.[10] That the girl is spared the equivalent of the boy's traumatic resolution of his Oedipal complex under threat of castration is, said Freud, a mixed blessing; for it is only by undergoing a sexual trauma of these proportions—by being pushed, albeit out of fear, to internalize the father's values—that an individual can develop a strong superego, which gives rise to the traits marking a civilized person. Because women remain at odds with men's laws, women are supposedly more resistant than men to the civilizing forces of the superego. Speculating in this fashion, Freud concluded:

> For women the level of what is ethically normal is different from what it is in men. Their super-ego is never so inexorable, so impersonal, so independent of its emotional origins as we required to be in men. Character traits which critics of every epoch have brought up against women—that they show less sense of justice than men, that they are less ready to submit to the great necessities of life, that they are more influenced in their judgements by feelings of affection or hostility—all these would be amply accounted for by the modification of their super-ego which we have already inferred.[11]

In other words, female moral inferiority is due to girls' lack of a penis. Because they do not have to worry about being castrated, girls are not nearly so motivated as boys supposedly are to become obedient rule followers whose "heads" always control their "hearts."

Standard Feminist Critiques of Freud

Because penis envy and related ideas paint such an unflattering portrait of women, many feminists were and still are angered by traditional Freudian theory. In the 1970s feminists with otherwise widely different agendas—for example, Betty Friedan, Shulamith Firestone, and Kate Millett—made Freud a common target. They argued women's social position and powerlessness relative to men had little to do with female biology and much to do with the social construction of femininity.

According to Betty Friedan, Freud's ideas were shaped by his culture, which she described as "Victorian," even though Freud wrote many of his most influential essays about female sexuality in the 1920s and 1930s. What most disturbed Friedan about Freud, however, was his supposed biological determinism. As she interpreted it, Freud's aphorism "Anatomy is destiny"[12] means a woman's reproductive role, gender identity, and sexual preference are determined by her lack of a penis and any woman who does not follow the course nature sets for her is in some way "abnormal."[13]

Not only did Friedan reject Freud's methodology, she also rejected what she regarded as his "fixation" on sex. By encouraging women to think female discontent and dissatisfaction have their roots in women's lack of the penis per se rather than in the privileged socioeconomic and cultural status its possession confers on men, Freud led women to believe, falsely, that women are defective. Moreover, by suggesting to women that in lieu of possessing the penis, they can instead have a baby, Freud lured women into the trap of the feminine mystique. Thus, Friedan faulted Freud for making a specific sexual experience she termed "vaginalism" the be-all and end-all of women's existence. In particular, she condemned him for encouraging women to be receptive, passive, dependent, and ever ready for the supposed "final goal" of their sexual life: impregnation.[14]

Blaming neo-Freudian therapists even more than Freud for justifying female subordination, Shulamith Firestone claimed women's sexual passivity is not natural but simply the social result of women's physical, economic, or emotional dependence on men.[15] Rather than "helping" depressed women and children adjust themselves to the status quo, said Firestone, neo-Freudian therapists should encourage them to rebel against it.[16] In particular, neo-Freudian therapists should not use their considerable skills to "fit" rebellious women and children into the patriarchal structure known as the nuclear family. Rather, they should challenge men's abuse of women and children within the confines of "home, sweet home."[17]

The more she reflected on the causes of women's and children's oppression, the more Firestone became convinced that human beings should abolish the nuclear family and with it the incest taboo, "the root cause of the Oedipus complex."[18] No longer having to "successfully" resolve the Oedipus complex, children would not be forced to distinguish between "bad," *sexual* feelings for their parents and "good," *loving* feelings for their parents. Were children permitted to combine their sexual and loving feelings for their parents, said Firestone, the power dynamics between men and women as well as parents and children would be fundamentally altered.

Like Firestone, Millett directed her critique of Freudianism more against neo-Freudian therapists than Freud himself. In particular, she faulted neo-Freudian therapists for claiming male sexual aggression is rooted in the "biological . . . necessity for overcoming the resistance of the sexual object."[19] She observed that in their attempt to prove this claim, they sometimes went to ridiculous extremes, looking for "male aggression" everywhere, including in such unlikely species as the prehistoric cichlid fish. The males of this species are able to impregnate the females of their species supposedly only because the latter respond to their advances with "awe." Millett used this "fishy" example to show, as Friedan might, that there is little sound evidence to support the theory that nature has determined men play first fiddle.[20]

Decidedly resistant to all types of biological determinism, Millett found the concept of penis envy a transparent instance of male egocentrism. Instead of celebrating woman's power to give birth, said Millett, neo-Freudian therapists interpret it as a pathetic attempt to possess a substitute penis: "Freudian logic has succeeded in converting childbirth, an impressive female accomplishment . . . into nothing more than a hunt for a male organ."[21] Had Freud made the clitoris, not the penis, the center of his analysis of female sexuality, mused Millett, he might have been better able to understand, for example, the "problem" that truly ailed his eighteen-year-old "hysterical" patient, Dora.

A bright and intelligent woman, Dora was a member of a typical Viennese middle-class family: father, mother, son, daughter. From Freud's point of view, Dora's family exhibited all the classic signs of "Oedipal behavior," with father and daughter aligned against mother and son. To make matters even worse, Dora's father had a lover, a longtime family friend, Frau K., whose husband, Herr K., had had sexual designs on Dora from the time she was fourteen. Although Dora had a close relationship with Frau K.—indeed, she found in her the affectionate "mother" her own mother had never been—she terminated this relationship as soon as she realized Frau K. was her father's lover and Herr K. had sexual designs on her. When she confronted her father about his infidelity and Herr K.'s lechery, he denied everything and attributed his daughter's "fantasies" to her being "hysterical." Brought to Freud for "treatment," Freud believed Dora's account of her father's adulterous behavior and Herr K.'s lecherous advances. Nevertheless, he failed to reassure Dora the bad behavior of these two men was the cause of her "hysteria." Instead, Freud told Dora her *real* problems were her sexual jealousy of Frau K. and her inability to be sexually aroused by Herr K.'s advances. Apparently unimpressed by Freud's diagnosis, Dora terminated treatment with him after three months, announcing she would rather be dead than married. Freud interpreted her abrupt termination of treatment as an instance of transference, causing Dora to shift her negative feelings toward her father and Herr K. to Freud himself. She would wreak revenge on all men by rejecting Freud.[22]

Proclaiming Freud's treatment of Dora unacceptable, Millett suggested that Dora's so-called hysteria was probably a simple case of justifiable anger. A feminist psychotherapist would likely regard Dora's reasons for not wishing to get married as quite rational given the emotional wringer through which she had been squeezed. At the very least, a feminist psychotherapist would tell Dora she had every right to accuse her father of adultery and Herr K. of a form of sexual harassment akin to rape.[23] Told that Freud suspected Herr K. and Dora's father were in "cahoots," a feminist psychotherapist would probably conclude Freud failed to serve the best interests of his patient precisely because Freud belonged to Herr K.'s and Dora's father's patriarchal club.

Pursuing Psychoanalysis in Feminist Directions

Psychoanalytic feminists concede that Freud, but most especially his disciples Helene Deutsch[24] and Erik Erikson,[25] contributed to women's oppression. Nonetheless, they believe that Freudian texts can be used to achieve ist as opposed to nonfeminist goals, provided feminists reinterpret these texts by rejecting the doctrine of biological determinism, by emphasizing the pre-Oedipal as opposed to the Oedipal stage of human sexual development, or by telling the Oedipal tale in a nonpatriarchal voice.

Rejecting Freud's Biological Determinism

Early feminist psychoanalysts such as Alfred Adler, Karen Horney, and Clara Thompson all contended that women's (and men's) gender identity, gender behavior, and sexual orientation are not the result of biological fact. Rather, they are the product of social values. By insisting that woman's biology is not her destiny—that her lack of a penis is important only because society happens to privilege men over women—each of these three theorists helped empower women.

Alfred Adler. According to Adler, men and women are basically the same because all human beings are born helpless. Our infantile experiences of powerlessness and "inferiority" are the sources of our lifelong struggles against feelings of overwhelming impotence. In striving for "superiority," the experience of powerfulness, nothing is determined by the mere fact some people have penises and others have vaginas. A person's biological contours do not lead logically or inevitably to certain psychological traits. Rather, said Adler, each human being has a "creative self" that assigns any number of possible meanings to his or her biological "givens." We are a species shaped more by our visions of the future than by our roots in the past. Our biology is not, he said, our destiny; it is simply the material we use to shape our unique selves.[26]

Given his philosophical assumptions about the plasticity of human nature, Adler was able to provide nondeterministic interpretations for why so-called neurotic women suffer from a sense of inferiority, for why they are plagued by "masculinity complexes." Acknowledging ours is a patriarchal society in which women "are determined and maintained by privileged males for the glory of male domination,"[27] Adler hypothesized that so long as patriarchy exists, "neurotic" women will exist; for a "neurotic" woman is simply a woman whom patriarchy has thwarted in her struggle to overcome her feelings of infantile helplessness. By recognizing that all human beings, be they women or men, have "creative selves" and desire to empower themselves through thought and action, Adler provided so-called neurotic women with the rationale to heal themselves: Not they but patriarchal society is sick.

Karen Horney. Like Adler, Karen Horney emphasized the role environment plays in a person's growth as a person. A medical school student in turn-of-the-century Berlin, Horney experienced firsthand the ways in which society constricts women's creative development. She claimed women's feelings of inferiority originated not in women's recognition of their "castration" but in realization of their social subordination. Although Horney conceded women are symbolically castrated in that they have been denied the power the penis represents, she refused to accept that ordinary women are radically defective beings simply because they lack penises. She instead argued that patriarchal culture first forces women to be feminine (passive, masochistic, narcissistic) and then tries to convince women they *like* being feminine. In this light, women who want what society considers truly valuable—namely, masculine things—will be labeled "sick," as suffering from a "masculinity complex," as "flying from womanhood."[28] Refusing to consider women who want to be "movers and shakers" in society as "sick," Horney instead described them as persons struggling to achieve a balance between three different pulls in their character: the self-effacing pull, the resigned pull, and the expansive pull. Not content with their powerless status in society, their behind-the-scenes role, women who choose to move beyond "femininity" are in the process of creating an ideal self that will include masculine as well as feminine traits. Far from being mentally "sick," such women are amazingly healthy. Their self-conception is without false, neurotic, or idealized components. In other words, these women know that society, not biology, has caused women to be the way they are. As soon as women learn how to view *themselves* as men's equals, society will have little if any power over them.[29]

Clara Thompson. Clara Thompson sided with Adler and Horney in portraying development as a process of growth away from one's biology and toward mastery of one's environment; human development is, she said, the task of self-formation. In the tradition of interpersonal psychology—which views our relationships with others as crucial to our development and well-being—Thompson explained female passivity as the product of a set of asymmetrical male-female relationships in which constant deferral to male authority causes women to have weaker egos than men do. Female and male identities do not emanate from unchanging female and male biologies. Rather, they emerge from ever-changing social ideas about what it means to be male or female. Along with Adler and Horney, Thompson believed women's guilt, inferiority, and self-hatred are grounded not in biological facts but in culture's interpretation of them. Thus, the transformation of the legal, political, economic, and social structures that constitute culture is a necessary step in the transformation of women's psychology.[30]

   In the process of reinterpreting Freud's observations, Adler, Horney, and Thompson moved beyond their "master." First, they spoke of masculine bias and male dominance and offered a political as well as psychoanalytic analysis of women's situation, something Freud did not do. Second, they proposed a unitary theory of human development that did not set men and women traveling down separate developmental tracks toward separate developmental goals. Instead, Adler, Horney, and Thompson insisted that all human beings—men *and* women—want the same thing, the opportunity to shape their own destiny creatively and actively. Last, and perhaps most interesting, all three of these psychoanalysts claimed the self is an identity that develops uniquely and individually in each person, growing out of the interface between nature and culture. For Adler, Horney, and Thompson, there is not *one* universally healthy, normal, and natural male self for men and *another* universally healthy, normal, and natural female self for women. Rather, there are as many human selves as there are individual people.[31]

The Feminist Cases for and Against Dual Parenting

Psychoanalytic feminists Dorothy Dinnerstein and Nancy Chodorow maintained that by focusing less on the Oedipal stage and more on the pre-Oedipal stage of psychosexual development, they could achieve a better understanding of how patriarchal society constructs sexuality and gender in ways that create and maintain male dominance. Much of what is wrong with men and women as individuals and as a society, according to Dinnerstein and Chodorow, is traceable to the fact that women do all or most of the mothering. Were men to mother just as much as women do, boys and girls would grow up realizing fathers as well as mothers have both weaknesses and strengths and neither men nor women are to blame for the human condition.

Dorothy Dinnerstein: *The Mermaid and the Minotaur*.   According to Dinnerstein, our culture's gender arrangements strongly influence how men and women conceive of themselves and each other, and the resulting portrait is not pretty. In it, women are "mermaids" and men are "minotaurs." Dinnerstein wrote: "The treacherous mermaid, seductive and impenetrable female representative of the dark and magic underwater world from which our life comes and in which we cannot live, lures voyagers to their doom. The fearsome minotaur, gigantic and eternally infantile offspring of a mother's unnatural lust, male representative of mindless, greedy power, insatiably devours live human flesh."[32]

Because Dinnerstein found this portrait so ugly, she sought to explain why we continue to paint it over and over again, albeit in different hues. The answer to our pathological need to make monsters of ourselves is buried, she speculated, deep in our psychosexual development, in the pre-Oedipal stage. The infant's relationship with her or his mother is profoundly symbiotic because the infant is initially incapable of distinguishing between her- or himself and the mother. Because the maternal body is the infant's first encounter with the material or physical universe, the infant experiences it as a symbol of an unreliable and unpredictable universe. The mother is the source of pleasure and pain for the infant, who is never certain whether the mother will meet his or her physical and psychological needs. As a result, the infant grows up feeling very ambivalent toward mother figures (women) and what they represent (the material/ physical universe, or nature).

Not wanting to reexperience utter dependence on an all-powerful force, men seek to control both women and nature, to exert power over them. Fearing the power of the mother within themselves, women concomitantly seek to be controlled by men. Men's need to control women and women's need to be controlled by men tragically leads, said Dinnerstein, to a *mis*shapen set of six gender arrangements, which serve as a paradigm for destructive human relations in general.

As the first characteristic of current gender relationships, Dinnerstein pointed to men's greater sexual possessiveness. Men hope to overcome their past inability totally to control their mothers by totally controlling their wives or girlfriends. Given men's intense desire to control women, when a woman is unfaithful to a man, the man feels the same despair he felt upon realizing his mother had a self separate from his own, a self whose will often conflicted with his. This refelt sense of despair, said Dinnerstein, explains men's violent reactions to their wives' or girlfriends' infidelities, ranging from extramarital affairs with male lovers to pajama parties with female friends.

Curiously, although many women accept men's sexual possessiveness as some sort of right, they do not generally claim the same right for themselves. Dinnerstein explained this asymmetry as follows: Because a woman fears the power of the mother within herself, she is always in search of a man who can control her. But because a man does not represent "mother" to her in the way she represents "mother" to him, she needs him less than he needs her. No matter how deep the symbiosis she achieves with him, it will not equal the kind of symbiosis she had with her mother in the past or that she could have with another woman/ mother now or in the future. Consequently, if a man leaves a woman, she will not feel the same intensity of grief she felt when her original mother left her.[33]

The second mark of current gender arrangements is, according to Dinnerstein, the muting of female erotic impulsivity. A muted female eroticism is one oriented exclusively toward male pleasure. Through sexual intercourse, the woman seeks to satisfy the man, and whatever pleasure she experiences is experienced vicariously as delight in his satisfaction. Her own sexual wants and needs must go unattended; for were she to insist on their fulfillment, she and the man would be in for a shock. They would both reexperience the rage they felt as infants when they first recognized their mothers as independent selves who had lives and interests of their own. Moreover, were she to let her partner satisfy her, the woman would feel enormous guilt for having abandoned her primary love object (mother and women) for a secondary love object (father and men). Better to deprive herself of sexual pleasure, she senses, than suffer the pangs of conscience.[34]

This guilt on the part of women contributes to the third feature of what Dinnerstein identified as current gender relations: the idea that sexual excitement and personal sentiment must be tied together for women but not for men. Because of the guilt she feels about abandoning her mother, a woman refuses to allow herself even vicarious pleasure in sex unless the relationship is infused with the same type of all-encompassing love that existed between her and her mother. In order to feel good about a sexual liaison, a woman must believe the relationship underlying it is like the one she initially had with her mother: deep, binding, and strong. Only such a sexual liaison can possibly justify her rejection of her mother. To abandon mother for a one-night stand, for example, would be to settle for a superficial intimacy that cannot approximate the deep intimacy of the mother-child symbiosis.

In contrast to women, men are notorious for their ability to separate sex from intense emotional commitment. This ability is also rooted in the mother-infant relationship, especially in the loss of the illusion of infant omnipotence. In the male-female sexual relationship, the man feels especially vulnerable because a woman "can reinvoke in him the unqualified, boundless, helpless passion of infancy."[35] Depending on how much a man needs to be in charge of his destiny, he will be threatened by the overwhelming powers of sexual passion. Once again, he will fear being overwhelmed by a woman able to shatter his ego by withdrawing herself from him. Thus, he will seek to remain in control of the sexual act, distancing himself from the woman with whom he is having intercourse.

Dinnerstein claimed the fourth hallmark of current gender arrangements is that a woman is viewed as an "it," whereas a man is seen as an "I." Because the child encounters a woman before the child is able to distinguish an "I" from an "it" (that is, a center of sentience and perception from an impersonal force of nature), Dinnerstein speculated that a child initially perceives the mother not as a person but as an object. In contrast, because the father usually plays a small role in an infant's upbringing, taking on a larger part in his child's life only after the child has made the I-it distinction, the child has less difficulty recognizing him as an "I," not an "it." Children perceive their fathers, but apparently not their mothers, as persons with lives of their own. Dinnerstein also hypothesized that human beings fear the power of an "it" more than the power of an "I." In her estimation, this state of affairs explains why "it-like" female power, in the private or public realm, is ultimately more threatening to both men and women than male power. Thus, not only do men feel a need to control women; women feel a need to be controlled by men.[36]

The fifth characteristic of current gender arrangements is rooted in our general ambivalence toward the flesh, according to Dinnerstein. We hate it because it limits our control and because we know it will ultimately die; yet we love it because it gives us pleasure. Our general ambivalence toward the body is, however, intensified in the case of woman. On the one hand, woman's body is powerful because it represents the forces of life; on the other hand, woman's body is disgusting because it bleeds and oozes. Because men's bodies do not carry as much symbolic baggage as women's do, men can imagine their bodies to be largely free of the impurities and problems associated with women's bodies. Rather unfairly, men dispel any remaining ambivalence they may have about the male body by displacing all their fears of the flesh onto the female body. The denigration of the female body as dirty, foul, and sinful causes woman to deny her bodily core of self-respect, which deprives her of the ability to reject confidently all the negative feelings being projected onto her body. As a result, woman comes to hate the body and to punish it in many and sundry ways.[37]

Dinnerstein observed the final characteristic of current gender arrangements is the tacit agreement between men and women that men should go out into the public world and women should stay behind within the private sphere. Women funnel their energies into symbiosis, into relationships, eschewing enterprise for fear of putting power back into the hands of women, while men funnel their passions into enterprise, eschewing symbiosis, or relationships, for fear of losing control. Regrettably, the terms of this bargain permit both men and women to remain perpetual children. Rather than taking responsibility for themselves and their world, men and women spend their days playing the kind of sex and gender games they should have stopped playing a long time ago.

As Dinnerstein saw it, our destructive gender arrangements are the direct result of women's role in child-rearing and our subsequent tendency to blame women for everything wrong about ourselves, especially that we are limited beings destined to err, decay, and die. We blame mother/woman for our limitations, speculated Dinnerstein, because it is mother/woman who presides when we skin our knees, when we get scolded for losing our gloves, when we get the flu, and when merciless waves destroy our sand castles. Dinnerstein insisted in order to overcome our destructive gender arrangements—a set of relationships symptomatic of our increasing inability to deal with each other and our world—we must stop blaming mother/woman for the human condition. Dinnerstein's interesting solution to the scapegoating of women was to propose a dual parenting system. She believed that such a system would have four positive consequences.

First and foremost, said Dinnerstein, dual parenting will enable us to stop projecting all of our ambivalence about carnality and mortality onto one parent, the female. Because both parents will be involved in the parenting process from the infant's birth onward, we will no longer associate our bodily limitations with the female parent only. It will not even occur to us to blame our carnality and mortality on women. Thus, we will be forced to deal with the human condition as a given that has nothing to do with gender. No longer will we feel compelled to blame Eve for tempting Adam with the apple.

Second, in Dinnerstein's estimation, dual parenting will enable us to overcome our ambivalence about growing up. We remain childish because we approach life as if it were a drama in which women are assigned one role to play and men another. Women play the nurturant mother-goddess role, while men play the mighty world-builder role. Yet both sexes not only doubt whether they can perform these roles satisfactorily; they also wish to break free of them. With the institution of dual parenting, these roles will no longer be split along gender lines. As a result, women will no longer feel totally responsible for nurturing, and men will no longer feel totally responsible for making the world go round. When men as well as women engage in mothering and women as well as men engage in enterprise, the roles of mother goddess and of world builder will be divested of their destructive mystique.

Third, Dinnerstein insisted that dual parenting will also help us overcome our ambivalence toward the existence of other separate beings. In the present situation, we do not fully acknowledge each other as autonomous agents. We tend to view other people as means toward an end—the end of making ourselves feel better about ourselves—rather than as separate beings, each of whom is an end unto himself or herself. With the inception of dual parenting, we will not require others to validate our existence. In other words, once we are free to choose whatever combination of nurturing and enterprising activities we prefer, we will no longer need as much confirmation and reinforcement from each other that our actions are valuable and necessary.

Finally, Dinnerstein believed that dual parenting will help us overcome our ambivalence about enterprise. All people, but especially men, tend to use world building as a defense against death. Indeed, the wonders of civilization can be read as the tragic testimony of a species that strives to achieve the good, the true, and the beautiful, knowing full well everyone and everything are doomed to disintegration. Given his traditional role as world builder, society has not permitted man to express reservations about the ultimate worth of his worldly projects. But given her traditional role as mother goddess—the "wise one" who is not easily deceived by the pomp and circumstance of civilization—society has permitted woman to articulate her misgivings about civilization. Indeed, said Dinnerstein, women have played the part of court jesters, poking fun at the games men play; women's irreverence has served to release the tension that ripples through the world of enterprise. As a result, things have never seemed bad enough for us to change the course of history. Dual parenting will enable us to see just how bad the world situation is. Because men and women will have an equal role in world building as well as child-rearing, women will no longer be able to play court jesters. With nowhere to hide, not even in laughter, both sexes will be required to put aside their games in order to reshape what is, fundamentally, a misshapen world.[38]

Nancy Chodorow: *The Reproduction of Mothering.* Less interested in sexual relationships than Dinnerstein, Nancy Chodorow wondered why women *want* to mother even when they do not have to do so.[39] Rejecting Freud's idea that for women babies are substitutes for penises, Chodorow sought the answer to her question in a careful analysis of the pre-Oedipal rather than the Oedipal stage of human psychosexual development. She pointed to the different "object-relational" experiences infants have with their mothers. According to Chodorow, the infant boy's pre-Oedipal relationship with his mother is sexually charged in a way that it is not for the infant girl. Feeling a sexual current between himself and his mother, the infant boy senses his mother's body is not like his body. As he enters the Oedipal stage, the growing boy senses how much of a problem his mother's otherness is. He cannot remain attached to her (i.e., overwhelmingly in love with her) without risking his father's wrath. Not willing to take this risk, the son separates from his mother. What makes this process of separation less painful for the son than it might otherwise be is his dawning realization that power and prestige are to be had through identification with men—in this case, the father. The boy's increasing contempt for women supposedly helps him define himself in opposition to the female sex his mother represents.[40]

In contrast to the mother-son pre-Oedipal relationship, the mother-daughter pre-Oedipal relationship is characterized by what Chodorow termed "prolonged symbiosis" and "narcissistic over-identification." Because both the daughter and mother are female, the infant girl's sense of gender and self is continuous with that of her mother. During the Oedipal stage, however, the mother-daughter symbiosis is weakened as the growing girl begins to desire what her father symbolizes: the autonomy and independence that characterizes a subjectivity, or I, on the one hand and the ability to sexually satisfy a woman—in this case, her mother—on the other. Thus, as Chodorow interpreted it, penis envy arises for the girl both because the penis symbolizes male power *and* because it is the sexual organ that apparently satisfies her mother: "Every step of the way . . . a girl develops her relationship to her father while looking back at her mother—to see if her mother is envious, to make sure she is in fact separate, to see if she is really independent. Her turn to her father is both an attack on her mother and an expression of love for her."[41]

Although most girls do finally transfer their primary love from a female to a male object, Chodorow suggested this transfer of love is never complete. Whether a girl develops into a heterosexual woman or not, she will tend to find her strongest emotional connections with other women. Thus the pre-Oedipal mother-daughter relationship provides a reference point for female friendships and lesbian relationships: The original mother-daughter symbiosis is never totally severed.[42]

Chodorow theorized that the psychosexual development of boys and girls has several social implications. The boy's separateness from his mother is the cause of his limited ability to relate deeply to others; this emotional deficiency, however, prepares him well for work in the public sphere, which values single-minded efficiency, a "survival-of-the-fittest" mentality, and the ability to distance oneself from others so as to assess them objectively and dispassionately.[43] In contrast, the girl's connectedness to her mother is the cause of her ability to relate to others, to weave intimate and intricate human connections—the kind of relationships that hold the private sphere together. Unfortunately, this very ability is also what makes it difficult for a girl to create a place for herself in the public world. Precisely because women develop permeable ego boundaries, women will tend to merge their own interests with the interests of others, making the identification and pursuit of any independent interests discomfiting.

Because of her view that woman's capacity for relatedness is overdeveloped and man's underdeveloped and that man's capacity for separateness is overdeveloped and woman's underdeveloped, Chodorow, like Dinnerstein, hypothesized that a dual parenting system would eliminate these asymmetries. Were children reared by both their mothers and fathers, boys and girls would grow up equally capable of merging and separating, of valuing their relationships to others and taking pride in their autonomy. More specifically, boys and girls reared equally by both of their parents would realize men and women need to balance their own self-interests against those of others.[44] Finally, coparented children would no longer view the home as woman's domain and the public world as man's domain. On the contrary, they would grow up thinking that all human beings should spend some of their time out in the world working and the rest of it at home with their families and friends.

Comparison and Contrast of Dinnerstein and Chodorow. Common to both Chodorow and Dinnerstein is the conviction that the oppression of *women* originates in the female monopoly on mothering. Explanations of female subordination that focus on differences in physical strength, on the workings of capital, or on the laws of society miss this crucial point. Despite this agreement, differences of substance as well as style characterize Dinnerstein's and Chodorow's respective analyses.

Dinnerstein drew a stark picture of current gender relations, accentuating some of the sadder moments in our self-development. Because our experience of being mothered has been so overwhelming and even terrifying, Dinnerstein described our transition from infancy to adulthood as the slow and painful process of rejecting the mother, of devaluing women and all things female. On account of his sexual *dissimilarity* to his mother, a boy can make this break completely, thereby realizing his desire for independence, for omnipotence. On account of her sexual *similarity* to her mother, however, a girl can never totally break from her mother. A woman, precisely because she is a woman, will remain less than autonomous so long as the experience of self-definition is understood largely as the process of maternal and therefore female rejection.

In contrast, Chodorow painted a portrait of mothering less preoccupied with the image of the omnipotent mother who must be controlled if not by domination, then by rejection. As Chodorow saw it, the infant's connection with his or her mother is not precipitously shattered, with all of the rage and vindictiveness such a sharp break entails. Instead, the connection is gradually eroded, especially for girls. This more temperate approach suggests that for Chodorow the measure of difference between males and females is how *connected* they are to their mothers, whereas for Dinnerstein it is how *separate* they are from their mothers.

In the main, Chodorow's and Dinnerstein's differences from each other are more a matter of emphasis than substance. Dinnerstein focused on men's *and* women's inability to overcome in adulthood the sense of powerlessness they felt as infants whose very life depended on the capricious female will of their mothers; Chodorow emphasized men and women's unconscious need to reproduce in adulthood their infantile experience of symbiosis with their mothers. Dinnerstein viewed the mother-child relationship as basically pathological, whereas Chodorow viewed it as fundamentally healthy.

Despite their differences, however, Dinnerstein and Chodorow were equally insistent that dual parenting is the solution to the problems associated with female mothering. Mothering must become *parenting* if women are to cease being the scapegoats of wailing infants and raging men. Men must become equal parents with women in order to free women from *sole* responsibility for "loving" and men from *sole* responsibility for "working." Dual parenting will, in the estimation of Dinnerstein and Chodorow, break down the sexual division completely. Men will be required to spend as much time "fathering" as women spend "mothering," and women will be expected to work alongside men in the workaday world. As a result, men and women will develop into autonomous, nurturant people who are equally comfortable in both the private and the public domains.

Critiques of Dinnerstein, Chodorow, and Dual Parenting. Critics faulted both Dinnerstein and Chodorow for three reasons. First, they complained that these two theorists emphasized that the root causes of women's oppression are psychological rather than social.[45] According to Dinnerstein and Chodorow, our legal, political, economic, and cultural systems would be dramatically different if women did not *want* or *need* to mother. Women are not mothers because law, politics, economics, or culture has forced them to be mothers; women are mothers because they think of themselves as mothers. The critics countered by insisting that a woman's "want" or "need" to mother is caused not by "mind" but "matter"—that is, by specific social conditions such as men's typically higher pay in the public labor force. In a society that gives economic rewards to men but not women, it makes sense for women to try to convince themselves they *like* staying at home with their children while Daddy "makes a living" for them.[46] Women would stop wanting and needing to mother if social conditions were such that women were paid as much as or more than men in the public labor force, for example.

Second, critics objected to what they perceived as Dinnerstein's and Chodorow's failure to appreciate the diverse forms the family takes interculturally as well as intraculturally. When Dinnerstein and Chodorow explained the pre-Oedipal and Oedipal stages, they apparently had in mind the two-parent, heterosexual family. Just because children raised in this type of family structure experience the Oedipus and castration complexes in a certain sort of way, however, does not mean that children raised in a single-parent family or a lesbian- or homosexual-couple family or an extended family will experience them in precisely the same way. Chodorow and Dinnerstein, said the critics, carelessly named the particular families they knew best "*the* family," as if all families were like their own families.

Third, critics objected to Dinnerstein's and Chodorow's preferred solution for women's oppression, the creation and maintenance of a dual-parenting system. Jean Bethke Elshtain singled out Dinnerstein for particularly strong words. Dinnerstein, said Elshtain, believed women have less of a need to control things and people than men have. As a result of their special symbiotic relationships to their mothers, daughters grow up to be nurturant, affectionate, and caring persons who are "less avid than men as hunters and killers, as penetrators of Mother Nature's secrets, plunderers of her treasure, outwitters of her constraints."[47] If this is indeed the case about women, queried Elshtain, what will happen to all of women's positive qualities, as well as men's negative qualities, when children are no longer intensely and exclusively mothered by women? Will children be better or worse off after women abandon the nursery to be replaced there by men?

Dinnerstein's answer to this kind of query was optimistic. Dual parenting will have positive effects on both boys and girls. No longer overwhelmed by the omnipotent mother, boys will grow up needing neither to control women nor to curb the feminine voice within themselves. As a result, men will be able to forge intense relationships with women (and also other men) without feeling threatened, and women will remain caring, compassionate, and considerate, "even as they gain public roles, authority, power."[48]

Unsatisfied by Dinnerstein's response, Elshtain asked why we should suppose men are capable of developing all the wondrous feminine qualities previously denied to them, whereas women are incapable of developing all the horrendous male qualities previously spared them? If men will become more nurturant by taking care of their babies, then perhaps women will become more aggressive by doing battle in the nation's boardrooms, courtrooms, and hospitals. In sum, according to Elshtain, Dinnerstein failed to ask herself what will be lost as well as gained in a dual parenting system.

Whereas Elshtain singled out Dinnerstein for special criticism on the point of dual parenting, Alice Rossi targeted Chodorow. Rossi claimed that Chodorow failed to take seriously the possibility that, in the end, allowing men to care for infants may prove disastrous.[49] Women's biology as well as psychology equips women to perceive their infants' needs so as to better serve them. Men's biology as well as psychology does not. Thus, Rossi stressed that the traditional caricature of the bumbling father pinning the diaper on his baby may have some basis in biosocial fact.[50]

Rossi also faulted Chodorow for thinking that provided girls and boys are dual parented, girls will have no more difficulty separating from their mothers than boys will. Once again appealing to women's biology as well as psychology, Rossi emphasized that the daughter's *female body* will always cause her to identify with her mother in a way that her brother with his *male body* cannot. Even if men as well as women mothered, this would still be the case. It is, for example, women's breasts, not men's, that swell with milk. Still, conceded Rossi, entrusting babies to men—giving dual parenting a try—is probably preferable to parents' handing their babies over to institutionalized childcare, where the biological ties currently holding human beings together would be maximally weakened.[51] As bad as it is to replace breastfeeding with bottle feeding so that dad gets to play "mom," it is even worse, in Rossi's estimation, to replace a child's biological parents with childcare attendants.

Another critic, Janice Raymond, offered a critique of dual parenting that applied equally well to Dinnerstein and Chodorow. Raymond observed that dual parenting *seems* like a reasonable solution to distorted gender relations. After all, if Dinnerstein is right that "male absence from child rearing" is leading the world to nuclear war and ecological chaos, then by all means let father spend at least as much time in the nursery as mother. However, warned Raymond, to insist dual parenting is the solution to the human malaise is to elevate men once again to the status of "saviors." This solution gives men even more power than they now have—personal and psychic power within the family as well as political and economic power outside the family. Additionally, to advocate dual parenting is once again to thwart "gyn-affection," or woman-to-woman attraction and interaction.[52] It is to suggest, among other things, that a lesbian couple cannot raise their children successfully or that a single woman assisted by her mother, for example, cannot raise a happy and healthy child.

As Raymond saw it, that *women* mainly mother is not the problem. Rather, the real problem, as Adrienne Rich suggested in *Of Woman Born*, is that women mother when, where, and how *men* want them to. The aim of resolving the Oedipus complex, claimed Raymond, is to teach girls how to direct their love away from women and toward men. What motivates a girl to reject her mother is that she sees her mother loving her father in a special way—so special that she surmises men must be worthy of a love women are not. Raymond speculated that were the girl to see her mother loving other women in an equally special way, the girl would grow up with extremely positive feelings about herself and other women. Despite their mutual claim that female bonds are stronger and deeper than male bonds, stressed Raymond, neither Dinnerstein nor Chodorow envisioned powerful and strong women joining together in communities of care—communities supportive enough to give women as well as children the kind of love they would not otherwise find.[53] Women do not need men to help them mother.

Toward a Feminist Reinterpretation of the Oedipus Complex

Juliet Mitchell: *Psychoanalysis and Feminism*.   Although Juliet Mitchell did not share Dinnerstein's and Chodorow's interest in dual parenting, she, too, sought to use the feminist ideas buried in the "unconscious" of Freud's writings.[54] As Mitchell understood Freud's theory, it is not some simpleminded enunciation of the slogan "Biology is destiny." On the contrary, his is a theory that demonstrates how social beings emerge from merely biological ones. Psychosexual development is a process of the "social interpretation" of biology, *not* the inexorable manifestation of biological destiny.[55] Although Freud studied psychosexual development among a specific group of people (the petite bourgeoisie of nineteenth-century Vienna), said Mitchell, his analysis applies to psychosexual development among any group of people. However, continued Mitchell, it is important to separate the particular emphases of Freud's analysis, its incidental features, from its general parameters, its essence. There are, after all, certain things about nineteenth-century, Viennese, petite bourgeois psychosexual development that are unique to it; that do not apply, for example, to twentieth-century, American, middle-class psychosexual development. Still, the American nuclear family, like the Viennese nuclear family, seems to reflect the pattern Freud names the Oedipal situation.[56]

When Mitchell agreed with Freud that the Oedipal situation is universal, she meant that without a prohibition on incest, human society is an impossibility. According to anthropologist Claude Lévi-Strauss, upon whose work Mitchell relied, if sexual relations are permitted within the biological family, there will be no impetus for the family to expand beyond its narrow confines, to form reproductive alliances between itself and other biological families in order to create the expanded network we call "society."[57]

As Lévi-Strauss explained, the incest taboo is the impetus that, by forbidding sexual relations within the family, forces people to form other, larger, social organizations. Of course, a mere ban on sexual intercourse within families is not enough. There must also be some way to facilitate sexual intercourse among families. Lévi-Strauss claimed this facilitation takes the form of an exchange system among biological families—specifically, the exchange of women among men. If a woman is forbidden by the incest taboo from marrying her brother or father, she will be pushed to marry some man outside of her biological family. If women were not exchanged (married off), the biological family unit would keep reproducing itself in simple form, and society as we know it would never take shape. So it is not because "there is anything biologically 'wrong' with incest" that there is an incest taboo; it is just "the command to exchange exogamously forbids the cul-de-sac of endogamy."[58] The exchange of women among men, according to Lévi-Strauss, constitutes humans' "decisive break" with the beasts and, added Mitchell, that men exchange women rather than vice versa accounts for the *patriarchal* character of human society.[59]

The laws for the exchange of women are, said Mitchell, anchored deep in the unconscious, surfacing during the individual's painful resolution of the Oedipus complex. Because men no longer need to exchange women in order to create society, Mitchell speculated the Oedipus complex might now be otiose:

> In economically advanced societies, though the kinship-exchange system still operates in a residual way, other forms of exchange—i.e., commodity exchange—dominate, and class, not kinship structures, prevail. It would seem that it is against a background of the remoteness of a kinship system that the ideology of the biological family comes into its own. In other words, the relationship between two parents and their children assumes a dominant role when the complexity of a class society forces the kinship system to recede.[60]

Because men do not have to exchange women in order to link biological families one to the other, the incest taboo is unnecessary, a fact that renders the Oedipus complex all the more traumatic. The only positive feature of this lamentable state of affairs, said Mitchell, is that it makes clear the "social non-necessity" of patriarchy because the construction of society no longer depends on men's exchanging women.[61]

The Limits of Mitchell's Analysis.   Mitchell's critics find much of her analysis useful, but they remain unconvinced by it. Lacking in her discussion of psychoanalysis and patriarchy, they say, is an adequate explanation for why *women* are exchanged and why the *father* has power over the family. Mitchell sought the answers to these questions in Freud's *Totem and Taboo*, in which Freud described the primal murder of an original mythical father. The totem is the symbol of the father; and associated with it are two taboos, one against destruction of the totem and one against incest. In the myth a group of brothers bands together in order to kill the feared and envied father—feared because of his power, envied because of his harem. Following their act of patricide, the brothers, feeling very guilty and not knowing quite what to substitute for the law of the father, collectively reestablish his two taboos. Freud commented that whereas the brothers' reinscription of the *totem* taboo is "founded wholly on emotional motives," their reinscription of the *incest* taboo is founded on a "practical" as well as an emotional basis.

> Sexual desires do not unite men but divide them. Though the brothers had banded together in order to overcome their father, they were all one another's rivals in regard to the women. Each of them would have wished, like his father, to have all women to himself. The new organization would have collapsed in a struggle of all against all, for none of them was of such overmastering strength as to be able to take on his father's part with success. Thus the brothers had no alternative, if they were to live together, but—not, perhaps, until they had passed through many dangerous crises—to institute the law against incest, by which they all alike renounced the women whom they desired and who had been their chief motive for dispatching their father.[62]

In sum, the brothers must refrain from incest; only then can patriarchy, in which they have a vested interest, thrive.

Although Mitchell's critics tend to dismiss the myth of the primal crime as *only a myth*, many do concede this myth's power. What the father symbolizes may indeed be universal in human society—namely, the desire to be transcendent, to assert one's will triumphantly, to be, in some sense of the term, "the boss." The father (and here Mitchell was borrowing from Jacques Lacan) is "he who is ultimately capable of saying 'I am who I am.'" The father represents success in the "symbolic order"; he is disentangled from confusions and struggles. He is clear-thinking, farseeing, and powerful. Because he can say, "I am who I am," he can name things for what they are.[63]

But as seductive as the image of the transcendent father and the omnipotent patriarch may be, the image is also oppressive, asserted Mitchell. Insofar as the Oedipus complex is the vehicle of patriarchy, a substitute must be found for it. There must, implied Mitchell, be some way to provide for individuals' "civilization," their entry into an orderly society, that does not require women's oppression.[64]

Sherry Ortner, a noted feminist anthropologist and theorist, disagreed with Mitchell that the Oedipus complex must be destroyed. On the contrary, as Ortner saw it: "The Oedipus complex is part of a theory of the development of the person. It is powerful, and significantly, an eminently dialectical theory: the person evolves through a process of struggle with and ultimate supersession . . . of symbolic figures of love, desire, and authority. As a general structure . . . (without gender valences attached to the particular figures), there seems no need to dispose of (and . . . probably no possibility of disposing of) this process."[65] Ortner theorized that because gender valences are historical accretions, they can be changed; and with their transformation, the Oedipal process can be freed from its current patriarchal agenda.[66] There is, in other words, no law that "maleness" and "femaleness" must be understood in one and only one way or that "maleness" must be privileged over "femaleness."

In developing her argument, Ortner insisted that labeling authority, autonomy, and universalism as male and love, dependence, and particularism as female is not essential to the Oedipus complex. Gender valences are simply the consequences of a child's experience with men and women. A society changes children's *ideas* about "maleness" and "femaleness" by changing their experiences with men and women. Does this mean, then, that Chodorow's and Dinnerstein's pleas for dual parenting will provide us with a new version of the old Oedipal tale? Or must our society effect a more radical social transformation than this to eliminate the kind of pernicious gender valences that favor one sex over the other? Must we, for example, enter the world of Mattapoisett that Marge Piercy described in *Woman on the Edge of Time,* a world in which children are gestated ex utero and reared by three comothers (two men and one woman or two women and one man)? In other words, is changing gender as easy as Ortner, Chodorow, and Dinnerstein suggest, or as difficult as Mitchell suggests? The force of Mitchell's work is her conviction that the original attribution of social and symbolic roles on the basis of gender is buried *very* deep in the human psyche. Changing our system of parenting to a dual-parenting arrangement may not change our ideas about men and women. We may, as Mitchell suggested, have to risk revolution against the entire Oedipal process.

Gender Feminism

Like psychoanalytic feminists, gender feminists (sometimes referred to as cultural feminists) are interested in the differences that distinguish the female psyche from the male psyche. However, unlike psychoanalytic feminists, gender feminists do not emphasize boy's and girl's psycho*sexual* development. If they stress any aspect of children's development in particular, it is what I would term boys' and girls' psycho*moral* development. According to gender feminists, boys and girls grow up into men and women with gender-specific values and virtues that (1) reflect the importance of separateness in men's lives and of connectedness in women's lives and (2) serve to empower men and disempower women in a patriarchal society. Thus, one question to ask is whether women's liberation will be best served by women's adopting male values and virtues, by men's adopting female values and virtues, or by everyone's adopting a mix of both female and male values and virtues. If the answer to this crucial question is that men and women should share a morality encompassing an equal mix of female and male virtues and values, then who should inculcate this morality in boys and girls? Is dual parenting the best means to achieve the end of gender equity in everything, including the practice of morality? Or do gender feminists propose another means to achieve this worthy goal?

Carol Gilligan: In a Different Voice

According to Carol Gilligan, men's emphasis on separation and autonomy leads them to develop a style of moral reasoning (and thinking) that stresses justice, fairness, and rights. In contrast, women's emphasis on connections and relationships leads them to develop a style of moral reasoning (and thinking) that stresses the wants, needs, and interests of particular people. Hypothesizing women's moral style is no less valid than men's, Gilligan claimed because most experts in moral development theory have mistakenly used *male* norms as opposed to human norms to measure women's as well as men's moral development, they have mistakenly concluded women are less morally developed than men. As Gilligan saw it, however, such appearances do not constitute reality. She argued that not women but the standards used to judge women's growth as moral persons must be changed.[67]

In defending her position that women's moral language is just as meaningful as men's, Gilligan singled out her former mentor, Harvard's Lawrence Kohlberg, for particular criticism. According to Kohlberg, moral development consists of a six-stage, *measurable* process through which a child must pass to become a fully functioning moral agent. Stage one is "the punishment and obedience orientation." To avoid the "stick" of punishment and/or receive the "carrot" of a reward, the child does as he or she is told. Stage two is "the instrumental relativist orientation." Based on a limited principle of reciprocity ("you scratch my back and I'll scratch yours") the child does what satisfies his or her own needs and occasionally the needs of others. Stage three is "the interpersonal concordance or 'good boy–nice girl' orientation." The adolescent conforms to prevailing mores because he or she seeks the approbation of other people. Stage four is "the 'law and order' orientation." The adolescent begins to do his or her duty, show respect for authority, and maintain the given social order for its own sake. Stage five is "the social-contract legalistic orientation." The adult adopts an essentially utilitarian moral point of view according to which individuals are permitted to do as they please, provided they refrain from harming other people in the process. Stage six is "the universal ethical principle orientation." The adult adopts an essentially Kantian moral point of view that provides a moral perspective universal enough to serve as a critique of any conventional morality. The adult is no longer ruled by self-interest, the opinion of others, or the force of legal convention but by self-legislated and self-imposed universal principles such as justice, reciprocity, and respect for the dignity of human persons.[68]

Gilligan took exception to Kohlberg's sixfold scale not because she regarded it as entirely without any merit but because the girls and women tested on it rarely got past stage three. Fearing people would interpret this curious result as somehow confirming Freud's sense women are less moral than men, Gilligan determined to prove that women's low scores on Kohlberg's test had little to do with any deficiency in women's ability to reason morally. She hypothesized women did poorly on Kohlberg's scale because of its flawed design. It had, in her estimation, been mistakenly constructed to measure *men's* method of moral reasoning. As a result, Kohlberg's scale was deaf to women's moral voice. The solution, said Gilligan, is not to measure men and women on a scale constructed to measure *women's* method of moral reasoning, with women taking vengeful delight in men's failure on it. Rather, the solution is to develop a scale that can accurately measure differences in men's and women's moral development. But in order to devise such a scale, claimed Gilligan, researchers must take into account the way gender affects the moral reasoning process.

Eager to understand more about the way in which women make moral decisions, Gilligan conducted an empirical study of twenty-nine pregnant women. Each of these women were in the process of deciding whether to abort or not to abort their fetuses. She interviewed them as they were making their decision and on several occasions after they had done so. Gilligan eventually concluded that no matter their age, social class, marital status, or ethnic background, each of these women manifested a way of thinking about moral matters that differed markedly from that of the men who had been tested on Kohlberg's moral development scale. Rather than approaching the issue of abortion analytically as if they were trying to solve a math problem about whose rights "weigh" more, the fetus's or the woman's, the women in Gilligan's study approached it as a human relations problem. They stressed how their decision about their fetus's fate would affect not only it but them in connection to their partners, parents, friends, and so on. Gilligan noted that each of the women in her abortion study moved between three levels of moral reasoning, seeking first to make and then to justify or excuse her decision to herself and others. The women who failed to come fully to terms with their abortion decision remained stuck either in level-one moral reasoning, in which the moral agent overemphasizes her own interests, or in level-two moral reasoning, in which the moral agent overemphasizes others' interests. In contrast, the women who engaged in level-three moral reasoning, in which the moral agent strikes a balance between her own interests and those of others, appeared at peace with their abortion decision.[69]

The more Gilligan reflected on the words of the twenty-nine women she interviewed, the more able she was to describe the differences between a level-one, a level-two, and a level-three mode of moral reasoning. At level one, she said, the self is the sole object of a woman's concern. This self is a beleaguered self, a powerless and disappointed self, so afraid of being hurt it prefers isolation to connectedness. As one woman in Gilligan's abortion study asserted, this is a self that wants *above all* to survive: "I think survival is one of the first things in life that people fight for. I think it is the most important thing, more important than stealing. Stealing might be wrong, but if you have to steal to survive yourself or even kill, that is what you should do. . . . Preservation of oneself, I think, is the most important thing. It comes before anything in life."[70] No wonder, observed Gilligan, that some of her subjects initially regarded a baby as someone who would help them survive by loving them. However, as these women struggled through their abortion decisions, many of them concluded a baby, no less than themselves, is a vulnerable person in need of love. They slowly began to reinterpret their *self-interest* as *selfishness*. So, for example, a seventeen-year-old who at first wanted to carry her baby to term to assuage her loneliness finally decided it would be wrong for her to do so because she did not have the means to take care of a baby: "What I want to do is to have the baby, but what I feel I should do, which is what I need to do, is have an abortion right now, because sometimes what you want isn't right. Sometimes what is necessary comes before what you want, because it might not always lead to the right thing."[71]

Like this seventeen-year-old, any woman making the transition from "wish" to "necessity"—from "the 'selfishness' of willful decision" to "the 'responsibility' of moral choice"[72]—will, in Gilligan's estimation, probably manifest a level-two style of moral reasoning. In her desire to establish or to maintain her connections to other people, a woman will start to focus on others' interests instead of her own interests. In many ways the woman who stops at the second level of moral reasoning is the conventional, nurturant woman who equates goodness with self-sacrifice and who tries to subjugate her wants to those of other people. In extreme cases such a woman comes to believe it is *always* "selfish" for her to do what she wants.

Gilligan provided the example of a woman in her study whose lover wanted her to have an abortion despite her desire to bring the fetus to term. Because this woman wanted both the baby and her lover's approval, she found herself in a moral "no-win" situation. On the one hand, aborting the fetus would be "selfish." She would thereby secure one of *her* wants, her lover's approval. On the other hand, not aborting the fetus would also be "selfish." She would thereby secure another of *her* wants, a baby. The woman reasoned that no matter what she decided to do, she would hurt someone: either her lover or her fetus. In the end the woman decided to have the abortion, consoling herself it was not really *her* decision but her lover's. Because the woman resented her lover's "decision," however, her resentment gradually turned to anger, souring the very relationship for which she had sacrificed her child.[73]

Pondering this woman's abortion decision, Gilligan speculated that a woman can suppress her wants only so long before she reaches a destructive boiling point. To avoid becoming a resentful, angry, even hateful person, Gilligan claimed a woman needs to push beyond level two to level three of moral reasoning, in which she will take into account her own as well as others' interest. As a woman moves to level three, the decision to abort, for example, becomes a choice she must make about how best to care for the fetus, herself, and anyone likely to be deeply affected by her decision. One of the women in Gilligan's study explained her decision to have an abortion as just such a choice: "I would not be doing myself or the child or the world any kind of favor having this child. I don't need to pay off my imaginary debts to the world through this child, and I don't think that it is right to bring a child into the world and use it for that purpose."[74] Gilligan characterized this woman's move from level-two to level-three moral reasoning as a transition from goodness to truth. A woman moves from simply pleasing others—being the conventionally good, always self-sacrificing women—to honestly recognizing her own needs as part of any relationship.

It is clear that in Gilligan's estimation women's type of moral reasoning is no worse than men's. It is simply different. Moreover, stressed Gilligan, although a moral agent might as an individual or as a member of a group (e.g., "women") prefer a certain style of morality, fully developed moral agents are very likely to display a marked ability to speak the languages of care and justice equally well. Had Gilligan stopped her research on moral development with this observation,[75] we could confidently conclude that, for her, the *morally androgynous* person is the paradigm moral agent. However, subsequent to writing *In a Different Voice*, Gilligan hinted that the ideal moral thinker might after all be more inclined to an ethics of care than an ethics of justice. She expressed considerable concern in her anthology *Mapping the Moral Domain* that a high percentage of today's adolescents "tended to characterize care-focused solutions or inclusive problem-solving strategies as utopian or outdated."[76] In her estimation, because our culture overvalues scientific, objective, and rational thinking, teachers tell students to use their heads rather than their hearts in the process of moral deliberation. Doubting the wisdom of this approach to children's moral development, Gilligan suggested that in many ways children seemed *more* moral than adults. Precisely because of their strong attachments to family members and friends, children seem not only really to care about the feelings, wants, needs, and interests of those to whom they are related but also to act upon these sentiments. That girls are more likely than boys to grow into adults who continue to put other people first is probably not a sign of women's moral inferiority but of women's moral depth.

Nel Noddings: Caring and Women and Evil

Like Gilligan, gender feminist Nel Noddings claimed that women and men speak different moral languages and that our culture favors a masculine ethics of justice over a feminine ethics of care. Although women can speak the language of justice as well as men can, said Noddings, this language is not women's native moral tongue. Indeed, women seem to enter the moral realm through a "different door" than men do, focusing less on "principles and propositions" and "terms such as justification, fairness, and justice" and more on "human caring and the memory of caring and being cared for."[77] As a result, women's style of moral reasoning is far less "rational" and far more "emotional" than men's. For example, said Noddings, when faced with a decision about further medical treatment for her dying child, a woman is not likely to approach this intensely personal decision as she would approach an extremely difficult math problem. On the contrary, as she struggles to discern what is in her child's best interest, she will prefer to consult her "feelings, needs, impressions, and . . . sense of personal ideal"[78] rather than some set of moral axioms and theorems. Her goal will be to identify herself as closely as possible with her dying child so that her decision will in fact be her or his decision.

Ethics, insisted Noddings, is about particular relations, where a "relation" means "a set of ordered pairs generated by some rule that describes the affect—or subjective experience—of the members."[79] When all goes well, the one cared for actively *receives* the caring deeds of the one caring, spontaneously sharing her or his aspirations, appraisals, and accomplishments with the one caring. Caring is not simply a matter of feeling favorably disposed toward humankind in general, of being concerned about people with whom we have no concrete connections. There is a fundamental difference between the kind of care a mother has for her child and the kind of "care" a well-fed American adult has for a starving Somali child she has never met. Real care requires active encounter with specific individuals; it cannot be accomplished through good intentions alone.

Unlike Gilligan, Noddings unambivalently claimed that an ethics of care is not only *different* from but also ultimately *better* than an ethics of justice. In her estimation, we must reject rules and principles as major guides to ethical behavior and with them the accompanying notion of universalizability. For Noddings, human relationships are not about persons' abstract rights but about particular individuals' concrete needs. Noddings qualified her rejection of "universals" and affirmation of "particulars," however. She claimed not to be a relativist, since there is something properly "universal" about the "caring attitude" that underpins her ethics. A child's memories of caring are not memories peculiar to him or her alone. On the contrary, they are the kind of memories to which virtually all human beings have access. "Indeed, I am claiming that the impulse to act in behalf of the present other is itself innate. It lies latent in each of us, awaiting gradual development in a succession of caring relations."[80]

Because our memories of caring and being cared for can fade, Noddings emphasized that we must use education to enhance our natural tendency to care. She noted our initial experiences of care come easily, almost unconsciously. We act from a *natural* caring that impels us to help others because we *want* to: "The relation of natural caring will be identified as the human condition that we, consciously or unconsciously, perceive as 'good.' It is that condition toward which we long and strive, and it is our longing for caring—to be in that special relation—that provides the motivation for us to be moral. We want to be moral in order to remain in the caring relation and to enhance the ideal of ourselves as one-caring."[81] The little boy helps his exhausted mother fold the laundry simply because she is his mommy. He wants to be connected to her and to have her recognize him as Mommy's helper. Later, when he is an adolescent, his memories both of caring *for* Mommy and being cared for *by* Mommy as a child flood over him "as a feeling—as an 'I must.'"[82] In "remembrance" of his little-boy "sentiments," he chooses to be late for a party so that he can help his mother instead. The deliberateness of *ethical* caring replaces the spontaneity of *natural* caring.

We might note that Noddings did not describe moral development as the process of *replacing* natural caring with ethical caring. Although ethical caring requires efforts natural caring does not, Noddings disagreed with philosopher Immanuel Kant's view that ethical caring is better than natural caring because doing things because we *ought* to do them is better than doing things because we *want* to do them.[83] In contrast to Kant, Noddings argued our "oughts" build on our "wants." She wrote: "An ethic built on caring strives to maintain the caring attitude and is thus dependent upon, and not superior to, natural caring."[84] Morality is not about affirming others' needs through the process of denying one's own interests. Rather, morality is about affirming one's own interests through the process of affirming others' needs. When we act morally (engage in ethical caring), we act to fulfill our "fundamental and natural desire to be and to remain related."[85] If we have any "duty" when our interests conflict with others' needs, it is not some obligation to these others but our self-imposed obligation to try to be as moral as possible, to be and to remain related. We meet others' needs not because mere inclination *impels* us to do so or because rationality instructs us we *must* do so but because, *on reflection*, we *choose* to do so.

In addition to her book on caring, Noddings wrote a book on evil in which she claimed women are more capable of withstanding evil than men are. According to Noddings, women's understanding of evil is concrete, whereas men's understanding of evil is abstract. For women, an evil event is a harmful event, something that hurts someone. For men, an evil event is a rule-breaking event—a violation of God's commandments or the state's laws. Wanting to replace the abstract *idea* of evil as sin, guilt, impurity, and fault with the concrete *experience* of evil as "that which harms or threatens harm,"[86] Noddings insisted eliminating evil is not about punishing sinners. Rather, it is about reducing the kind of pain, separation, and helplessness infants typically feel. Evil is isolation in one's hour of need, and the way to overcome isolation is through relationship.

In her attempt to further elucidate the differences between the "masculine" idea of evil and the "feminine" experience of evil, Noddings interpreted one of the stories Doris Lessing tells in *The Diary of a Good Neighbor*. In Lessing's story, Jane, a middle-aged, highly successful novelist and magazine editor, tries to alleviate the suffering of Maudie, a skinny, dirty, lower-class, ninety-year-old woman. Several female nurses and nurses' aides assist Jane's efforts. In contrast to the male physician who views Maudie as a "case," these women view Maudie as a unique individual who needs their help to fight the infirmities of old age and the ravages of disease. Reflecting on the women's healing ministry to Maudie, Noddings noted none of them found "meaning" in their patient's suffering since it was without instructional value. Nor did any of them speak of "God's will," as if Maudie's suffering were the price she must pay for her "sins." On the contrary, they simply worked "to relieve her pain, alleviate her loneliness, and preserve—as nearly as they [could]—her autonomy."[87] For Maudie's female healers, evil is "the deliberate or negligent failure"[88] to help someone whose body is racked with pain, whose spirit is in anguish, or whose dignity as a person is in jeopardy.

Interwoven among the pages of *Women and Evil* as well as the pages of *Caring* is a relational ethics, a type of ethics to which Noddings believed women are predisposed. In the course of discussing the evils of poverty, Noddings issued a call to end the kind of nonrelational, dichotomous thinking at the root of all human conflicts. Too often we cast the evils of poverty as the black-and-white struggle of the "oppressed" versus the "oppressors." Thus, some blame poverty on the sloth, genetic weakness, or sins of the poor, whereas others blame it on the indifference, ruthlessness, or crimes of the wealthy. In either instance the distorted nature of such unreflected stereotypes offers only half of the actual problem and half of the possible solution.

Noddings repeatedly noted that the kind of "us-versus-them" thinking described above often leads the rich (or relatively rich) to condemn the poor by interpreting the poor's hunger, disease, and isolation as somehow merited or deserved. So prevalent is our society's tendency to blame the victim that even organized religion adds its voice to the hue and cry directed against the "unworthy" poor. Saints in rags might hope for glory in heaven, but bag ladies and homeless men need not apply. The solution to this destructive state of affairs is not for the poor to rebel against the rich and to become rich themselves. Nor is it for the rich to become like the poor. Rather, the solution is for the rich and poor to come together and expose the lie embedded in the belief that poverty is an ineliminable feature of the human condition. Noddings summoned women to take the lead in bridging the gap that separates the oppressed poor from the oppressive rich, since for centuries women have lived "with both oppressors and oppressed in their own families."[89] Women mediate between their powerful husbands and their powerless children. Lacking political and economic power, women have learned how to "persuade, plead, appeal and sympathize, interpret, reward, and above all attribute the best possible motive consonant with reality to both parties to the dispute."[90] If anyone can bring the rich and the poor together, claimed Noddings, it is the women whose survival has depended on their ability to reach a loving compromise between weak and strong.

Like poverty, war is another evil whose roots Noddings traced to a morally distorted worldview. With Homer's *Iliad* begins the celebration of the warrior hero, a celebration that paradoxically couples Greek rationality and moderation on the one hand with Greek irrationality and violence on the other. Rather than challenging the warrior hero and his deadly projects, Western philosophy tended to honor him. Indeed, even philosopher William James, who sought for war's "moral equivalent"— that is, for "something heroic that will speak to men as universally as war does"[91]—nonetheless praised the warrior's virtues: his boldness, energy, and valor. Wondering whether it is morally better to be a monk than a soldier, James initially opted for the military as opposed to the ascetic ideal. Only after he managed to reconceive the ascetic life in heroic rather than "effeminate" terms did James produce a convincing argument against war and on behalf of peace. Provided that the monk, like the soldier, goes about his business like a *man*, his path is the one to follow since blood is not spilled on it senselessly. In order to feel good about himself, a man supposedly must strive to do his perceived duty no matter what the cost to himself or others. If a man is a warrior, he is to emulate the soldier who fought the hardest. If he is a monk, he is to emulate the martyr who suffered the most: "To reach the extremes by choice, whether of war or pacifism, of poverty or wealth, requires[s] striving, and striving for extremes has been a mark of manhood."[92]

As Noddings saw it, war will not be discarded in favor of peace until concerted caring aimed at uniting replaces strenuous striving aimed at dividing people, at making some individuals "winners" and other individuals "losers." Only when the unappreciated art of relational ethics, of working together to maintain connection, comes into its own will peace have a chance. It is not that women do not strive. They do. It is just that when they strive, they do so not with the unrealistic intention of vanquishing their external foes or internal demons once and for all but with the realistic intention of continuing as best they can: "A woman knows that she can never win the battle against dust, that she will have to feed family members again and again (and that no meals are likely to go down in history), that she must tend the garden every year, and that she cannot overcome most of its enemies but must treat them with the sort of moderation that encourages harmony."[93] She who knows her loved ones' survival will sometimes depend on her good relations with her opponents also knows that bad relations—quintessentially, war—are not a genuine solution to the problems underlying the "us-versus-them" dichotomy.

Caring does not give birth to rivals. Striving to be the best, the invidious competition hidden within the Greek idea of excellence, does not promote caring. On the contrary, the rivalry prevalent in our society quickly leads to enmity, and enmity leads to disaster. Noddings insisted that in order to avoid war, we must stop trying to be "number one," instead contenting ourselves with our good human relationships.

Noddings realized we cannot *eliminate* all evil, since it stems foremost from a separation of ourselves from other human beings, from an objectification of those around us. We can only *reduce* evil by accepting and combating our own penchant for evil. Suppose, said Noddings, your child was going to be killed in one hour unless you found her, and you had a man before you who knew where she was but would not tell you. Would you be able and willing to "torture" the information out of him? Noddings admitted she, for one, would be up to this "challenge."[94] But she asked herself whether this one exception to her rule of "do no evil" would lead her to make a series of exceptions, the sum total of which would negate the very rule upon which she had built her own morality.

For an answer to this disturbing question, Noddings turned to a story in Simon Wiesenthal's novel *The Sunflower*. Here, a young Jewish man, who turns out to be Simon himself, comes to the bedside of a Nazi. The Nazi, guilt-ridden and verging on death, beseeches the Jew, Simon, to forgive him. Simon wrestles with pity and repugnance and then leaves without saying a word. Simon invites his readers to plumb their own souls and answer the question, "What would you have done in my place?" Haunted by the memory of his choice, Simon asks us to struggle with the limits and requirements of forgiveness.

As Noddings saw it, because Simon viewed himself *symbolically*, as a representative of the Jewish people, he could not see the situation that confronted him *relationally*, a state of affairs involving one identifiable human being seeking forgiveness from another identifiable human being. "Seeing each other and ourselves as symbols," observes Noddings, "is . . . part of what sustains our capacity to inflict suffering."[95] Simon's rejection of the Nazi's pleas for forgiveness only compounded suffering and evil. Indeed, according to Noddings, Simon could combat the evil in the world only through a *genuine* forgiveness of the Nazi. If we forgive someone not because we empathize with his suffering but because some sort of God-imposed duty, for example, requires us to do so, our action is improperly motivated. We seek to maintain our relationship with God rather than with the human being before us, viewing him as a morally inferior version of ourselves. Had Simon forgiven the Nazi simply because it was his duty to do so, he would not have overcome the fundamental separation within himself that leads to evils such as the Holocaust. The Nazi sought absolution from *Simon*, in particular, and not from Jews in general, precisely because he wanted to establish a one-on-one relation with Simon: "He needed a genuine human response."[96] In Noddings's estimation, even if Simon could only have yelled, wept, or screamed at the Nazi, a relation of sorts might have been established. Noddings explained: "Then gradually each might have seen the full horror of their situation. They both might have seen that the possibility of perpetrating unspeakable crimes lay in Simon as well as in Karl and that the possibility and thus the responsibility to resist lay also in both."[97]

When we anesthetize our souls to the cries of other human beings in pain—to men, women, and children who feel separate and helpless—we succumb to evil, concluded Noddings. Evil is not an abstract phenomenon; it is a concrete reality taking at least one of the three following forms:

1. Inflicting pain (unless it can be demonstrated that doing so will or is at least likely to spare the victim greater pain in the future)
   A. Inducing the pain of separation
   B. Neglecting relation so that the pain of separation follows or those separated are thereby dehumanized
   C. Deliberately or carelessly causing helplessness
   D. Creating elaborate systems of mystification that contribute to the fear of helplessness or to its actual maintenance[98]

These actions, said Noddings, are evil. No higher or better "good" can ever justify our causing each other pain or rendering each other separate or helpless. Men must learn what women have known for some time, that "one's soul dies as soon as it detaches from the concrete persons who stretch out their hands in need or friendship."[99] Ethics is about overcoming pain, separation, and helplessness—a task which requires human beings to relate to each other as creatures whose goodness requires a sense of community.

Critiques of Gilligan's and Noddings's Ethics of Care

Toward the beginning of *In a Different Voice*, Gilligan declared it was not her intention to make sex-based generalizations to the effect, for example, that all and only men espouse an ethics of justice and that all and only women espouse an ethics of care: "The different voice I describe is characterized not by gender but theme. Its association with women is an empirical observation, and it is primarily through women's voices that I trace its development. But this association is not absolute, and the contrasts between male and female voices are presented here to highlight a distinction between two modes of thought and to focus a problem of interpretation rather than to represent a generalization about either sex."[100] But even if it was not Gilligan's *intention* to make sex-based generalizations about men's and women's moralities, critics noted her literary examples and research data nonetheless communicated the notion that *men* focus on rights, claims, self-interested demands, strict duties, obligations, burdens, and limits on autonomy, whereas *women* focus on responsibilities and the importance of responding empathetically to others, showing concern in close relations, and nurture and give aid. Thus, Gilligan must take some responsibility for the passionate debates triggered by her work.

The first of these debates focused on Gilligan's methodology, with critics faulting her for not raising enough of the right issues. They claimed that because the women in Gilligan's abortion study came from a variety of ethnic backgrounds and social classes, ranged in age from fifteen to thirty-three, differed in marital status and educational background, Gilligan should have questioned how these differences among the women in her sample might affect their style of moral reasoning. She should have asked, for example, if African American women's "morality" is closer to that of African American *men* than to *white* women.[101] The critics also faulted Gilligan for failing to raise questions about men's moral attitudes toward abortion (in this case, the lovers, husbands, fathers, and friends of the women in her sample) and how they did and did not differ from women's. A "pro-life" woman might think about abortion in the way a "pro-life" man does, rejecting as alien to herself the way a "pro-choice" woman thinks about abortion. In the critics' estimation, Gilligan's failure to focus on the differences among the women in her study is a sign she was, despite her disclaimers, intent on establishing that *men's* moral reasoning is different from *women's*. Not wanting to "complicate" her analysis with facts that would weaken her hypothesis, she chose at some level to ignore these facts.

The second of the debates occasioned by Gilligan's work centered on the negative consequences of associating women with an ethics of care. Critics claimed that even if women *are* better "carers" than men (for whatever reasons), it might still be epistemically, ethically, or politically unwise to associate women with the value of care. To link women with caring is to promote the view that women care by nature. It is also to promote the view that because women can and have cared, they should always care no matter the cost to themselves.

In *Femininity and Domination*, Sandra Lee Bartky sought to determine whether women's experience of feeding men's egos and tending men's wounds ultimately disempowers or empowers them. She noted the kind of "emotional work" practiced by female flight attendants often leads "to self-estrangement, an inability to identify one's own emotional states, even to drug abuse or alcoholism."[102] To pay a person to be "relentlessly cheerful"[103]—to smile at even the most verbally abusive and unreasonably demanding passengers—means paying a person to feign a certain set of emotions. A person can pretend to be happy only so many times before the person forgets how it feels to be genuinely or authentically happy.

Conceding that the kind of emotional work female flight attendants do for passengers may be more alienating and disempowering than the kind of emotional work wives do for their husbands, Bartky noted that many wives find the experience of caring for their husbands empowering. The better caregiver a wife is, the more she may regard herself as the pillar without whom her husband would crumble. But, cautioned Bartky, subjective feelings of empowerment are not the same as the objective reality of actually having power. Women's androcentric emotional work probably *harms* women far more than it *benefits* them. According to Bartky, caring women reinforce men's status through a variety of "bodily displays," including "the sympathetic cocking of the head; the forward inclination of the body; the frequent smiling; the urging, through appropriate vocalizations, that the man continue his recital, hence, that he may continue to commandeer the woman's time and attention."[104] Men do not accord women similar status, however, and because they do not, women's care of men amounts to "a collective genuflection by women to men, an affirmation of male importance that is unreciprocated."[105]

In Bartky's estimation, the epistemic and ethical consequences of women's unreciprocated care of men is most worrisome. The more emotional support a woman gives a man, the more she will tend to see things as he sees them. She will participate in *his* projects, share *his* friends, rejoice in *his* successes, and feel badly about *his* failures. But women do not need yet another reason to lose their sense of self or to doubt their own vision of reality and version of the truth. Men's and women's interests are not identical in a patriarchal society, and it is important for women, who tend "to get the short end of the stick," to realize this.

As bad as it is, from an epistemic point of view, to know the world only or primarily through someone else's eyes, especially someone who looks down on you, it is even worse, from an ethical point of view, to affirm someone else's morality no matter the goodness or badness of his or her values. Bartky pointed to Teresa Stangl, wife of Fritz Stangl, commandant of Treblinka, as an exemplification of her point. Although her husband's monstrous activities horrified her, she continued to "feed" and "tend" him dutifully, even lovingly. She played "footloose and fancy free" with her own soul as she helped him deaden his conscience. Quoting a passage from Jill Tweedie's *In the Name of Love*, Bartky observed that one cannot remain silent about evil and expect to keep one's goodness entirely intact: "Behind every great man is a woman, we say, but behind every monster there is a woman too, behind each of those countless men who stood astride their narrow worlds and crushed other human beings, causing them hideous suffering and pain. There she is in the shadows, a vague female silhouette, tenderly wiping blood from their hands."[106] Because horror perpetrated by a loved one is still horror, women need to analyze "the pitfalls and temptations of caregiving itself" before they embrace an ethics of care wholeheartedly.[107]

For reasons related to Bartky's general concerns about any and all ethics of care, philosopher Bill Puka singled out Gilligan's ethics of care for specific criticism. He claimed care can be interpreted in two ways: (1) in Gilligan's way, "as a general orientation toward moral problems (interpersonal problems) and a track of moral development";[108] or (2) in his way, "as a sexist service orientation, prominent in the patriarchal socialization, social conventions, and roles of many cultures."[109] Those who interpret care as Gilligan does will trace women's moral development through the three levels presented earlier in this chapter. In contrast, those who interpret care as Puka does will view these supposed levels of moral development largely as coping mechanisms or defensive strategies that women use in a patriarchal world structured to work against their best interests.

Puka developed a persuasive case for his view of care. First, he reinterpreted Gilligan's self-oriented level one of moral reasoning as those strategies of self-protection and self-concern women use to avoid rejection or domination. "I'm out for myself" and "If I don't care about myself, no one else will" are statements likely to be uttered by a woman who feels she has to privilege herself over other people simply because other people, especially men, are not likely to concern themselves about her.[110]

Second, Puka reinterpreted Gilligan's other-directed level two of moral reasoning as a resumption of the "conventional slavish approach" that women typically adopt in a patriarchal society.[111] Although level-two moral reasoning is frequently described as altruistic, as if women always *freely* choose to put other people's needs and interests ahead of their own, in reality such moral reasoning is simply another coping mechanism. Within a patriarchy, women learn men will reward, or at least not punish, the women who faithfully serve them.

Finally, Puka reinterpreted Gilligan's self-and-other moral reasoning as a coping mechanism involving elements of both self-protection and slavishness: "Here a woman learns where she can exercise her strengths, interest, and commitments (within the male power structure) and where she would do better to comply (with that structure). A delicate contextual balance must be struck to be effective here."[112] Insofar as a woman is rationally calculating her chances of surviving and possibly even thriving within a patriarchy, level-three moral reasoning constitutes a degree of *cognitive* liberation for her. It does not, however, signal *personal* liberation for her. As long as society remains patriarchal, women will not be able to strike an appropriate and abiding balance between rights and responsibilities in their moral lives. On the contrary, women will tend to practice not so much the moral virtue of care as either its vicious excess of slavishness or its vicious defect of self-preservation.

Although some of the criticisms directed against Noddings echo those directed against Gilligan, others, such as the criticisms offered by Sarah Lucia Hoagland, are quite distinct. Hoagland claimed, for one, that Noddings erred in advancing a fundamentally unequal relationship, in this instance the mother-child relationship, as the paradigm moral relationship. Unequal relationships such as the parent-child, teacher-student, and therapist-client relationships, said Hoagland, are meant to be transcended, not maintained.[113] As personified by the child, student, or client, the cared-for submits to the parent, teacher, or therapist, trusting there is really a method in the "madness" of these authorities (drink this nasty penicillin, read this boring book, dredge up all your phobias). Hoagland repeatedly noted dependency relationships are ethically problematic.[114] If the cared-for is to achieve full moral development, she or he must break these relationships of dependency as quickly as possible, which makes them an unviable paradigm for what constitutes a morally good relationship. There is more to the moral life than being a follower; one must be a leader.

Hoagland further challenged Noddings's assumption that it is at least morally permissible and sometimes even morally required for the one caring to *control* the relationship with the one cared for. She claimed instead that often the cared-for *is* the best judge of his or her own good. Morally good relationships are not about the caring playing the role of "giver" and "leader" and the cared-for playing the role of "taker" and "follower." As long as this sort of "role-playing" occurs, said Hoagland, we can be sure the relationship being described is less than morally good.

Third, Hoagland questioned Noddings's view that inequalities in *ability* make a relationship unequal. She instead claimed that inequalities in *power* make a relationship unequal. A student might know more than a teacher, but it will still be the teacher who grades the student and not vice versa. Hoagland asserted it is a mistake to choose an unequal relationship as the paradigm for a moral relationship. In doing so we increase rather than decrease problems of power, since "we live in a society premised on the dominance and subordination, and oppression emerges in many forms . . . when decisions are made 'for another's own good.'"[115] This is particularly true of parent-child relationships, observed Hoagland. In nearly one-third of American households, fathers (or stepfathers) rape their female children, and mothers are just as likely to feel anger as tenderness toward their children.[116] The parent-child relationship is far from being totally innocent and purely good. The person with the power—that is, the one caring—is often reluctant to relinquish her or his power over the cared-for and may, depending on the circumstances, be tempted to wield it arbitrarily and abusively.

Hoagland argued as well that, paradoxically, unequal relationships often work against the totality of the interests of the one caring as well as those of the cared-for. Hoagland noted that in Noddings's view reciprocity is the only thing needed for the solidification of a caring relationship, a condition the cared-for can meet simply by acknowledging that he or she is indeed the focus of attention for the one caring. Thus, a baby need only smile to complete its mother's caring acts. Hoagland claimed, however, since a baby's smile is more likely an instinctual than a cognitive response to the caring acts of its mother, the mother-child relationship is, at least at its inception and for some time thereafter, an ethically diminished one. There is, as Claudia Card observed, a major difference between receptivity and reciprocity. When a baby smiles at its mother, it is receiving her caring acts but not reciprocating her for them:

> Reciprocity, in the ordinary sense, refers to doing to or for another something that is either equivalent in value or in some sense, "the same thing" that the other did to or for oneself. That characterization can be rough and abstract, as in returning a favor, where the favor returned differs from the original favor. However, in the ordinary sense, we do not say people have *reciprocated* when they have simply received and acknowledged what others have given. Receptivity *complements,* or *completes,* others' behavior but reciprocates it only if equivalent in value.[117]

However sweet a baby's fleeting smile may be, it is not equivalent in value to a mother's unending work. One should not try to read into a relationship more than is actually there.

Like Card, Hoagland has fundamental reservations about "the promotion of infant nonreciprocity-beyond-acknowledgment as a model for ethically relating to others."[118] Such a model does not communicate the kind of respect necessary for a morally good relationship. Unless I expect from my intimate what I demand from myself, and unless what I demand from myself is what my intimate expects from me, our relationship cannot be an entirely good one, morally. Certainly, it cannot be an equal one. No matter what she says about the one caring and the cared-for switching roles, the overall picture Noddings draws, according to Hoagland, is of the one caring consistently giving and the cared-for consistently taking.

Indeed, continued Hoagland, Noddings even implied the obligation of the cared-for is not to attend to the needs and wants of the one caring but simply to do her or his "own thing."[119] As Noddings wrote, "The cared-for is free to be more fully himself in the caring relation. Indeed, this being himself, this willing and unselfconscious revealing of self, is his major contribution to the relation. This is his tribute to the one-caring."[120] Such a "tribute" gives little to either party, in Hoagland's estimation. A unidirectional mode of caring does little to teach the cared-for about the burdens of the one caring, and it does even less to teach the one caring about the legitimacy of her or his own needs and wants.

Finally, Hoagland faulted Noddings for implying that the *best* caregivers never stop caring, no matter the cost to themselves. Although Noddings protested that she thinks there *are* circumstances justifying the withdrawal of care, Hoagland countered that such justifications were accepted only inasmuch as the withdrawal of the care enabled the caregiver to become a *better* carer. The self-interest and self-concern of the one caring are nothing more or less than disguised forms of other-directed care, insisted Hoagland. I am permitted to care about myself only when such action is important to the other. If this is true, said Hoagland, "then I get my ethical identity from always being other-directed,"[121] and "being moral" becomes another term for "being exploited."

Hoagland cautioned there is more to the moral life than being responsive to other persons' needs and wants. She argued that Noddings erred by implying that although it is morally permissible for an abused wife to leave her abusive husband and even to kill him in self-defense, she is not necessarily a better person for doing so.[122] In Hoagland's estimation, however, an abused wife is not simply morally permitted to withdraw from a destructive relationship; she is morally required to do so if at all possible. In no way, shape, or form should the mother who withdraws from the incestuous father or the wife who withdraws from the abusive husband, for example, feel "ethically diminished"[123] or less good as a person for her act of withdrawal. The naive view that "down deep he is a really great person who needs a good woman to save him" traps and destroys women. Told that she will probably compromise her moral ideals if she leaves her abusive husband, the abused wife's guilt, coupled with her fear of reprisal, may deprive her of the moral courage to leave him. Hoagland had nothing at all negative to say about women who leave abusive relationships. She stated: "I must be able to assess any relationship for abuse/oppression and withdraw if I find it to be so. I feel no guilt, I have grown, I have learned something. I understand my part in the relationship. I separate. I will not be there again. Far from diminishing my ethical self, I am enhancing it."[124] Ethics is about knowing when not to care as well as when to care.

Conclusion

What is enormously appealing about the writings of Dinnerstein, Chodorow, Mitchell, Gilligan, and Noddings is how they mesh with many of our ordinary intuitions about sexual behavior, mothering, and moral conduct. Many a woman has found in *The Mermaid and the Minotaur*, *The Reproduction of Mothering*, *Psychoanalysis and Feminism*, *In a Different Voice*, and *Caring* persuasive explanations for her need to love and be loved, for her willingness to give up a high-powered career for an intimate family life, for her willingness to forgive and to forget male abuse and neglect, and for her tendency to give too much and take too little.

To be sure, psychoanalytic explanations for women's oppression do not provide a total explanation for female subordination. Legal, political, and economic institutions and structures must also be taken into account. Nevertheless, to free herself from what is holding her back, a woman must do more than fight for her rights as a citizen; she must also probe the depths of her psyche in order to exorcise the original primal father from it. Only then will she have the space to think herself anew and become who she has the power to be.

Similarly, gender identity explanations for women's oppression are problematic. In expressing concern about the dangers of care, Gilligan's critics echo Elizabeth Cady Stanton's nineteenth-century admonition that given society's tendency to take advantage of women, it is vital that women make self-development rather than other-directed self-sacrifice their first priority.[125] Still, it is important not to overemphasize the problems associated with retrieving feminine or woman virtues from the webs of patriarchy. Whatever weaknesses Gilligan's and Noddings's ethics of care may have, there are serious problems with women's abandoning all of their nurturant activities. The world would be a much worse place tomorrow than it is today were women suddenly to stop meeting the physical and psychological needs of those who depend on them. Just because men and children have more or less routinely taken advantage of some women's willingness to serve them does not mean every woman's caring actions should be contemptuously dismissed as yet another instance of women's "pathological masochism" or "passivity."[126] Care can be rescued from the patriarchal structures that would misuse or abuse it. If it is to be rescued, however, we need to recognize the differences between what Sheila Mullett terms "distortions of caring" on the one hand and "undistorted caring" on the other.[127]

According to Mullett, a person cannot truly care for someone if she is economically, socially, or psychologically forced to do so. Thus, genuine or fully authentic caring cannot occur under patriarchal conditions characterized by male domination and female subordination. Only under conditions of sexual equality and freedom can women care for men without men in any way diminishing, disempowering, or disregarding women. Until such conditions are achieved, women must care cautiously, asking themselves whether the kind of caring in which they are engaged:

1. Fulfills the one caring
2. Calls upon the unique and particular individuality of the one caring
3. Is not produced by a person in a role because of gender, with one gender engaging in nurturing behavior and the other engaging in instrumental behavior
4. Is reciprocated with caring, and not merely with the satisfaction of seeing the ones cared for flourishing and pursuing other projects
5. Takes place with the framework of consciousness-raising practice and conversation[128]

Care can be freely given only when the one caring is not taken for granted. As long as men demand and expect caring from women, both sexes will fail to actualize their moral potential. Neither men nor women will be able to care authentically.

CHAPTER FIVE

■

Existentialist Feminism

Shortly before Simone de Beauvoir died, Margaret A. Simons and Jessica Benjamin interviewed her for the journal *Feminist Studies*. In their background commentary, Simons and Benjamin commented on the significance of de Beauvoir's major theoretical work, *The Second Sex*:

> De Beauvoir's analysis of women's oppression in *The Second Sex* is open to many criticisms: for its idealism—her focus on myths and images and her lack of practical strategies for liberation; for its ethnocentrism and androcentric view—her tendency to generalize from the experience of European bourgeois women, with a resulting emphasis on women's historic ineffectiveness. Still, we have no theoretical source of comparable sweep that stimulates us to analyze and relentlessly question our situation as women in so many domains—literature, religion, politics, work, education, motherhood, and sexuality. As contemporary theorists explore the issues raised in *The Second Sex*, we can see that in a sense all feminist dialogue entails a dialogue with Simone de Beauvoir. And a discussion with her can be a way of locating ourselves within our feminist past, present, and future.[1]

Within a short forty-year span, *The Second Sex* clearly achieved the status of a classic in feminist thought. Thus, no introduction to feminist thought would be nearly complete without a discussion of this work, which has helped many feminists understand the full significance of woman's otherness.

Over the years there have been questions about the precise relationship between de Beauvoir's *Second Sex* and Jean-Paul Sartre's *Being and Nothingness*. The first and ultimately mistaken view is that *The Second Sex* is simply an application of *Being and Nothingness* to women's specific situation. Because Sartre was de Beauvoir's lover and mentor, the misconception she dutifully followed his philosophical lead clouds the history of her own works. To be sure, Sartre and de Beauvoir were on-and-off lovers for many years and, initially, Sartre was de Beauvoir's teacher. However, by the time they both became well-known authors, de Beauvoir was anything but Sartre's student. On the contrary, she was his intellectual companion and at times his teacher.[2]

Even if it is misleading to overemphasize the contribution of Sartre's philosophy to that of de Beauvoir's, *The Second Sex* remains an existentialist text. De Beauvoir used many Sartrean terms in her book, modifying their meanings in order to fit her feminist agenda. Thus, it is helpful to understand Sartre's philosophy in order to fully appreciate de Beauvoir's.

Sartre's *Being and Nothingness*: A Backdrop to *The Second Sex*

Sartre popularized a body of ideas rooted in the philosophies of G.W.F. Hegel, Edmund Husserl, and Martin Heidegger. Chief among these ideas was Hegel's description of the psyche as "self-alienated spirit." Hegel saw consciousness presiding in a divided arena. On the one hand lies the observing ego; on the other hand lies the immanent self, or the observed ego.[3] Sartre made this distinction between the observer and the observed by dividing being into two parts: being-for-itself (*pour-soi*) and being-in-itself (*en-soi*). Being-in-itself refers to the repetitive, material existence humans share with animals, vegetables, and minerals; being-for-itself refers to the moving, conscious existence humans share only with other humans.[4]

The distinction between being-in-itself and being-for-itself is useful in an analysis of the human person, particularly if we associate being-in-itself with the body. The body has constant and objective being. Because it can be seen, touched, heard, smelled, and tasted, the body is the perceived. In contrast, the perceiver—the entity that does the seeing, touching, hearing, smelling, and tasting—is not itself a perceptible object but, according to Sartre, still has a certain kind of being: being-for-itself. To appreciate being-for-itself fully, picture someone momentarily conscious of the fingers on her hand. Her "I" is identified with her fingers because they are, after all, *her* fingers, not anyone else's. However, her "I" is also distinct from her fingers because she is at the same time more than, or other than, her fingers. According to Sartre, what separates one's "I"— one's consciousness or one's mind—from one's body is, paradoxically, nothing (literally, *no-thing*, or nothingness).

To the first two forms of being, Sartre added a third, being-for-others. Sartre sometimes described this mode of being *positively* as *Mit-sein*, as a communal being-with. More frequently, however, he described it *negatively*, as involving "a personal conflict as each For-itself seeks to recover its own Being by directly or indirectly making an object out of the other."[5]

Because each being-for-itself establishes itself as a subject, as a self, precisely by defining other beings as objects, as others, the action of consciousness sets up a system of fundamentally conflictual social relations. Thus, the process of self-definition is one of seeking power over other beings. "While I attempt to free myself from the hold of the Other, the Other is trying to free himself from mine; while I seek to enslave the Other, the Other seeks to enslave me. . . . Descriptions of concrete behavior must be seen within the perspective of conflict."[6] In establishing its self *as* a self, each self describes and prescribes roles for the other. Moreover, each subject conceives of itself as transcendent and free and views the other as immanent and enslaved.

Freedom, the distinguishing characteristic of a self, is, according to Sartre, more of a curse than a blessing. It is a curse because so long as a person is conscious, there is no relief from the freedom to choose and affirm. There are no answers in life, just questions. Worse, there is no such thing as *human nature*, an essence common to all human persons, determining what a person ought to be. Rather, there is only a *human condition*, into which all persons are thrown equally and without self-definition. Existence, said Sartre, precedes essence. In other words, we exist only as amorphous, living organisms until we create separate and essential identities for ourselves through conscious action—through making choices, coming to decisions, reaffirming old purposes and projects, or affirming new ones.

Sartre saw an intimate connection between his conception of freedom—so different from either the liberal or the Marxist—and his conception of nothingness.[7] He insisted that because nothing compels us to act in any one way, we are absolutely free. Our futures are totally open; none of the blanks have been filled in for us. However, as we start filling in these blanks, we are overcome with a sense not so much of finding ourselves as of losing ourselves. When we elect one possibility for ourselves, we simultaneously annihilate all the others. We buy the future at the cost of our past, a cost that burdens our psyches. If we insist we do not experience any of the psychic burdens—dread, anguish, nausea—he described, Sartre will accuse us of "bad faith," a state of being akin to self-deception, false consciousness, or delusion.

Sartre analyzed several types of bad faith, the most typical being hiding oneself in a *role* that seems to leave one no room for choice. For example, anyone who has ever been to a four-star French restaurant has probably met "the waiter," Sartre's favorite example of role-playing taken to its extreme.[8] Everything about the quintessential French waiter is highly stylized: He will present the wine list with the requisite flourish; he will grimace if the diner selects the wrong combination of courses; and he will behave in an overly solicitous manner should the diner's soup arrive lukewarm. The waiter acts in these ways not only because his job depends on it but also because his role-playing helps him avoid the fundamental uncertainties and ambiguities of human existence. As noted above, all conscious beings, or beings-for-themselves, are without essence or definition. They must define themselves through the mutually related processes of decisionmaking and action-taking. In contrast, all nonconscious beings, or beings-in-themselves, are *massif*. In other words, they are what they are. Conscious beings supposedly yearn for the safe, uncomplicated state of nonconscious beings. The questions that afflict conscious beings, the possibilities that haunt them are, said Sartre, their painful "freedoms." The power to choose nags conscious beings, summoning them to decide who they want to be. Thus, the aim of bad faith is to escape this awful condition. The waiter avoids varying his role and pretends there is only one kind of waiter he can ever be.

Another mode of bad faith occurs when we pretend we are thinglike, that we are just a body or object in the world that we can observe. Sartre used the example of a young woman dating an old man who desires sex with her. To preserve the particular excitement of the occasion—such as "I have been noticed by this man . . . how interesting I must be"—the woman wards off her dawning realization she has a decision to make about whether to sleep with him. Each time her companion makes a leading statement—for example, "I find you so attractive"—she attempts to "disarm" the phrase of its sexual implications. She is controlling the situation quite well, until the man takes her hand. The moment of decision has come. To leave the hand there is to "engage herself" in the flirtation; to withdraw the hand is to ruin the evening. But then bad faith comes to the woman's rescue. She leaves her hand in the man's hands, but "she does not notice that she is leaving it."[9] She achieves this state of nonconsciousness, of blissful oblivion, of thinghood by engaging her companion in lofty intellectual and spiritual conversation, thereby achieving the separation of her soul from her body. "The hand," said Sartre, "rests inert between the warm hands of her companion—neither consenting nor resisting—a thing."[10] By divorcing herself from her hand, the woman masks from herself that she is a free subject, not a determined object.

The problem with trying to live in bad faith is twofold. First, no matter how hard the conscious subject tries to live in bad faith, in the final analysis complete bad faith is an ontological impossibility. *Pour-soi*, the conscious subject, cannot be *en-soi*, the nonconscious object. Only death, the foreclosure of all possibilities, permits the conscious subject to escape freedom once and for all. Second, no matter how the conscious subject tries to excuse or justify it, bad faith is an ethical horror. If freedom has any meaning, it is in taking responsibility for one's actions, in realizing there is always room for some sort of choice, no matter how constricted one's circumstances.

Sartre had no patience with Freudians who would destroy the ethical project by permitting people to hide from their responsibility in the so-called unconscious. For Sartre, not only our decisions and actions but also our feelings are conscious. We use our emotions to work magic tricks. When our lives get too difficult to handle, we consciously work ourselves up into a rage or down into a depression. We then use these emotional extremes as excuses for our unreadiness and unwillingness to cope with life. Similarly, said Sartre, if manic-depressives or obsessive-compulsives cannot explain their afflictions, it is because they are repressing these explanations. Whereas Freud spoke of unconscious wishes unconsciously repressed, Sartre spoke of falsehoods, of people refusing to admit what they know are ultimately the reasons or explanations for their actions.[11]

Of all Sartre's categories, being-for-others is probably the most suited for a feminist analysis. According to Sartre, human relations are variations on two basic themes of conflict between rival consciousnesses, between self and others. First, there is love, which is essentially masochistic. Second, there are indifference, desire, and hate, which are essentially sadistic.[12]

Fools that we are, most of us start out with very grand ideas about love, about harmonizing the self and the other, said Sartre. The quest for love, we believe, is our attempt to be one with the other. This attempt is similar to the Christian mystic's effort to become one with God without forsaking his or her unique personal identity. Mystical union, we believe, is a very mysterious state. The mystic is at one and the same time himself or herself *and* God. It is this mysterious state we wish to create for ourselves. At the physical level, such union without absorption would mean my lover, for example, would live my body as he simultaneously lives his own. My lover would know my body in such a way he would erase all separation between us without depriving either of us of our quality of otherness. Similarly, at the psychological level, such union without absorption would mean my lover would know my psychic states, would know me and be me and still not rob me of my identity or lose his own.

According to Sartre, such union without absorption is an impossible dream. We live in a very nonmystical world. There is no possibility of harmony, or union, between the self and the other; the self's need for total freedom is too absolute to be shared. Our attempts at love—at union without absorption—will always deteriorate to mutual possession or to mutual objectification. Exhausted by the struggle to maintain our subjectivity and freedom but still desiring a relationship (albeit one that is literally self-destructive) with the other, we may be led to masochism, the prospect of losing our subjectivity altogether in that of the other, who is now invited to treat us as a mere object.

Masochism is, for Sartre, not the perversion of love but its essential consequence. Through pain and humiliation, we hope to erase our subjectivity, to actually become the object that the other, the torturer, perceives as us. Our suffering may seem to testify we have no choice in the matter; however, as Sartre explained, this is a delusion. In order to be masochists, we must *choose* to apprehend ourselves as objects. Thus, as a flight from subjectivity, masochism is a dead end. The more we try to reduce ourselves to mere objects, the more we became aware of ourselves as subjectivities who are attempting this reduction.[13]

Defeated in our attempt to exist either as lovers or as failed lovers (masochists), we may be driven to indifference-desire or sadism-hate, the attempt to defy the freedom of the other. Our defiance begins quietly with indifference, a form of what Sartre called "blindness," or the nonrecognition of the subjectivity of others. Blind, we make no attempt to apprehend the other as anything but an object: "I scarcely notice [others]; I act as if I were alone in the world."[14] This solipsism is ego building, for it allows us to overlook that we are determined by others, shaped by the look of those others among whom we strut. When we are indifferent to others, we pretend they do not exist, that they cannot define us or pigeonhole us. Nevertheless, what occurs even without our acknowledgment still in fact occurs: There *are* others in whose eyes we are objects. What we refuse to recognize, then, may at any moment intrude upon us. The other may at any moment direct at us an altogether human look, and we may receive it. "Brief and terrifying flashes of illumination," said Sartre, may rip through the shroud of our indifference, forcing us to recognize the subjectivity and freedom of the other.[15]

Receiving the look of the other ruins our attempt at total indifference, at times so much so that we come to desire the other sexually. To desire the other sexually is to want the other as mere flesh, as total object. There is, said Sartre, something sadistic about this desire. But no sooner do we possess the other as body than we discover it was not the other as body but the other as self we desired: "To be sure, I can grasp the Other, grab hold of him, knock him down. I can, providing I have the power, compel him to perform this or that act, to say certain words. But everything happens as if I wished to get hold of a man who runs away and leaves only his coat in my hands. It is the coat, it is the outer shell which I possess. I shall never get hold of more than a body, a psychic object in the midst of the world."[16] Just when we think we are about to triumph over the other—just when the other's consciousness as well as flesh seems ready to yield to us—the other may look us in the eye and make of us an object. By reestablishing itself as a subject, insisted Sartre, the other frustrates our attempt at sadism.

Unable to eliminate the threat or independence of the other even through sadism, our only recourse is hate—the wish for the death of the other. We want to wipe out forever the self who has, by looking at us as the other, threatened our freedom. If we feel we have been ridiculous or evil or cowardly in the other's consciousness, we may wish to wipe out the embarrassment by destroying that consciousness. Sartre pointed out that hatred of a particular other is, in reality, hatred of all others. If we wish not to be a self-for-others, logically we should have to annihilate all others. But hate is also futile, for even if all others ceased to exist, the memory of their looks would live on forever in our consciousness, inseparable from whatever ideas we might try to form about ourselves. So even our last resource does not suffice. "Hate does not enable us to get out of the circle. It simply represents the final attempt, the attempt of despair. After the failure of this attempt nothing remains for the for-itself except to re-enter the circle and allow itself to be infinitely tossed."[17]

Simone de Beauvoir: Existentialism for Women

In adopting the ontological and ethical language of existentialism, de Beauvoir observed that men named "man" the self and "woman" the other. If the other is a threat to the self, then woman is a threat to man. Therefore, if man wishes to remain free, he must subordinate woman to him. To be sure, gender oppression is not the only form of oppression. Far from it. Blacks know what it is to be oppressed by whites, and the poor know what it is to be oppressed by the rich. Nonetheless, insisted Dorothy Kaufmann McCall, women's oppression by men is unique for two reasons. "First, unlike the oppression of race and class, the oppression of woman is not a contingent historical fact, an event in time which has sometimes been contested or reversed. Woman has always been subordinate to man. Second, women have internalized the alien point of view that man is the essential, woman the inessential."[18]

Destiny and History of Woman

A good way to test de Beauvoir's characterization of woman's oppression as unique is to ponder her analysis of how woman became the other. In the first three chapters of The Second Sex, which she entitled "The Data of Biology," "The Psychoanalytic Point of View," and "The Point of View of Historical Materialism," de Beauvoir discussed how women became not only different and separate from man but also inferior to him. She claimed that although biologists, Freudian psychoanalysts, and Marxist economists helped illuminate the reasons for woman's "otherness," existentialist philosophers provided the best explanation for it.

De Beauvoir noted that biology provides society with facts, which society then interprets to suit its own ends. For example, biology describes the respective reproductive roles of males and females:

The sperm, through which the life of the male is transcended in another, at the same instant becomes a stranger to him and separates from his body, so that the male recovers his individuality intact at the moment when he transcends it. The egg, on the contrary begins to separate from the female body when, fully matured, it emerges from the follicle and falls into the oviduct; but if fertilized by a gamete from outside, it becomes attached again through implantation in the uterus. First violated, the female is then alienated—she becomes, in part, another than herself.[19]

Although these reproductive "facts" might explain why it is oftentimes harder for a woman to become and remain a self, especially if she has a child, in de Beauvoir's estimation they in no way prove the societal myth that women's capacity for selfhood is somehow intrinsically less than men's.

De Beauvoir repeatedly observed that although biological and physiological facts about woman—such as her primary role in reproduction relative to man's secondary role, her physical weakness relative to man's physical strength, and her inactive role in heterosexual intercourse relative to man's active role—are true enough, how much value we attach to these facts is up to us as social beings. She wrote:

The enslavement of the female to the species and the limitations of her various powers are extremely important facts; the body of woman is one of the essential elements in her situation in the world. But that body is not enough to define her as woman; there is no true living reality except as manifested by the conscious individual through activities and in the bosom of a society. Biology is not enough to give an answer to the question that is before us: why is woman the Other?[20]

In other words, since woman is being-for-herself as well as being-in-itself, we must look for causes and reasons beyond those suggested by female biology and physiology to fully explain why society has selected *woman* to play the role of the other.

When de Beauvoir looked beyond biology to psychology, especially psychoanalysis, for a better explanation of woman's otherness, she was disappointed. According to de Beauvoir, traditional Freudians all tell essentially the same story about woman: She is a creature who must struggle between her "viriloid" and her "feminine" tendencies, the first expressed through clitoral eroticism, the second through vaginal eroticism. To win this battle—to become normal—woman must overcome her "viriloid" tendencies and transfer her love from a woman to a man. Although de Beauvoir conceded Freud's genius—which, for her, consisted in his having forwarded the bold idea that sexuality is the ultimate explanation for the human condition—she nevertheless rejected this notion as simplistic:

There is no need of taking sexuality as an irreducible datum, for there is in the existent a more original "quest of being," of which sexuality is only one of the aspects. The psychoanalysts hold that the primary truth regarding man is his relation with his own body and with the bodies of his fellows in the group; but man has a primordial interest in the substance of the natural world which surrounds him and which he tries to discover in work, in play, and in all the experiences of the "dynamic imagination." Man aspires to be at one concretely with the whole world apprehended in all possible ways. To work the earth, to dig a hole, are activities as original as the embrace, as coition, and they deceive themselves who see here no more than sexual symbols.[21]

In other words, civilization cannot be explained merely as the product of repressed or sublimated sexual impulses. Civilization is more complicated than this, and so are the relations between men and women.

In particular, de Beauvoir viewed Freud's explanation for woman's otherness as incomplete. She faulted Freudians for teaching that women's low social status relative to men is due simply to women's lack of the penis. Anticipating by decades a central tenet of the U.S. woman's movement, de Beauvoir refused to concede it is women's anatomy that consigns women to second-class personhood and citizenship. Women "envy" those who possess a penis, said de Beauvoir, not because they want a penis per se but because they desire the material and psychological privileges society accords to penis possessors. The social status of men is not to be traced to certain features of the male anatomy; rather, the "prestige of the penis" is to be explained "by the sovereignty of the father." Women are the other not because they lack penises but because they lack power.[22]

Finally, de Beauvoir considered the Marxist explanation for why woman is the other and found it nearly as unsatisfying as Freud's. Engels contended that from the beginning of time women performed *en-soi*-like tasks such as cooking, cleaning, and child-rearing, whereas men performed *pour-soi*-like tasks such as hunting and fighting, most of which involve the use of tools to subdue the world. As a result of this particular division of labor, men seized the means of production; they became the "bourgeois" and women became the "proletariat." Capitalism favors this state of affairs since it does not have to pay women for the work they do in the home. The "system" gets women's housework for free. Thus, men will remain the "bourgeois" and women the "proletariat" until capitalism is overthrown and the means of production are owned equally by men and women. Then and only then, said Engels, will work be divided not on the basis of individuals' gender but on the basis of individuals' ability, readiness, and willingness to perform certain jobs.

Disagreeing with Engels, de Beauvoir insisted a move from capitalism to socialism would not automatically change the relations between men and women. Women are just as likely to remain the other in a socialist society as in a capitalist society, for the roots of women's oppression are more than economic; they are ontological. Thus, de Beauvoir stressed: "If the human consciousness had not included . . . an original aspiration to dominate the Other, the invention of the bronze tool could not have caused the oppression of woman."[23] Women's liberation requires far more than the elimination of the institution of private property; it requires nothing less than the elimination of men's desire to control women.

Unsatisfied by the traditional biological, psychological, and economic explanations of women's oppression, de Beauvoir sought a deeper explanation for why men named man the self and woman the other. She speculated that in perceiving themselves as subjects capable of risking their lives in combat, men perceived women as objects, capable only of giving life. "It is not in giving life but risking life," said de Beauvoir, "that man is raised above the animal; that is why superiority has been accorded in humanity not to the sex that brings forth but to that which kills."[24] In addition, de Beauvoir surmised there was probably another, even more basic explanation for men's relegation of woman to the sphere of otherness. She observed that as soon as man asserted himself "as subject and free being, the idea of the Other [arose]"[25]—specifically, the idea of *woman* as the other. Woman became for man everything man was not, an alien power that man had best control lest woman become the self and man the other.

Myths About Woman

As civilization developed, men discovered they could control women by creating myths about woman: her irrationality, complexity, and opaqueness. Throughout her analysis of men's myths about woman, de Beauvoir emphasized that each man is in search of the ideal woman—that is, the woman who can make him whole. But because men's basic needs are so similar, their ideal women tend to look the same. Literature attests to this fact, said de Beauvoir.

Focusing on five male authors, de Beauvoir noted that: "Montherlant, the solar spirit, seeks pure animality in her; Lawrence, the phallicist, asks her to sum up the feminine sex in general; Claudel defines her as a soul-sister; Breton cherishes Mélusine, rooted in nature, pinning his hope on the woman-child; Stendhal wants his mistress intelligent, cultivated, free in spirit and behavior: an equal."[26] As different as these ideal women may seem, said de Beauvoir, they share certain fundamental traits. In each case the woman is urged to forget, deny, or in some way *negate* herself. Montherlant's woman exists in order to make her man feel virile. Lawrence's woman gives up her dreams so that her man can fulfill his. Claudel's woman is the handmaid not only of God but also of her man. Breton's woman is burdened with a heavy guilt trip: Only if her love is deep enough will she be able to save her man; otherwise, he will be damned. Stendhal's woman risks life and limb in a passionate attempt to save her lover from ruin, prison, and death. In sum, the ideal woman, the woman whom men worship, is the woman who believes it is her *duty* to sacrifice herself for her man.[27]

In addition to idealizing/idolizing the self-sacrificial woman, man's myths about woman betray a fundamental ambivalence about her nature. In words anticipating those of psychoanalytic feminist Dorothy Dinnerstein and ecofeminist Susan Griffin, de Beauvoir described the ways in which men connect nature to women. Like nature, woman reminds men of both life and death. At one and the same time, woman is innocent angel and guilty demon. Because her natural body reminds man he is subject to disease, disintegration, death, and decay, man delights in her artificial body. Feathered and furred, powdered and perfumed, the "animal crudity" of woman (her "odor") is hidden from man in his flight from carnality and the mortality to which her body points.[28]

If woman could simply scoff at the image of her "ideal," then the situation would not be so perilous for her. But woman is unable to do so because man has the power to control her—to use her for his own purposes no matter the cost she has to pay. Honoré de Balzac, said de Beauvoir, summarized man's attitude toward woman when he wrote, "Pay no attention to her murmurs, her cries, her pains; *nature has made her for our use and for bearing everything*: children, sorrows, blows and pains inflicted by man. Do not accuse yourself of hardness. In all the codes of so-called civilized nations, man has written the laws that ranged woman's destiny under his bloody epigraph: '*Vae victis!* Woe to the weak!'"[29] Finally, what makes the myth of woman so horrific is that many women come to internalize it as an accurate reflection of what it means to be woman.

Woman's Life Today

Unlike Sartre, de Beauvoir specified social roles as the primary mechanisms the self, or subject, uses to control the other, or object. She labeled woman's tragic acceptance of her own otherness the feminine "mystery," which passes from generation to generation through the painful socialization of girls. De Beauvoir spoke from her own experience—that of a bourgeois French girl growing up between two world wars. She claimed girls recognize their bodily differences from boys very early on. With puberty, with the swelling of their breasts, and with the beginning of their menstrual flows, girls are compelled to accept and internalize as shameful and inferior their otherness. This otherness is cemented, said de Beauvoir, in the institutions of marriage and motherhood.

As de Beauvoir saw it, the role of wife blocks women's freedom. Although de Beauvoir believed men and women are capable of deep love, she claimed the institution of marriage perverts couples' relationships. It transforms freely given feelings into mandatory duties and shrilly asserted rights. Marriage is a form of slavery, said de Beauvoir. It gives women (at least French bourgeois women) little more than "gilded mediocrity lacking ambition and passion, aimless days indefinitely repeated, life that slips away gently toward death without questioning its purpose."[30] Marriage offers women contentment, tranquillity, and security, but it also robs women of the chance to be great. In return for their freedom, women are given "happiness." Gradually, women learn how to settle for less:

> It is not without some regret that she shuts behind her the doors of her new home; when she was a girl, the whole countryside was her homeland; the forests were hers. Now she is confined to a restricted space; Nature is reduced to the dimensions of a potted geranium; walls cut off the horizon. But she is going to set about overcoming these limitations. In the form of more or less expensive bric-a-brac she has exotic countries and past time; she has her husband representing human society, and she has her child, who gives her the entire future in portable future.[31]

If the role of wife limits women's self-development, the role of mother does so even more.[32] Although de Beauvoir conceded *rearing* a child to adulthood can be existentially engaging, she insisted *bearing* a child is not an action but a mere event. De Beauvoir stressed the ways in which pregnancy alienates a woman from herself, making it difficult for her to chart, unencumbered, the course of her destiny. Like radical-libertarian feminist Shulamith Firestone, de Beauvoir questioned the supposed joys of pregnancy, observing that even women who want to have children seem to have a tough time of it. Also like Firestone, de Beauvoir worried about the way in which the mother-child relationship is so easily distorted. At first the child seems to liberate the mother from her object status because she "obtains in her child what man seeks in woman: an other, coming nature and mind, who is to be both prey and *double*."[33] As time goes on, however, the child becomes a demanding tyrant—a toddler, an adolescent, an adult, a conscious subject who, by looking at mother, can turn her into an object, into a machine for cooking, cleaning, caring, giving, and especially sacrificing. Reduced to an object, the mother, not unexpectedly, begins to view and to use her child as an object, as something that can make up for her deep sense of frustration.

It is clear that "wifing" and "mothering" are, in de Beauvoir's estimation, two feminine roles that limit woman's freedom, but so, too, is the role of "career" woman. De Beauvoir stressed a career woman can no more escape the cage of femininity than a wife and mother can. Indeed, in some ways, the career woman is in a worse situation than the stay-at-home wife and mother because she is at all times and places expected to be and act like a woman. In other words, a career woman is expected to add to her professional duties those "duties" implied in her "femininity," by which society seems to mean a certain sort of pleasing appearance. As a result, she develops an internal conflict between her professional and feminine interests. If the career woman devotes herself to her professional interests so much so that she neglects her appearance, she will see herself as falling very short of the standards set by beautiful women. She will find fault with her hair, teeth, nails, complexion, figure, and clothes. Panicked by her lack of good looks and sex appeal, the career woman will be tempted to cut her workday short so she has more time for beauty treatments. If she reallocates her time in this fashion, however, the career woman will soon find herself playing second fiddle to the career man who, unlike her, is not required to cultivate narcissism as a virtue.[34]

Although all women engage in feminine role-playing, according to de Beauvoir, three kinds of women play the role of "woman" to the hilt. They are the prostitute, the narcissist, and the mystic. De Beauvoir's analysis of the prostitute was complex. On the one hand, the prostitute is a paradigm for woman as the other, as object, as the exploited one; on the other hand, the prostitute, like the man who purchases her services, is a self, a subject, an exploiter. She prostitutes herself, suggested de Beauvoir, not simply for the money but for the homage men pay to her "otherness." Unlike men's wives and girlfriends, prostitutes get something for yielding their bodies to men's dreams: "wealth, and fame."[35]

Conceding that the so-called streetwalker often sells her body because it is the only thing she has to sell, de Beauvoir stressed that in contrast the so-called call girl, the hetaira, who regards her whole self as capital, usually has the upper hand in any relationship.[36] Men need her more than she needs them. De Beauvoir's point seems to be that even if the hetaira, like the wife and the mother, cannot escape being the other, at least she is able to use her otherness to her own personal advantage. (As disturbing as I find de Beauvoir's account and as much as I want to resist it, I am reminded of a former colleague of mine, a brilliant and beautiful Third World woman who used her "otherness" to capture the imagination of many of my male colleagues. At one point she said to me, "I make them pay for my otherness." And pay they did, for she had a way of trivializing and humiliating them both as men and as intellectuals.)

A feminine role even more problematic than the prostitute is the narcissist. De Beauvoir claimed that women's narcissism results from her otherness. Woman is frustrated as a subject because she is not allowed to engage in self-defining activity and because her feminine activities are not fulfilling. "Not being able to fulfill herself through projects and objectives, [woman] is forced to find her reality in the immanence of her person. . . . She gives herself supreme importance because no object of importance is accessible to her."[37]

Woman then becomes her own object of importance. Believing herself to be an object—a belief confirmed by most everyone around her—she is fascinated by, and perhaps even fixated on, her own image: face, body, clothes. The sense of being a subject and object simultaneously is, of course, illusory. Nevertheless, the narcissist somehow believes that *she* is the impossible synthesis of being-for-itself and being-in-itself.

At first narcissism is helpful for woman. As an adolescent, she "can draw from the worship of her ego the courage to face the disquieting future."[38] In the end, however, narcissism hinders woman's self-development. She becomes enchained by the need to fulfill man's desires and to conform to society's tastes. The narcissist's self-worth depends on man's and society's approval of her. She is only as beautiful as they say she is beautiful. She has no power to declare herself beautiful.

Probably the most problematic feminine role is the mystic who seeks to be the supreme object of a supreme subject. The mystic, wrote de Beauvoir, confuses God with man and man with God. She speaks of divine beings as if they were human beings, and she speaks of men as if they were gods. What the mystic seeks in divine love, said de Beauvoir, is "first of all what the *amoureuse* seeks in that of man: the exaltation of her narcissism: this sovereign gaze fixed attentively, amorously, upon her is a miraculous godsend."[39] The mystic does not pursue transcendence through God. Instead, she seeks to be possessed supremely by a God who would have no other woman before him. What the mystic wants from God is the exaltation of her objecthood.

In reflecting upon her descriptions of the wife, the mother, the career woman, the prostitute, the narcissist, and the mystic, de Beauvoir concluded the tragedy of these roles is they are not fundamentally of woman's own making. Not a maker herself, woman has been offered up to the masculine world of productive society for approval. She has, said de Beauvoir, been constructed by man, by his structures and institutions. But because woman, like man, has no essence, she need not continue to be what man has made her to be. Woman can be a subject, can engage in positive action in society, and can redefine or abolish her roles as wife, mother, career woman, prostitute, narcissist, and mystic. Woman can create her own self because there is no essence of eternal femininity prescribing a ready-made identity for her. All that is holding woman back from self-creation is society—a patriarchy that is, in de Beauvoir's estimation, reaching its end: "What is certain is that hitherto woman's possibilities have been suppressed and lost to humanity, and that it is high time she be permitted to take her chances in her own interest and in the interest of all."[40] Woman, like man, is a subject rather than an object; she is no more being-in-itself than man is. She, like man, is being-for-itself, and it is high time for man to recognize this fact.

There are, of course, no easy ways for woman to escape what de Beauvoir repeatedly described as woman's immanence—the limits, definitions, and roles that society, propriety, and men have imposed on her. Nevertheless, if woman wants to cease being the second sex, the other, she must overcome the forces of circumstance; she must have her say and her way as much as man does. On the way to transcendence, there are, said de Beauvoir, four strategies women can employ.

First, women can go to work. To be sure, de Beauvoir recognized that work in a capitalist patriarchy is oppressive and exploitative, particularly when it results in women's working a double day: one shift in the office or factory and one shift at home. Nonetheless, de Beauvoir insisted no matter how taxing or tiring a woman's job is, it still opens up possibilities for her that she would otherwise lack. By working outside the home alongside men, woman "regains her transcendence"; she "concretely affirms her status as subject, as someone who is actively charting the course of her destiny."[41]

Second, women can become intellectuals, members of the vanguard of change for women. Intellectual activity is, after all, the activity of one who thinks, looks, and defines, not the nonactivity of one who is thought about, looked at, and defined. De Beauvoir encouraged women to study writers such as Emily Brontë, Virginia Woolf, and Katherine Mansfield, who took themselves seriously enough as writers to probe death, life, and suffering.[42]

Third, women can work toward a socialist transformation of society. Like Sartre, de Beauvoir held out hope for an end to the subject-object, self-other conflict among human beings in general and between men and women in particular. In *Being and Nothingness*, Sartre added a footnote to his conclusion that all attempts at love or union are bound to lapse into either masochism or sadism. Sartre explained his "considerations do not exclude the possibility of an ethics of deliverance and salvation. But this can be achieved only after a radical conversion which we cannot discuss here."[43] The radical conversion he had in mind is a Marxist revolution. The struggle between one human being and another, which in *Being and Nothingness* arose from a psychological necessity derived from the nature of consciousness itself, became, in Sartre's *Critique of Dialectical Reason*, a struggle between workers and capitalists caused not by psychological but by economic necessity. Sartre implied that if all people had adequate food, clothing, and shelter, they might be able to overcome the psychological barriers separating them. Love might be possible after all.

Like Sartre, de Beauvoir believed one of the keys to women's liberation is economic, a point she emphasized in her discussion of the independent woman. De Beauvoir reminded women that their circumstances will, of course, limit their efforts to define themselves. Just as a sculptor's creativity is limited by the marble block at hand, a woman's freedom is limited by the size of her bank account, for example. If a woman wants to be all that she can possibly be, she must help create the kind of society that will provide her with the material support to transcend her present limits.

Finally, in order to transcend their limits women can refuse to internalize their otherness—that is, to identify themselves through the eyes of the dominant group in society. To accept the role of the other, said de Beauvoir, is to accept being an object. It is, as Josephine Donovan wrote, "to deny the subject-self that is autonomous and creative" and risk the kind of "madness and schizophrenia" that results from "engaging in a perpetual lie."[44] On the one hand, woman's *inauthentic* self lives as the "object-self" seen by the male world; on the other hand, woman's *authentic* self lives as a "withdrawn-invisible self—invisible at times even to oneself."[45] As a result, woman's person is split.

According to Donovan, Meredith Tax's analysis of women's "splitness" is particularly insightful. Tax described a woman forced to put up with men's catcalls and whistles as she walks down a public street. In such a situation, the woman has but two choices: "Either she remains sensitive and vulnerable to the pain; or she shuts it out by saying, 'It's only my body they are talking about. It doesn't affect me. They know nothing about me.' Whatever the process, the solution is a split between the mind and the body."[46] Reinforcing Tax's analysis, Sandra Bartky observed that the phenomenon of catcalling or whistling demonstrates just how pervasive women's objectification is in our society. No matter where they go, women can't seem to escape men's eyes.

In an attempt to further elucidate how the "gaze of the Other" petrifies women's self into an object, Bartky speculated that in our society the other that is internalized in women takes a particular form; it is the other created by the "fashion-beauty complex." Women are, she said, "presented everywhere with images of perfect female beauty—at the drugstore cosmetics display, the supermarket magazine counter, on television";[47] and it is these images women internalize, mercilessly measuring their imperfect bodies against the supposedly perfect bodies of high fashion. What women in our society—indeed in any society in which cosmetics and fashion exist—fail to realize, said Bartky, is something de Beauvoir knew only too well. De Beauvoir asserted that "costumes and styles are often devoted to cutting off the feminine body from any possible transcendence."[48] The mobility of the foot-bound or high-heeled woman is limited; the dexterity of the long-finger-nailed or bejeweled woman is impeded. Women are so busy attending to their deficient bodies they have no time to improve their minds. Thus, the only way for a woman to become a self in a society such as ours is for her to *free* her self from her body, to refuse to fritter away her time at the beauty salon when she could be engaged in some sort of creative or service-oriented project.

Critiques of Existentialist Feminism

A Communitarian Critique of Existentialist Feminism

Jean Bethke Elshtain faulted de Beauvoir's *Second Sex* for three reasons. She noted for one that the book was not accessible to the majority of women. "Immanence" and "transcendence," "essence" and "existence," "being-for-itself" and "being-in-itself" are ideas that do not arise directly out of woman's lived experience but are abstractions that emerge from the philosopher's armchair speculations. De Beauvoir's technical words, said Elshtain, are more likely to "pummel" less formally educated women into agreeing with her than to persuade them they are indeed the second sex.[49]

Elshtain also strongly objected to de Beauvoir's treatment of the body, especially the female body. She claimed de Beauvoir presents all bodies but particularly female bodies as negative: unfortunate, insignificant, dirty, shameful, burdensome, inherently alienating. Elshtain speculated de Beauvoir's general distrust of the body was rooted in her existentialist anxieties about the carnality and mortality of the flesh. The body is a problem within the existentialist framework insofar as it is a stubborn and unavoidable object limiting the freedom of each conscious subject. De Beauvoir recorded in her memoirs her own war against the flesh: her squashed sexual urges, her attempts to do without sleep, her sense of horror as she relentlessly aged.[50] Because the slow disintegration of the body signals the coming of death—the end of consciousness, of freedom, of subjectivity—existentialists such as de Beauvoir have little desire to celebrate a body that represents to them the forces of death.

De Beauvoir's general distrust of the body, claimed Elshtain, became a very particular mistrust of the *female* body. According to de Beauvoir, woman's reproductive capacities rob her of her personhood. In contrast, a man's reproductive capacities do not threaten his personhood. After sexual intercourse the man remains exactly as he was before sexual intercourse. But if fertilization takes place after sexual intercourse, a woman is no longer the same person she was before: "Ensnared by nature, the pregnant woman is plant and animal, a stock-pile of colloids, an incubator, an egg; she scares children proud of their young, straight bodies and makes young people titter contemptuously because she is a human being, a conscious and free individual, who has become life's passing instrument."[51] In focusing on this passage and others like it, Elshtain commented that de Beauvoir's description of pregnancy is profoundly alienating to the bulk of pregnant women, most of whom view their "swelling with child" positively. One does not win many converts to feminism by claiming pregnant women are akin to vegetables.

Last, Elshtain criticized de Beauvoir for celebrating largely male norms. All of de Beauvoir's complaints about woman's character as passive, submissive, and immanent translate into a valorization of man's character as active, dominant, and transcendent. The denigration of woman's body arises from the elevation of man's mind. The deploring of woman's association with nature contrasts with the admiration of man's construction of culture. Thus, de Beauvoir prescribed women achieve freedom by rejecting their bodies and connections to nature. As Elshtain saw it, de Beauvoir's prescription for women's oppression was flawed. To ask women to give up their female identities without considering the ramifications of trading in sisterhood for brotherhood is, Elshtain said, irresponsible.[52]

A Philosophical Critique of Existentialist Feminism

In *Man of Reason*, a book about the construction of gender in Western philosophy, Genevieve Lloyd argued de Beauvoir's philosophical categories were at odds with some fundamental feminist needs. Transcendence, Lloyd said, is a male ideal by definition. To accept the ideal of transcendence as liberating places the feminist in a paradox rooted in the existentialist opposition between the looker and the looked-at, between self and other. One is either looking, acting, and transcending or being looked at, passive, and immanent. Since there is no way to exist *in-between* these two ways of being, the only way for someone to become a self instead of an other is to leap from immanence into transcendence.

Lloyd thought the leap into transcendence creates special problems for women. Even if women are by *nature* no more immanent and *en-soi* than men are, women are still culturally linked with this way of being in the same way that men are still culturally linked with a transcendent and *pour-soi* way of being. Because "'transcendence,' in its origins, is a transcendence of the feminine,"[53] said Lloyd, transcendence for women is very risky business: "Male transcendence . . . is different from . . . female transcendence. . . . It is breaking away from a zone which for the male, remains intact—from what is for him the realm of particularity and merely natural feelings. For the female, in contrast, there is no such realm which she can both leave and leave intact."[54] Small wonder, then, that Lloyd faulted de Beauvoir for asking women to destroy themselves.

Conclusion

The critics of de Beauvoir invite us to ponder whether it is more liberating to think of woman as the product of a cultural construction or instead to think of woman as the result of a natural arrangement. They also invite us to wonder whether the realm of transcendence is better, worse, or simply different than the realm of immanence. Finally, they invite us to consider, as others already have, whether women's liberation requires women to reject the "feminine" entirely or to embrace it yet more wholeheartedly.

Despite the force of Elshtain's and Lloyd's critiques, much can and has been said in defense of de Beauvoir's existentialist feminism. De Beauvoir is, admittedly, a challenging, even intimidating feminist thinker. But just because she spoke in her own voice—that of a highly educated, bourgeois, French woman—does not mean her words cannot speak to women whose life circumstances depart dramatically from her own.

De Beauvoir was dismayed when some of her supposedly nonsexist friends—for example, the existentialist Albert Camus—met the publication of *The Second Sex* coldly, rejecting it as a simpleminded assault upon masculinity.[55] She was also disheartened by the chilly response of the local Communist Party, which regarded her book as yet another trivial catalogue of female complaints intended to distract women from genuine class struggle.[56] To be sure, de Beauvoir also had her supporters; 22,000 copies of *The Second Sex* were sold in the first week following its publication. However, what pleased de Beauvoir the most, according to one of her biographers, were the letters she received from grateful women of *every social class* whose lives had changed in positive directions after reading her reflections. Whether de Beauvoir's prose is difficult to read or not, these women found in her book a liberating message addressed to them in particular.[57]

The assertion that de Beauvoir was hostile to the body, especially to the female body, is one for which ample textual evidence exists. When de Beauvoir observed women have within their bodies a "hostile element"—namely, "the species gnawing at their vitals"—her words evoked feelings of fear, weakness, and disgust.[58] Nevertheless, despite her valorization of the mind over the body, de Beauvoir's rejection of the body was less virulent than Sartre's rejection of the body. In fact, de Beauvoir told Sartre that his attitude toward the body, especially the emotions, was *too* inflexible: "I criticized Sartre for regarding his body as a mere bundle of striated muscles, and for having cut it out of his emotional world. If you gave way to tears or nerves or seasickness, he said, you were simply being weak. I, on the other hand, claimed that stomach and tear ducts, indeed the head itself, were all subject to irresistible forces on occasion."[59]

Of course de Beauvoir's concession that "it's good to demand that a woman should not be made to feel degraded by, let's say, her monthly periods; that a woman refuse to be made to feel ridiculous because of her pregnancy; that a woman be able to be proud of her body, and her feminine sexuality"[60] does not mean that, after all, she really did love the body in general and the female body in particular. On the contrary, when informed that like many French feminists, many U.S. feminists made woman's body the centerpiece of their feminism, de Beauvoir commented that she was opposed to any privileging of a special female way of being.

> There is no reason at all to fall into some wild narcissism, and build, on the basis of these givens, a system which would be the culture and the life of women. I don't think that women should repress their givens. She has the perfect right to be proud of being a woman, just as man is also proud of his sex. After all, he has the right to be proud of it, under the condition, however, that he does not deprive others of the right to a similar pride. Everyone can be happy with her or his body. But one should not make this body the center of the universe.[61]

As de Beauvoir saw it, the problem with making woman's body the linchpin of women's liberation is that it mistakes a biological fact for a social fact. Woman's body—as wonderful as it is—should not prescribe, or mandate, a definite mode of existence for all women. Rather, each woman should shape a unique mode of existence for herself.

This last point—that each woman should shape the course of her own destiny—must be carefully understood. De Beauvoir recognized the legal, political, economic, social, and cultural circumstances that restrain and constrain women. She also recognized the ways in which women have let themselves be restrained and constrained by these circumstances. Nonetheless, de Beauvoir insisted none of these limitations are capable of totally imprisoning women. Women are both determined by and free of patriarchy. "People," wrote Carol Ascher, "make decisions to break out of or remain within varying degrees of constraint, at times no positive decision may be possible. Yet the decision is made, and the individual is responsible for it."[62] Thus, when de Beauvoir asked women to transcend the limits of their immanence, de Beauvoir was not asking women to negate themselves but rather to cast off the weights impeding their progress toward authentic selfhood. To be sure, some of these weights are too heavy for any individual woman to cast off, but they can be disposed of through small and large acts of collective empowerment. What is now does not always have to be. No one or no thing can forever hold back a determined group of women.

CHAPTER SIX

■

Postmodern Feminism

Since the relationship between postmodernism and feminism is an uneasy one, feminists who classify themselves as postmodern feminists often have difficulty explaining how they can be both postmodern and feminist. Postmodern feminists, like all postmodernists, seek to avoid in their writings any and all reinstantiations of phallogocentric thought, ideas ordered around an absolute word (logos) that is "male" in style (hence the reference to the phallus). Thus, they view with suspicion any mode of feminist thought that aims to provide *the* explanation for why woman is oppressed or *the* ten steps *all* women must take to achieve liberation. Some postmodern feminists are so suspicious of traditional feminist thought that they reject it altogether. For example, Hélène Cixous wanted nothing to do with terms such as *feminist* and *lesbian*. These words are, she claimed, parasitic upon phallogocentric thought because they connote "deviation from a norm instead of a free sexual option or a place of solidarity with women."[1] Better for women seeking liberation to avoid such terms, which suggest a unity that blocks difference. Although postmodern feminists' refusal to develop one overarching explanation and solution for women's oppression poses major problems for feminist theory, this refusal also adds needed fuel to the feminist fire of plurality, multiplicity, and difference. Postmodern feminists invite each woman who reflects on their writings to become the kind of feminist she wants to be. There is no single formula for being a "good feminist."

Some Major Influences on
Postmodern Feminist Thought

Anglo-American feminists initially referred to postmodern feminism as "French feminism" because so many of its exponents were either French nationals or women living in France (especially Paris).[2] When British and American audiences realized what "French feminists" had in common was not so much their "Frenchness" as their philosophical perspective, however, they began to consider French feminism postmodern feminism.

To a considerable degree such postmodern feminists as Hélène Cixous, Luce Irigaray, and Julia Kristeva take their intellectual cues from existentialist Simone de Beauvoir, deconstructionist Jacques Derrida, and psychoanalyst Jacques Lacan. Like de Beauvoir, they focus on woman's "otherness"; like Derrida, they delight in attacking the "ordinary notions of authorship, identity and selfhood";[3] and like Lacan, they commit themselves to interpreting traditionally Freudian thought iconoclastically. That Cixous, Irigaray, and Kristeva rely to some extent on de Beauvoir's, Derrida's, and Lacan's philosophies does not imply, however, that they espouse the politics of any of these thinkers.[4] Far from it. Moreover, enormous political differences exist among Cixous, Irigaray, and Kristeva, as well as other less-well-known postmodern feminists. Although some postmodern feminists write simply to spin theory as an art form, others write primarily to motivate women to change their ways of being and doing in the real world.

Anglo-American audiences still retain a somewhat skewed view of postmodern feminism because initial translations of postmodern feminist writings were few and selective. An organization called Psychanalyse et politique (known as "Psych et po"), with which Hélène Cixous is closely associated, served for many years as a gatekeeper for what Anglo-American audiences regard as "postmodern feminist" texts. If a writer did not share Psych et po's interest in semiotics and psychoanalysis and if a writer was judged too "feminist" (too concerned about women's actual lot),[5] then that writer's work was usually rejected for publication. Although writers with philosophical perspectives and political sensitivities different from those of Psych et po found other publishers to market their books, their writings did not always reach the Anglo-American market. As a result, many British and American feminists dismissed postmodern feminist texts as self-indulgent academic treatises addressed not to ordinary women but only to highly educated women with doctoral degrees in philosophy, for example.

Nevertheless, even if it is wrong to think that all postmodern feminists are interested in feminist theory to the exclusion of feminist practice, most postmodern feminists are exceptionally good at theory. Since postmodern feminists insist that it is their aim to write something new about women, a primary goal of this chapter is to determine whether Cixous's, Irigaray's, and Kristeva's thought is original. To what degree is postmodern feminism a truly unique mode of thought and to what degree is it simply Derridian, Lacanian, or de Beauvoirian?

Postmodern Feminism and Existentialist Feminism

Some of postmodern feminism's roots are found in the works of Simone de Beauvoir, who phrased the essential question of feminist theory as, "Why is woman the *second* sex?" Rephrased in postmodern terms, the question becomes, "Why is the woman the other?" Why does woman remain earthbound, immanent and determined, as she watches man fly off into the realm of transcendence, the zone of freedom? De Beauvoir's answers to these questions may or may not prove convincing, but no reader of *The Second Sex* can turn to its last page without concluding that to be "second," or "other," is not the best way for a person to be.

Postmodern feminists take de Beauvoir's understanding of otherness and turn it on its head. Woman is still the other, but rather than interpreting this condition as something to be transcended, postmodern feminists proclaim its advantages. The condition of otherness enables women to stand back and criticize the norms, values, and practices that the dominant culture (patriarchy) seeks to impose on everyone, including those who live on its periphery—in this case, women. Thus, otherness, for all of its associations with oppression and inferiority, is much more than an oppressed, inferior condition. It is also a way of being, thinking, and speaking allowing for openness, plurality, diversity, and difference.

Postmodern Feminism and Deconstruction

Being able to see the advantages of *not* being one of society's favored members—of being excluded, shunned, frozen out, disadvantaged, unprivileged, rejected, unwanted, abandoned, dislocated, and marginalized—is a major theme in deconstruction. Deconstructionists take a critical attitude toward everything that society regards as good, true, and beautiful, suggesting that it might actually be better for individuals to be "bad," "false," and "ugly." Among the most radical assumptions of deconstruction is the view that the entire conceptual and therefore linguistic scheme of the West is fundamentally flawed. Deconstructionists regard the West's predilection for "dualistic" thinking, speaking, and writing as utterly misguided. As much as possible, they challenge arbitrary boundaries between concepts such as reason and emotion, mind and body, and self and other, as well as senseless barriers between art and science, psychology and biology, and literature and philosophy.

So complete is the antiessentialism of the deconstructionists that they question the two most basic assumptions of Western thought: namely, that there is an essential unity of self through time and space termed *self-identity* and that there is an essential relationship between language and reality termed *truth*. They challenge the notion of a unified, or integrated, self by reference to the idea that the self is fundamentally split between its conscious and unconscious dimensions. In turn, they challenge the notion of truth by reference to the idea that language and reality are variable and shifting, missing each other in a Heraclitean flux. Words do not stand for things, for pieces of reality. Rather, reality eludes language, and language refuses to be pinned down or limited by reality. It is clear that these ideas are philosophically unsettling.

The deconstructionist belief that there is neither self-identity nor truth—that the order within our lives and our language is an imposed structure—caught the attention of writers/theorists such as Cixous, Irigaray, and Kristeva. They were also impressed by Lacan's and Derrida's many references to the ways in which language excludes the "feminine" from it. Therefore, in order to fully understand the writings of postmodern feminists, it is helpful to summarize Lacan's and Derrida's thoughts about the "excluded feminine."

Jacques Lacan

Building upon anthropologist Claude Lévi-Strauss's contention that every society is regulated by a series of interrelated signs, roles, and rituals, Lacan termed this series "the Symbolic Order."[6] For a child to function adequately within society, he or she must internalize the symbolic order through language; and the more a child submits to the linguistic rules of society, the more those rules will be inscribed in his or her unconscious. In other words, the symbolic order regulates society through the regulation of individuals; so long as individuals speak the language of the symbolic order—internalizing its gender roles and class roles—society will reproduce itself in fairly constant form.[7]

Emphasizing our unconscious acceptance and internalization of the symbolic order, Lacan, claimed the symbolic order *is* society, a system of relationships that antedates us. If we are to fit into this order, said Lacan, we must go through three stages, slowly submitting to the "law of the father."

In the first, or pre-Oedipal, phase—called the imaginary phase, which is the antithesis of the symbolic order—an infant is completely unaware of her or his own ego boundaries. Indeed, the infant has no sense of where the mother's body ends and her or his own body begins. As far as the infant is concerned, he or she and the mother are one.

In the second, or mirror, phase (also part of the imaginary phase), the infant thinks the image of her- or himself, as reflected through the "mirror" of the mother's gaze, is her or his real self. According to Lacan, this is a normal stage in self-development. The infant must first see the self as her or his mother sees it—as the other—before the infant can see her- or himself as a self.[8] Lacan claimed that the process of infantile self-discovery serves as a paradigm for all subsequent relations; the self always finds itself through its reflections in the other.

The third, or Oedipal, phase includes a period of growing estrangement between mother and infant, as the infant matures into a child. Unlike the infant, the child does not view her- or himself as a unity; rather, the child regards the mother as the other—someone to whom it must communicate wishes and, therefore, someone who, due to the limitations of language, can never truly fulfill them. During the Oedipal phase proper, the already weakened mother-child relationship is further eroded by the intervention of the father.[9] Fearing *symbolic* castration (the loss of the phallic signifier for all that is gratifying), the child separates from the mother in return for a medium (language) through which the child can maintain some connection with the mother—the original, never-to-be-had-again source of total gratification.[10]

Boys experience the process of splitting from the mother differently than do girls. In the Oedipal phase the boy rejects identification with his mother, eschewing the undifferentiated and silent state of the womb, and bonds with his anatomically similar father, who represents the symbolic order, the word. Through identification with his father, the boy not only enters into subjecthood and individuality but also internalizes the dominant order, the value-laden roles of society. In sum, the boy is born again—this time to language.

On account of their anatomy, girls cannot wholly identify with their fathers in the psychosexual drama. As a result, girls cannot fully accept and internalize the symbolic order. From this situation we can draw one of two conclusions. On the one hand, we can conclude that women are excluded from the symbolic order or confined to its margins. This seemed to be Freud's point when he claimed that because girls do not undergo the castration complex in the same way that boys do, their moral sense is not as developed. On the other hand, we can conclude that women are repressed within the symbolic order, forced into it unwillingly. Because women refuse to internalize the "law of the father," this law must be imposed from the outside. Women are given the same words men are given: masculine words. These words cannot express what women *feel*, however; they can express only what men *think*. Lacking feminine words, women must either babble or remain silent within the symbolic order.

Like Freud, Lacan could not find a comfortable place for women within his framework. Because women cannot completely resolve the Oedipal complex, they remain outside the symbolic order, beyond thought and words. [11] They are, therefore, unknowable. Lacan speculated that were we to try to do the impossible—to know women—we would have to begin our inquiry at the level of feminine sexual pleasure (*jouissance*). But like women, *jouissance* cannot be known because it can be neither thought nor spoken in the phallic language of the fathers. It leads a totally repressed existence at the margins of the symbolic order, seeking a nonphallic language capable of thinking and speaking it. Were *jouissance* to find the words to express itself, it would burst out of captivity, destroying, once and for all, the symbolic order and its major prop, patriarchy.

Jacques Derrida

Although postmodern feminists faulted Derrida for mystifying and romanticizing woman, they found his overall critique of the symbolic order useful for some of their own purposes.[12] Derrida criticized three aspects of the symbolic order: (1) logocentrism, the primacy of the spoken word, which is less subject to interpretation than the written word; (2) phallocentrism, the primacy of the phallus, which connotes a unitary drive toward a single, supposedly reachable goal; and (3) dualism, the expression of everything in terms of binary oppositions. Derrida traced these three isms to traditional Western philosophy's search for meaning, a search he rejected as pointless because for him meaning does not exist. Language does not, said Derrida, provide us with the meanings or essences of objects, concepts, or persons somehow located outside of it. Rather, language creates meaning, the only meaning to which it can refer. Because there is no being (presence) to be grasped, there is, continued Derrida, no nothingness (absence) with which to contrast it. Were we able to liberate thought from the fundamental binary opposition, being-nothingness, we would no longer be compelled neatly to oppose our thoughts, one against the other (male-female, nature-culture, speech-writing). Rather, we would find ourselves free to think new and different thoughts.

Derrida wanted to liberate thinking from the assumption of singularity—the view that one single truth or essence, a "transcendental signified," exists, in and of itself, as a giver of meaning. Because the only language available to him was the logocentric, phallocentric, binary language constricting his thought, Derrida was pessimistic about destroying the symbolic order. Nevertheless, he believed he could weaken the symbolic order by providing suppressed alternative interpretations of texts (for Derrida, anything communicated through language is a text).[13] Theorizing that we cannot overcome the kind of difference (in French, *différence*) that separates the object of perception from our perception, Derrida coined the term *différance* to describe the ineliminable gap between reality and language that confounds us. Postmodern feminists immediately appropriated this novel term. They noted that if they agreed on anything, it was that woman, the other, the feminine, had been left unthematized and silent in the void between language and reality, and the time had come for her to emerge from this abyss.

Postmodern Feminism: Three Perspectives

Postmodern feminists admit it is extremely difficult to challenge the symbolic order when the only words available to do so are words that have been issued by this order. For example, in insisting that all is plural, multiple, and different, postmodern feminists, like the "fathers," risk making a universal truth claim. This risk prompts some postmodern feminists to reject any label ending in *ism*, including *feminism* and *postmodernism*. Labels, they fear, always carry with them the "phallologocentric drive to stabilize, organize and rationalize our conceptual universe."[14] Yet no matter how much writers such as Cixous, Kristeva, and Irigaray insist on the uniqueness of their particular philosophies and politics, the public continues to classify them as postmodern feminists—that is, as writers offering women the most fundamental liberation of all: freedom from oppressive thought.

Hélène Cixous

Hélène Cixous is primarily a novelist experimenting with literary style. In applying Derrida's notion of *différance* to writing, she contrasted feminine writing (*l'écriture féminine*) with masculine writing (*littérature*). Understood psychoanalytically, masculine writing is rooted in a man's genital and libidinal economy, which is emblemized by the phallus. For a variety of sociocultural reasons, masculine writing has reigned supreme over feminine writing. In the words of Ann Rosalind Jones, man (white, European, and ruling class) has claimed, "I am the unified, self-controlled center of the universe. The rest of the world, which I define as the Other, has meaning only in relation to me, as man/father, possessor of the phallus."[15]

Cixous has objected to masculine writing and thinking because they are cast in binary oppositions. Man has unnecessarily segmented reality by coupling concepts and terms in pairs of polar opposites, one of which is always privileged over the other. In her essay "Sorties," Cixous listed some of these dichotomous pairs:

> Activity/Passivity
> Sun/Moon
> Culture/Nature
> Day/Night
> Thought has always worked through opposition.
> Speaking/Writing
> Parole/Ecriture
> High/Low
> Through dual, hierarchical oppositions.[16]

According to Cixous, each of these dichotomies finds its inspiration in the dyad man-woman in which man is associated with all that is active, cultural, light, high, or generally positive and woman is associated with all that is passive, natural, dark, low, or generally negative. Moreover, the first term of man-woman is the term from which the second departs or deviates. Man is the self; woman is the other. Thus, woman exists in man's world on his terms. She is either the other for man, or she is unthought. After man is done thinking about woman, "what is left of her is unthinkable, unthought."[17]

Cixous challenged women to write themselves out of the world *men* constructed for women. She urged women to put themselves—the unthinkable/unthought—into words. The kind of writing Cixous identified as woman's own—marking, scratching, scribbling, jotting down—connotes movements that bring to mind Heraclitus' ever-changing river. In contrast, the kind of writing Cixous associated with man composes the bulk of the so-called accumulated wisdom of humankind. Stamped with the official seal of social approval, masculine writing is too weighted down to move or change.

For Cixous, feminine writing is not merely a new style of writing; it is "the very possibility of change, the space that can serve as a springboard for subversive thought, the precursory movement of a transformation of social and cultural standards."[18] Women can, she insisted, change the way the Western world thinks, speaks, and acts by developing feminine writing. This is no easy task, however. Trying to write the nonexistent into existence, to "foresee the unforeseeable," may, after all, strain women writers to the breaking point.[19]

In the process of further distinguishing woman's writing from man's, Cixous drew many connections between male sexuality and masculine writing and female sexuality and feminine writing. Male sexuality, which centers on what Cixous called the "big dick," is ultimately boring in its pointedness and singularity.[20] Like male sexuality, masculine writing, which Cixous usually termed phallogocentric writing, is also ultimately boring. Men write the same old things with their "little pocket signifier"— the trio of penis/phallus/pen.[21] Fearing the multiplicity and chaos that exist outside their symbolic order, men always write in black ink, carefully containing their thoughts in a sharply defined and rigidly imposed structure.

In contrast, female sexuality is, for Cixous, anything but boring. She stated in no uncertain terms that: "Almost everything is yet to be written by women about femininity: about their sexuality, that is, its infinite and mobile complexity; about their eroticization, sudden turn-ons of a certain minuscule-immense area of their bodies; not about destiny, but about the adventure of such and such a drive, about trips, crossings, trudges, abrupt and gradual awakenings, discoveries of a zone at once timorous and soon to be forthright."[22] Like female sexuality, feminine writing is open and multiple, varied and rhythmic, full of pleasures and, more important, full of possibilities. When a woman writes, said Cixous, she writes in "white ink,"[23] letting her words flow freely where she wishes them to go: "Her writing can only keep going, without ever inscribing or discerning contours. . . . She lets the other language speak—the language of 1,000 tongues which knows neither enclosure nor death. . . . Her language does not contain, it carries; it does not hold back, it makes possible."[24]

Running through Cixous's writing are an optimism and joy lacking in both Derrida, for whom logocentrism is inevitable, and Lacan, for whom the phallus will always dominate. Cixous insisted women writers have the ability to lead the Western world out of the dichotomous conceptual order that causes it to think, speak, and act in terms of someone who is dominant and someone else who is submissive. If woman explores her body "with its thousand and one thresholds of order," said Cixous, she "will make the old single-grooved mother tongue reverberate with more than one language."[25] The id, implied Cixous, is the source of all desires. "Oral drive, anal drive, vocal drive—all these drives are our strengths, and among them is the gestation drive—just like the desire to write: a desire to live self from within, a desire for the swollen body, for language, for blood."[26] For Cixous, desire, not reason, is the means to escape the limiting concepts of traditional Western thought.

Luce Irigaray

Although Luce Irigaray agreed with Cixous that feminine sexuality and the female body are sources of feminine writing, there are substantial differences between Cixous and Irigaray. Unlike Cixous, who is first and foremost a writer, Irigaray is first and foremost a psychoanalyst. Through psychotherapy as well as writing, her aim is to liberate the feminine from masculine philosophical thought, including the thought of Freud and Lacan.[27]

We will recall that, in Lacan, the imaginary phase is the pre-Oedipal domain of prelinguistic, specular identifications in which the child initially mistakes her- or himself for her or his own mirror image, gradually coming to the realization that the image is not the real self. With this realization, the child enters the symbolic order prepared to assume the "I" in language—that is, to assert the self as a distinct subjectivity, separate from other subjectivities, or Is. Like Lacan, Irigaray drew contrasts between the imaginary and the symbolic; but unlike Lacan, Irigaray claimed there is *within* the imaginary a male imaginary and a female imaginary.[28]

For Lacan, the imaginary is a prison within which the self is the captive of illusory images. After successfully completing the Oedipal phase, boys are liberated from the imaginary and enter the symbolic order, the realm of language and selfhood. Because they never completely resolve the Oedipal phase, however, girls remain behind in the imaginary. In opposition to Lacan, Irigaray refused to view women's life in the imaginary as a state of affairs to bemoan. Instead, she viewed women's life in the imaginary as full of untapped possibilities for women.

Irigaray noted that at present anything we know about the imaginary and woman, including her sexual desire, we know from a male point of view. In other words, the only woman we know is the "masculine feminine," the phallic feminine, woman as man sees her. But, said Irigaray, there is another woman to know, the "feminine feminine," woman as women see her.[29] This woman must not be defined, however, through any statement definitively asserting what the true "feminine" is. Defining "woman" in any one way will recreate the "phallic" feminine: "To claim that the feminine can be expressed in the form of a concept is to allow oneself to be caught up again in a system of 'masculine' representations, in which women are trapped in a system or meaning which serves the auto-affection of the (masculine) subject."[30] What obstructs the progression of women's thought out of the imaginary is the concept of sameness, the thought product of masculine narcissism and singularity.

Irigaray used the word *speculum* (a concave mirroring medical instrument often used in vaginal examinations) to capture the nature and function of the idea of sameness in Western philosophy and psychoanalysis. "Specularization," commented Toril Moi, "suggests not only the mirror-image that comes from the visual penetration of the speculum inside the vagina" but also "the necessity of postulating a subject that is capable of reflecting on its own being."[31] Because of narcissistic philosophical "specularization"—which is epitomized in the medieval description of God as thought thinking thought—masculine discourse has never been able to understand woman, or the feminine, as anything other than a reflection of man, or the masculine. Therefore, it is impossible to think the "feminine feminine" within the structures of patriarchal thought. When men look at women, they see not women but reflections, or images and likeness, of men.

In her study of Western philosophy and psychoanalysis, Irigaray found sameness everywhere: in thinkers as various as Plato, René Descartes, G.W.F. Hegel, Friedrich Nietzsche, Sigmund Freud, and Jacques Lacan. Her analysis of sameness in Freud's theory was particularly important because she used it to criticize his theory of female sexuality. Freud saw the little girl as a deficiency or negativity, as a "little man" without a penis. He suppressed the notion of difference, characterizing the feminine as a lack. Woman is a reflection of man, the same as a man except in her sexuality. Female sexuality, because it does not mirror the male's, is an absence, or lack, of the male's. Where woman does not reflect man, she does not exist and, stressed Irigaray, will never exist until the Oedipus complex is exploded.[32]

Irigaray claimed that if women want to experience themselves as something other than "waste" or "excess" in the little structured margins of man's world,[33] three courses of action are available to them. First, women can create a female language eschewing gender-neutral language as forcefully as they eschew male language. Not only is the search for "neutrality" pointless (because no one is really neutral about anything), claimed Irigaray, but it is also morally misguided. Trying to hide the identity of the speaker from the reader/listener is cowardly. Stressing the fact that women will not find liberation in objectivity, Irigaray noted that "neither *I* nor *you*, nor *we* appears in the language of science."[34] Science forbids the "subjective," often because it wishes to mask the identities of its agents. Distressed by the unwillingness of science—and, for that matter, traditional philosophy and psychoanalysis—to take responsibility for its own words and deeds, Irigaray urged women to find the courage to speak in the active voice, avoiding at all costs the false security, and ultimate inauthenticity, of the passive voice.

Second, women can create a female sexuality. Like Cixous, Irigaray contrasted the singularity the male sexual organ implies with the multiplicity the female sexual organs imply. In particular, she localized the feminine voice in the labia, "two lips" that reveal woman to be "neither one nor two." Woman is not two, because the labia belong to a single woman's body, "which keeps woman in touch with herself, but without any possibility of distinguishing what is touching from what is touched." However, woman is not one either, because the labia represent a woman's multiple and diffuse (nonphallic sexuality): "So woman does not have a sex organ? She has at least two of them, but they are not identifiable as ones. Indeed, she has many more. Her sexuality is always at least double, goes even further; it is plural."[35]

Irigaray did not simply contrast the plural, circular, and aimless vaginal/clitoral libidinal economy of women with the singular, linear, and teleological phallic libidinal economy of men. She also argued that the expression of these libidinal economies is not restricted to sexuality but instead extends to all forms of human expression, including social structures. Just as the penetration of the penis prevents the lips from touching, so the phallic unity of the symbolic order represses the multiplicity of female sexuality. Thus, patriarchy is the social manifestation of masculine libidinal economy and will remain the order of the day until the repressed "feminine feminine" is set free. Women can unshackle this potentiality, however, through lesbian and autoerotic practice. As women explore the multifaceted terrain of the female body, they will learn to think thoughts, speak words, and do deeds powerful enough to displace the phallus.

Third, in their efforts to be themselves, women can mime the mimes men have imposed on women. Women should take men's images of women and reflect them back to men in magnified proportions. Through miming, women can "*undo* the effects of phallocentric discourse simply by *overdoing* them."[36] For example, if men view women as sex objects, fetishizing women's breasts in particular, then women should pump up their breasts as big as possible and walk into church on Sunday, their breasts fully exposed in all their naked glory, as if to say, "Here, boys; we know what is on your minds. So look. See if we care." To be sure, conceded Irigaray, mimicking is not without its perils. The distinction between mimicking the patriarchal definition of woman in order to subvert it and merely fulfilling this definition is not clear. In her attempts to overdo this definition, woman may be drawn back into it, however. Nevertheless, despite this risk, no woman should lose the opportunity to break out of the male imaginary and into a female one.

Throughout Irigaray's work, there is a tension between her conviction that we must finally end the process of labeling and categorizing and her competing conviction that we cannot help but engage in this process.[37] Because Irigaray dared to express both of these convictions, sometimes in the same breath, her critics describe her as self-contradictory. Rather than feeling embarrassed by the ambiguities and ambivalences in her writing, however, she took increasing pleasure in them. For Irigaray, self-contradiction is a form of rebellion against the logical consistency required by phallocentrism. "'She' is indefinitely other in herself. This is doubtless why she is said to be whimsical, incomprehensible, agitated, capricious . . . not to mention her language, in which 'she' sets off in all directions leaving 'him' unable to discern the coherence of any meaning. Hers are contradictory words, somewhat mad from the standpoint of reason, inaudible for whoever listens to them with ready-made grids, with a fully elaborated code in hand."[38] Refusing to be pinned down even by her own theory, Irigaray vowed to liberate her life from the phallocentric concepts that would squeeze its multiple meanings—its exciting differences—into boring sameness.

Julia Kristeva

Of all the postmodern feminists, Julia Kristeva is the most controversial. She explicitly rejected "feminism" as it is defined by French theorists and activists. However, just because Kristeva disavowed feminism as it is understood in France does not mean that she necessarily opposed the goals and strategies of feminism as it is understood in the United States. For this reason, and also because Kristeva's "rejection of feminism can teach us some important lessons about feminism,"[39] it is important to consider Kristeva's ideas in addition to those of Cixous and Irigaray.

Using Lacan's psychoanalytic framework, Kristeva drew a contrast between the "semiotic," or pre-Oedipal, stage and the "symbolic," or post-Oedipal, stage.[40] For Kristeva, the maternal "semiotic" is not strictly opposed to the symbolic order but is a part of the symbolic order. It exists inside as well as outside the symbolic order. According to Kristeva, the symbolic order, which is the order of signification, or the social realm, is composed of two elements: the semiotic element that seeps in from the "territory" of the pre-Oedipal and the symbolic element that exists only in the symbolic order. The symbolic element is that aspect of meaning-making that permits us to make rational arguments; it produces linear, rational, objective, and very grammatical writing. The symbolic is the element of stasis within the Symbolic order.

In contrast to the symbolic element, the semiotic element is the aspect of meaning-making that permits us to express feelings. It is "the drives as they make their way into signification";[41] it produces the rule-breaking writing: its syntax and grammar. The semiotic is also the element of rejection—what Kristeva termed the "abject"—within the symbolic order. Kristeva believed that a liberated person is someone able to "play" between the maternal, semiotic, pre-Oedipal realm and the patriarchal Oedipal realm on the one hand and the dialectic between the semiotic and symbolic aspects of meaning-making *inside* the symbolic order on the other hand.[42] In other words, she suggested that the liberated person is able to move freely between the "feminine" and the "masculine," chaos and order, revolution and the status quo.

Unlike Cixous and Irigaray, Kristeva resisted identification of the "feminine" with biological women and the "masculine" with biological men. She maintained that when the child enters the symbolic order, he or she may identify with either the mother or the father. Depending on the "choice" the child makes, the child will be more or less "feminine" or "masculine." Thus, boys can exist and write in a "feminine" mode, and girls can exist and write in a "masculine" mode. Perhaps most interesting and controversial is Kristeva's claim that the "feminine" writings of men have more revolutionary potential than those of women. Culture is more upset when a man speaks like a woman than when a woman speaks like a man. In other words, as Kelly Oliver put it, Kristeva thought that "whereas in males an identification with the maternal semiotic is revolutionary because it breaks with traditional conceptions of sexual difference, for females an identification with the maternal does not break traditional conceptions of sexual difference."[43]

Kristeva's main emphasis is on difference in general rather than sexual difference in particular. Rejecting traditional accounts of two binary sexes, of two *opposed gender identities*, Kristeva admitted it is nonetheless true that there are male and female *sexual differences*. Like psychoanalytic feminists Dinnerstein and Chodorow, Kristeva located the beginnings of sexual difference in the child's relation to the mother; but in her version of this relationship, a child's sexual identity is specifically formed through a struggle to separate from the mother's body. The male does this not by rejecting his mother's body but by "abjecting" it, reconceiving it as an object that represents everything that is disgusting about being a human being (excrement, blood, mucous).[44] In contrast, the more the female identifies with her mother's body, the more trouble she has rejecting or abjecting it. To the degree that the rejected or abjected maternal body is associated with women per se, women are grouped with society's "misfits"—the Jews, Gypsies, homosexuals, deformed, diseased—an identification that would, contrary to what Kristeva has said elsewhere, seem to fit women, far more than men, for revolution.

Just because Kristeva conceded that men and women have different sexual identities does not mean she believed these identities are manifested in exactly the same way by each "female" or "male." For example, Kristeva maintained that the concept "woman" makes no sense at the ontological level but only at the political level: "The belief that 'one is a woman' is almost as absurd and obscurantist as the belief that 'one is a man.' I say 'almost' because there are still many goals which women can achieve: freedom of abortion and contraception, daycare centers for children, equality on the job, etc. Therefore, we must use 'we are women' as an advertisement or slogan for our demands. On a deeper level, however, a woman cannot 'be'; it is something which does not even belong in the order of being."[45] Acknowledging that past feminists successfully invoked the term *woman* to improve the lot of many women, Kristeva nonetheless stressed that current feminists should invoke the term more judiciously lest the "politics of liberation" become the "politics of exclusion and counterpower."[46] Oliver explained: "Feminists in the United States are struggling with this very issue. The feminist movement has had to realize that it is a white middle class movement that has worked to exclude women whose interests and needs are somehow different. Paradoxically as soon as feminism defines 'woman' it excludes all sorts of women."[47] Thus, Kristeva ultimately endorsed only those aspects of the feminist movement that break down or render ambiguous identity, especially sexual identity.

Critiques of Postmodern Feminism

Some critics reject postmodern feminism as "feminism for academicians." As they see it, postmodern feminists are deliberately opaque, viewing clarity as one of the seven deadly sins of the phallogocentric order. These critics tend to dismiss postmodern feminists as contemporary Epicureans who withdraw from real revolutionary struggle—marches, campaigns, boycotts, protests—into a garden of intellectual delights. Surrounded by friends, by people who share their philosophical perspective, postmodern feminists "use language and ideas in such a specific way that no one else can understand what they are doing."[48] Rarely do they leave their blissful surroundings, and as time passes their sayings become increasingly irrelevant to the majority of women.

Other critics are not particularly disturbed by the opacity of postmodern feminist texts. Instead, they fault postmodern feminists for taking the "wrong" side not only in the so-called sameness-difference debate—are women essentially the same as men or fundamentally different from men?—but also in the so-called antiessentialism-essentialism debate—is woman's "nature" "plastic" (mutable, ever changing, always becoming something different, in Heraclitean flux) or "fixed" (immutable, unchangeable, always remaining the same, in Parmidean status)? Is *gender* ("femininity") an organic outgrowth of sex ("femaleness"), an arbitrary cultural imposition on sex or, more radically, a determinant of sex?

In an article entitled "Sexual Difference and the Problem of Essentialism," Elizabeth Grosz noted that in the past, so-called egalitarian feminists such as Simone de Beauvoir, Betty Friedan, Eva Figes, Kate Millett, Shulamith Firestone, and Germaine Greer promulgated the view that there is nothing distinctive about woman's nature. Women's subordinate status is the result not of biological nature but of cultural construction and can, therefore, be changed. In other words, stressed Grosz, egalitarian feminists maintained "that the 'raw materials' of socialization are fundamentally the same for both sexes: each has analogous biological or natural potential, which is unequally developed because the social roles imposed on the two sexes are unequal. If social roles could be readjusted or radically restructured, if the two sexes could be resocialized, they could be rendered equal. The differences between the sexes would be no more significant than the differences between the individuals."[49] Women can be "unfeminine"; men can be "unmasculine."

In their attempts to delink sex and gender, observed Grosz, egalitarian feminists made several mistakes. First, egalitarian feminists took "male achievements, values and standards as the norms to which women should aspire."[50] But why, in the name of equality, did they urge "women" to become "men" and not "men" to become "women"? Did they not value women's ways as much as men's? Second, they minimized women's specific needs and interests, including those that arise from "women's corporeality and sexuality."[51] In erasing women's bodies—women's reproductive and sexual identities—said Grosz, egalitarian feminists also erased the visible signs of women's oppression as women and therefore women's concrete rallying points for justice between the sexes.

As a result, women's struggle for gender justice became a mere moment in the struggle for human justice, and feminism receded into the bowels of humanism.

Sketching the contrast between egalitarian feminists on the one hand and so-called difference feminists on the other, Grosz implied that the latter feminists sought to prevent feminism's devolution into humanism and woman's (re)absorption into man. Difference feminists, especially postmodern feminists, celebrated women's bodies, reproductive rhythms, and sexual organs. Women and men are different and women have no interest in forsaking their differences, they said. Women do not want the right to be the *same* as men. Rather, women want the right to be as *free* as men—to construct themselves apart from, not in opposition to, men; to be opposite of men yet to be themselves.[52] Thus, Grosz claimed that as she understood the postmodern feminist idea of difference, it is a notion that among other things

> resists the homogenization of separate political struggles—insofar as it implies not only women's differences from men, and from each other; but also women's differences from other oppressed groups. It is not at all clear that, for example, struggles against racism will necessarily be politically allied with women's struggles or, conversely, that feminism will overcome forms of racist domination. This, of course, does not preclude the existence of common interests shared by various oppressed groups, and thus the possibility of alliances over specific issues; it simply means that these alliances have no prior necessity.[53]

Woman is not to be subsumed into man or vice versa, and feminism is not to be viewed as humanism dressed in a skirt.

Grosz's interpretation of the postmodern feminist understanding of difference is far more sympathetic than that of other readers. Whereas Grosz argued that difference feminists see difference "not as difference from a pre-given norm but as pure difference, difference itself, difference with no identity,"[54] critics of postmodern feminism claim that if the truth be told, difference feminists use the term *difference* in an "essentialist" way. To say that difference feminists are "essentialists," however, is to say that unlike more "enlightened" or "politically correct" feminists, difference feminists are incapable of "carefully holding apart the poles of sex and gender,"[55] of femaleness and femininity.

Rejecting the label of "essentialist," most postmodern feminists maintain that in their writings they *do* attempt to distinguish between "(1) women as biological and social entities and (2) the 'female,' 'feminine' or 'other,' where 'female' stands metaphorically for the genuinely other in a relation of difference (as in the system consciousness/unconsciousness) rather than opposition."[56] In other words, postmodern feminists insist that they describe woman's nature "not as some sort of 'thing-in-itself' to which all the 'sensible properties' of 'woman's nature' actually cling but as the 'totality of the properties, constituent elements,'"[57] and so on without which it would be impossible consistently and coherently to refer to 'woman's nature' at all.

Explaining that difference feminists are "nominalists" as opposed to "realists," Teresa de Lauretis stated that as the majority of difference feminists see it,

> the "essence" of woman is more like the essence of the triangle than the essence of the thing-in-itself: it is the specific properties of (e.g., a female-sexed body), qualities (a disposition to nurturance, a certain relation to the body, etc.), or necessary attributes (e.g., the experience of femaleness, of living in the world as female) that women have developed or have been bound to historically, in their differently patriarchal sociocultural contexts, which makes them women, and not men. One may prefer one triangle, one definition of women and/or feminism, to another and, within her particular conditions and possibilities of existence, struggle to define the triangle's existence, struggle to define the triangle she wants or wants to be—feminists do want differently.[58]

Just as we have no access to a triangle as it exists in itself but only to the enormous variety of particular triangles we can conceive of, we have no access to woman as she exists in herself. Yet in the same way we can recognize a triangle, we know a woman when we see one.

De Lauretis stressed that like feminist realism/essentialism, feminist nominalism/postmodernism, too, is problematic. Whereas the former implies that all women must be the same, the latter suggests that women have nothing in common and therefore no basis for collaborative political action. In de Lauretis's estimation, however, there is a way to avoid both the pitfalls of realism and the pitfalls of nominalism, a way suggested in the notion of "woman as position."[59] In becoming feminists, said de Lauretis, women assume a position, a point of view or perspective termed "gender," from which "to interpret or (re)construct values and meanings."[60] Proceeding from their specific sociohistorical locations—their concrete interests—feminist women *consciously* use the category of gender to forge political alliances aimed at increasing each other's freedom and well-being at particular places and times. For de Lauretis, the (female) sex/(feminine) gender relationship is such that gender is neither an unproblematic procession from biologically determined sex nor an imaginary construct that is purely arbitrary. Rather, gender is the "product and process of a number of social technologies" that "create a matrix of differences and cross any number of languages."[61] Gender points to a conception of women as neither already unified nor inseparably divided but as multiple and therefore *capable* of unifying and dividing at will. Furthermore, said de Lauretis, if postmodern feminists wish to remain "feminist," they must in some way privilege the category of gender so that women have some ground to stand on when they come together to improve their "estate."[62] Political action requires a platform—some sort of launching pad.

Conclusion

Despite all the criticisms raised against postmodern feminism, it remains one of the most exciting developments in contemporary feminist thought. Although postmodern feminists have distinctively different agendas, they share certain tendencies, such as an appreciation for the possibilities latent in nothingness, absence, the marginal, the peripheral, the repressed. Moreover, they share a common desire to think nonbinary, nonoppositional thoughts, the kind that may have existed before Adam was given the power to name the animals, to determine the beginnings and ends of things: "And out of the ground the Lord God formed every beast of the field, and every fowl of the air; and brought them unto Adam to see what he would call them—and whatsoever Adam called every living creature, that was the name thereof."[63] We can imagine this original state prior to Adam's intrusion either as a Taoist undifferentiated "uncarved block,"[64] as a Lacanian imaginary, as a Kristevian abject, or as any number of disordered conditions—the point being that there was, in the beginning, *no word* but only myriad voices waiting for time and space to interpret their meaning.

Whether women can, by breaking the silence, by speaking and writing, help overcome binary opposition, phallocentrism, and logocentrism, is not certain. What is certain, however, is that the time has come for a new conceptual order. Bent upon achieving unity, we human beings have excluded, ostracized, and alienated so-called abnormal, deviant, and marginal people. As a result of this policy of exclusion, the human community has been impoverished. It seems, then, that men as well as women have much to gain by joining a variety of postmodern feminists in their celebration of multiplicity. Yet as Christine di Stefano emphasized, women may also have something to lose in their embrace of the enriching differences of race, class, sexual preference, ethnicity, culture, age, religion, and so on: They may lose themselves.[65] For the time being, it might be wise for women to heed di Stefano's caution: For women, whatever their differences,

> gender is basic in ways that we have yet to fully understand, . . . it functions as "a difference that makes a difference," even as it can no longer claim the legitimating mantle of *the* difference. The figure of the shrinking woman may

perhaps be best appreciated and utilized as an aporia within contemporary theory: as a recurring paradox, question, dead end, or blind spot to which we must repeatedly return, because to ignore her altogether is to risk forgetting and thereby losing what is left of her.[66]

Women exist *as* women; at least I know I exist, and "ain't I a woman?"

■

CHAPTER SEVEN

Multicultural and Global Feminism

MULTICULTURAL AND GLOBAL FEMINISTS share with postmodern feminists a view of the self as fragmented. However, for multicultural and global feminists, the roots of this fragmentation are primarily cultural, racial, and ethnic rather than sexual, psychological, and literary. There are many similarities between multicultural and global feminism. Both challenge "female essentialism," the view that the idea of "woman" exists as some sort of Platonic form each and every flesh-and-blood woman somehow fits; and both disavow "female chauvinism," the tendency of some women, privileged on account of their race or class, for example, to presume to speak on behalf of all women.

Despite the important similarities that link multicultural and global feminists, there are nonetheless some major differences that distinguish them. Multicultural feminism is based on the insight that even in one nation—the United States of America, for instance—all women are not created or constructed equal. Depending on her race and class but also on her sexual preference, age, religion, education attainment, occupation, marital status, health condition, and so on, each and every woman in the United States will experience her oppression as an American woman differently. Adding to the insights of multicultural feminists, global feminists further stress that depending on whether a woman is a citizen of a First World or a Third World nation, an advanced industrial or a developing nation, a nation that is colonialist or colonized, she will experience oppression differently.

Multicultural Feminism: An Overview

Because my experiences are those of an American woman, in this chapter I write about multicultural feminism in the United States. Moreover, I

212

stress issues of race and class not because I think race and class are always of more concern to American women than sexual preference and age, for example, but because issues of race and class have a particularly long history in the United States. Furthermore, many multicultural feminists have themselves focused on these issues. In a similar vein I focus on the differences between black and white women for largely pragmatic reasons. It is not that I am totally unaware of or disinterested in the issues confronting Asian American women, Native American women, Hispanic women, lesbian women, old women, women from religious traditions other than Christianity, or disabled women. It is simply that I am unable effectively to communicate the thoughts of the large number of different kinds of women who have themselves written about their unique experiences of oppression. I apologize to those women whose voices are not explicitly heard in these pages and ask them, as well as those whose voices are heard here, to read my reflections on multicultural feminism simply as the attempt of one woman to understand how she both is and is not like other women.

The Roots of Multicultural Feminism
in the United States

In some ways multicultural *feminist* thought is related to multicultural thought, an ideology that supports diversity and is currently highly popular in the United States. However, Americans have not always celebrated diversity. Unity was the goal of earlier generations, who maintained that the United States represented the idea of *e pluribus unum*, "out of many, one." According to historian Arthur M. Schlesinger Jr., early immigrants to the United States wanted to become a new people. He specifically noted the eighteenth-century French immigrant J. Hector St. John de Crèvecoeur, who spoke eloquently about trading in his old identity for a new one:

> Crèvecoeur's conception was of a brand new nationality created by individuals who, in repudiating their homelands and joining to make new lives, melted away ancient ethnic differences. Most of those intrepid Europeans who had torn up their roots to brave the wild Atlantic and attain America wanted to forget a horrid past and to embrace a hopeful future. They *expected* to become Americans. Their goals were escape, deliverance, assimilation. They saw America as a transforming nation, banishing old loyalties and forging a new national identity based on common political ideals.[1]

During the nineteenth century and for the first half of the twentieth century, the trend toward "escape, deliverance, assimilation" continued. Indeed, until the end of World War II, the majority of immigrants to the

United States willingly jumped into America's so-called melting pot, first described by Israel Zangwill in a 1909 play:

> There she lies, the great melting pot—listen! Can't you hear the roaring and the bubbling? There gapes her mouth—The harbor where a thousand feeders come from the ends of the world to pour in their human freight. Ah, what a stirring and a seething! Celt and Latin, Slav and Teuton, Greek and Syrian,—black and yellow—. . . East and West, North and South, the palm and the pine, the pole and the equator, the crescent and the cross—how the Great Alchemist melts and fuses them with his purging flame! Here shall they all unite to build the Republic of man and the Kingdom of God. . . . Peace, peace, to all you unborn millions, fated to fill this giant continent.[2]

For a variety of reasons, most of them having to do with how "the Great Alchemist" seemed to be cooking a homogeneous, white cream soup rather than a heterogeneous gumbo or minestrone, the old many-united-into-one gospel gave way to a new one-divided-into-many gospel by the second half of the twentieth century. Schlesinger noted this new gospel condemned Crèvecoeur's "vision of individuals of all nations melted into a new race in favor of an opposite vision: a nation of groups, differentiated in their ancestries, invisible in their diverse identities."[3] Assimilation gave way to ethnicity, and integration deferred to separatism as the "salad bowl" or "quilt" metaphor for the United States displaced the old melting-pot metaphor.[4] Multiculturalism had been born.

Usually defined as a "social-intellectual movement that promotes the value of diversity as a core principle and insists that all cultural groups be treated with respect and as equals,"[5] multiculturalism met with much criticism during the late 1980s and throughout the 1990s. Of all the arguments raised against multiculturalism, those focusing on its tendency to undermine social solidarity were the strongest. For example, Joseph Raz, himself a supporter of multiculturalism, conceded to his critics: "Without a deep feeling of solidarity, a political society will disintegrate into quarreling factions. Solidarity is required if people are to feel concerned about each other's fortunes and to be willing to make sacrifices for other people. Without such willingness the possibility of a peaceful political society disappears."[6] Critics of multiculturalism insisted labels such as *African American, Asian American, Hispanic American,* and *Native American* were perniciously divisive. These critics longed for a homogeneous America and "American Americans."

In support of multiculturalism, its defenders noted that all too often "mainstream" Americans presume the "all-American kid" is a baseball-playing, apple-pie-eating, blue-eyed, blond-haired, very white kid. In reaction to this sketch of the typical American, Americans who do not look "all-American" but who nonetheless regard themselves as true Americans emphasize or celebrate their native roots as essential to their *unique* way of looking "American." They assert, "We should learn to think of our [society] as consisting not of a majority and minorities but of a plurality of cultural groups."[7] We do not all have to look, act, speak, and think alike to be American. What we need instead is to cultivate mutual toleration, respect, and knowledge of each other's cultures and to make sure we *all* possess the skills and rights necessary to compete in the economic market and the political arena.[8]

Multicultural feminists applaud multicultural thinkers' celebration of difference, lamenting that traditional feminist theorists often failed to distinguish between the condition of white, middle-class, heterosexual, Christian women in advanced and affluent Western industrialized countries and the very different conditions of other women with varying backgrounds. In *Inessential Woman: Problems of Exclusion in Feminist Thought*, Elizabeth Spelman sought to explain the reasons for this puzzling failure. In her estimation, traditional feminist theorists went wrong because they thought they could overcome women's oppression simply by maintaining not only women's *sameness* to men but also women's *sameness* to each other. They reasoned, said Spelman, that if all people are the same, then all people are equal. No one is anyone else's "superior" or "inferior." Unfortunately, continued Spelman, traditional feminist theorists did not realize that it is possible to oppress people by denying human difference as well as by denying human sameness.[9] Referring to women's oppression in particular, she explained her point about difference and sameness as follows:

> The assertion of differences among women can operate oppressively if one marks the differences and then suggests that one of the groups so differentiated is more important or more human or in some sense better than the other. But on the other hand, to stress the unity of women is no guarantee against hierarchical ranking, if what one says is true or characteristic of some as a class is only true or characteristic of some women: for then women who cannot be so characterized are in effect not counted as women. When Stanton said that women should get the vote before Africans, Chinese, Germans, and Irish, she obviously was relying on a concept of "woman" that blinded her to the "womanness" of many women.[10]

Spelman urged contemporary feminist theorists to resist the impulse to gloss over women's differences, as if there exists some sort of "woman" into whom all of women's autobiographical differences flow and dissolve. In particular, she pleaded with them not to make the mistake historian Kenneth Stampp made when he asserted "that innately Negroes are, after all, only white men with black skins, nothing more, nothing else."[11] Why, asked Spelman, is it that *Negroes* are only white men with black skins, nothing more, nothing else? Why is it not instead that *Caucasians* are only black men with white skins, nothing more, nothing else? If a white man can imagine himself protesting his reduction to a black man with white skin, why does he have trouble imagining a black man protesting his reduction to a white man with black skin? Could it be that whites still think "white" is definitely the best way to be, that is, that white people are somehow the gold standard for all people? Noting there are many well-intentioned "Stampps" within the ranks of traditional feminist theorists, Spelman observed: "If, like Stampp, I believe that the woman in every woman is a woman just like me, and if I also assume that there is no difference between being white and being a woman, then seeing another woman 'as a woman' will involve seeing her as fundamentally like the woman I am. In other words, the womanness underneath the Black woman's skin is a white woman's, and deep down inside the Latino woman is an Anglo woman waiting to burst through a cultural shroud."[12] No wonder, said Spelman, that so many women of color reject traditional feminist thought. A valid feminist theory must take the differences among women seriously; it cannot claim all women are "just like me."

Black Women and Feminism:
The Interlocking Systems of Gender, Race, and Class

Although a wide variety of feminists in the United States expressed dissatisfaction with "white" feminism, black feminists were among the first to voice their grievances systematically and extensively. To be sure, the concerns that black feminists, including African American feminists, raised about "white" feminism were not *identical* to those raised by Hispanic American, Asian American, and Native American feminists, for example. Nevertheless, they resonated well enough with the concerns of these and other U.S. minority women (for example, lesbians and disabled women) to constitute a major challenge to "white" feminism. Black feminists told white feminists that women of color and other minority women see the world differently than do white women and other privileged women and that unless "white" feminism stopped being "white," its message would be meaningless to women of color and other minority women.

Among the central claims of black feminists is the inseparability of the structures and systems of gender, race, and culture. Most black feminists deny it is possible for women to focus exclusively on their oppression *as women*. On the contrary, each woman, or each relatively distinct group of women, needs to understand how everything about her—the color of her skin, the amount of money in her purse, the condition of her body, the sex of the person(s) with whom she is intimate, the date on her birth certificate—provides part of the explanation for her subordinate status. As Spelman commented: "It is not as if there is a goddess somewhere who made lots of little identical 'woman' units and then, in order to spruce up the world a bit for herself, decided to put some of the units in black bodies, some in white bodies, some in the bodies of kitchen maids in seventeenth-century France some in the bodies of English, Israeli, and Indian prime ministers."[13] On the contrary, implied Spelman. The "goddess" made *millions* of women—a far more demanding and creative process.

When black feminists tell white feminists they need to understand more fully the intersection of racism, sexism, classism in the lives of black women, not all white feminists respond appropriately to U.S. black women's "multiple jeopardy."[14] Some white feminists react in the nineteenth-century style of Elizabeth Cady Stanton, who, we will recall, insisted that the fight against sexism must take priority over the fight against all other isms, including the very ugly racism and classism. These white feminists accuse black feminists of too easily forgiving the sexist sins of black men, of feeling sorry for their most immediate and intimate oppressors. Other white feminists react in an overly apologetic way, vowing to fight against racism (and to a lesser degree classism) before mounting an attack on sexism. They beg black women to forgive them for their racist (and classist) sins.

Distressed and dismayed by the apparent inability of many white feminists to *understand* what black feminists actually mean by expressions such as "multiple jeopardy" and "interlocking systems of oppression," bell hooks claimed in no uncertain terms that racism, sexism, and classism are not separable in fact, even if they are separable in theory. No one of these forms of oppression can be eliminated prior to the elimination of any other.[15] Oppression is a many-headed beast capable of regenerating any one of the heads temporarily severed from its bloated body. The *whole body* of the beast is the appropriate target for those who wish to end its reign of terror. In an equally direct manner, Audre Lorde noted that "as a forty-nine-year-old Black lesbian feminist socialist, mother of two, including one boy, and a member of an interracial couple," she understood the concept of multiple jeopardy all too well, since she usually found herself a member of some group "defined as other, deviant, inferior, or just plain wrong."[16] The way to overcome this kind of marginality, said Lorde, is not "to pluck out some one aspect of [oneself] and present this as [a] meaningful whole,"[17] as if one could solve all of one's problems simply by fighting racism *or* sexism *or* classism *or* homophobia *or* ableism (Lorde experienced even more alienation subsequent to a mastectomy).[18] Rather, the way to overcome one's otherness is to "integrate all the parts of who I am, openly, allowing power from particular sources of my living to flow back and forth freely through all my different selves, without the restrictions of externally imposed definition."[19] Lorde asserted she fights indiscriminately against the forces of oppression, including "that piece of the oppressor"[20] within herself. Her one and only priority is to create a society in which everyone is truly equal and where "different" does not mean "inferior" but instead "unique."

Furthering the analyses of hooks and Lorde, Patricia Hill Collins argued that in the United States black women's oppression is systematized and structured along three interdependent dimensions. First, the *economic* dimension of black women's oppression relegates black women to "ghettoization in service occupations."[21] Second, the *political* dimension of black women's oppression denies black women the rights and privileges routinely extended to all white men and many white women, including the very important right to an equal education.[22] Third, the *ideological* dimension of black women's oppression imposes a freedom-restricting set of "controlling images" on black women, serving to justify as well as explain white men's and (to a lesser extent) white women's treatment of black women. Commented Collins: "From the mammies, Jezebels, and breeder women of slavery to the smiling Aunt Jemimas on pancake mix boxes, ubiquitous Black prostitutes, and ever-present welfare mothers of contemporary popular culture, the nexus of negative stereotypical images applied to African-American women has been fundamental to Black women's oppression."[23] Collins theorized the ideological dimension was more powerful in maintaining black women's oppression than either the economic or political dimension. She stated that "race, class, and gender oppression could not continue without powerful ideological justification for their existence"[24] and stressed that black feminists must work to free African American women from the "mammy," "matriarch," welfare recipient, and "hot momma" stereotypes. Until blacks as well as whites stop thinking in stereotypical terms about black women, black women will not be free to be themselves.

Although black feminists often focus on economic and political issues, contrary to some misconceptions they also address many sexual issues. To be sure, black feminists have been loathe to make a "public issue" of sexism in the black community for fear of feeding some whites' misperception that black men are more sexually voracious and violent than white men or, the related view, that black women, like their "menfolk," have enormous sexual appetites.[25] Nevertheless, many black feminists have decided to risk such misperceptions. Among the most eloquent of them has been hooks.

Noting the extent to which black men have used disturbing gendered metaphors to describe the nature of blacks' struggle for freedom, hooks explained:

> The discourse of black resistance almost always equated freedom with manhood, the economic and material domination of black men with castration,

emasculation. Accepting these sexual metaphors forged a bond between oppressed black men and their male oppressors. They shared the patriarchal belief that revolutionary struggle was really about the erect phallus, the ability of men to establish political dominance that could correspond to sexual dominance. . . . Many of us have never forgotten that moment in *Soul on Ice* when Eldridge Cleaver, writing about the need to "redeem my conquered manhood," described raping black women as practice for the eventual rape of white women. Remember that readers were not shocked or horrified by this glamorization of rape as a weapon of terrorism men might use to express rage about other forms of domination, about their struggle for power with other men. Given the sexist context of the culture, it made sense.[26]

But, continued hooks, that black men have suffered does not negate that black women have also suffered, not only at the hands of their white oppressors but also at the hands of black men. This latter suffering, no less than the former, must be addressed, in hooks's estimation. In other words, the black community must confront its own sexism, and black women must challenge black as well as white pornographers, sexual harassers, and rapists, for example, by holding them accountable for their role in oppressing women, particularly black women.

Although white and black feminists define pornography differently, they agree it is degrading when it represents depersonalized sexual exchanges devoid or nearly devoid of mutual respect, that is, when it describes or depicts sexual exchanges in which the desires and experiences of at least one participant are not regarded by the other participant(s) as having a validity and importance equal to his/her/their own. Although some black feminists dismiss the radical-cultural feminist antipornography campaign as an instance of misplaced "white" outrage—a spewing of venom that only white, middle-class, "spoiled" women who have adequate food, shelter, clothing, education, and jobs can afford—other black feminists regard pornography as a relevant and significant issue. For example, Tracey Gardner expressed the view that more black women would take pornography seriously if they realized just how bad it is.[27] She claimed that many black women, like many white women, *think* they know what pornography is. They may have seen copies of *Playboy* or *Jiveboy*; they may have attended an X-rated movie; they may have heard about urban "combat zones" or even visited them. But it is unlikely that these same women have also seen violent porn (in which women are tortured) or have spent time cruising New York City's Forty-Second Street or its equivalent. Pornography is not so much about cute *Playboy* bunnies as it is about depicting women as raw meat or a cluster of dismembered body parts.

Over and beyond sexist pornography, there exists a whole genre of racist pornography. Unlike those feminists who assume pornography primarily affects white women, Collins argued that "the treatment of Black women's bodies in nineteenth-century Europe and the United States may be the foundation upon which contemporary pornography as the representation of women's objectification, domination, and control is based."[28] She noted that in antebellum America, at least in the South, men did not need pornographic representations because they "could become voyeurs of black women on the auction block."[29] Collins described the objectification of the black female body in the person of Sarah Bartmann, the so-called Hottentot Venus. Bartmann, an African woman, was often displayed at fashionable Parisian parties as a sexual curiosity. Wealthy Europeans gladly paid royal sums to view her genitalia and buttocks, which remain on display in Paris to this day. In other words, stressed Collins, many white men (and also white women) paid to see a live pornographic show in which the sexuality of Bartmann was represented as *the* sexuality of all African women (and men): a physical, animal-like sexuality, supposedly different from the sexuality of white men and women. No wonder, then, when black women appear in pornographic magazines targeted for white men, they are frequently portrayed as animals (usually cats such as tigers, leopards, and cheetahs) being chained or caged by the "great white hunter."

Even worse than the kind of racist pornography white men use, said writer Alice Walker, is the kind of racist pornography black men use. Sometimes black men's racist pornography shows a black man getting a white woman to perform a sexual act no white man would dare ask her to perform. Here the racist message is that when black men get power, they intend to have "their way" with white women. At other times black men's racist pornography depicts even more hurtful scenes: for example, one showing a black man defecating or urinating on a black woman. Here the racist message is that black men do not take pride in anything or anyone black. In her moving essay "Coming Apart," Walker described a black man's feelings as he finally comes to terms with his use of racist pornography:

> What he has refused to see . . . is that where white women are depicted in pornography as "objects," black women are depicted as animals. Where white women are at least depicted as human bodies if not beings, black women are depicted as shit. He begins to feel sick. For he realizes that he has bought some if not all the advertisements about women, black and white. And further, inevitably, he has bought the advertisements about himself. In pornography the black man is portrayed as being capable of fucking anything . . . even a piece of shit. He is defined solely by the size, readiness and unselectivity of his cock.[30]

In degrading women, but particularly his own women, the black man degrades himself. He also helps set the stage for black women's sexual harassment.

Like white women, black women are not strangers to sexual harassment, defined as unwanted sexual attention of a nondiscriminatory or discriminatory sort. Nondiscriminatory sexual harassment occurs when the harasser has no official control over the women he harasses. Discriminatory sexual harassment occurs when the harasser is in a position of authority or power allowing him to make better or worse the educational or occupational situation of the women he harasses.

When it comes to discriminatory sexual harassment, the focus of this analysis, black women are leaders in the efforts to stop its incursions into the workplace and into academia. As in pornography, power plays directed against black women are likely to have racist as well as sexist overtones. Black women, especially poor black women, are particularly vulnerable to sexual harassment because of their pressing need for education and employment. When white men harass black women, they use sex not only to control black women as *women* but also to demean them as *black* women (racism + sexism) or as *poor* black women (classism + racism + sexism). Sexual harassers tend to take advantage of those whom they perceive as most vulnerable; and whether "white" America cares to face it or not, black women epitomize as well as enflesh the vulnerability of their people's slave past.[31]

Black men, too, sexually harass women.[32] However, the sexual harassment of a black woman by a black man is qualitatively different from the sexual harassment of a black woman by a white man; it is also qualitatively different from the sexual harassment of a white woman by a black man.[33] When a white woman is sexually harassed by a black supervisor or employer, "being white" will probably work to her advantage in the same way "being white" works to a white woman's advantage when she is raped by a black man. The "system" will be more inclined to believe her story; "white" society assumes black men *want* white women as "trophies." In contrast, when a black woman is sexually harassed by a powerful white man, "being black" will probably not work to her advantage, although it should, given that in the past white slave owners usually got their "way" with their black female slaves. The rewards for pleasing the master and the punishments for displeasing the master were such that black female slaves quickly learned to say yes to their masters' sexual advances. Nevertheless, even though the legacy of slavery continues to distort sexual relations between blacks and whites, so powerful is the stereotype of the black "hot mamma" that judges and juries are inclined to believe that the guilty party is the black female employee, not her white male employer. She is the supposed temptress who threw her black body at him to give him a taste of what his uptight, lily-white wife could never give him. Similarly, when black female employees charge black male employers with sexually inappropriate behavior, courts are far more likely to see an instance of sexual attraction gone sour than an instance of genuine sexual harassment. In this connection, the Anita Hill–Clarence Thomas case is most instructive.

In 1991 Anita Hill, a young black lawyer with an impeccable personal and professional record, alleged Clarence Thomas sexually harassed her when she was under his supervision. At the time Hill made these allegations, Thomas was a candidate for a seat on the Supreme Court. Indeed, one of the reasons Hill gave for the time lag between Thomas's alleged harassment and her coming forward with her complaints was precisely that she could no longer keep silent about her abuse. In her estimation a sexual harasser had no business serving on the U.S. Supreme Court. However reluctant she had previously been to air her story in public because of possible risks to her career, she felt she could not continue to hold her tongue.

Criticism of Hill's decision to go public was particularly strong among blacks. They considered her disloyal to the black community and held her in disdain for jeopardizing the confirmation of the *only* black candidate President George Bush would nominate to the Supreme Court.[34] Moreover, Thomas himself linked Hill's allegations against him with the lynching of black men in the "old days." At his Senate confirmation hearings, he declared, "I will not provide the rope for my own lynching."[35] After hearing Hill's and Thomas's divergent accounts of their relationship, the fourteen white men on the Senate committee in charge of Thomas's confirmation hearings unanimously endorsed his candidacy to the Supreme Court. In the process of doing so, several members of the committee attacked Hill's character. One went so far as to suggest she had fabricated the whole story as part of a *liberal* plot to ruin *conservative* Thomas's chances for Senate confirmation. Reflecting on these attacks, journalist Jack E. Hill commented:

> Black women's complaints about sexist behavior are taken even less seriously than white women's. Held down by racism and the sexism of both black and white males, black females are one of society's most oppressed groups. Yet their attempts to call attention to their plight routinely provoke storms of energy denial of the legitimacy of their complaints. An example: the denunciations that were heaped on Alice Walker for her novel *The Color Purple* and the film that was based on it. Some critics falsely charged that Walker was a lesbian who hated black men because she created a heroine who was savagely mistreated by nearly every black male she encountered.[36]

To make matters even worse for Hill, polls revealed that although *feminists* supported her, 49 percent of American women, black and white, either sided with Thomas or proclaimed the Hill-Thomas "showdown" a draw.[37] In particular, less-advantaged women felt that despite her humble roots, the highly educated and very successful Hill was not really one of them. Anne Rungold, media director for the Democratic Party, stated: "Both working-class women and highly educated women put up with sexual harassment every day. . . . But the perception among working-class women is that a Yale degree just gives you the right to make a federal case out of it. Besides, if you can't get a good-paying job somewhere else, what good is that degree anyway?"[38] In some ways the Hill-Thomas case played out as it did because these two blacks were perceived as "white" and "rich" and therefore as not *really* black.

Like pornography and sexual harassment, rape assumes different forms in black and white women's lives. In her book *Women, Race and Class*, Angela Davis claimed white feminists ranging from Susan Brownmiller to Jean MacKellar to Diana Russell helped resuscitate the "old racist myth of the Black rapist" who yearns to abuse white women sexually.[39] MacKellar, for example, noted that 90 percent of all reported rapes in the United States are committed by black men, even though the FBI's corresponding figure is 47 percent.[40] Similarly, of the twenty-two rape cases Diana Russell described, more than 50 percent involved women who had been raped by men of color, even though only 26 percent of the original ninety-five cases she studied involved men of color.[41] By presenting their statistics in such ways, Davis observed, MacKellar and Russell obscured the real social causes of rape. Since only a small fraction of rapes are ever reported, it could be women are more inclined to report poor or black rapists than rich or white rapists. Although this is conjecture, it is not idle speculation. The law prefers not to catch rich, respected, or powerful men in its snares. Therefore, a woman who is raped by a pillar of the community, especially a white pillar, is likely to leave bad enough alone by not reporting her rapist to the authorities. As a result, there is no way of estimating how many women are raped by "nice" white doctors, lawyers, professors, and businessmen.

Davis was most distressed by what she perceived as the contributions of Brownmiller, MacKellar, and Russell to white society's irrational fears about the "violent black man." She took particular exception to some passages in Brownmiller's influential book on rape, *Against Our Will: Men, Women, and Rape*. She claimed that Brownmiller implied, for example, that the average black man agrees with Eldridge Cleaver's statement that rape is an "insurrectionary act" against "white society." Commented Davis: "It seems as if she [Susan Brownmiller] wants to intentionally conjure up in her readers' imaginations armies of Black men, their penises erect, charging full speed ahead toward the most conveniently placed white woman."[42] Such a view of black men, stressed Davis, is one that feeds the flames of the racist fires continuing to warm the passions of big-oted people.

In the nineteenth century, wrote Davis, thousands of black men were lynched by white men. For several years, these lynchings were justified as necessary to prevent "Negro conspiracies, Negro insurrections, Negro schemes to murder all the white people, Negro plots to burn the town and to commit violence generally."[43] When it became obvious that no such conspiracies, insurrections, schemes, or plots were brewing, another reason was offered to justify white society's lynching of black men: to save white women from black men's sexual assaults. These sexual as-saults were often "trumped up," if not by white women then by white men. Nevertheless, the lynchings continued despite the concerted efforts of black antilynching crusaders such as Ida B. Wells, Mary Church Terrell, and Mary Talbert, all of whom did their best through the 1890s and early 1900s to expose these "justified lynchings" for what they really were—un-justified murders of innocent black men. Not until 1930, when white women, under the leadership of Jessie Daniel Ames, established the Asso-ciation of Southern Women for the Prevention of Lynching, did the tide of lynching reverse itself and abate. These white women refused to "allow those bent upon personal revenge and savagery to mount acts of violence and lawlessness in the name of women."[44] Commending these white women for their convictions and courage, Davis nonetheless expressed regret it took white women so long to respond to the repeated pleas of their black sisters.

Currently, many black women are not certain whether they should press for more stringent rape laws. On the one hand, they are well aware that black men who rape white women (or who are accused of raping white women) are often treated more harshly than white men who rape black women (or white women). Since 1930, of the 455 men who were legally executed in the United States for a rape conviction, 89 percent were black. In a majority of these cases, the rape victim was a white woman. In Florida alone, between 1940 and 1964, six white men who raped white women were executed; in comparison, eighty-four blacks were prosecuted for raping white women and forty-five were executed. And no rapist, white or black, who violated a black woman received the death penalty.[45] In view of such statistics, black women want white femi-nists to work with them to make certain that new rape laws will be en-forced fairly, irrespective of skin color.

On the other hand, black women are also well aware that most rapes are intraracial, not interracial, and that however hard it is for a white woman to "prove" she has been raped by a white man, it is even harder for a black woman to "prove" she has been raped by a black man. Not only is the white community likely to trivialize her complaints, dismissing her rape as just "one of those things *those* people do to each other," but the black community is likely to condemn her as a "traitor," urging her to set her priorities straight.

Focusing on black women's confusion about what to do about rape, Barbara Omolade analyzed the heavily publicized Central Park jogger case. On April 19, 1989, a young white female jogger was brutally assaulted and raped by a group of young black men in New York's Central Park. Both the black and white community were appalled by the attack. Indeed, said Omolade, Mayor Koch spoke of "a whole city filled with distress and pain at the plight of this young girl."[46] Because this was a black-on-white rape, the media predictably turned a "polarized racial lens on the crime,"[47] describing the alleged assailants as "animals" and "their actions in the park a form of wilding."[48] As it turned out, the alleged assailants were seemingly "good" black boys who came from hardworking, churchgoing families and whose guilt was far from certain.

Although black feminists expressed concern that the alleged rapists of the Central Park jogger were being "railroaded," they were still eager to consider the *sexist* as well as *racist* implications of the case, said Omolade. Acknowledging that the law is often unfair to black men, Omolade nonetheless stressed that black men are *victimizers* as well as *victims* and that no one knows this better than black women. She commented:

> The . . . case occurred during a social science blitz about "endangered" Black males being poor, jailed, uneducated, and despised. The Black man then became a heroic and besieged "victim" of white racism whose "endangered status" is used to rationalize and justify his violence. The pain of Black women and children who are "endangered" by these same Black men is ignored.
>
> Although the young Black men of the [Central Park jogger] case are from a community with little economic, political, or social power, and have been found guilty of raping a woman from a *race* and community with all such power, they are also from a *gender* which can rape and abuse women of their race with the same impunity white men use in murdering or judging Black men. What construct other than sexism can be offered to explain Black resistance to condemning all forms of rape irrespective of the victim's color? What other than rejection of the value of the Black female body can explain the Black community's protests and furor about the guilt or innocence of the . . . boys who allegedly raped a white woman, and its lack of concern about the boys who harass and rape Black women every day![49]

Omolade emphasized that sexism within the black community has to be confronted. There comes a time when black women's concerns should be moved from the back burner to the front burner. However serious the concerns of black men are, the concerns of black women are equally serious.

Global Feminism: An Overview

Global feminism differs from multicultural feminism because it focuses on the oppressive results of colonial and nationalist policies and practices, how Big Government and Big Business divide the world into the so-called First World (the realm of the haves) and the so-called Third World (the realm of have-nots). Agreeing with multicultural feminists that the definition of feminism must be broadened to include all the things that oppress women, whether based on race or class or resulting from imperialism or colonialism, global feminists stress "the oppression of women in one part of the world is often affected by what happens in another, and that no woman is free until the conditions of oppression of women are eliminated everywhere."[50] Committed to the task of dispelling misunderstandings and creating alliances between Third World women and First World women, global feminists aim to widen the scope of feminist thought.

Believing that First World women are interested only in sexual issues or in making the case that gender discrimination is the worst form of oppression a woman can experience, many Third World women emphasize they are far more concerned about political and economic issues than sexual issues. They also stress that in their experience their oppression as women is not nearly so bad as their oppression as Third World people. Thus, many Third World women reject the label *feminist*. In its stead, they embrace Alice Walker's term *womanist*. Walker defined a "womanist" as "a Black feminist or woman of color" committed to the "survival and wholeness of entire people, male and female."[51]

In reaction to Third World women's critique of feminism, some First World feminists object that "womanists" do women a disservice by minimizing gender discrimination. However, most First World feminists are highly receptive to Third World women's reservations about feminism. They admit the time has come for feminists to redefine "feminism." In fact, some First World feminists are so eager to make up for their past neglect of Third World women's issues that they insist *only* Third World women's issues are important. First World women should, they claim, simply count their blessings and beg Third World women's forgiveness for their contributions to Third World women's and men's oppression. Not only are First World men guilty of exploiting Third World people, so, too, are First World women.[52]

Other First World feminists believe that it is not necessary for First World women to deny the legitimacy of their own concerns in order to acknowledge their role in oppressing Third World people. They stress that global feminism is not about privileging the concerns of Third World women over those of First World women. Rather, global feminism is about women, from all over the world, coming together as true equals to discuss their commonalities and differences as honestly as possible in a mutual effort to secure what Charlotte Bunch identified as the two long-term goals of global feminism:

1. . . . the right of women to freedom of choice, and the power to control our own lives within and outside of the home. Having control over our lives and our bodies is essential to ensure a sense of dignity and autonomy for every woman.
2. . . . the removal of all forms of inequity and oppression through the creation of a more just social and economic order, nationally and internationally. This means the involvement of women in national liberation struggles, in plans for national development, and in local and global struggles for change.[53]

For global feminists, the personal and the political are one. What goes on in the privacy of one's home, including one's bedroom, affects the ways in which men and women relate in the larger social order. Sexual and reproductive freedom should be of no more or less importance to women than economic and political justice. Socialist feminist Emily Woo Yamaski made this point most forcefully when she stated: "I cannot be an Asian American on Monday, a woman on Tuesday, a lesbian on Wednesday, a worker/student on Thursday, and a political radical on Friday. I am all these things every day."[54]

Over and beyond emphasizing the interconnections among the various kinds of oppression each woman faces in her own life, global feminists stress the links among the various kinds of oppression women in all parts of the world experience. For global feminists, the local is global and the global is local. What an individual woman does in the United States affects the lives of women all over the world; and, correlatively, what women all over the world do affects the life of the woman in the United States. Bunch explained:

To make global feminist consciousness a powerful force in the world demands that we make the local, global and the global, local. Such a movement is not based on international travel and conferences, although these may be useful, but must be centered on a sense of connectedness among women active at the grass roots in various regions. For women in industrialized countries, this connectedness must be based in the authenticity of our struggles at home, in our need to learn from others, and in our efforts to understand the global implications of our actions, not in liberal guilt, condescending charity, or the false imposition of our models on others. Thus, for example, when we fight to have a birth control device banned in the United States because it is unsafe, we must simultaneously demand that it be destroyed rather than dumped on women in the Third World.[55]

Feminist *practice* is a theme global feminists repeatedly announce.

Diversity and Commonality

Although global feminists insist women are interconnected, they caution women that in order to understand what binds them together, women must first understand what separates them. Women cannot work together *as true equals* to resolve issues concerning them unless women first recognize the depths of their differences. According to Audre Lorde, when a feminist walks into a room filled with women from all over the world, she probably does not want to confront her differences from all of them. It is simply too threatening to her notions about "sisterhood" to focus on women's "manyness," so she strains to focus on women's "oneness." Lorde stressed that it is precisely this type of behavior that explains feminists' inability to forge the kind of alliances necessary to create a better world. She stated:

> Advocating the mere tolerance of difference between women is the grossest reformism. It is a total denial of the creative function of difference in our lives. Difference must not be merely tolerated, but seen as a fund of necessary polarities between which our creativity can spark like a dialectic. Only then does the necessity for interdependency become unthreatening. Only within that interdependency of different strengths, acknowledged and equal, can the power to seek new ways of being in the world generate, as well as the courage and sustenance to act where there are no charters.[56]

Just because a feminist wants to work with women very different from her—who may, for example, have suffered oppressions far more harmful to body, mind, and spirit than the ones she suffered—does not mean she should deny who she is. Nor does it mean she should keep her counsel for fear of offending others. On the contrary, to refuse to reveal one's self to others is to assume that others are not capable of coming to terms with one. "Although I think I have what it takes to understand others, I doubt that they share this ability": To think in such a fashion is the height of arrogance in global feminists' view.

"Women's Issues" Versus "Political Issues"

Among the differences global feminists address is the tendency of some women to stress sexual and reproductive issues and other women to stress economic and political issues. In 1975 the United Nations declared the years 1975–1985 the Decade of Women, instructing all its members to give women the same opportunities for advancement in the economic, cultural, religious, political, and judicial fields that men have. Three international women's conferences punctuated the Decade of Women: a beginning conference held in Mexico City (1975); a midpoint conference held in

Copenhagen (1980); and a final, twelve-day conference held in Nairobi, Kenya (1985). More than 2,000 delegates from 140 countries attended the final meeting. In addition, some 13,000 delegates participated in Forum 85, a loosely confederated group of 157 nongovernmental organizations. Although global feminists generally looked forward to each of these conferences, many of them worried that a women's conference sponsored by a "patriarchal" organization like the United Nations was subject to problems. It was bound to serve, as Robin Morgan claimed, not women's interests but Big Brother's interests.[57]

As it turned out, problems between First World women and Third World women did emerge at each of the international women's conferences held between 1975 and 1985. In the estimation of several First World women who attended these meetings, so-called political issues often took center stage, as so-called women's issues were shunted aside. They claimed, for example, that at the Mexico City conference the delegates of communist, Asian, Latin American, and African states were instructed by their respective governments to engage solely in "politics" and to eschew issues related to women's human rights; that at the Copenhagen conference "more heat was generated about 'Zionism,' 'racism,' and 'Western imperialism' than about the basic rights of women and their legally deprived status in over 75 of the 118 countries attending";[58] and that at the Nairobi conference, as well as at Forum 85, "once again, political cliches and ideological harangues, associated with East-West and North-South disputes in the General Assembly of the U.N., dominated proceedings."[59] Referring in particular to the Nairobi conference and Forum 85, critic Eschel Rhoodie observed:

> Even the subject of the right of women to choose when and how many children to have did not make the grade. Yet this issue is one of the most important ones to be addressed by women's organizations and governments in the Third World. It failed to become a central rallying point in Kenya, the venue of the conference, the capital of a country where men's blind and irresponsible resistance to birth control has produced the highest birthrate in the world, creating catastrophic social and economic problems and condemning women to remain in a centuries-old stereotype.[60]

The leader of the U.S. delegation, Maureen Reagan, reportedly summed up the Nairobi conference as "an orgy of [political and ideological] hypocrisy."[61]

Global feminists urge First World women critical of the UN international women's conferences to reconsider their objections to them. Conceding that Big Brother indeed used some women at these meetings to support political causes that weaken rather than strengthen women's status, global feminists nonetheless remain convinced that so-called political issues and so-called women's issues are not necessarily opposed. They also remain convinced that it is a mistake to think that feminists must always privilege women's issues over political issues; sometimes sexual and reproductive issues must, as many Third World women presently believe, defer to economic and political issues.

Third World women's priorities help explain why some of them view First World women as arrogant know-it-alls, who are totally ignorant about real oppression. Nawal el Saadawi, an Egyptian writer, was particularly critical of First World women's supposed powers of perception. She noted: "Western women often go to countries such as Sudan and 'see' only clitoridectomy, but never notice the role of multinational corporations and their exploited labor."[62] In other words, First World women frequently fail to appreciate the extent to which *they* are the economic and political oppressors of women (and men) in the Third World. The same U.S. woman who is willing to attend protests against clitoridectomy might not be willing to attend protests against the multinational corporation that pays her or her husband a substantial salary.

Global feminists stress that the distinction between so-called political issues and so-called women's issues is false. There is, they say, no boundary between these two kinds of issues. On the contrary, they co-constitute each other.[63] In this connection, global feminist Angela Gillian quoted a Cape Verdean woman, who, together with several other women, had invited her to address their daughters about the importance of higher education:

> I want my daughter to take part in what is taking place in this country. If she gets married now, she will never participate in the change. I don't want her to be like me. I am married to a good man. As you know about 40 percent of Cape Verdian men are labourers in Europe, and my husband is in Holland. That house over there that we are building brick by brick right next to this little cabin is being made with the money he sends home. Every two years he gets one month's vacation, and comes home to meet the baby he made the last time, and to make a new one. I don't want that for my daughter. I've heard that it is possible to prevent pregnancy by knowing the calendar. Please teach our girls how to count the days so that they can control their pregnancies.[64]

Gillian commented that for this woman the issue was not *men's* oppression of women but how an inequitable international labor system causes both men and women to construct their family relations in deleterious ways. No wonder, said Gillian, that many Third World women are convinced that "the separation of sexism from the political, economic, *and* racial is a strategy of elites. As such it becomes a tool to confuse the real issues around which most of world's women struggle."[65]

Stressing that *everything* is a women's issue, many global feminists went to each of the three UN international women's conferences wanting very much to erase the arbitrary line between so-called women's issues and so-called political issues and to bridge the gap between the perspectives of First World and Third World women. For example, as Charlotte Bunch prepared for the Nairobi conference, she hoped to set a broad agenda not limited to sexual and reproduction issues. She said: "Racism is a woman's issue, just as is anti-Semitism, Palestinian homelessness, rural development, ecology, the persecution of lesbians, and the exploitive practices of global corporations. Domination on the basis of race, class, religion, sexual preference, economics, or nationality cannot be seen as a mere additive to the oppression of women by gender. Rather, all these factors help to shape the very forms of that oppression."[66]

Nowhere is the complex interplay between multiple forms of oppression more clear than with respect to the old reproduction-controlling technologies (contraception, sterilization, and abortion) and the new reproduction-aiding technologies (intrauterine donor insemination and in vitro fertilization). Whether such technologies and the social arrangements associated with some of them (e.g., surrogate motherhood) are women-liberating or women-oppressing depends largely on a woman's class, race, sexual preference, religion, and nationality. For example, although virtually all U.S. women express concerns about the safety, efficacy, convenience, and availability of contraception, sterilization, and abortion, most white, middle-class heterosexual women believe they would be far less free and well-off without these reproduction-controlling technologies.

But the largely positive view that white, middle-class, heterosexual women hold regarding reproduction-controlling technologies is *not* the view *all* U.S. women share. All too often, some racist and classist (as well as sexist) American healthcare practitioners and politicians have used (or sought to use) the reproduction-controlling technologies for eugenic or cost-saving purposes. For example, in the 1960s the so-called rule of 120, which precluded sterilization of a woman unless her age times the number of her living children equaled 120 or more,[67] was widely followed by obstetricians and gynecologists when it came to healthy, white, middle-class, married women—a fact that angered these advantaged women. They wanted physicians to adopt more permissive sterilization policies. What these advantaged women failed to realize, at least initially, was that the same obstetricians and gynecologists who were reluctant to sterilize them were often only too happy to sterilize women of color, especially indigent ones. Indeed, in some southern states, sterilizations of indigent black women were so common that they were irreverently referred to as "Mississippi appendectomies."[68] More recently, but in the same manner, some legislators have drafted policies and laws linking fertile women's welfare eligibility to their willingness to use the contraceptive Norplant. In the estimation of these lawmakers, unless a woman agrees to use this long-term contraceptive implant, she and any children she might already have should be denied Aid to Families with Dependent Children.[69]

The kind of policies and laws described above caused many U.S. women of color, particularly those whose incomes are very low, to suspect "white" America has eugenic designs on "black" America. Some of these women claim that "white" America is so eager to limit the growth of the black population that it forces the abortion "choice" as well as the contraception "choice" and sterilization "choice" on black women and other women of color. In support of their claim, they note that some of the most fervent right-to-lifers also advocate limiting or cutting benefits to welfare mothers—even though such limits and cuts might cause more than a few welfare mothers to terminate their pregnancies. Realizing the extent to which a woman's race and class affects the scope of her reproductive freedom, Alison Jaggar commented: "A real choice about abortion requires that a woman should be able to opt to have her child, as well as to abort it. This means that the full right to life of the child must be guaranteed, either by community aid to the mother who wishes to raise it herself, or by the provision of alternative arrangements that do not put the child who is not raised by its own mother at any significant disadvantage."[70]

If the situation with respect to women's use of reproduction-controlling and reproduction-assisting technologies is unclear in the United States, it is even more unclear worldwide. In the former Soviet Union, women have the right to abort. However, most of them are forced to exercise this right routinely (on average twelve to fourteen times during their lifetimes) because contraceptives, although legal, are extremely difficult to obtain.[71]

Even more worrisome than the former Soviet Union's policies are those of China, where a one-child-per-family policy remains on the books, enforced more strenuously in some regions of the country than in others. In the early 1980s Chinese government officials decided to monitor the fertility of approximately 340 million Chinese women, going so far as to track their menstrual cycles. They also decided to punish couples who had more than one child and to reward those who complied with the one-child policy. A variety of economic penalties were levied against the former; in contrast, the latter were given pay raises of up to 40 percent, extended maternity leaves, and better housing.[72] In 1995 a new generation of Chinese government officials stepped up the effort to decrease the size of China's population. They posted signs warning women to report every three months to a local clinic for a pregnancy test or else face a large fine. In addition, officials urged women with one child either to be sterilized or to accept an intrauterine device. Failure to comply with such urgings proved to be no small matter in some rural outposts. After blasting into rubble the home of a family with three children, government dynamiters in the village of Xiaoxi warned its shocked inhabitants, "Those who do not obey the family planning policies will be those who lose their fortunes."[73]

Equally if not even more threatening to women's reproductive freedom are India's amniocentesis policies. First developed to discover genetic abnormalities in the fetus, amniocentesis is now routinely used in India as a sex determination test with the purpose of eliminating female fetuses. The test is inexpensive, and women supposedly "want" it, particularly if they already have one or more daughters, each of whom will eventually require a costly wedding dowry.

When Indian feminists campaigned for a ban on sex determination, their protest was heard, but in a way that backfired on them. GAMETNICS, a U.S. company with clinics in many Third World countries, devised a preconception sex-selection technology. Using this method, technicians separate Y chromosomes, which are the male sex determinants, from X chromosomes. At present they are able to select sperm containing 80 percent of Y chromosomes, which are then injected into the woman. Although this method is more costly than amniocentesis followed by abortion and although it, like its predecessor method, promises to make Indian women an "endangered species," it struck many Indians as more "humane" than amniocentesis and abortion. Reflecting on this new technology, Maria Mies, who is both an ecofeminist and a global feminist, commented: "This example shows clearly that the sexist and racist ideology is closely interwoven with capitalist profit motives, that the logic of selection and elimination has a definite economic base. Patriarchy and racism are not only ethically rejectable ideologies, they mean *business* indeed."[74]

No less a woman's issue than reproduction is production. As Robin Morgan noted, "Women are the world's proletariat."[75] Even though housework constitutes 60 to 80 percent of most nations' economies, housework continues to suffer from "gross national product invisibility." To deny that women work, stressed Morgan, is absurd. Women constitute almost the totality of the world's food producers and are responsible for most of the world's hand portage of water and fuel. In most nations handicrafts are largely or solely the products of female labor, and in most nations women compose a large portion of tourist industry workers, particularly the sex tourism industry in Asia (catering to businessmen who pay for the sexual services of women in the countries they visit).[76] In addition multinational corporations use women as a cheap source of labor, failing to provide them with the training they provide men and firing them whenever it proves profitable to do so. Women are migrant and seasonal workers in agrarian countries and part-time laborers in industrialized countries.

Worldwide, women work a so-called double day, doing eight or more hours of "invisible" work at home (housework, childcare, eldercare, sick care) and eight or more hours of "visible" work outside the home. When governments and businesses respond to women's complaints about having to work too hard, they typically do so in ways that do not improve women's situations. They tell overworked women to work part time or to get on a mommy track, strategies that often render women virtually ineligible for substantial promotions and pay increases. Or, worse, governments and businesses pass laws and develop policies that "protect" women from supposedly "harmful" high-paying jobs. As if this is not bad enough, governments and businesses often fail to understand women's complaints about their "double day" of work, recommending ridiculous or insulting solutions. For example, Cuba's Fidel Castro once proposed that "hairdressers remain open during the evening to ease the burden of the woman who is employed during the day but needs to be attractive in her house wifing role at night."[77]

Reflecting on how hard women work and how little government and business has done to ameliorate women's lot, Morgan concluded this state of affairs obtains because Big Brother's interests are not served by providing women the same kind of work and economic security it provides men. Whether Big Brother lives in the First World or Third World, "a marginal female labor force is a highly convenient asset: cheap, always available, easily and callously disposed of."[78] In Morgan's estimation, women's oppression as producers is clearly equal to if not greater than their oppression as reproducers.

Although First World women are disadvantaged workers relative to First World men, Morgan conceded that they are advantaged workers relative to Third World people, including Third World men. She also acknowledged that First World proposals to solve the Third World's economic problems—in particular so-called development economics strategies—often work to the detriment of Third World people, especially Third World women. (However, Morgan did not discuss the specific ways in which development economics strategies help consolidate the First World's power in the Third World.)

Detailing how the First World's "you-can-catch-up-to-us" policies serve the interests of the First World far more than the interests of the Third World, Maria Mies claimed that First World economists make promises to Third World people they have no hope of keeping. They tell Third World people that they can attain the same standard of living First World people enjoy. But down deep, First World economists doubt the truth of their stories about endless progress and limitless growth.[79] For example, observing that the world's population will swell to 11 billion after the year 2050, Mies stated: "If of these eleven billion people the per capita energy consumption was similar to that of Americans in the mid-1970s, conventional oil resources would be exhausted in 34–74 years."[80]

Because the First World already finds it difficult to maintain its high standard of living, Mies speculated that whatever the First World gives the Third World in the way of benefits, it extracts in the way of costs. Specifically, the First World passes on to its Third World "partners" the economic, social, and ecological costs it cannot afford to pay without dropping from First World status to something more akin to Third World status. Commented Mies:

> The relationship between colonized and colonizer is based not on any measure of partnership but rather on the latter's coercion and violence in its dealings with the former. This relationship is in fact the secret of unlimited growth in the centers of accumulation. If externalization of all the costs of industrial production were not possible, if they had to be borne by the industrialized countries themselves, that is if they were internalized, an immediate end to unlimited growth would be inevitable.[81]

In sum, stressed Mies, "catching-up development" is not feasible, and this for two reasons: (1) There are only so many resources to divide among humankind, and they are currently inequitably distributed and consumed; and (2) the existing "colonial world order" needs to maintain the economic gap it promises to eliminate in order to maintain its present power.

What is more, not only is "catching-up development" not feasible, it is not *desirable* in Mies's estimation. She claimed the First World's "good life" is actually a very *bad* life insofar as human relationships are concerned. First World people are too busy making money to spend time with each other. They are so strained and stressed they gradually lose any sense of selfhood or ultimate meaning. First World people run the rat race, day after day, until the day they die. Their children inherit their considerable material goods, and the meaningless cycle of running and dying continues.

Mies also stressed that "catching-up development" has a role within the First World as well. First World women are offered the opportunity to catch up to First World men. However, to keep this promise, like the similar one to Third World people, is, once again, neither feasible nor desirable. First, whether promises of freedom, equality, and self-determination are kept depends on who controls the money and who has the power in a society; and in the First World *men* still control most of the money and most of the power. In order for First World women to "catch up" to First World men, First World men would have to be willing to share all of society's resources *equally* with First World women. At present such willingness on the part of First World men is not apparent.

Second, even in the affluent First World the "system" can afford only so many women to get the kind of money and power they need to be as free, equal, and self-determining as men are. Since First World men are not currently willing to share their money and power equally with First World women, First World women's best chance for "liberation" would then seem to depend to a greater or lesser extent on Third World people's, especially Third World women's, oppression. Mies explained: "Only while women in Asia, Africa or Latin America can be forced to work for much lower wages than those in affluent societies—and this is made possible through the debt trap—can enough capital be accumulated in the rich countries so that even unemployed women are guaranteed a minimum income; but all unemployed women in the world cannot expect this. Within a world system based on exploitation 'some are more equal than others.'"[82]

Third, because money and power are limited goods for which self-interested human beings will inevitably compete, there is no ethical basis for solidarity among human beings in general or women in particular. Mies offered the following example:

> It may be in the interest of Third World women working in the garment industry for export, to get higher wages, or even wages equivalent to those paid in the industrialized countries; but if they actually received these wages then the working-class woman in the North could hardly afford to buy those garments, or buy as many of them as she does now. In her interest the price of these garments must remain low. Hence the interests of these two sets of women who are linked through the world market are antagonistic.[83]

As long as the possession of material goods and power is equated with human happiness, there will be the kind of competition and antagonism that inevitably leads to conflict and even war. Women will be set against women multiculturally and globally and against their own men nationally.

From the perspective of global feminists, stressed Mies, the First World must abandon its view of the "good life" and substitute for it a view predicated not on the *quantity* of one's possessions and power but on the *quality* of one's relationships. In addition the First World must confront the material world's limits and vow to live within these limits. Only then will it be possible to create a new world order, in which divisions such as First World–Third World are incomprehensible. Finally, from the perspective of global feminists, women should take the lead in devising and implementing the systems, structures, policies, and programs needed to effect this transformation. In their estimation, it is women, particularly Third World women, who seem to know better than men, including Third World men, that the truly good life is not the rich, powerful life. In this connection, Mies described the experiences of her collaborator, Vandana Shiva, during a conference about the "green movement" in South Africa:

> While the male leaders and speakers seemed to expect South Africa's economic and ecological problems to be solved through full integration into the growth-oriented world economy, the women, who had so far borne the burden of modernization and development, were much more sceptical. One 60-year-old woman said that, 'The (government's) betterment scheme has been the best strategy to push us into the depth of poverty. It accelerated the migratory system.'
>
> The men were forced to migrate to the cities in search of jobs, whereas the women, together with the old and the children, had to try to survive in the rural areas. Meanwhile, the white government destroyed all assets and possessions by which the women tried to maintain their subsistence. 'We were dispossessed of our goats, donkeys and other animals. They were taken away by force and we got only 20 cents as compensation per head.'
>
> This woman had experienced the contradictory impact of 'betterment' or development as the government understood it. She knew that some must always pay the price for this development and that usually its victims are the women. Therefore she was not enthusiastic about further integration of the new non-racist democratic South Africa into the world market. Rather she demanded land and the security of independent subsistence.[84]

Production, no less than reproduction, is clearly a woman's issue.

The One and the Many: Ethical Absolutism Versus Ethical Relativism

That women are different and that they have different priorities is a tenet of global feminism. So, too, is the view that depending on where, when, how, and with whom she lives a woman will experience forms of oppression unique to those who share her circumstances. All this suggests that in order to be a global feminist, one must first be a multicultural feminist. According to Mies and Shiva, the East-West confrontations that preoccupied us from World War I onward and the North-South tensions that currently confront us effectively ended not only "all socialist dreams and utopias" but also "all universal" ideologies based on the conception of a common human nature.[85] Belief in oneness, as many postmodern feminists insist, is Eurocentric, egocentric, and phallogocentric. We must deconstruct the "one" so people can be *themselves*—not the other. Moreover, as many environmentalists claim, because natural and cultural diversity is a precondition for the maintenance of life on the planet, we must oppose the "homogenization of culture on the U.S. coca-cola and fast-food model" and the destruction of life forms "according to the demands of profit-oriented industries."[86]

Attracted to the view that the "many" needs to replace the "one," global feminists theorize that by parity of reasoning ethical relativism, the theory that ethical judgments are applicable only to the time and place in which they arise, needs to replace ethical absolutism, the theory that ethical judgments are applicable to all times and all places. But this is easier said than done. Ethical relativism poses a serious threat to feminism. For example, Mies and Shiva noted the total espousal of ethical relativism implies that global feminists "must accept even violence, and such patriarchal and exploitative institutions and customs as dowry, female genital mutilation, India's caste system. . . . Taken to extremes the emphasis on 'difference' could lead to losing sight of all commonalities, making even communication impossible."[87] In other words, if the idea of difference makes it impossible for women in one culture to communicate with women in another culture, global feminists might as well forget their plans to build a new world order. Such an order is neither viable nor welcome if people are so different they cannot even make sense of each other's words.

To get even clearer on why ethical relativism is a stumbling block for global feminists in particular, it is useful to focus on female circumcision/genital mutilation, a practice that has prompted some heated disputes between First World and Third World women. In her book *No Longer Patient*, feminist bioethicist Susan Sherwin noted it is indeed true that most feminists, not just global feminists, tend toward ethical relativism. Feminists supposedly regard ethical relativism as less oppressive than ethical absolutism. Yet according to Sherwin, feminists who rightly flee from the oppressiveness of an ethical absolutism that refuses to recognize difference may also wrongly flee from the universality of an ethical absolutism that permits them to say that oppression is always wrong. Feminists, she said, need to be able to say something is *wrong* before they try to make it *right*. A relativist critic is an oxymoron. If your decisions are as good as mine, then how can I possibly criticize you, or you me? asked Sherwin. We two are perfect; there is simply no need for either one or both of us to change our minds or course of action. Socially speaking, ethical relativism would seem to cost all feminists, including global feminists, the possibility of moral progress—of a better tomorrow, of a new world order.

In an attempt to elucidate just how difficult it is for a feminist to steer a course between the Scylla of ethical absolutism and the Charybdis of ethical relativism, Sherwin focused on the widespread practice of female circumcision/genital mutilation in many African and Middle Eastern countries. She noted more than 84 million women now living have undergone this painful, frequently unsanitary, often harmful surgical procedure. Among the justifications for female circumcision/genital mutilation are "custom, religion, family honor, cleanliness, aesthetics, initiation, assurance of virginity, promotion of social and political cohesion, enhancement of fertility, improvement of male sexual pleasure, and prevention of female promiscuity."[88] Although large numbers of women as well as men within these countries endorse this practice, Sherwin still judged it wrong. In proclaiming the wrongness of female circumcision/genital mutilation, however, Sherwin realized she was walking down a perilous path. All too often "moral absolutism" has been used to support cultural dominance. Oppressors make the leap from "There is a truth" to "*I know* that truth, but you do not." Nevertheless, Sherwin claimed that in their desire to show proper respect for cultural diversity and to eschew the role of oppressor, feminists must be careful not to pull the moral carpet out from under themselves. Surely, some actions are so egregiously wrong— for example, rape—that feminists must simply say, "Rape is *wrong*," even if some culture or another happens to endorse rape. In taking this step, however, feminists must explain why they decided to violate their general rule of respect for cultural difference.[89]

Sherwin conceded it is easier to be a traditional ethical relativist than a feminist ethical relativist. Whereas the traditional ethical relativist is willing to live with his or her inability to condemn a practice such as female circumcision/genital mutilation (or, I suppose, even rape) if the majority of a population accepts it, the feminist ethical relativist is not. Sherwin agreed with traditional ethical relativists "that we do not have access to anything more foundational than community standards in ethics,"[90] but she claimed some communities are morally worse than other communities. A community that structures its relations in terms of patterns of domination and subordination, she said, is not worthy of moral trust; and unless a community is morally trustworthy, feminist relativists are not obligated to tolerate, let alone respect, its standards.

Before feminists decide to trust a community's standards, they must, emphasized Sherwin, make some baseline judgments about its moral methodology. If the community's standards are the result of a truly democratic conversation, then those standards, however disconcerting, ought to be tolerated, indeed respected, by feminist relativists. So, for example, if it turns out all segments of a society practicing female circumcision/ genital mutilation truly endorse it—that no affected group has been forced to support this practice as the result of "coercion, exploitation, ignorance, deception, or even indifference"[91]—then it is a nonoppressive practice. However, in Sherwin's estimation, it is doubtful that *all* the segments of the societies practicing female circumcision/genital mutilation truly support it. Indeed, there is increasing evidence that support for female circumcision/genital mutilation is waning even in those nations that currently practice it. For example, over a decade ago, Kenyan president Daniel Moi condemned female circumcision/genital mutilation. Like many other people in his government, he believed the practice harms women and children physically and psychologically. Urging his people to put aside one of their long-standing traditions, Moi stressed that no nation, especially a developing one like Kenya, can afford to harm its own human resources. Kenya's future depends on each of its citizens' being as healthy and happy as possible.[92]

Conceding it is not simple to determine whether a community is oppressive or nonoppressive—or just *how* oppressive a community must be before feminist ethical relativists mistrust its moral judgments—Sherwin sought additional guidance for feminists from David Wong, a nontraditional (but still nonfeminist) moral philosopher. Wong claimed that two equally justified, equally true, opposed moral positions can exist side by side. The individuals who espouse these two separate positions, however, should not interfere with each other's ends unless such interference would be "acceptable to them were they fully rational and informed of all relevant circumstances."[93] In order to clarify his meaning, Wong gave the example of abortion. As he saw it, people fight endlessly over abortion, but neither the anti-abortion nor the pro-choice camps can rationally convert the other side. Both positions are grounded in reflective, well-established moral systems. Both positions, therefore, are probably morally justified. Referring to his own "justification principle," Wong again stressed that since no fully rational and informed person is willing to accept active interference with his or her ends, both the conservatives and the liberals should confine themselves to verbal volleying.[94] Each side should simply respect the moral convictions of the other and make it impossible, or nearly impossible, for the other side to follow its own ethical lights.

What is wrong with Wong's otherwise helpful position on ethical relativism, said Sherwin, is its acceptance of the conservatives' and liberals' respective moral systems as equally well established. In her estimation, Wong failed to ask certain crucial questions: namely, How did the systems come to be? Whose interests do they foster? And whose interests do they impede?[95] These questions are the kind of questions feminist ethical relativists should ask. The answers will probably reveal not only that the conservative position favors fetuses' and men's interests over women's interests but also that the conservative goal of stopping abortion limits liberals in ways that the liberal goal of safe, affordable, and accessible abortion does not limit conservatives.

The conservatives would block liberals from doing something they believe is right—having an abortion because one is not ready, willing, or able to be a parent; yet the liberals would not stop the conservatives from doing something they believe is right—not having an abortion because of their beliefs about the personhood of fetuses. The bumper sticker that reads "Don't like abortion? Don't have one!" comes close to making Sherwin's distinction succinctly. To the degree conservative abortion policies block liberals in a way liberal abortion policies do not block conservatives, feminists may actively interfere with conservatives on the grounds that conservative abortion policies are less "democratic" than liberal abortion policies.

> A feminist moral relativism demands that we consider who controls moral decision-making within a community and what effect that control has on the least privileged members of that community. Both at home and abroad, it gives us grounds to criticize the practices that a majority believes acceptable if those practices are a result of oppressive power differentials. It will not, however, always tell us precisely what is the morally right thing to do, because there is no single set of moral truths we can decipher. Feminist moral relativism remains absolutist on the question of the moral wrong of oppression but is relativist on other moral matters; in this way, it is better able to incorporate feminist moral sensibilities.[96]

Apparently, not all differences are created equal.

However promising the future of feminist relativism may be, at present it cannot escape all of its absolutist tendencies. Feminist moral relativists want to respect difference, but they reserve the right to judge *which* differences among individuals or groups should be respected. They imply that "consent" plays the crucial role in determining whether oppression does or does not exist and therefore whether a culture's practice should or should not be respected. But is "consent" really the only factor or even the most important factor in determining whether a practice is absolutely wrong? Or is there another equally important or even more important factor that makes certain states of affairs absolutely right or absolutely wrong? Are there, for example, certain things to which all people have a moral claim, no matter when, where, or how they live?

According to Mies and Shiva, there is a basis for claiming that at its most basic level morality is indeed absolute and universal. Its fundamental function is to meet the physical and psychological needs *all* people have in common, for unless these needs are met, a human being cannot give meaningful "consent." An absolutism or universalism built on meeting fundamental human needs is, in Mies and Shiva's estimation, very different from an absolutism or universalism based on recognizing human rights. They explained:

> This universalism does not deal in abstract universal human "rights" but rather in common human needs which can be satisfied only if the life-sustaining networks and processes are kept intact and alive. These symbioses, or "living interconnectednesses," both in nature and in human society are the only guarantee that life in its fullest sense can continue on this planet.

These fundamental needs: for food, shelter, clothing; for affection, care and love; for dignity and identity, for knowledge and freedom, leisure and joy, are common to all people, irrespective of culture, ideology, race, political and economic system and class.[97]

Thus, global feminists must ask themselves if female circumcision/genital mutilation serves a fundamental human need before they make any proclamation about its rightness or wrongness. More important, they must assume that if women in one culture are capable of recognizing fundamental human needs, so, too, are women in every other culture. If I think I can know that female circumcision/genital mutilation, as practiced, does not serve any fundamental human need, then I must assume women in other cultures can come to the same conclusion.

Conclusion

Multicultural and global feminism present a great challenge to feminism: how to unite women in, through, and despite their differences. In general, multicultural and global feminists have offered women two ways to achieve unity in diversity. The first consists in working toward sisterhood or friendship. For example, in the introduction to *Sisterhood Is Global*, Robin Morgan stressed that when all is said and done, women are not really so very different. Provided women ask each other *"sincere* questions about difference," said Morgan, they will see each other as searching for the same thing: namely, a *self* ("self-identity," "an articulation of selfhood," "self-realization," "self-image," "the right to be oneself").[98]

Furthering Morgan's point, Elizabeth Spelman itemized the kind of "sincere" questions multicultural and global feminists must ask. Among these questions are the following: "What do I and can I know about women from whom I differ in terms of race, culture, class, ethnicity?"[99] "What happens when oppressors want to undo racism or other oppression; how do they go about acquiring knowledge about others, knowledge whose absence is now regretted?"[100] Among the many ways to find answers to these questions, said Spelman, is to "read books, take classes, open your eyes and ears or whatever instruments of awareness you might be blessed with, go to conferences planned and produced by the people about whom you wish to learn and manage not to be intrusive."[101] Other ways are to try to imagine what other women's lives are like and to be tolerant of difference no matter how much it threatens one. Of course, said Spelman, imagining how it is with others and tolerating others is far different from perceiving others and welcoming others. She explained the difference between imagining and perceiving as follows:

When I am perceiving someone, I must be prepared to receive new information all the time, to adapt my actions accordingly, and to have my feelings develop in response to what the person is doing, whether I like what she is doing or not. When simply imagining her, I can escape from the demands her reality puts on me and instead construct her in my mind in such a way that I can possess her, make her into someone or something who never talks back, who poses no difficulties for me, who conforms to my desires much more than the real person does.[102]

Later Spelman elucidated the important distinction between tolerating someone's opinion and welcoming someone's opinion. She claimed that merely to tolerate a viewpoint is to fail "actively" to seek it out as a *serious* critique of one's own viewpoint. If I am just tolerating you, I am not open to really changing myself. I am not prepared to be your friend; instead, I am simply willing not to be your enemy.

In a dialogical essay she coauthored with Maria Lugones, Spelman stressed that in order to develop an adequate (multicultural and global) feminist theory, a wide variety of women have to formulate it together. But in her sections of the essay, Lugones asked Spelman what motive the women who were previously left out of theory-making would have for doing this. Perhaps they want to be left alone to do theory themselves, in their own voices. Furthermore, Lugones wondered, what motive would the women who were previously the ones in charge of theory-making have for doing this? Why would they want to join women who told them they could come and listen to their discussions, provided they were, as they had once been, "unobtrusive, unimportant, patient to the point of tears," yet willing to learn new lessons from women who might view them "as of no consequence except as an object of mistrust?"[103] Would the motive of the former theory-makers be self-interest, either in the sense of getting to know the other so as to better dominate her or in the sense of "self-growth or self-expansion," feeding off the rich "difference" of the other? If so, stressed Lugones, white women and First World women need to know they will not be *tolerated,* let alone *welcomed* by women of color and Third World women.

Moreover, continued Lugones, white women and First World women need to know that if they wish to do theory with women of color and Third World women out of a sense of duty, understood as an act of noblesse oblige or as an anemic substitute for love, then they should be prepared for rejection. There will be no opportunity for sisterhood, for entering the world of the other. Lugones stressed that First World women and white women who use the language of duty do little more than agree *not* to use their "education" to "overwhelm," "research," and keep on the defensive Third World women and women of color.[104]

If the feminists who have been at the center of theory want to do theory with the feminists who have been at the margins of theory, their motive must be nothing short of friendship, according to Lugones. Unless one woman wants to be another woman's friend, she will be unable to summon the psychic energy to travel to that woman's world in order to see her living her life there as a self rather than the other. According to Morgan, Spelman, and Lugones, the chief task of multicultural and global feminists is, therefore, to inspire women to want to be each other's friends.

Disagreeing with Morgan's, Spelman's, and Lugones's views on the essential goal of multicultural and global feminism are a variety of thinkers, including bell hooks, Audre Lorde, and Iris Young. Although hooks and Lorde sometimes employed the language of sisterhood in their writings, for them sisterhood is a *political* rather than a *personal* concept. Women can be sisters in the sense of being political comrades, but only if they are willing to truly confront their differences. "Imagining," "perceiving," "tolerating," and "welcoming" are fine, insofar as they go; but confronting differences requires far more painful activities, like being enraged and being shamed. There is a difference, hooks emphasized, between "bourgeois-women's-liberation" sisterhood and multicultural-and-global-feminist sisterhood. The former focuses on women's "supporting" each other, where support serves "as a prop or a foundation for a weak structure" and where women, emphasizing their "shared victimization," give each other "unqualified approval."[105] The latter rejects this sentimental brand of sisterhood and offers in its stead a type of sisterhood that begins with women's confronting and combating each other's differences and ends with their using these very same differences to "accelerate their positive advance" toward the goals they share in common. As hooks explained: "Women do not need to eradicate difference to feel solidarity. We do not need to share common oppression to fight equally to end oppression. . . . We can be sisters united by shared interests and beliefs, united in our appreciation for diversity, united in our struggle to end sexist oppression, united in political solidarity."[106] Lorde also stressed the importance of maintaining women's differences rather than trying to transcend them. She claimed, for example, that feminists don't have to love each other in order to work with each other.[107] In the same vein, Iris Young observed that although women should not be enemies, they should not expect to be friends. They should simply be content to be "strangers."[108]

Rejecting the homogenizing, conformist tendencies of the language of community and family, Young argued that feminists should not try to be "sisters" and "friends" with women whose worlds are radically different than their own. As Nancie Caraway noted, for Young "insistence on the ideal of shared subjectivity . . . leads to undesirable political implications."[109] Young repeatedly urged feminists, among other political theorists and activists, to distrust the desire "for reciprocal recognition and identification with others . . . because it denies differences in the concrete sense of making it difficult for people to respect those with whom they do not identify."[110] She claimed, said Caraway, that multicultural and global feminists should not want to be sisters or friends because such desires "thwart our principled calls for heterogeneity in feminism."[111]

The choice between the sisterhood of friendship and the sisterhood of political solidarity is an important one. Multicultural and global feminists might need to make this choice once and for all in the future, but for now the overall consensus seems to be a both-and approach in which political alliances become opportunities for women to form personal friendships. In this connection it might be the case that none other than Aristotle had some good advice for feminists. There are, according to Aristotle, three kinds of friendship: the kind of friendship people who are of *use* to each other have (for example, professional colleagues); the kind of friendship people who enjoy the same sorts of pleasures have (for example, "drinking buddies" and dance partners); and the kind of friendship people who share meaningful goals and tasks in common have (for example, famine relief workers and women against oppression). To be this last kind of friend, said Aristotle, is to be a "partner in virtue and a friend in action."[112] Perhaps this is precisely the kind of friends multicultural and global feminists should want to be.

CHAPTER EIGHT

— ∎ —

Ecofeminism

LIKE MULTICULTURAL AND GLOBAL FEMINISM, ecofeminism strives to show the connections among all forms of human oppression, but it also focuses on human beings' attempts to dominate the nonhuman world, or nature. Because women have been culturally tied to nature, ecofeminists argue there are conceptual, symbolic, and linguistic connections between feminist and ecological issues. According to Karen J. Warren, the Western world's basic beliefs, values, attitudes, and assumptions about itself and its inhabitants have been shaped by an oppressive patriarchal conceptual framework, the purpose of which is to explain, justify, and maintain relationships of domination and subordination in general and men's domination of women in particular. The most significant features of this framework are:

> (1) value-hierarchical thinking, i.e., "up-down" thinking which places higher value, status, or prestige on what is "up" rather than on what is "down"; (2) value dualisms, i.e., disjunctive pairs in which the disjuncts are seen as oppositional (rather than as complementary) and exclusive (rather than as inclusive), and which place higher value (status, prestige) on one disjunct rather than the other (e.g., dualisms which give higher value or status to that which has historically been identified as "mind," "reason," and "male" than to that which has historically been identified as "body," "emotion," and "female"); and (3) logic of domination, i.e., a structure of argumentation which leads to a justification of subordination.[1]

Patriarchy's hierarchical, dualistic, and oppressive mode of thinking has harmed both women and nature in Warren's opinion. Indeed, because women have been "naturalized" and nature has been "feminized," it is difficult to know where the oppression of one ends and the other begins. Warren emphasized women are "naturalized" when they are described in animal terms such as "cows, foxes, chicks, serpents, bitches, beavers, old bats, pussycats, cats, bird-brains, hare-brains."[2] Similarly, nature is "feminized" when "she" is raped, mastered, conquered, controlled, penetrated, subdued, and mined by men, or when "she" is venerated or even worshiped as the grandest "mother" of all. If man is the lord of nature, if he has been given dominion over it, then he has control not only over nature but also over nature's human analog, woman. Whatever man may do to nature, he may also do to woman.

Similar to the manner in which radical-cultural feminists and radical-libertarian feminists disagree about whether women's association with the work of childbearing and child-rearing is ultimately a source of power or disempowerment for women, "cultural," "nature,"[3] or "psychobiologistic"[4] ecofeminists disagree with "social-constructionist"[5] or "social" ecofeminists about the wisdom of stressing women's association with nature. Yet despite their often divergent views on our particular responsibilities to the environment (must we live as simply as possible?), to animals (must we be vegetarians and antivivisectionists?), and to future generations (must we be pacifists and strict population controllers?), all ecofeminists agree with Rosemary Radford Ruether that women's and nature's liberation are a joint project. In the words of Ruether: "Women must see that there can be no liberation for them and no solution to the ecological aims within a society whose fundamental model of relationships continues to be one of domination. They must unite the demands of the women's movement with those of the ecological movement to envision a radical reshaping of the basic socioeconomic relations and the underlying values of this [modern industrial] society."[6]

The Roots of Ecofeminism

In her 1962 book, *The Silent Spring*, Rachel Carson warned Americans that unless they began to take care of their environment, then "all man's assaults upon the environment [including] the contamination of air, earth, rivers, and sea with dangerous and even lethal materials . . . [will undoubtedly] shatter or alter the very material . . . upon which the shape of the future depends."[7] As ecological concerns about global warning, ozone depletion, waste disposal, animal farming, endangered species, energy conservation, and wilderness preservation grew, an environmental movement took hold in the United States and throughout the world. Though all environmentalists believe human beings should respect nature, so-called human-centered environmentalists provide reasons for respecting nature based on furthering human interests, whereas so-called earth-centered environmentalists provide reasons for respecting nature based on the intrinsic value of the earth itself.

Human-centered environmentalists emphasize that we harm ourselves when we harm the environment. If we exhaust our natural resources or pollute our skies and water, not only we but also our progeny will suffer. If we want to have the material goods and life-styles that industrialization makes possible, we must devise some means to handle the toxic wastes it produces as a by-product. If we want to have the benefit of bountiful and inexpensive energy, we must harness new sources of energy like the sun and wind, lest we use the entire supply of oil and natural gas currently fueling our economy. If we want to experience the wilderness and to see uncultivated vegetation and undomesticated animals, then we must prevent commercial enterprises from transforming every piece of wild land into a Disneyland or Club Med. And if we want to preserve the rich diversity of nature and the treasures it might still hold for us, then we must safeguard all life forms, refusing to imperil their existence.

Viewing themselves as "realistic" or "pragmatic" about environmental concerns, human-centered environmentalists concede that from time to time we will have to sacrifice the environment in order to serve our interests. In other words, sometimes a forest must be cut down so we can use the trees to build homes; sometimes the air must be polluted so we can continue to drive our automobiles; sometimes a predatory species of wild animals must be eliminated or relegated to our zoos so our domesticated animals can graze safely. In short, the environment's value is *instrumental*; its meaning, significance, and purpose depends on our needs or wants. The environment exists not for itself but for human beings.

It is not surprising that critics of human-centered environmentalism condemn it as "arrogant anthropomorphism," generally faulting the Judeo-Christian tradition as one of the main players in the devaluation of the environment. They point, for example, to the biblical mandate that instructed *men* to "subdue" the earth and "have dominion over the fish of the sea and over the birds of the air and every living thing that moves upon the earth"[8] as promoting the view that nature has instrumental value only. These same critics also stress how the metaphors and models of mechanistic science, which gained sway during the pre-Enlightenment and Enlightenment periods, reinforced the Bible's anthropomorphic view of nature. They claim that prior to the seventeenth century we thought of nature organically, as a benevolent female or nurturing mother, as someone who gave freely and generously of *her* bounty to us, her children. Following the scientific revolution, however, we reconceived nature mechanistically, as an inert, lifeless machine. As a result of this paradigm shift, we found it easier to justify not only our use but also our misuse and abuse of nature. We reasoned there is nothing morally wrong with treating a mere "object" in whatever way we wish.

René Descartes's philosophy, which privileged mind over matter, further bolstered the mechanistic conception of nature, according to critics of human-centered environmentalism. His belief that our ability to think ("I think, therefore I am") makes us "special" led to the view that "things" that think (*res cogitans,* or human beings) are meant to control things that do not think (animals, trees, and rocks). Gradually, we convinced ourselves that human beings are indeed the highest life form: the center of the universe. As a result of our exalted self-conception, we took it upon ourselves to decide not only when to protect and preserve the environment for our use but also when to sacrifice it for our greater glory and good.

Human-centered, or anthropomorphic, environmentalism, sometimes termed "shallow ecology," remained the order of the day until the late 1940s, when a new generation of environmentalists forwarded an earth-centered environmentalism they termed "deep ecology." This post-Enlightenment view of nature repudiated the modern conception of nature as a machine, reverting to medieval and even ancient conceptions of nature as an organism that has intrinsic as well as instrumental value.

In his much-anthologized essay "The Land Ethic," Aldo Leopold wrote that we should think about the land as "a fountain of energy flowing though a circuit of soils, plants, and animals."[9] Leopold believed the earth is a life system, an intricately interwoven and interdependent intersection of elements that functions as a whole organism. If one element of this system becomes diseased, the whole system is probably sick; and the only way to heal the system is to treat or cure the diseased part, whether that diseased part is an excessively flooded plain, a severely overpopulated herd of deer (or human beings), or a heavily polluted river. To be sure, a treatment or cure for the diseased element will not always be found, but that is to be expected. In fact, the ecosystem's laws of death and decay *require* that its old elements be extinguished in order to provide space for the new elements its laws of regeneration and life continually bring into being. It is not important for each particular *part* to continue, said Leopold, but only for the *whole* to continue.

From nature's perspective, as opposed to man's (to use Leopold's term) perspective, flows an environmental ethics best termed "biocentric" or "ecocentric," in Leopold's opinion. He claimed "a thing is right when it tends to preserve the integrity, stability, and beauty of the biotic community. It is wrong when it tends to do otherwise."[10] To illustrate his point, Leopold gave the example of a river sandbar, a very particular and small environmental system. Such a system has an identifiable integrity; it is a unity of interdependent elements combining together to make a whole with a unique character. It has a certain stability, not because it does not change but because it changes only gradually. Finally, it has a particular beauty in its harmonious, well-ordered form: a unity in diversity. When envisioned on a larger scale, this small environmental system interlocks with other small environmental systems, together constituting the very large ecosystem of which human beings are simply a part. This, the largest of all ecosystems, is none other than "nature," and morality becomes a matter of conscious (or thinking) beings' preserving its integrity, stability, and beauty.

Leopold's thinking was at the forefront of the conceptual revolution that replaced the anthropomorphism of "shallow ecology" with the biocentrism of "deep ecology." Arne Naess and George Sessions articulated the principal tenets of deep ecology:

1. The well-being and flourishing of human and non-human life on earth have value in themselves (synonyms intrinsic value, inherent value). These values are independent of the usefulness of the non-human world for human purposes.
2. Richness and diversity of life forms contribute to the realization of these values and are also values in themselves.
3. Humans have no right to reduce this richness and diversity except to satisfy vital needs.
4. The flourishing of human life and cultures is compatible with a substantial decrease of the human population. The flourishing of non-human life requires such a decrease.
5. Present human interference with the non-human world is excessive, and the situation is rapidly worsening.
6. Policies must therefore be changed. These policies affect basic economic, technological, and ideological structures. The resulting state of affairs will be deeply different from the present.
7. The ideological change is mainly that of appreciating life quality (dwelling in situations of inherent value) rather than adhering to an increasingly higher standard of living. There will be a profound awareness of the difference between big and great.
8. Those who subscribe to the foregoing points have an obligation directly or indirectly to try to implement the necessary changes.[11]

Critics of deep ecology fault both the theory underlying deep ecology and some of its tactics. They demand to know what the *source* of nature's intrinsic value is, rejecting nature's mere "is-ness" as an inadequate answer to their question. Just because something exists, they say, does not make it intrinsically valuable. In an effort to persuade these critics that nature is indeed intrinsically valuable, Peter Wenz argued there is something intuitively wrong about destroying an ecosystem when there is no good reason to do so. He claimed that if the last surviving human being after a worldwide disaster had a choice between saving or not saving all the remaining plant and animal life on the earth, it would not be "a matter of moral indifference" whether he chose to save these life forms.[12]

Although critics of deep ecology agree with Wenz that the earth has value independent of us, they do not agree with the view that the earth's interests are equal to or even more important than ours. For example, critic Luc Ferry vehemently objected to some deep ecologists' proposal that if we fail or refuse to control the size of our population voluntarily, the government should force us to do so, so that *nonhuman* animals have enough food and space. Does this mean, asked Ferry, that in order to get the ideal human-nonhuman population ratio,[13] our government should do nothing to stop the kind of "massive human die backs" caused by famine, disease, and war?[14] Are we to be handled like an overpopulated herd of deer?

Ecofeminism:
New Philosophy or Ancient Wisdom?

Ecofeminism is a relatively new variant of ecological ethics. In fact, the term *ecofeminism* first appeared in 1974 in Françoise d'Eaubonne's book *Le Féminisme ou la mort*. In this work she expressed the view that there exists a direct link between the oppression of women and the oppression of nature. She claimed the liberation of one cannot be effected apart from the liberation of the other.[15] A decade or so after Eaubonne coined the term, Karen J. Warren further specified the core assumptions of ecofeminism. She claimed: "(1) There are important connections between the oppression of women and the oppression of nature; (2) understanding the nature of these connections is necessary to any adequate understanding of the oppression of women and the oppression of nature; (3) feminist theory and practice must include an ecological perspective; and (4) solutions to ecological problems must include a feminist perspective."[16]

In many ways ecofeminism resembles deep ecology, yet ecofeminists generally fault deep ecologists for missing one crucial point. According to ecofeminists, deep ecologists mistakenly oppose anthropocentrism in general when the real problem is not so much or only the Western world's *human*-centeredness but its *male*-centeredness. Androcentrism, not anthropomorphism, is the chief enemy of women and nature.

Although she praised deep ecologists' "concerted effort . . . to rethink Western metaphysics, epistemology, and ethics," ecofeminist Ariel Kay Salleh nonetheless proclaimed their rethinking "deficient."[17] Noting that most of deep ecology's spokespersons are *men*, Salleh accused them of being afraid to confront the sexism as well as naturism causing our current environmental crisis. The "deep ecology movement will not truly happen," she said, "until men are brave enough to rediscover and to love the woman inside themselves."[18] Salleh's thesis, which is shared by many ecofeminists, is "that the hatred of women, which ipso facto brings about that of nature, is one of the principal mechanisms governing the actions of men (of 'males') and, thus, the whole of Western/patriarchal culture."[19]

Problems in Ecofeminism:
To Link or Not to Link Women with Nature—

Although ecofeminists agree the association of women with nature is the root cause of both sexism and naturism, they disagree about whether women's connections to nature are primarily biological and psychological or primarily social and cultural. They also disagree about whether women should deemphasize, emphasize, or reconceive their connections with nature. According to Ynestra King, "The recognition of the connections between women and nature and of women's bridge-like position between nature and culture poses three possible directions of feminism."[20] The first direction is to sever the woman-nature connection by totally integrating women into culture and the realm of production. The second is to reaffirm the woman-nature connection, proposing that female nature is not only different than but somehow better than male culture. The third is, in King's estimation, the truly ecofeminist way and consists in

> a recognition that although the nature-culture dualism is a product of culture, we can nonetheless consciously choose not to sever the woman-nature connection by joining male culture. Rather, we can use it as a vantage point for creating a different kind of culture and politics that would integrate intuitive, spiritual, and rational forms of knowledge, embracing both science and magic insofar as they enable us to transform the nature-culture distinction and create a free, ecological society.[21]

Implicit in King's understanding of true ecofeminism is the postmodern feminist belief that ultimately all forms of human oppression are rooted in those dichotomous conceptual schemes that privilege one member of a dyad over another (e.g., male *over* female, nature *over* culture, science *over* magic).

The Argument for Severing the Woman-Nature Connection

Simone de Beauvoir. Among the feminists who have pondered women's association with nature are some who seem to reside outside the ecofeminist camp. For example, Simone de Beauvoir urged women to "transcend" their links to nature in order to overcome their status as the other, or second, sex. De Beauvoir speculated woman's identity as the other derived partly from her biology—especially her reproductive capacity—and partly from her socially imposed child-rearing responsibilities. De Beauvoir did not view woman's body as woman's friend. On the contrary, she viewed woman's body as fundamentally alienating, as an energy drain leaving women too tired to participate in the kind of creative activity men enjoy.[22]

Following Sartre, de Beauvoir stressed that men and women are cast in a *pour-soi–en-soi* dialectic (see Chapter Five). *Pour-soi* (being-for-itself) entails being a self, consciously aware of the possibilities for self-creation that the future presents; *en-soi* (being-in-itself) entails being the other, a thing without a future and therefore without any possibilities for transformation whatsoever. Although all human beings are *pour-soi*, or conscious, Western culture tends to view only men as fully *pour-soi* and women as somehow still *en-soi*.

Since it is anxiety producing to be *pour-soi*, both men and women engage in various modes of so-called bad faith in an attempt to hide from the fact they alone are the creators of their destinies. Men seek refuge from their freedom in the *idea* of woman's "it-ness," or *en-soi* immanent "nature." In other words, men see in "woman" what they would like to be: a person who simply *is* and who is relieved of the burdensome task of perpetually becoming something new or different or better, a person who is "finished" and thus totally absorbed in her body's repetitive, cyclical motion and altogether oblivious of her mind's urges to transcend the present known into the future unknown.

Knowing full well that they are as free as men, women nonetheless engage in bad faith by gladly accepting their role as the other. De Beauvoir noted that "along with the ethical urge of each individual to affirm his subjective existence, there is also the temptation to forgo liberty and become a thing."[23] If women are ever to be liberated from the status of the second sex, they must, she said, resist the temptation of the "easy way out." By refusing to be the other—the "it," the *en-soi*, the immanent one, the natural one—women will not only liberate themselves but also men. No longer will men be able to hide from their freedom in the bosom of "woman."

Reflecting on de Beauvoir's suggested program for women's liberation, ecofeminist Val Plumwood reproached de Beauvoir for giving women who care about nature the wrong advice:

> For Simone de Beauvoir woman is to become fully human in the same way as man, by joining him in distancing from and in transcending and controlling nature. She opposes male transcendence and conquering of nature to woman's immanence, being identified with and passively immersed in nature and the body. The "full humanity" to be achieved by woman involves becoming part of the superior sphere of the spirit and dominating and transcending nature and physicality, the sphere of freedom and controllability, in

contrast to being immersed in nature and in blind uncontrollability. Woman becomes "fully human" by being absorbed in a masculine sphere of freedom and transcendence conceptualized in human-chauvinist terms.[24]

Plumwood feared that by rejecting the *en-soi* realm, the world of immanence, women will gain not true personhood but merely the "opportunity" to become men's full partners in the campaign to control or dominate nature. The male-female dichotomy will not be bridged or healed into wholeness. Rather, the female member of this long-standing dyad will simply be erased into the male member. Moreover, the culture-nature dichotomy will not be eliminated. Instead, it will be worsened. Abandoned by woman, nature will find itself utterly defenseless against the forces of culture.

Sherry B. Ortner. According to Sherry B. Ortner, it will not be easy for women to disassociate themselves from nature, since virtually all cultures believe women are closer to nature than men are.[25] There are, she said, three reasons for the near universality of this belief. First, woman's *physiology* is "more involved more of the time with 'species of life'; it is woman's body that nurtures humanity's future."[26] Second, woman's *place* is more the domestic context, the place where "animal-like infants" are slowly transformed into cultural beings and where plant and animal products are shaped into food, clothing, and shelter. Third, woman's *psyche*, "appropriately molded to mothering functions by her own socialization,"[27] tends toward more relational, concrete, and particular modes of thinking than man's.

In Ortner's opinion, that woman is viewed as somehow existing *between* nature and culture has several consequences, each of them suggesting a different interpretation of the term *intermediate*. First, *intermediate* can simply mean women have a "middle status" lower than man but higher than nature. Second, it can instead mean women "mediate," or perform some set of synthesizing or converting functions between nature and culture—for example, the socialization of children. Unless children are properly socialized, culture cannot survive; it needs its members to conform to its rules and regulations. For this reason, hypothesized Ortner, culture seeks to restrict women's sexual, reproductive, educational, and occupational choices. The more conservative women are, the more conservative their children will be. Third, and finally, *intermediate* can mean "of greater symbolic ambiguity." Because culture cannot quite understand women, it is not certain whether to associate women with life or death, good or evil, order or chaos.[28] Are women ultimately culture's friends or its foes?

Since culture's view of women as intermediaries between itself and nature is, in Ortner's estimation, the product of "social actuality"—that is, women's reproductively special physiology, domestic role, and feminine psyche—women's social actuality must change in order to change culture's view of women. Only then will women be viewed as "cultural," and only then will women enjoy the same high human status men have traditionally enjoyed. However, stressed Ortner, it is impossible to change women's social actuality unless culture's view of women as intermediaries between itself and nature changes. Women will never escape this circular trap unless their situation is simultaneously attacked from both sides: from the social actuality side (women's reproductively special physiology, domestic role, and feminine psyche) *and* the conceptual or ideological side (women as occupying middle status, as performing mediating functions between nature and culture, as carrying ambiguous symbolic baggage).

Explaining her point as forcefully as possible, Ortner claimed:

> Efforts directed solely at changing the social institutions—through setting quotas on hiring, for example, or through passing equal-pay-for-equal-work laws—cannot have far-reaching effects if cultural language and imagery continue to purvey a relatively devalued view of women. But at the same time efforts directed solely at changing cultural assumptions—through male and female consciousness-raising groups, for example, or through revision of education materials and mass-media imagery—cannot be successful unless the institutional base of the society is changed to support and reinforce the changed cultural view.[29]

Ortner believed that the effect of this two-pronged attack on women's situation would be to involve both men and women equally "in projects of creativity and transcendence."[30] At last, women as well as men would be seen as "cultural," and women no less than men would participate "in culture's ongoing dialectic with nature."[31]

Like de Beauvoir's line of reasoning, Ortner's led to the conclusion that women can be liberated without nature's being liberated. Had Ortner thought otherwise, she would have been concerned to show not only that women as well as men are "cultural" but also that men as well as women are "natural." In other words, she would have wanted to change men's actuality and the ideology that supports it as much as she wanted to change women's. If we need to bridge women's "distance" from culture by involving women in "creative" and "transcendent" tasks, then we also need to bridge men's distance from nature by involving men in "repetitive" and "immanent" tasks.

The Argument for Emphasizing the Woman-Nature Connection: Nature, or Cultural, Ecofeminism

In general, ecofeminists with a radical-cultural feminist background seek to strengthen rather than weaken women's connections to nature. Unlike

de Beauvoir and Ortner, nature, or cultural, ecofeminists (most often referred to simply as "nature ecofeminists") believe the traits traditionally associated with women—such as caring, nurturing, and intuitiveness—are not so much the result of cultural constructions as the product of women's actual biological and psychological experiences. The problem is not that women have a closer relationship with nature than men do but that this relationship is undervalued. Nature ecofeminists reject the assumed inferiority of both women and nature as well as the assumed superiority of both men and culture. Instead, they insist nature/woman is at least equal to and perhaps even better than culture/man, implying that traditional female virtues, not traditional male virtues, can foster improved social relations and less aggressive, more sustainable ways of life.

Mary Daly: *Gyn/Ecology.*   As Mary Daly moved toward a lesbian separatist feminism perspective, she began to reject male culture as evil and to embrace female culture as good. She speculated that prior to the establishment of patriarchy, there existed an original matriarchy. In this gynocentric world women flourished. They controlled their own lives, bonded with each other and with the nonhuman world of animals and nature, and lived both freely and happily. Thus, Daly saw the process of women's liberation as putting women back in touch with women's original "wild" and "lusty" natural world and freeing them from men's "domesticating" and "dispiriting" cultural world.[32]

Daly contrasted women's life-giving powers with men's death-dealing powers. She claimed women have the capacity for a fully human life, a vigorous life lived in dynamic communion with animals, earth, and stars. Men, she maintained, lack this capacity. They are, she said, parasites who feed off of women's energy in order to fuel their destructive activities and constricting thoughts. Because they are not able to bring life into the world and because they are incapable of bonding with nature, men substitute artificial life for flesh-and-blood life and, in acts of envious rage directed against women, seek not only to control and destroy women but also to control and destroy all that is natural. Male culture is everything female nature is not; it is about disease and death rather than health and life. Daly wrote:

> The products of necrophilic Apollonian male mating are of course the techno-
> logical "offspring" which pollute the heavens and the earth. Since the passion
> of necrophiliacs is for the destruction of life and since their attraction is to all
> that is dead, dying, and purely mechanical, the fathers' fetishized "fetuses"
> (reproductions/replicas of themselves), with which they passionately identify,
> are fatal for the future of this planet. Nuclear reactors and the poisons they
> produce, stockpiles of atomic bombs, ozone-destroying aerosol spray propel-
> lants, oil tankers "designed" to self-destruct in the ocean, iatrogenic medica-

tions and carcinogenic food additives, refined sugar, mind pollutants of all kinds—these are the multiple fetuses/feces of stale male-mates in love with a dead world that is ultimately co-equal and consubstantial with themselves. The excrement of Exxon is everywhere. It is ominously omnipresent.[33]

Daly linked men's pollution of nature with men's "pollution" of women, contrasting man's gynecology with woman's "gyn/ecology." Man's gynecology is about segmenting and specializing reproduction as if it was just another mode of production; it is about substituting the fake for the real, the artificial for the natural; it is about cutting wholes into parts. In contrast, woman's "gyn/ecology" is about "dis-covering, de-veloping the complex web of living/loving relationships *of our own kind*. It is about *women* living, loving, creating our Selves, our cosmos."[34] Whereas man's gynecology depends upon "fixation and dismemberment," woman's gyn/ecology affirms everything is connected.[35]

According to Daly, women must work hard to stop the patriarchal forces of necrophilia—that is, of death. Most females, she claimed, have been seduced into cooperating with the "phallocentric" system of "necrophilia"; they have become men's "fembots," permitting themselves to be drained of their life forces.[36] In the days of matriarchy, Daly said, women reproduced through parthenogenesis, their eggs dividing and developing independently of sperm. Now, in the days of patriarchy, men have persuaded women to exchange natural reproduction for artificial reproduction. They invite women to enter a world in which *male* gynecologists snatch women's eggs from women's wombs in order to hatch them in technology's wombs, or artificial placentae. With this "advance" in science, said Daly, men move closer to achieving what they really seek— death—and unless women refuse to become men's "fembots," men will consume them as well as nature.

Although Daly claimed women do not have a special mission to save the world from ecological disaster,[37] it would seem that on account of what Daly termed the "spring" within women, women *are* in fact nature's only hope. Women should free themselves from men for their own sakes, but unless women accomplish this task, nature seems doomed indeed.

Susan Griffin. Susan Griffin maintained that she was not an "essentialist" who believed in *biological* connections between women and nature,[38] but her writings nonetheless imply deep, even *ontological* connections between women and nature. For example, Griffin wrote: "We know ourselves to be made from this earth. We know this earth is made from our bodies. For we see ourselves. And we are nature. We are nature seeing nature. We are nature with a concept of nature. Nature weeping. Nature speaking of nature to nature."[39] In addition to implying women have a special way of knowing and perceiving reality because of their special connections to nature, Griffin suggested it is women who must help human beings escape the false and destructive dualistic world into which men (i.e., Western philosophers) have led us.

In particular, Griffin used poetry to challenge dualistic thinking, instrumental rationality, and unbridled technology. She countered the objective, dispassionate, and disembodied voice of male culture with the subjective, passionate, embodied voice of female culture. If men can identify with machines and wonder whether machines (e.g., computers and robots) have feelings as well as thoughts, then women can identify with animals and wonder whether animals have thoughts as well as feelings. In *Woman and Nature* Griffin often spoke through the voice of an animal:

> He says that woman speaks with nature. That she hears voices from under the earth. That wind blows in her ears and trees whisper to her. That the dead sing through her mouth and the cries of infants are clear to her. But for him this dialogue is over. He says he is not part of this world, that he was set on this world as a stranger. He sets himself apart from woman and nature.
>
> And so it is Goldilocks who goes to the home of the three bears, Little Red Riding Hood who converses with the wolf, Dorothy who befriends a lion, Snow White who talks to the birds, Cinderella with mice as her allies, the Mermaid who is half fish, Thumbelina courted by a mole. (*And when we hear in the Navaho chant of the mountain that a grown man sits and smokes with bears and follows directions given to him by squirrels, we are surprised. We had thought only little girls spoke with animals.*)
>
> *We are the bird's eggs. Bird's eggs, flowers, butterflies, rabbits, cows, sheep; we are caterpillars; we are leaves of ivy and sprigs of wallflower. We are women. We rise from the wave. We are gazelle and doe, elephant and whale, lilies and roses and peach, we are air, we are flame, we are oyster and pearl, we are girls. We are woman and nature. And he says he cannot hear us speak.*
>
> *But we hear.*[40]

Griffin sought to overcome dualism by providing what David Maccauley has termed an "antidote to Plato's epistemological hierarchy." In his *Republic* Plato led Western man out of what he regarded as an inferior sensory realm, the world of appearances, into what he regarded as a superior intellectual realm, the world of forms. In this latter world *ideas* such as beauty, truth, and goodness supposedly reside. However, in book one of *Woman and Nature* Griffin suggested Plato led us astray by incorrectly insisting that spirit is superior to matter and by prompting us to view man as mind and woman as body. Plato's dualistic hierarchy, stressed Griffin, is behind Western's society's view that women are men's inferiors.[41]

Emphasizing the links between men's ideas about nature and their attitudes toward women, Griffin saw similarities between men's domestication of animals and their "domestication" of woman. She also noted ways in which women have either actively participated in or passively accepted their own "taming." For example, in a chapter entitled "Cows: The Way We Yield," Griffin suggested that the words used to describe a cow can be used equally well to describe a woman:

> She is a great cow. She stands in the midst of her own soft flesh, her thighs great wide arches, round columns, her hips wide enough for calving, sturdy, rounded, swaying, stupefied mass, a cradle, a waving field of nipples, her udder brushing the grass, a great cow, who thinks nothing, who waits to be milked, year after year, who delivers up calves, who stands ready for the bull, who is faithful, always there, yielding at the same hour, day after day, that warm substance, the milk white of her eye, staring, trusting, sluggish, bucolic, inert, bovine mind dozing and dreaming, who lays open her flesh, like a drone, for the use of the world.[42]

Asked why she chose to describe woman in terms of domestic rather than wild animals, Griffin responded that her two-year experience as a housebound wife and mother caused her to identify with domestic animals, whom she viewed as well taken care of but decidedly unfree.[43]

Viewing Western thought's "decision" to privilege culture (man) over nature (woman) as a disastrous one, Griffin proceeded in book two of *Woman and Nature* to discuss all the "separations" that Platonic philosophy generated: mind/body, intellect/emotion, city/wilderness, knower/known. She also critiqued scientific knowledge, ridiculing the importance men attach to numbers, in particular how they quantify everything in the universe and in their possession. Everything is reducible to a sum, a statistic, a cost-benefit ratio, said Griffin. Horrified by the thought of a world ruled by and reduced to numbers, Griffin urged women to journey out of culture—the labyrinth of dualistic thinking—back into nature—the cave where matter and spirit merge into one, the true habitat of human beings who are more than mere "ideas."

Finally, in the third and fourth books of *Woman and Nature*, Griffin claimed we can overcome the kind of thinking that belittles nature, materiality, the body, and women, but only if women learn to speak for themselves and for the natural world. She insisted we need to replace "his certainty"—quantity, probability, and gravity—with (her?) "possibility," his "land" and "timber" with "this earth" and "the forest,"[44] and his reason with her emotion. Griffin wrote:

> They said that in order to discover truth, they must find ways to separate feeling from thought *Because we were less* That measurements and criteria must be established free from emotional bias *Because they said our brains were smaller* That these measurements can be computed *Because we were built closer to the ground* according to universal laws *Because according to their tests we*

> *think more slowly, because according to their criteria our bodies are more like the*
> *bodies of animals, because according to their calculations we can lift less weight,*
> *work longer hours, suffer more pain, they said,* constitute objectivity *because we*
> *are more emotional than they are* and based they said only on what *because our*
> *behavior is observed to be like the behavior of children* is observably true *because*
> *we lack the capacity to be reasonable* and emotions they said must be distrusted
> *because we are filled with rage* that where emotions color thought *because we cry*
> *out* thought is no longer objective *because we are shaking* and therefore no
> longer describes what is real *shaking in our rage because we are shaking in our*
> *rage and we are no longer reasonable.*[45]

Nature has a value that cannot be reduced to its usefulness to culture, and woman has a value that cannot be reduced to her usefulness to man.

In some of her later work, Griffin revisited the nature-culture dichotomy, depicting pornography as culture's revenge against nature as well as men's revenge against women. "We will see," said Griffin, "that the bodies of women in pornography, mastered, bound, silenced, beaten, even murdered, are symbols for natural feeling and the powers of nature which the pornographic mind hates and fears."[46] Commenting on Griffin's analysis of the pornographic mind, David Maccauley urged us to ask ourselves, "Whether there now exists . . . a kind of earth pornography, since the gendered planet, the 'mother of life' or 'our nurse' as Plato referred to it, is not only violated literally by strip mining, deforestation, and radioactive waste but subjected increasingly to the circulation of a voyeuristic media—as the image of a bounded, blue sphere is re-placed (away from natural context) on billboards or commercials in order to sell computers, hamburgers, or candidate's positions."[47] Just as women's violated bodies are used to sell all sorts of commodities, such as cars, boats, and designer jeans, so, too, is nature's violated "body" similarly used. Women, implied Griffin, must refuse to let themselves and nature be exploited in such ways. Reform, indeed revolution, begins with saying no to what *is* in order to seek what *might be.*

Spiritual Ecofeminists

Closely allied to so-called cultural, or nature, ecofeminists are a variety of so-called spiritual ecofeminists, two of the most prominent being Starhawk and Charlene Spretnak.[48] Reflecting on the ways in which an anthropocentric perspective tries to justify the harms human beings inflict upon nature as well as on the ways in which an androcentric perspective tries to justify the harms men inflict upon women, spiritual ecofeminists posit a close connection between environmental degradation and the Judeo-Christian conviction that God gave humans "dominion" over the earth. Inspired by Mary Daly's *Gyn/Ecology* and Rosemary Radford

Ruether's *New Woman, New Earth*, they insist that no matter which theology, religion, or spirituality women adopt, it must be an *embodied* rather than a *disembodied* way of relating to the ultimate source or deepest wellspring of meaning. Implicit in the thought of most spiritual ecofeminists, therefore, is the view that unless "patriarchal" religions such as Judaism and Christianity can purge themselves of the idea of an omnipotent, disembodied male spirit, women should abandon the oppressive confines of their synagogues and churches and run to the open spaces of nature, where they can practice any one of a number of earth-based spiritualities.

Although spiritual ecofeminists draw strength from a variety of earth-based spiritualities, they tend to gravitate toward ancient goddess worship and nature-oriented Native American ritual. They believe that cultures that view the female body as sacred also view nature as sacred, honoring its cycles and rhythms. Spiritual ecofeminists often draw an analogy between the role of women in biological production and the role of an archetypical "Earth Mother" or "birth-mother" (usually referred to as "Gaia")[49] in giving life and creating all that exists. Because women's role is analogous to Gaia's role, women's relationship to nature is privileged over men's relationship to nature, according to spiritual ecofeminists.

Starhawk.   Among the best-known spiritual ecofeminists who stress the woman-nature link is Starhawk. In one of her poems, she wrote that nature's and women's work are one and the same:

> *As your labor has become her labor*
> *Out of the bone, ash*
> *Out of the ash, pain*
> *Out of the pain, the swelling*
> *Out of the swelling, the opening*
> *Out of the opening, the labor*
> *Out of the labor, the birth*
> *Out of the birth, the turning*
> *wheel the turning tide.*[50]

Through their uniquely female bodily experiences—their monthly menses, the demanding symbiosis of pregnancy, the pain of childbirth, and the pleasure of breast-feeding their infants—women supposedly come to know, in a way men cannot, that human beings are one with nature.

Starhawk claimed the kind of earth-based spirituality she practices as a witch (by which she means a woman charged with the task and possessing the skill to "bend" and "reshape" Western culture) provides a good deal of the energy still left in the feminist movement.[51] In her estimation, earth-based spirituality has three core concepts. The first is *immanence*.

The Goddess is *in* the living world, in the human, animal, plant, and mineral communities. Therefore, each being has value, and each conscious being also has power. Understood not as power-over but as power-from-within, this power is "the inherent ability . . . to become what we are meant to be—as a seed has within it the inherent power to root, grow, flower, and fruit."[52] We grow in this kind of creative power, claimed Starhawk, when we take on responsibility for everyone and everything to which we are related and also when we strive to achieve personal integrity by prioritizing our needs and those of our entire relational network. Spirituality is not an "opiate"; it is an energizer and stimulus to action. Starhawk explained: "When what's going on is the poisoning and destruction of the earth, our own personal development requires that we grapple with that and do something to stop it, to turn the tide and heal the planet."[53]

The second feature of earth-based spirituality is *interconnection* and the expanded view of self it encourages. Not only are our bodies natural, but so, too, are our minds, Starhawk stressed: "Our human capacities of loyalty and love, rage and humor, lust, intuition, intellect, and compassion are as much a part of nature as the lizards and the redwood forests."[54] The more we understand that we are nature, wrote Starhawk, the more we will understand our oneness with all that exists: human beings, natural cycles and processes, animals, and plants. We will make the mistake neither of allying ourselves with human beings against nature nor of allying ourselves with nature against human beings, as some environmentalists do when they engage in extreme forms of so-called ecoterrorism. Killing animal research scientists in the name of animal liberation is not better than killing animals in order to find cures for the diseases threatening human beings. There is, implied Starhawk, almost always a way to serve the interests of one and all. Our own interests "are linked to black people in South Africa as well as to forest-dwellers in the Amazon, and . . . their interests in turn are not separate from those of the eagle, the whale, and the grizzly bear."[55]

The third and probably most important feature of earth-based spirituality is the kind of *compassionate life-style* women typically lead. Starhawk claimed that unless we care for each other, we can forget about "reweaving the world" or "healing the wounds." Thus, she faulted deep ecologist Daniel Connor for suggesting "the AIDS virus may be Gaia's tailor-made answer to human overpopulation," as well as deep ecologist Dave Foreman for opposing the provision of famine relief to starving African nations.[56] She commented: "When environmentalists applaud the demise of Africans and homosexuals, they ally themselves with the same interests that are killing people of color, gay people, women, and other vulnerable groups. Those same interests are destroying the earth's ecosystems and raping the wilderness."[57] According to Starhawk, spiritual ecofeminists—especially those who regard themselves as witches—bring to the environmental movement a compassionate perspective that permits them "to identify powerlessness and the structures that perpetuate it as the root cause of famine, of overpopulation, of the callous destruction of the natural environment."[58]

The nature-culture dichotomy, indeed all dichotomies, must be dissolved so we can appreciate the "oneness" of reality. Starhawk implied, however, that it is not a matter of indifference how this "oneness" is achieved. Culture ought to be subsumed into nature rather than vice versa, for unless we all live more simply, some of us will not be able to live at all. Starhawk also suggested that even though women are probably more ready, willing, and able to take the lead in generating improved social relations and a less violent and more sustainable way of life than men are, there is certainly room for feminist men in the save-the-earth movement:

> *The labor is hard, the night is long*
> *We are midwives, and men who tend*
> *the birth and bond with the child.*
> *We are birthing, and being born*
> *We are trying to perform an act of*
> *magic—*
> *To pull a living child out of a near-corpse of the mother we are*
> *simultaneously poisoning, who is ourselves.*[59]

With Mary Daly, Starhawk declared her total opposition to necrophilia and her wholehearted and whole-minded embracing of life.

The Argument for Deemphasizing the Nature-Woman Connection: Social, or Social-Constructionist, Ecofeminism

Like nature, or culture, ecofeminists, including spiritual ecofeminists, so-called social, or social-constructionist, ecofeminists ponder woman's connection to nature. Unlike the former ecofeminists, however, the latter seek to deemphasize the nature-woman connection. They imply that unless women minimize their socially constructed and ideologically reinforced *special* connections to nature, not only will women continue to be subordinated to men, but nature will continue to be subordinated to culture. All human beings—male and female—must understand they are just as much natural as they are cultural.

Dorothy Dinnerstein. Western dichotomous thought, said Dorothy Dinnerstein, must be exploded in order to end the oppression of everyone and everything currently devalued. This explosion must begin with the deconstruction of the male-female dichotomy, for it is the fundamental source of "the silent hatred of Mother Earth which breathes side by side with our love for her, and which, like the hate we feel for our human mothers, poisons our attachment to life."[60] As noted above, Dinnerstein claimed that as a result of our nearly exclusively female practice of mothering, all infants (be they male or female) come to view women as the cause of their most positive *and* most negative feelings. When she is available for her child, the mother will, if she can, meet her child's needs almost immediately and completely; but when she is unavailable for her child, the mother will not, even if she can, meet her child's needs. Instead, she will discomfort, frustrate, or anger him or her. As it is with the mother—that is, woman—so it is with nature, the realm of reality with which woman is identified. Mother Nature can bestow blessings on us, but "she" can also mete out harms and hardships to us: hurricanes, volcanoes, floods, fires, famines, disease, death. Thus, the only way for human beings—especially men who do not bodily resemble the mother in the ways women do—to deal with "mother" or "nature" is to seek to control her, to separate her from all that is male or identified as "masculine," including culture.

However, Dinnerstein asserted the attempt to exclude women and nature from men and culture has caused us (she includes women as complicit in this psychopathological arrangement) not only to *maim and exploit women, and stunt and deform men* " but also to proceed *"toward the final matricide—the rageful, greedy murder of the planet that spawned us."*[61] Borrowing an idea from Lewis Mumford, she observed that most of us are firm believers in the "megamachine" myth. This myth entails the view that human beings can use their minds and tools not only to extend control over nature and everything identified with nature—woman, the body, life, death, and so on—but also to make huge monetary profits in the course of doing so. According to Dinnerstein, this myth will continue to rule our thoughts and actions unless we end the present division of the world into male and female (culture and nature) and the assignments of women to nature (child-rearing as well as childbearing) and men to culture (world building). Women must bring nature into culture (by entering the public world), and men must bring culture into nature (by entering the private world). Then and only then will we see that men and women (culture and nature) are *one* and that it is counterproductive for half of reality to try to dominate the other half. A reality, divided and at war with itself, cannot and will not survive. Thus, Dinnerstein proclaimed, "The core meaning of feminism . . . lies, at this point, in its relations to earthly life's survival."[62] Unless men and women get their act together and start behaving like adults instead of infants, the human species can expect a rapid demise.

Karen J. Warren.   Like Dinnerstein, Karen J. Warren emphasized that the dualisms threatening to destroy us are social constructions. In a capitalist patriarchal society, women and nature, men and culture, have certain meanings, but these meanings are far from necessary. They would be very different in a socialist nonpatriarchal society. For example, they would be very different in the kind of society Marge Piercy posited in *Woman on the Edge of Time*, a work of fiction in which people rejected all dualisms, beginning with the male-female dichotomy. As noted above (see Chapter Two) in Mattapoisett, Piercy's utopia, babies are born from brooders and raised by three co-mothers (of both sexes). Since both men and women mother—the men even lactate and nurse—both men and women also work. Piercy's society is also one in which the line between nature and culture is largely nonexistent. Although Mattapoisett is agriculturally oriented, it is also technologically advanced. Almost totally mechanized factories do the society's drudge work and heavy labor, producing the tools and commodities necessary to sustain a system of military *defense* (not offense), agricultural production, a limited (nonpolluting) transportation system, and a comfortable life-style for one and all. People's work is both socially useful and personally rewarding, and there is nothing that resembles a sexual division of labor. Work is based entirely on people's abilities and proclivities, with a modicum of unpleasant work (e.g., waste disposal) equally distributed to all people. As the result of serious efforts to control the size of the population, Mattapoisett's communities are small, self-sufficient, and very democratic. People have time for play as well as work. Indeed, inhabitants of Mattapoisett are anything but workaholics. They enjoy both the serenity of the natural world and the excitement of the "holies," a highly developed cinematic/multisensory experience. Persons are both masculine and feminine; society is both natural and cultural.[63]

Wanting very much to reconceptualize nature and culture as well as man and woman—without insisting, as Piercy did, that women must forsake their special role in biological reproduction—[64] Warren claimed feminists must be ecofeminists. She argued that, *logically*, feminism is just as much a movement to end naturism as it is a movement to end sexism:

(C1) Feminism is a movement to end sexism.
(C2) But sexism is conceptually linked with naturism (through an oppressive conceptual framework characterized by a logic of domination).
(C3) Thus, feminism is (also) a movement to end naturism.[65]

All forms of oppression are interlocked and intertwined. Oppression is a many-headed beast that will continue to exist and regenerate itself until human beings manage *completely* to behead it.

Focusing on the kind of ecoethics currently informing environmentalism, Warren commented there are within it many sexist elements, or male biases, that undermine its ability to "save the earth." Only an ecofeminist ethics—an ecoethics free of androcentric as well as anthropocentric distortions—can overcome naturism once and for all. Such an ethics must be

1. antinaturist, rejecting "any way of thinking about or acting toward nonhuman nature that reflects a relationship to the logic, values, or attitude of domination"
2. contextualist, emphasizing human beings' *relationships* to nonhuman nature instead of stressing human beings' *rights* over or *duties* to nonhuman nature
3. structurally pluralistic, recognizing the differences among humans as well as the differences between humans and nonhumans
4. theoretically "in-process," favoring first-person narrative and the active voice over third-person analysis and the passive voice
5. inclusivist
6. subjectively "biased," identifying "patriarchal conceptual frameworks" such as the female-male and nature-culture splits as the fundamental cause of naturism and sexism, both of which are wrong
7. attentive to and appreciative of traditionally "feminine" values
8. interested in reconceiving humans as creatures who are dependent on the environment and whose "essence" is no less material and earthy than it is spiritual and other-worldly.[66]

Warren claimed ecofeminists are able to relate to nonhumans in ways that overcome the nature-culture split without denying their differences from nonhumans. In one example she contrasted rock climbers who climb in order to conquer mountains and rock climbers who climb in order to know mountains (and therefore themselves) in new ways. When an ecofeminist climbs a mountain, said Warren, she assumes she has a genuine *relationship* to it. Her concern is not in showing it who is "boss" by making it to the top but in becoming its friend, someone who cares about it. Thus, an ecofeminist does not look at the mountain with an "arrogant eye," viewing it as a hunk of inert matter trying to get the best of her by exhausting her. Rather, she sees it with a "loving eye," viewing it as a unique reality with much to tell her about her strengths and weaknesses.[67]

In another example Warren told the story of a young Sioux boy sent by his father to learn "the old Indian ways" from his grandfather. Among other things, the boy's grandfather taught him how to hunt by instructing him

to shoot your four-legged brother in his hind area, slowing it down but not killing it. Then, take the four-legged's head in your hands, and look into his eyes. The eyes are where all the suffering is. Look into your brother's eyes and feel his pain. Then, take your knife and cut the four-legged under his chin, here, on his neck, so that he dies quickly. And as you do, ask your brother, the four-legged, for forgiveness for what you do. Offer also a prayer of thanks to your four-legged kin for offering his body to you just now, when you need food to eat and clothing to wear. And promise the four-legged that you will put yourself back into the earth when you die, to become nourishment for the earth, and for the sister flowers, and for the brother deer. It is appropriate that you should offer this blessing for the four-legged and, in due time, reciprocate in turn with your body in this way, as the four-legged gives life to you for your survival.[68]

The lesson the Sioux grandfather taught his grandson about hunting is clearly far more ecofeminist (antinaturist and antisexist) than the lesson the typical "great white hunter" would teach his grandson about hunting for the "fun" or "sport" of it, for the "pleasure" of the kill. The Sioux hunting lesson is one that informs us how people whose conceptual schemes are not oppositional see themselves in *relationship* to nonhuman nature. Nevertheless, the Sioux hunting lesson is not fully ecofeminist, for it does not proceed from a gender analysis. Moreover, it arose in a culture that treats women as less than men's equals. This last fact suggests, contra Warren, that even in a culture where women are no more identified with nature than men are, sexism might still exist.

Socialist Ecofeminists

According to Warren, of the four major branches of feminist thought—liberal, Marxist, radical, and socialist—the socialist comes closest to providing the theoretical basis from which to launch ecofeminist practices. Liberal feminism is deficient, in Warren's estimation, because it maintains dualisms such as culture/nature, mind/body, and rational/emotional. Like liberalism, liberal feminism emphasizes the value of individualism and independence as opposed to the importance of weblike relationships and the connectedness of all forms of life and natural resources.[69] Thus, liberal feminism is not particularly compatible with ecology; indeed, its theoretical basis seems to be at odds with ecology.

Marxist feminism is inadequate for very different reasons, noted Warren. Marxist feminists, like Marxists, believe physical labor is the essential human activity that transforms natural, material resources into products for human exchange and consumption. This theoretical approach allows little if any room for concerns about nature, since Marxists and Marxist feminists place liberated "men and women, as one class, over and against nature."[70] Moreover, in setting the human world over and against the nonhuman world, Marxist feminism fails to appreciate just how closely women's oppression is linked with nature's oppression. To set women in opposition to nature is to set women in opposition to themselves in a profound way.[71]

Finally, observed Warren, radical feminism is inadequate because it unwittingly "assumes the very nature-culture split that ecofeminism denies"[72] by requiring women either to embrace (radical-cultural feminists) or to reject (radical-libertarian feminists) their biological connections to nature. Stressing that women's interests are served neither by identifying nor by disidentifying women with nature, Warren insisted ecofeminism must view both men and women as equally "natural" and equally "cultural."

Warren stressed that socialist feminism is fundamentally antidualist. Its goal is, as Alison Jaggar stated, "to abolish the social relations that constitute humans not only as workers and capitalists but also as women and men."[73] Yet, observed Warren, socialist feminism does not seem intent on abolishing the human-nonhuman dichotomy, failing to recognize the extent to which the oppression of women by men is linked to the oppression of nonhumans by humans. For this reason, Warren called for a "feminism" even more comprehensive than socialist feminism, a feminism she termed "transformative feminism."[74]

According to Warren, transformative feminism has six features. First, it recognizes and makes explicit the interconnections between all systems of oppression. Second, it stresses the diversity of women's experiences, forsaking the search for "woman" and her unitary experience. Third, it rejects the logic of domination. Fourth, it rethinks what it means to be a human being, courageously reconsidering whether humans should view "consciousness" (and rationality) as not only that which distinguishes them from nonhumans but somehow makes them better than nonhumans. Fifth, it relies on an ethic that stresses those traditional "feminine" virtues that tend to weave, interconnect, and unite people. Finally, it maintains science and technology be used only to the extent they preserve the earth.[75] Given Warren's analysis of transformative feminism, it would seem to constitute a "thinking space" where men and women from all over the world can gather together to mix and match multiple feminist insights.

Maria Mies and Vandana Shiva.   Among the social ecofeminists who may already have bridged the gap between socialist ecofeminism and transformative ecofeminism are Maria Mies, a sociologist known for her work on development economics, and Vandana Shiva, a physicist known for her interests in spirituality, a fact that has generated some tension between Mies and Shiva. Like many global feminists, Mies and Shiva stressed that since women, more than men, are engaged in the work of sustaining daily *life*, women, more than men, are concerned about the elements: air, water, earth, fire. In order to bear and rear healthy children and in order to provide their families with nourishing food, adequate clothing, and sturdy housing, women need fertile soil, lush plant life, fresh water, and clean air. In addition, like many postmodern feminists, Mies and Shiva lamented Western culture's obsession with the idea of "sameness"—the universal "I," the overarching "one." Capitalism and patriarchy, they observed, are systems that stamp out difference, doggedly cloning themselves, their ideas, and their salable goods wherever they go. Finally, like many socialist feminists, Mies and Shiva observed how people in capitalist patriarchies tend to be alienated from everything: the products of their labor, nature, each other, and even themselves. As a result, human beings in capitalist patriarchies often engage in some fairly bizarre behavior. For example, in an essay entitled "White Man's Dilemma: His Search for What He Has Destroyed,"[76] Mies claimed people in capitalist patriarchies (especially men, because their alienation from nature tends to be greater than women's) want to be closer to nature, but they have no idea about how to bridge the gap between themselves and it.

First, there is "the flight into 'Nature', the 'wilderness', 'underdeveloped' countries of the South, to areas where White Man . . . has not yet 'penetrated.'"[77] Thus, tourist agents promote "Third World" trips to nations such as Senegal as follows: "European tourists can live in villages in close contact with the 'natives' in African-style huts with minimum comfort, African food, no running water and where European and African children play together. The 'real' Africa to be touched!"[78] Second, explained Mies, rather than trying to unite with the "mundane" nature right in his backyard, white man seeks the kind of nature he (or she) perceives as "colony, backward, exotic, distant and dangerous, the nature of Asia, Africa, South America."[79] Those who yearn for this special kind of nature do not desire to relate to it productively by working on it or tending to it but rather by absorbing it or consuming it—by locking it in the chambers of their cameras or by marketing it to others as souvenirs. Third, white man—and here Mies means biological males—yearns for yet another kind of nature, the space known as woman's body. It, too, is wild terrain, the "dark continent." But once again, when white man relates to woman's body, he relates to it as he relates to nature. Prostitution tourism is the perfect example of this type of pathological behavior, noted Mies: Rich white men pay to colonize the bodies of poor, dark women.

According to Mies, sex is white man's last hope to connect to nature because there is nothing else deeply sensual in his or her life (here Mies refers to all people in capitalist patriarchies). In general, people in capitalist patriarchies have little direct physical contact with plants, the earth, animals, and the elements. Their relationship to nature tends to be mediated through machines, which function to further alienate them from nature. However, because people in capitalist patriarchies, like people everywhere, are bodily creatures, they yearn for physical intimacy. Sex becomes their obsession, for it is the *only direct* physical contact they have with nature. Commented Mies:

> The growing sex-obsessing apparent in all industrial societies is . . . a direct consequence of alienation from nature, the absence of a sensual interacting with nature in people's work life. Sexuality is supposed to be the totally "other" from work, sexuality should not interfere with work, should be strictly separated from the work life. Sexuality is the "transcendence" of work, the "heaven" after the "valley of tears and sweat" of work, the real essence of leisure. . . . The tragedy is, however, that this "heaven" is also a commodity, to be bought like any other. And like the acquisition of other consumer goods, ultimately, it disappoints. . . . Therefore, the constantly disappointed striving to attain this "heaven" transforms need into an addiction.[80]

Reflecting on Mies's comments, we may find it easy to view her and her coauthor, Shiva, as socialist-*transformative* ecofeminists. Shiva as well as Mies believed there are enough similarities among women to motivate women to work together against capitalist patriarchy and the destructive isms it spawns. As evidence that all women share similar interests in preserving nature, Mies and Shiva provided numerous examples of Third World and First World women struggling against ecological destruction and deterioration. Women, they noted, have led the battle to preserve the bases of life wherever and whenever military and/or industrial interests have threatened them.

Among the case studies Shiva presented to demonstrate why trees, for example, are a feminist issue and not simply an ecological issue was the 1974 protest of twenty-seven northern Indian women to stop the felling of their homeland's small, indigenous trees.[81] These women intended to cling physically to the trees had lumberjacks attempted to cut them down. The women's protest, known as the *chipko* (a Hindi word meaning "to hug") movement, saved thousands of square kilometers of sensitive watershed. Because wood is inextricably connected to their rural and household economies, providing food, fuel, fodder, products for the home, and income, the *chipko* women were willing to die to keep the indigenous trees from being replaced by imported trees too large for them to fell. According to outsiders, it was in the best interests of northern Indians to plant "income-generating" eucalyptus trees, which produce a marketable fiber. But even if it was in the interests of some northern Indian men to switch their "allegiance" to the eucalyptus, it was not in the best interests of northern Indian women to do so, said Shiva. They and their families needed and wanted trees for all sorts of purposes: to use as fence poles; to provide materials for baskets, dyes, medicines, and decorations; for shade; for food;

and most important, to symbolize who the people of northern India are and stand for as a unique people. Shiva used poetic words to express the *chipko* women's intense feelings about their trees.

> *A fight for truth has begun*
> *At Sinsyaru Khala*
> *A fight for rights has begun*
> *In Malkot Thano*
> *Sister, it is a fight to protect*
> *Our mountains and forests*
> *They give us life*
> *Embrace the life of the living trees*
> *And streams to your hearts*
> *Resist the digging of mountains*
> *Which kills our forests and streams*
> *A fight for life has begun at*
> *Sinsyaru Khala.*[82]

If life is a theme for socialist-transformative ecofeminists, so, too, is freedom. The freedom to which Mies and Shiva referred is not the kind of Marxist freedom that requires man to master nature and therefore woman's body. Rather, it is the kind of freedom that asks all of us to recognize and accept our "naturalness," our physicality and materiality, our carnality and mortality. Because nature is an exhaustible good, we must learn to conserve it by living as simply as possible and by consuming as little as possible. If we care about our descendants' lives, we must develop a so-called subsistence perspective.

It is not surprising that Mies and Shiva proposed a subsistence perspective as the key to dissolving all the practices and systems that threaten to destroy the earth. They are, after all, *socialist*-transformative ecofeminists for whom "transformation" must be material as well as spiritual. Mies claimed people in capitalist patriarchies need to take ten steps if they are serious about developing a subsistence life-style:

1. People should produce only enough to satisfy fundamental human *needs*, resisting the urge to produce "an ever-growing mountain of commodities and money (wages or profit)"[83] in a futile attempt to still people's endless and insatiable *wants*.
2. People should use only as much of nature as they need to, treating it as a reality with "her own subjectivity;"[84] and people should use each other not to make money but to create communities capable of meeting people's fundamental needs, especially their need for intimacy.

3. People should replace representative democracy with participatory democracy so each man and woman has the opportunity to express his or her concerns to everyone else.
4. People should develop "multidimensional or synergic"[85] problem-solving approaches, since the problems of contemporary society are interrelated.
5. People should combine contemporary science, technologies, and knowledge with ancient wisdom, traditions, and even magic.
6. People should break down the boundaries between work and play, the sciences and the arts, spirit and matter.
7. People should view water, air, earth, and all natural resources as community goods rather than as private possessions.
8. Men as well as women should adopt the socialist-transformative ecofeminist view, the subsistence perspective. Commented Mies:

> Ecofeminism does not mean, as some argue, that women will clean up the ecological mess which capitalist-patriarchal men have caused; women will not eternally be the *Trummerfrauen* (the women who clear up the ruins after the patriarchal wars). Therefore, a subsistence perspective necessarily means men begin to share, *in practice*, the responsibility for the creation and preservation of life on this planet. Therefore, men must start a movement to redefine their identity. They must give up their involvement in destructive commodity production for the sake of accumulation and begin to share women's work for the preservation of life. In practical terms this means they have to share unpaid subsistence work: in the household, with children, with the old and sick, in ecological work to heal the earth, in new forms of subsistence production.[86]

9. Men as well as women should cultivate traditional feminine virtues (caring, compassion, nurturance) and engage in subsistence productions, for "only a society based on a subsistence perspective can afford to live in peace with nature, and uphold peace between nations, generations and men and women."[87]
10. Most important, people should realize that in order for each person to have enough, no person can "have it all." Mies claimed that Kamla Bhasin, an Indian feminist, expressed this thought in a particularly forceful manner when she stated that "sustainable development"

> is not compatible with the existing profit- and growth-oriented development paradigm. And this means that the standard of living of the North's affluent societies cannot be generalized. This was already clear to Mahatma Gandhi 60 years ago, who, when asked by a British journalist whether he would like India to have the same standard of living as Britain, replied: "To have its standard of living a tiny coun-

try like Britain had to exploit half the globe. How many globes will India need to exploit to have the same standard of living?" From an ecological and feminist perspective, moreover, even if there were more globes to be exploited, it is not even desirable that this development paradigm and standard of living was generalized, because it has failed to fulfil its promises of happiness, freedom, dignity and peace, even for those who have profited from it.[88]

Critiques of Ecofeminism

Nature, or Cultural, Ecofeminism

Because there are so many varieties of ecofeminism, no general critique is applicable. As noted above, the critiques raised against nature, or cultural, ecofeminism are similar to those raised against radical-cultural feminism. In the estimation of Janet Biehl, nature ecofeminists erred when they "biologize(d) women as presumably uniquely ecological beings"[89] who are able to relate to and understand nature in ways men simply cannot, and who are caring and nurturing in ways men, try as they might, can never be. There is, said Biehl, too much willingness among nature ecofeminists either to reduce women into mere bodies or to limit women's potentialities and abilities to those associated with their supposedly "caring nature." As Biehl saw it, nature ecofeminism is reactionary rather than revolutionary. Quoting Simone de Beauvoir, from whom many cultural (nature) ecofeminists borrowed their basic concept of women's and nature's "otherness," Biehl stressed that women celebrate the nature-woman connection at their own peril, for "that's the formula used to try and keep women quiet."[90] Biehl insisted that ecofeminists like Mary Daly misled women by suggesting women can by fiat "reclaim" the meaning of the nature-woman connection as an entirely positive one. The fact of the matter, insisted Biehl, is that the nature-woman connection has been "enormously debasing to women,"[91] and centuries of negative cultural baggage cannot be cast off by passionate "reclaiming" alone.

Spiritual Ecofeminism

Critics on the left fault spiritual ecofeminists for substituting religion for politics and for spending too much time dancing in the moonlight, casting "magic" spells, chanting mantras, doing yoga, "mindfully" meditating, and giving each other massages. Defenders of spiritual ecofeminism concede that some spiritual ecofeminists might have mistaken New Age or "spa" spirituality for genuine ecofeminist spirituality, but they insist such mistakes were the exception, not the rule. Goddess worship is not, said

Mies and Shiva, "luxury spirituality," "the idealist icing on top of the material cake of the West's standard of living."[92] It is not about turning the East's spiritual and cultural treasures into commodities for sale as exotica to privileged and pampered Western people who lack "meaning." Rather, Goddess worship is an attempt to break the culturally constructed dichotomy between spirituality and materiality and to recognize everything and everyone as worthy and deserving of respect. Spiritual ecofeminists, observed Ynestra King, are not other-worldly dreamers; they are this-worldly activists. Spiritual ecofeminists use such "community-building techniques" as performance art, kinesthetic observations (dancing and chanting), and ritual to enable people "to establish and maintain community with one another in contentious and difficult situations of political engagement in the public world."[93] Some spiritual ecofeminists may indeed choose to restrict their political activities to their local communities, insisting "theirs is the politics of everyday life, the transformation of fundamental relationships, even if that takes place only in small communities."[94] They claim so-called everyday politics is "much more effective than countering the power games of men with similar games."[95] But just because some spiritual ecofeminists refuse to play power games with men does not mean they should be dismissed as crystal gazers. Not everyone who cares about the earth and works to safeguard it needs to move to the Women's Peace Camp at Greenham Commons in England; there is work to be done in one's own backyard as well as in far away places.

Social and Social-Constructionist Ecofeminism

As noted above, social ecofeminists deny women are "naturally" caring and nurturing, instead claiming that women's feminine characteristics are the products of enculturation or socialization. For example, Carolyn Merchant repeatedly emphasized that "any analysis that makes women's essence and qualities special ties them to a biological destiny that thwarts the possibility of liberation. A politics grounded in women's culture, experience, and values can be seen as reactionary."[96] Women are no more "natural" than they are "cultural."

However, according to critics, deemphasizing the connections between women's and nature's life-giving capacities "somewhat diminish[es] the original ecofeminist passion to reclaim 'nature' in an organic sense—certainly when it comes to women's biology."[97] Moreover, an ecofeminism grounded in women's traditional feminine virtues, maternal roles, and special relationship to nature need not be "reactionary." Such an ecofeminism can be "revolutionary."

Alluding to the revolutionary potential of so-called maternal thinking, Sara Ruddick noted that when women become aware, for example, that the government is stockpiling nuclear weapons or letting major corporations pollute the environment, many women feel moved to protest, picket, and even riot against the military-industrial complex. Although such women often choose to fight alongside men, they sometimes fight alone, claiming that they, *as women*, have particularly strong reasons for resisting war and protecting the earth. Women, said Ruddick, "who bring to the public plazas of a police state pictures of their loved ones, like women who put pillowcases, toys and other artifacts of attachment against the barbed wire fences of missile bases, translate the symbols of mothers into political speech."[98]

"Maternal" political speech can be very effective. When a reasonable human being looks at a dead child's toys, he or she is likely to realize the senselessness as well as cruelty of most of the wars waged between nations. Indeed, even those ecofeminists who wish to deny that women are naturally more nurturant than men admit that they, too, have thought "maternally." For example, Ynestra King, a critic of cultural (nature) ecofeminism noted that throughout her entire pregnancy she kept thinking that in the time it took her to gestate one precious human being, 8,000 children in the Persian Gulf had starved to death or died of causes directly attributable to the weapons used by U.S. forces during the Gulf War. Overwhelmed by this thought, she realized that "thinking like an ecofeminist" requires one to make "abstract connections concrete."[99]

Socialist Ecofeminism and Transformative-Socialist Ecofeminism

Although critics find the perspective of socialist ecofeminists compelling, they suspect its demands are too challenging for ordinary people to accept. In particular, they note the degree of activism and changes in lifestyle transformative-socialist ecofeminism requires are ones typical citizens in affluent societies are neither ready nor willing nor able (on account of the ways in which they have been socialized) to embrace. For example, most people, including most feminists, are neither vegetarians nor pacifists nor "tree-huggers," and most of them do not want to radically change their life-styles.

In response to this objection, some socialist ecofeminists simply comment that people's reluctance to make life-style changes is not a moral justification for their not doing so. Altruism requires a certain measure of self-sacrifice. Other socialist ecofeminists soften this response by conceding that moral progress is often incremental. Even if a person is not willing to forsake eating meat altogether, he or she can at least refuse to eat animals that have been factory-farmed or grown under extremely cruel conditions.

Likewise, even if a person is not willing to devote the bulk of his or her time working for environmental causes or feels overwhelmed by them, there is *always* some positive difference, however small, he or she can make. Doretta Zemp, creator of the satirical comic strip *Roseanna of the Planet*, commented:

> Too often the environmental issues are bigger than we are, and we feel help-less in the face of their enormity, such as the greenhouse effect, the rape of the rain forests, and the Bophal pesticide lead, which killed 2500 people and permanently injured 17,000 more. What can we do about that? But Roseanna, my character, is down to our size. She and her best friend, stuffy old Egmont, wax in passion over concerns that are on our scale: chemicals in the home, neighborhood pollution, and the malathion spraying against our will. They disagree on everything except where to go for solutions. He uses ivory tower rhetoric and blind faith. I see Roseanna as every woman, and I see Egmont as exemplifying conventional wisdom, government, and big business.[100]

While Egmont stands idly by, trusting Big Brother will save everyone from environmental doom, Roseanna is busy throwing out the ozone-damaging deodorants in her bathroom, the poisonous bug sprays under her kitchen sink, and the herbicide-laden cosmetics on her bureau. There is, she insists, always something one can do.

Finally, even if a person is not a pacifist, he or she can be antimilitary. To be opposed to the waging of wars—the intention of which is domination by means of destruction of life—is not the same, explained Ruddick, as being opposed to participating in any act of violence whatsoever. Self-defense and wars waged for the purpose of liberating one's self and one's people from the forces of death are not incompatible with socialist ecofeminist ideals. To be sure, socialist ecofeminists will try to resolve conflicts creatively (i.e., nonviolently) and peacefully (i.e., through rational destruction). However, when they realize their voices will not be heard and the destruction of everything and everyone (especially their children) precious to them will continue, even the most peaceful ecofeminists will fight for *life*.

Conclusion

No matter the differences that exist between social-constructionist and nature ecofeminists or between socialist and spiritual ecofeminists, all ecofeminists believe human beings are connected to one another and to the nonhuman world: animal, vegetal, and inert. Unfortunately, we do not always acknowledge our relationships to and responsibilities for other people, let alone those we have to the nonhuman world. As a result, we do violence to each other and to nature, congratulating ourselves on protecting our self-interests. Meanwhile, each day, we kill ourselves by killing our brothers and sisters and by laying waste to the earth from which we originate and to which we will return.

Given the state of human affairs just described, ecofeminists wonder what it will take for the majority of human beings to realize how irrational as well as unfeeling human systems of oppression and domination are. These systems bring in their wake hate, anger, destruction, and death, yet we humans cling to our social constructs. Is the solution to this pathological state of affairs to create a culture in which we honor women and nature as some sort of saviors? Or is it instead to follow Dinnerstein's instructions and insist that men and women alike assume equal responsibility for both child-rearing and world building? What will it take for us to stop thinking dichotomously, to realize we are our own worst enemies? Are we wasting time waiting for the saving grace of some Godot when we should instead be using our own heads and hearts to stop destroying what we are in fact: an interdependent whole, a unity that exists in and through, and not despite, its diversity? Ecofeminists, especially transformative-socialist ecofeminists, have already made their decision. They stopped waiting for the revolution, the transformation, the miracle to happen a long time ago. They are busy at work (and play) doing what they can to eliminate the blights that brown the earth and kill the human spirit. The question remains, however, whether the rest of us are set to join them. No doubt the new millennium will bring the answer.

■

Conclusion:
Margins and Centers

THE PRIMARY PURPOSE OF THIS BOOK has been to highlight some of the main perspectives in feminist thought, without providing reasons for preferring *one* feminist perspective over all the others. This is not to suggest that readers will not find some schools of feminist thought more convincing than others. For example, I am personally attracted both to those forms of feminism that describe where women currently are—at the margins and on the periphery—and to those forms of feminism that describe where women could be—in the center. It is enormously appealing to be an outsider—to be uncorrupted by the system, to see and feel what other people do not see and feel, to be free of tight constraints and unnecessary restraints. But it is equally appealing to be an insider—to be a valued member of the team, to share a common vision, to have, as Aristotle said, "partners in virtue and friends in action."[1]

At the end of the first edition of this book, I wrote that I regarded socialist feminism as the most inclusive form of feminism, since it showed how the forces of sexism and classism interlock in a capitalist patriarchy and how woman's estate is determined by both her reproductive and productive role. What I did not notice ten years ago, however, was the extent to which socialist feminism did not emphasize issues related to racism, colonialism, and naturism. For this reason, I now think that ecofeminism is the most inclusive form of feminism, particularly the socialist-transformative ecofeminism of Maria Mies and Vandana Shiva. Thanks to them, I now understand the extent to which all systems and structures of oppression interlock, reinforcing each other and feeding off of each other's venom.

In a similar manner, ten years ago I thought that the margins of feminist thought were populated most exclusively by postmodern feminists—that they were *the* voice of difference, that they were feminism's best protection against permitting the "standpoint of woman" to degenerate into yet another instantiation of the phallus or logos. I now realize the multi-

278

cultural and global feminists are also voices that speak the language of difference. Together with postmodern feminists they remind us that as bad as it is for a woman to be bullied into submission by a patriarch's unitary truth, it is even worse for her to be judged not a real feminist by a matriarch's unitary truth. I know that I do not like to be accused of "false consciousness" or to be branded a "pseudofeminist," and I suspect that no feminist likes to be told that her explanation of women's oppression is benighted and befuddled. Likewise, I know that I do not like to be told what women think or should think about x, y, or z or to be called on the carpet every time I disagree with prevailing feminist sentiments. After all, there are things about me unique to me—I am not "woman"; I am Rosemarie Behensky/Tong/Putnam. Indeed, this is the "difference" postmodern, multicultural, and global feminists have permitted me.

So here I am again: stretched between women's samenesses and women's differences. But this time around, the stretching is not as painful as it was the first time around. I am a more flexible feminist now: one less worried about labeling things properly and more concerned about getting to know more about women who are not like me—women who live in lands I will probably never get to visit; women in the United States whose paths I will probably never cross; women at my workplace and in my neighborhood whom I should get to know. They all have something to teach me, if I let them. There is, I believe, a great need for women of color and working-class women as well as white and middle-class women to speak their own minds and to express their own feelings. Feminist theory is at its best when it reflects the lived experiences of a wide variety of women, when it bridges the gap between mind and body, reason and emotion, thinking and feeling.

As I see it, attention to difference is precisely what will help women achieve unity. Audre Lorde, whose very person is a celebration of difference—black, lesbian, feminist, disfigured by breast cancer—and whose poetry is a voice against the duality of mind versus body, wrote that as we come to know, accept, and explore our feelings, they will "become sanctuaries and fortresses and spawning grounds for the most radical and daring of ideas—the house of difference so necessary to change and the conceptualization of any meaningful action."[2] Feelings lead to ideas, and ideas lead to action, said Lorde.

There was a time when I viewed my white, middle-class, heterosexual, U.S. self as a permanent obstacle or wall isolating me from women of color, from working-class and upper-class women, from lesbian women, from women who live in different continents. But then I realized that difference does not necessarily mean separation. I think here of the kaleidoscope I used to play with as a child, and the delight I took in bringing together hundreds of chips of colored rocks into a single beautiful pattern—only to break that pattern and bring together an even more beautiful one. As I grew older, I no longer played with my kaleidoscope. The ephemerality of its patterns increasingly distressed me as I learned about *the* good, *the* true, and *the* beautiful. But today I no longer view ephemerality as a problem because I am no longer in quest for *the* meaning of life. Rather, I understand that change and growth are necessary to life and that what makes feminist thought liberating is its vitality, its refusal to stop changing, to stop growing.

As I look back over the pages of this book, I take vicarious pleasure and pride in the different thoughts women have conceived in order to liberate themselves from oppression. To be sure, some of these thoughts have sent women stumbling down cul-de-sacs; but most of them have brought women at least a few steps closer to liberation. Because feminist thought is kaleidoscopic, the reader's preliminary impression may be one of chaos and confusion, of dissension and disagreement, of fragmentation and splintering. But a closer inspection will always reveal new visions, new structures, new relationships for personal and political life, all of which will be different tomorrow than today. What I most treasure about feminist thought, then, is that although it has a beginning, it has no end; and because it has no predetermined end, feminist thought permits each woman to think her own thoughts. Not the truth but the truths will set women free.

Notes

Introduction

1. Mary Wollstonecraft, *A Vindication of the Rights of Women*, Carol H. Poston, ed. (New York: W. W. Norton, 1975).

2. John Stuart Mill, "The Subjection of Women," in John Stuart Mill and Harriet Taylor Mill, *Essays on Sex Equality*, Alice S. Rossi, ed. (Chicago: University of Chicago Press, 1970), pp. 184–185.

3. Catharine A. MacKinnon elaborated upon the sex/gender system in MacKinnon, "Feminism, Marxism, Method, and the State: An Agenda for Theory," *Signs: Journal of Women in Culture and Society* 7, no. 3 (Spring 1982): 515–516.

4. Linda Alcoff, "Culture Feminism Versus Poststructuralism: The Identity Crisis in Feminist Theory," *Signs: Journal of Women in Culture and Society* 13, no. 31 (1988): 408; Ann Ferguson, "The Sex Debate in the Women's Movement: A Socialist-Feminist View," *Against the Current* (September/October 1983): 10–16; Alice Echols, "The New Feminism of Yin and Yang," in *Powers of Desire: The Politics of Sexuality*, Ann Snitow, Christine Stansell, and Sharon Thompson, eds. (New York: Monthly Review Press, 1983), p. 445.

5. See Mary Vetterling-Braggin, ed., *"Femininity," "Masculinity," and "Androgyny"* (Totowa, N.J.: Rowman & Littlefield, 1982), p. 6.

6. Carol S. Vance, ed., *Pleasure and Danger: Exploring Female Sexuality* (Boston: Routledge & Kegan Paul, 1984).

7. Rosemarie Tong, *Women, Sex and the Law* (Totowa, N.J.: Rowman & Littlefield, 1984).

8. Mary Daly, *Gyn/Ecology: The Metaethics of Radical Feminism* (Boston: Beacon Press, 1978).

9. Charlotte Bunch, "Lesbians in Revolt," in *Women and Values*, Marilyn Pearsall, ed. (Belmont, Calif.: Wadsworth, 1986), pp. 128–132.

10. Shulamith Firestone, *The Dialectic of Sex* (New York: Bantam Books, 1970).

11. Adrienne Rich, *Of Woman Born* (New York: W. W. Norton, 1976); Sara Ruddick, "Maternal Thinking," in *Mothering: Essays in Feminist Theory*, Joyce Trebilcot, ed. (Totowa, N.J.: Rowman & Allanheld, 1984).

12. See, for example, Genea Corea, *The Mother Machine: Reproduction Technologies from Artificial Inseminating to Artificial Wombs* (New York: Harper & Row, 1985).

13. Friedrich Engels, *The Origin of the Family, Private Property and the State* (New York: International Publishers, 1972), p. 103.

14. Juliet Mitchell, *Woman's Estate* (New York: Pantheon Books, 1971).

15. Alison M. Jaggar, *Feminist Politics and Human Nature* (Totowa, N.J.: Rowman & Allanheld, 1983), pp. 316–317.

16. Dorothy Dinnerstein, *The Mermaid and the Minotaur: Sexual Arrangements and Human Malaise* (New York: Harper Colophon Books, 1977), p. 161.

17. Sherry B. Ortner, "Oedipal Father, Mother's Brother, and the Penis: A Review of Juliet Mitchell's *Psychoanalysis and Feminism*," *Feminist Studies* 2, nos. 2–3 (1975): 179.

18. Nancy Chodorow, *The Reproduction of Mothering* (Berkeley: University of California Press, 1978).

19. Simone de Beauvoir, *The Second Sex*, H. M. Parshley, trans. and ed. (New York: Vintage Books, 1974).

20. Ynestra King, "Healing the Wounds: Feminism, Ecology, and Nature/Culture Dualism," in *Feminism and Philosophy*, Nancy Tuana and Rosemarie Tong, eds. (Boulder, Colo.: Westview Press, 1995).

Chapter One

1. Douglas MacLean and Claudia Mills, eds., *Liberalism Reconsidered* (Totowa, N.J.: Rowman & Allanheld, 1983).

2. Susan Wendell, "A (Qualified) Defense of Liberal Feminism," *Hypatia* 2, no. 2 (Summer 1987): 65–94.

3. Alison M. Jaggar, *Feminist Politics and Human Nature* (Totowa, N.J.: Rowman & Allanheld, 1983).

4. Ibid., p. 33.

5. Michael J. Sandel, ed., *Liberalism and Its Critics* (New York: New York University Press, 1984), p. 4. I owe this reference to Michael Weber, who also clarified for me the distinction between the "right" and the "good."

6. Jaggar, *Feminist Politics and Human Nature*, p. 31.

7. According to Carole Pateman, the private world is one "of particularism, of subjection, inequality, nature, emotion, love and partiality" (Carole Pateman, *The Problem of Political Obligation: A Critique of Liberal Theory* [Berkeley: University of California Press, 1979], p. 190).

8. Again according to Pateman, the public world is one "of the individual, or universalism, of impartial rules and laws, of freedom, equality, rights, property, contract, self-interest, justice—and political obligation" (ibid., p. 198).

9. Sandel employed this terminology in *Liberalism and Its Critics*, p. 4.

10. Wendell, "A (Qualified) Defense of Liberal Feminism," p. 66.

11. Ibid., p. 90.

12. Zillah Eisenstein, *The Radical Future of Liberal Feminism* (Boston: Northeastern University Press, 1986), pp. 96–99.

13. Mary Wollstonecraft, *A Vindication of the Rights of Woman*, Carol H. Poston, ed. (New York: W. W. Norton, 1975).

14. Ibid., p. 56.

15. Ibid., p. 23.

16. Jean-Jacques Rousseau, *Emile*, Allan Bloom, trans. (New York: Basic Books, 1979).

17. Allan Bloom advanced a contemporary argument in support of sexual dimorphism. See Allan Bloom, *The Closing of the American Mind* (New York: Simon & Schuster, 1987), pp. 97–137.

18. Wollstonecraft, *A Vindication of the Rights of Woman*, p. 61.

19. Ibid.

20. Ibid., p. 152.

21. Immanuel Kant, *Groundwork of the Metaphysic of Morals*, H. J. Paton, trans. (New York: Harper Torchbooks, 1958).

22. Jane Roland Martin, *Reclaiming a Conversation: The Ideal of the Educated Woman* (New Haven, Conn.: Yale University Press, 1985), p. 76.

23. Wollstonecraft, *A Vindication of the Rights of Woman*, p. 152.

24. Judith A. Sabrosky, *From Rationality to Liberation* (Westport, Conn.: Greenwood Press, 1979), p. 31.

25. Wollstonecraft, *A Vindication of the Rights of Woman*, p. 147.

26. Ironically, Wollstonecraft's personal life was driven by emotions. As Zillah Eisenstein described it, Wollstonecraft "tried unsuccessfully to live the life of independence" (*The Radical Future of Liberal Feminism*, p. 106).

27. Wollstonecraft, *A Vindication of the Rights of Woman*, p. 34.

28. Kant, *Groundwork of the Metaphysic of Morals*, pp. 63–64, 79, 95–98.

29. Alice S. Rossi, "Sentiment and Intellect: The Story of John Stuart Mill and Harriet Taylor Mill," in John Stuart Mill and Harriet Taylor Mill, *Essays on Sex Equality*, Alice S. Rossi, ed. (Chicago: University of Chicago Press, 1970), p. 28.

30. John Stuart Mill and Harriet Taylor, "Early Essays on Marriage and Divorce," in ibid., pp. 75, 81, and 86.

31. Ibid., p. 75.

32. Harriet Taylor Mill, "Enfranchisement of Women," in ibid., p. 95.

33. Ibid., p. 104 (emphasis mine).

34. Ibid., p. 105.

35. Mill and Taylor, "Early Essays on Marriage and Divorce," pp. 74–75.

36. Taylor Mill, "Enfranchisement of Women," p. 105.

37. Richard Krouse, "Mill and Marx on Marriage, Divorce, and the Family," *Social Concept* 1, no. 2 (September 1983): 48.

38. Eisenstein, *The Radical Future of Liberal Feminism*, p. 131.

39. John Stuart Mill, "The Subjection of Women," in *Essays on Sex Equality*, p. 221.

40. Susan Moller Okin, *Women in Western Political Thought* (Princeton, N.J.: Princeton University Press, 1979), pp. 197–232.

41. Wollstonecraft, *A Vindication of the Rights of Woman*, p. 77.

42. Mill, "The Subjection of Women," p. 186.

43. Ibid., p. 154.

44. Ibid., p. 213.

45. John Stuart Mill, "Periodical Literature 'Edinburgh Review,'" *Westminster Review* 1, no. 2 (April 1824): 526.

46. Wollstonecraft, *A Vindication of the Rights of Woman*, p. 39.

47. See Mill's description of Harriet Taylor in John Stuart Mill, *Autobiography* (London: Oxford University Press, 1924), pp. 156–160.

48. Mill, "The Subjection of Women," p. 177.

49. Angela Y. Davis, *Women, Race and Class* (New York: Random House, 1981), p. 42.

50. Judith Hole and Ellen Levine, *Rebirth of Feminism* (New York: Quadrangle Books, 1971), p. 3.

51. Ibid., p. 434.

52. Ibid.

53. Ibid., p. 435.

54. Quoted in Elizabeth Cady Stanton, Susan B. Anthony, and Matilda Joslyn Gage, *History of Woman Suffrage*, vol. 1 (1848–1861) (New York: Fowler and Wells, 1881), pp. 115–117.

55. Davis, *Women, Race and Class*, p. 75.

56. Hole and Levine, *Rebirth of Feminism*, p. 14.

57. Maren Lockwood Carden, *The New Feminist Movement* (New York: Russell Sage Foundation, 1974), p. 3.

58. Ibid., p. 16.

59. Caroline Bird, *Born Female* (New York: David McKay Company, 1968), p. 1.

60. Betty Friedan, "N.O.W.—How It Began," *Women Speaking*, April 1967, p. 4.

61. "NOW (National Organization for Women) Bill of Rights (Adopted at NOW's first national conference, Washington, D.C., 1967)," in *Sisterhood Is Powerful*, Robin Morgan, ed. (New York: Random House, 1970), pp. 513–514.

62. "Report of the President, Second National Conference of NOW, Washington, D.C., November 18, 1967," cited in Hole and Levine, *Rebirth of Feminism*, p. 6.

63. Betty Friedan, National Organization for Women, Memorandum, September 22, 1969.

64. Carden, *The New Feminist Movement*, p. 113.

65. Patricia Ireland, "The State of NOW," *Ms.*, July/August 1992, pp. 24–27.

66. Betty Friedan, *The Feminine Mystique* (New York: Dell, 1974).

67. Ibid., pp. 69–70.

68. Ibid., pp. 22–27.

69. Ibid., p. 380.

70. Ibid., p. 330.

71. Betty Friedan, *The Second Stage* (New York: Summit Books, 1981).

72. Ibid., pp. 20–21.

73. Ibid., p. 67.

74. Ibid., p. 28.

75. Ibid., p. 27.

76. Eisenstein, *The Radical Future of Liberal Feminism*, p. 190.

77. Ibid.

78. Friedan, *The Second Stage*, p. 112.

79. Ibid., p. 148.

80. Friedan, *The Feminine Mystique*, p. 362.

81. Ibid., p. 363.

82. See Judith Stacey, "The New Conservative Feminism," *Feminist Studies* 9, no. 3 (Fall 1983): 562.

83. Friedan, *The Second Stage*, pp. 248, 249.

84. Ibid., p. 249.

85. Quoted in John Leo, "Are Women 'Male Clones'?" *Time*, August 18, 1986, p. 63.

86. Quoted in ibid., p. 64.

87. Betty Friedan, *The Fountain of Age* (New York: Simon & Schuster, 1993), p. 157.

88. Ibid., p. 638.

89. Friedan, *The Second Stage*, p. 342.

90. Ibid., p. 41.

91. Eisenstein, *The Radical Future of Liberal Feminism*, p. 176.

92. For a detailed discussion of the distinction between sex and gender, see Ethel Spector Person, "Sexuality as the Mainstay of Identity: Psychoanalytic Perspectives," *Signs: Journal of Women in Culture and Society* 5, no. 4 (Summer 1980): 606.

93. Cited in Hunter College Women's Studies Collective, *Women's Realities, Women's Choices: An Introduction to Women's Studies* (New York: Oxford University Press, 1983), p. 521.

94. Not all liberal feminists agree that women and minority male candidates should be viewed as equally disadvantaged. The more *liberal* a liberal feminist is, the more likely she is to view gender and race/ethnic disadvantages as on a par. The more *feminist* a liberal feminist is, the more likely she is to focus her attention exclusively on women.

95. Jane English, "Sex Roles and Gender: Introduction," in *Feminism and Philosophy*, Mary Vetterling-Braggin, Frederick A. Elliston, and Jane English, eds. (Totowa, N.J.: Rowman & Littlefield, 1977), p. 39.

96. There is much debate about how factors such as race, class, and ethnicity affect the social construction of gender. See Carol Stack, *All Our Kin* (New York: Harper & Row, 1974).

97. By no means has the interest in androgyny been confined to liberal feminists. Radical feminists have also explored this notion, expressing, however, more reservations about it.

98. Carolyn G. Heilbrun, *Toward the Promise of Androgyny* (New York: Alfred A. Knopf, 1973), pp. x–xi.

99. Sandra L. Bem, "Probing the Promise of Androgyny," in *Beyond Sex-Role Stereotypes: Reading Toward a Psychology of Androgyny*, Alexandra G. Kaplan and Joan P. Bean, eds. (Boston: Little, Brown, 1976), p. 51ff.

100. Although not a liberal feminist, Joyce Trebilcot has forwarded an analysis of androgyny that liberal feminists have found useful. See Joyce Trebilcot, "Two Forms of Androgynism," in *"Femininity," "Masculinity," and "Androgyny,"* Mary Vetterling-Braggin, ed. (Totowa, N.J.: Rowman & Littlefield, 1982), pp. 161–170.

101. In her *Feminist Politics and Human Nature*, Alison Jaggar reminded us that gender neutrality can go to ridiculous extremes. In 1976 the Supreme Court ruled that exclusion of pregnancy-related disabilities from an employer's disability plan is no more sex discriminatory than is exclusion of diabetes-, hepatitis-, or bronchitis-related disabilities. The Court counted as irrelevant the fact that whereas diabetes, hepatitis, and bronchitis are diseases that befall both women and men, only women are subject to pregnancy-related disabilities (*General Electric Co. v. Gilbert et al.*, 1976 *United States Reports* 42, n. pp. 161–170). Jaggar commented that "the accidental biological fact of sex does have political relevance and, in so doing, it challenges the liberal feminist ideal of the 'sex-blind' androgynous society" (p. 47).

102. Ireland, "The State of NOW," pp. 24–27.

103. Jean Bethke Elshtain, "Feminism, Family and Community," *Dissent* 29 (Fall 1982): 442.

104. Jean Bethke Elshtain, *Public Man, Private Woman* (Princeton, NJ: Princeton University Press, 1981), p. 252.

105. In the nineteenth century, many of the suffragists waxed eloquently about women's moral superiority. See *History of Woman Suffrage*, Ida Husted Harper, ed. (New York: National American Woman Suffrage Association, 1922), vol. 5, p. 126. See, for example, the section on feminist ethics in *Women and Values*, Marilyn Pearsall, ed. (Belmont, Calif.: Wadsworth, 1986), pp. 266–364.

106. Elshtain, *Public Man, Private Woman*, p. 253.

107. Ibid., p. 243.

108. Ibid., p. 251.

109. Ibid., p. 336.

110. Ibid., p. 237.

111. Jaggar, *Feminist Politics and Human Nature*, p. 28.

112. Ibid., pp. 40–42.

113. Ibid., p. 41.

114. Naomi Scheman, "Individualism and the Objects of Psychology," in *Discovering Reality: Feminist Perspectives on Epistemology, Metaphysics, Methodology, and the Philosophy of Science*, Sandra Harding and Merrill B. Hintikka, eds. (Dordrecht, Netherlands: D. Reidel, 1983), pp. 225–244.

115. Ibid., p. 232.

116. Wendell, "A (Qualified) Defense of Liberal Feminism," p. 66.

117. Ibid.

118. Ibid., p. 76.

119. Angela Y. Davis, "Reflections on the Black Woman's Role in the Community of Slaves," *Black Scholar* 3 (1971): 7.

120. Ireland, "The State of NOW," p. 26.

121. Elizabeth Erlich, "Do the Sunset Years Have to Be Gloomy?" *New York Times Book Review*, 1994, p. 18.

122. Ibid.

123. Quoted in Hole and Levine, *Rebirth of Feminism*, p. 94.

124. Ibid.

125. Ellen Willis, "The Conservatism of *Ms.*," in *Feminist Revolution*, Redstockings, ed. (New York: Random House, 1975), pp. 170–171.

126. One of these exceptions is Janet Radcliffe Richards, *The Skeptical Feminist* (London: Routledge & Kegan Paul, 1980).

127. Willis, "The Conservatism of *Ms.*," p. 170.

128. Wendell, "A (Qualified) Defense of Liberal Feminism," p. 86.

Chapter Two

1. See Judith Hole and Ellen Levine, *Rebirth of Feminism* (New York: Quadrangle, 1971), pp. 15–166.

2. Ibid., p. 108.

3. Elizabeth Cady Stanton, *The Woman's Bible*, 2 vols. (New York: Arno Press, 1972; originally published 1895 and 1899), vol. 1, p. 7.

4. Alison M. Jaggar and Paula S. Rothenberg, eds., *Feminist Frameworks* (New York: McGraw-Hill, 1984), p. 186.

5. Joreen as quoted in Anne Koedt, Ellen Levine, and Anita Rapone, eds., *Radical Feminism* (New York: Quadrangle, 1973), p. 52.

6. Alice Echols, "The New Feminism of Yin and Yang," in *Powers of Desire: The Politics of Sexuality*, Ann Snitow, Christine Stansell, and Sharon Thompson, eds. (New York: Monthly Review Press, 1983), p. 445.

7. Ibid.

8. Alison M. Jaggar, "Feminist Ethics," in *Encyclopedia of Ethics*, Lawrence Becker with Charlotte Becker, eds. (New York: Garland, 1992), p. 364.

9. Echols, "The New Feminism of Yin and Yang," p. 440.

10. Linda Alcoff, "Cultural Feminism Versus Poststructuralism: The Identity Crisis in Feminist Theory," *Signs: Journal of Women in Culture and Society* 13, no. 3 (1988): 408.

11. Gayle Rubin, "The Traffic in Women," in *Toward an Anthropology of Women,* Rayna R. Reiter, ed. (New York: Monthly Review Press, 1975), p. 159.

12. Hester Eisenstein, *Contemporary Feminist Thought* (Boston: G. K. Hall, 1983), p. 8.

13. Kate Millett, *Sexual Politics* (Garden City, N.Y.: Doubleday, 1970), p. 25.

14. Ibid., pp. 43–46.

15. Henry Miller, *Sexus* (New York: Grove Press, 1965), pp. 181–182.

16. Millett, *Sexual Politics*, p. 178.

17. Herbert Barry III, Margaret K. Bacon, and Irwin L. Child, "A Cross-Cultural Survey of Some Sex Differences in Socialization," in *Selected Studies in Marriage and the Family*, Robert F. Winch, Robert McGinnis, and Herbert R. Barringer, eds., 2d ed. (New York: Holt, Rinehart and Winston, 1962), p. 267.

18. In the 1970s Millett asserted that what society needs is a single standard of "sex freedom" for boys and girls and a single standard of parental responsibility for fathers and mothers. Without such unitary standards for sexual and parental behavior, equality between men and women will remain ephemeral (Millett, *Sexual Politics*, p. 62).

19. Ibid.

20. Shulamith Firestone, *The Dialectic of Sex* (New York: Bantam Books, 1970), p. 59.

21. Ibid., p. 175.

22. Ibid.

23. Ibid., p. 190.

24. Ibid., p. 191.

25. Ibid., p. 242.

26. Marilyn French, *Beyond Power: On Women, Men and Morals* (New York: Summit Books, 1985), p. 72.

27. Ibid., pp. 25–66.

28. Ibid., p. 67.

29. Ibid., p. 69.

30. Ibid., p. 68.

31. Ibid., p. 443.

32. Joyce Trebilcot, "Conceiving Wisdom: Notes on the Logic of Feminism," *Sinister Wisdom* 3 (Fall 1979): 46.

33. Alison M. Jaggar, *Feminist Politics and Human Nature* (Totowa, N.J.: Rowman & Allanheld, 1983), p. 252.

34. French, *Beyond Power*, pp. 487–488.

35. Dorothy Dinnerstein, *The Mermaid and the Minotaur: Sexual Arrangements and Human Malaise* (New York: Harper Colophon Books, 1977), p. 5.

36. French, *Beyond Power*, p. 538.

37. Mary Daly, *Beyond God the Father: Toward a Philosophy of Women's Liberation* (Boston: Beacon Press, 1973).

38. If we use French's terms here, we can say that an immanent God infuses women with the "power-to-grow" into their own image and likeness rather than be molded into the image and likeness of a transcendent God interested only in expressing his "power-over" others.

39. Alice Rossi, "Sex Equality: The Beginning of Ideology," in *Masculine/Feminine*, Betty Roszak and Theodore Roszak, eds. (New York: Harper & Row, 1969), pp. 173–186.

40. Daly, *Beyond God the Father*, p. 105.

41. Mary Daly, *Gyn/Ecology: The Metaethics of Radical Feminism* (Boston: Beacon Press, 1978), p. 59.

42. Ibid., pp. 107–312.

43. Ibid., p. xi.

44. Ibid., p. 68.

45. See Ann-Janine Morey-Gaines, "Metaphor and Radical Feminism: Some Cautionary Comments on Mary Daly's *Gyn/Ecology*," *Soundings* 65, no. 3 (Fall 1982): 347–348.

46. Daly, *Gyn/Ecology*, p. 334.

47. Ibid., p. 336.

48. Ibid., p. 337.

49. Friedrich Wilhelm Nietzsche, *On the Genealogy of Morals*, Walter Kaufmann and R. Hollingdale, trans. (New York: Vintage Books, 1969), p. 44.

50. Daly, *Gyn/Ecology*, pp. 14–15.

51. Mary Daly, *Pure Lust: Elemental Feminist Philosophy* (Boston: Beacon Press, 1984), p. 203.

52. Ibid., p. 2.

53. Ibid., pp. 2–3.

54. Ibid., p. 35.

55. Ibid., p. 204.

56. Betty Friedan, *The Feminine Mystique* (New York: Dell, 1974).

57. Daly, *Pure Lust*, p. 206.

58. See Carole S. Vance, "Pleasure and Danger: Toward a Politics of Sexuality," in *Pleasure and Danger: Exploring Female Sexuality*, Carole S. Vance, ed. (Boston: Routledge & Kegan Paul, 1984), pp. 1–27.

59. Ann Ferguson, "Sex War: The Debate Between Radical and Liberation Feminists," in *Signs: Journal of Women in Culture and Society* 10, no. 1 (Autumn 1984): 109.

60. Ibid., p. 108.

61. Ibid., p. 109.

62. Ibid.

63. Gayle Rubin, "Thinking Sex: Notes for a Radical Theory of the Politics of Sexuality," in *Pleasure and Danger: Exploring Female Sexuality,* Vance, ed., pp. 275–301.

64. Ibid., p. 275.

65. Ibid., p. 278.

66. Ibid., p. 275.

67. Ibid., p. 278.

68. Alice Echols, "The Taming of the Id," in *Pleasure and Danger: Exploring Female Sexuality,* Vance, ed., p. 59.

69. Ibid.

70. Ferguson, "Sex Wars," pp. 108–109.

71. Deirdre English, Amber Hollibaugh, and Gayle Rubin, "Talking Sex: A Conversation on Sexuality and Feminism," in *Socialist Review* 11, no 4 (July/August 1981): 53.

72. See the debate between Christina Hoff Sommers and Marilyn Friedman in Marilyn Friedman and Jan Narveson, *Political Correctness: For and Against* (Lanham, Md.: Rowman & Littlefield, 1995), pp. 36–37.

73. Catharine A. MacKinnon, "Francis Biddle's Sister: Pornography, Civil Rights, and Speech," in Catharine A. MacKinnon, *Feminism Unmodified: Disclosures on Life and Law* (Cambridge: Harvard University Press, 1987), p. 176.

74. Catharine A. MacKinnon, "Feminism, Marxism, Method, and the State: An Agenda for Theory," *Signs: Journal of Women in Culture and Society* 7, no. 3 (Spring 1982): 533.

75. Appendix I, Minneapolis, Minn., Code of Ordinances, title 7, ch. 139, 1 amending 39.10.

76. Stuart Taylor Jr., "Pornography Foes Lose New Weapons in Supreme Court," *New York Times,* February 25, 1986, p. 1.

77. Nan D. Hunter and Sylvia A. Law, Brief Amici Curiae of Feminist Anti-Censorship Task Force et al. to U.S. Court of Appeals for the Seventh Circuit, *American Booksellers Association, Inc. et al. v. William H. Hudnut III et al.* (April 18, 1985): 9–18.

78. Ibid., p. 11.

79. MacKinnon, "Feminism, Marxism, Method, and the State," p. 533.

80. Ann Koedt, "The Myth of the Vaginal Orgasm," *Notes from the Second Year: Women's Liberation—Major Writings of the Radical Feminists* (April 1970), p. 41.

81. Ibid.

82. Adrienne Rich, "Compulsory Heterosexuality and Lesbian Existence," in *Living with Contradictions: Controversies in Feminist Social Ethics,* Alison M. Jaggar, ed. (Boulder, Colo.: Westview Press, 1994), p. 488.

83. Hole and Levine, *Rebirth of Feminism,* p. 221.

84. English, Hollibaugh, and Rubin, "Talking Sex," p. 49.

85. See *Redstockings Manifesto,* in *Sisterhood Is Powerful,* Robin Morgan, ed. (New York: Random House, 1970), p. 534.

86. English, Hollibaugh, and Rubin, "Talking Sex," p. 50.

87. *Redstockings Manifesto,* p. 534.

88. *New York Covens' Leaflet* in *Sisterhood Is Powerful,* Morgan, ed., pp. 539–540.

89. Friedrich Engels, *Socialism: Utopian or Scientific,* quoted in Firestone, *The Dialetic of Sex,* pp. 1–12.

90. Firestone, *The Dialectic of Sex,* p. 12.

91. Because the claim that biology is the cause of women's oppression sounds similar to the claim that women's biology is their destiny, it is important to stress the difference between these two claims. Whereas conservatives believe that the constraints of nature exist necessarily, radical feminists insist that it is within women's power to overcome them. For some conservative views, see George Gilder, *Sexual Suicide* (New York: Quadrangle, 1973) and Lionel Tiger, *Men in Groups* (New York: Random House, 1969). For some feminist views, see Mary Vetterling-Braggin, ed., *"Femininity," "Masculinity," and "Androgyny"* (Totowa, N.J.: Rowman & Littlefield, 1982).

92. Firestone, *The Dialectic of Sex*, p. 12.

93. Ibid., pp. 198–199.

94. Marge Piercy, *Woman on the Edge of Time* (New York: Fawcett Crest Books, 1976).

95. Ibid., p. 102.

96. Ibid., pp. 105–106.

97. Ibid., p. 183.

98. Azizah al-Hibri, *Research in Philosophy and Technology*, Paul T. Durbin, ed. (London: JAL Press, 1984), vol. 7, p. 266.

99. Anne Donchin, "The Future of Mothering: Reproductive Technology and Feminist Theory," *Hypatia* 1, no. 2 (Fall 1986): 131.

100. Mary O'Brien, *The Politics of Reproduction* (Boston: Routledge & Kegan Paul, 1981).

101. Ibid., pp. 8, 20ff., and 35–36. See also Sara Ann Ketchum, "New Reproductive Technologies and the Definition of Parenthood: A Feminist Perspective" (photocopy, June 18, 1987).

102. Adrienne Rich, *Of Woman Born* (New York: W. W. Norton, 1979), p. 111.

103. Ibid., pp. 38–39.

104. Firestone, *The Dialectic of Sex*, p. 199.

105. Andrea Dworkin, *Right-Wing Women* (New York: Coward-McCann, 1983), pp. 187–188.

106. Margaret Atwood, *The Handmaid's Tale* (New York: Fawcett Crest Books, 1985).

107. Ibid., p. 164.

108. Genea Corea, *The Mother Machine: Reproduction Technologies from Artificial Insemination to Artificial Wombs* (New York: Harper & Row, 1985), pp. 107–119.

109. Genea Corea, "Egg Snatchers," in *Test-Tube Women: What Future for Motherhood?* Rita Arditti, Renate Duelli Klein, and Shelley Minden, eds. (London: Pandora Press, 1984), p. 45.

110. Robyn Rowland, "Reproductive Technologies: The Final Solution to the Woman Question," in *Test-Tube Women*, Arditti, Klein, and Minden, eds., pp. 365–366.

111. Ibid., p. 368.

112. Alison M. Jaggar, *Feminist Politics and Human Nature* (Totowa, N.J.: Rowman & Allanheld, 1983), p. 256.

113. Ann Oakley, *Woman's Work: The Housewife, Past and Present* (New York: Pantheon Books, 1974), p. 186.

114. Ibid., pp. 187, 199.

115. Ibid., p. 201.

116. Ibid., pp. 201–203.

117. Ibid., p. 203.

118. The claim that adopted children fare just as well as biological children is more controversial than Oakley believed. See, for example, Betty Reid Mendell, *Where Are the Children? A Close Analysis of Foster Care and Adoption* (Lexington, Mass.: Lexington Books, 1973).

119. The kibbutzim have come under fire, however. See, for example, "The Pathogenic Commune," *Science News* 122, no. 76 (July 3, 1982): 76.

120. Firestone, *The Dialectic of Sex*, p. 229.

121. Ibid., pp. 228–230.

122. Rich, *Of Woman Born*, p. 174.

123. Ibid., p. 13.

124. Ibid., p. 57.

125. Ibid., p. 13.

126. Ibid., p. 57.

127. Ibid., pp. 31–32.

128. Because the term *surrogate mother* suggests that such a woman is not a real mother but a substitute mother, many feminists prefer the term *contracted mother*.

129. Corea, *The Mother Machine*, pp. 213–249.

130. "A Surrogate's Story of Loving and Losing," *U.S. News & World Report*, June 6, 1983, p. 12.

131. *Boston Globe*, October 2, 1987, p. 1.

132. Jean Bethke Elshtain, *Public Man, Private Woman* (Princeton, N.J.: Princeton University Press, 1981), p 226.

133. Mary R. Beard, *Woman as Force in History* (New York: Collier Books, 1972).

134. Sheila Rowbotham, *Women, Resistance and Revolution* (New York: Vintage Books, 1972).

135. Elshtain, *Public Man, Private Woman*, p. 228.

136. Ibid., p. 213.

137. Audre Lorde, "An Open Letter to Mary Daly," in *This Bridge Called My Back*, Cherríe Moraga and Gloria Anzaldúa, eds. (Watertown, Mass.: Persephone Press, 1981), pp. 94–97.

138. Elshtain, *Public Man, Private Woman*, p. 226.

139. Ibid., p. 225.

140. Rich, "Compulsory Heterosexuality and Lesbian Existence," in *Living with Contradictions*, Jaggar, ed., p. 488.

141. Ann Ferguson, "The Sex Debate in the Women's Movement: A Socialist-Feminist View," *Against the Current* (September/October 1983): 12.

142. Ibid.

143. Ibid., p. 13.

144. Ibid. (emphasis mine).

145. Ibid.

Chapter Three

1. Richard Schmitt, *Introduction to Marx and Engels* (Boulder, Colo.: Westview Press, 1987), pp. 7–8.

2. Ibid., p. 14.

3. Karl Marx, *A Contribution to the Critique of Political Economy* (New York: International Publishers, 1972), pp. 20–21.

4. Nancy Holmstrom, "A Marxist Theory of Women's Nature," *Ethics* 94, no. 1 (April 1984): 464.

5. Robert L. Heilbroner, *Marxism: For and Against* (New York: W. W. Norton, 1980), p. 107.

6. Henry Burrows Acton, *What Marx Really Said* (London: MacDonald, 1967), p. 41.

7. Ernest Mandel, *An Introduction to Marxist Economic Theory* (New York: Pathfinder Press, 1970), p. 25.

8. Marx's discussion of surplus value and exploitation are found in his three-volume work *Capital*, particularly volumes 1 and 2. For a more detailed introduction to these concepts, see Wallis Arthur Suchting, *Marx: An Introduction* (New York: New York University Press, 1983).

9. Schmitt, *Introduction to Marx and Engels*, pp. 96–97.

10. For an elaboration of these points, see Mandel, *An Introduction to Marxist Economic Theory*.

11. Karl Marx, *The 18th Brumaire of Louis Bonaparte* (New York: International Publishers, 1968), p. 608.

12. Here the term *class* is being used in a sense that falls short of the technical Marxist sense. As we shall see, it is very debatable that women form a true class.

13. Allen W. Wood, *Karl Marx* (London: Routledge & Kegan Paul, 1981), p. 8.

14. Heilbroner, *Marxism: For and Against*, p. 72.

15. Karl Marx, "Economic and Philosophic Manuscripts," in *Early Writings*, T. B. Bottomore, ed. (New York: McGraw-Hill, 1964), p. 122. I owe this reference as well as several good analyses of alienation to Michael Weber.

16. Ann Foreman, *Femininity as Alienation: Women and the Family in Marxism and Psychoanalysis* (London: Pluto Press, 1977), p. 65.

17. Ibid., pp. 101–102.

18. Quoted in David McLellan, *Karl Marx* (New York: Penguin Books, 1975), p. 33.

19. Karl Marx and Friedrich Engels, *The German Ideology*, in *The Marx-Engels Reader*, Robert C. Tucker, ed. (New York: W. W. Norton, 1978), p. 199.

20. Schmitt, *Introduction to Marx and Engels*, p. 202.

21. Friedrich Engels, *The Origin of the Family, Private Property and the State* (New York: International Publishers, 1972), p. 103.

22. Ibid.

23. Notions of hunting and gathering as popularized from anthropological studies are often oversimplified. We should be aware, therefore, of the danger of attributing a rigid sexual division of labor to "hunting and gathering" societies, past and present. Women and children may contribute meat to the diet, just as men may contribute root or grain foods. Noticing Engels's dependence on stereotypical ideas of women's and men's work should lead readers to view Engels's account as less than accurate history. (I owe this reminder to Antje Haussen Lewis.)

24. Engels quoted approvingly the controversial thesis of a now largely discredited anthropologist that women in pairing societies wielded considerable political as well as economic power. "The women were the great power among the clans, [gentes], as everywhere else. They did not hesitate, when occasion required

'to knock off the horns,' as it was technically called, from the head of a chief, and send him back to the ranks of the warriors" (*The Origin of the Family, Private Property and the State*, p. 113). Apparently, it did not strike Engels as odd that a powerful matriarch would let herself be forcibly seized as a wife by a man whose "horns" she could have had "knocked off."

25. Ibid.

26. Lise Vogel, *Marxism and the Oppression of Women: Towards a Unitary Theory* (New Brunswick, N.J.: Rutgers University Press, 1983), p. 82.

27. Engels, *The Origin of the Family, Private Property and the State*, p. 117.

28. Jane Flax asked why a group of matriarchs would have let men control the tribe's animals and/or use the fact of their control to gain power over women (Jane Flax, "Do Feminists Need Marxism?" in *Building Feminist Theory: Essays from "Quest," a Feminist Quarterly* [New York: Longman, 1981], p. 176).

29. Engels, *The Origin of the Family, Private Property and the State*, p. 117.

30. Marx and Engels, *The German Ideology*, in *The Marx-Engels Reader*, Tucker, ed., p. 201.

31. Engels, *The Origin of the Family, Private Property and the State*, pp. 118–119.

32. Ibid., p. 120.

33. Ibid., p. 121.

34. Ibid., p. 137.

35. Ibid., p. 128.

36. Ibid., pp. 137–139.

37. Ibid., p. 79.

38. Barrett, *Women's Oppression Today: Problems in Marxist Feminist Analysis* (London: Verso, 1980), p. 49.

39. Engels, *The Origin of the Family, Private Property and the State*, p. 72 (emphasis mine).

40. Flax, "Do Feminists Need Marxism?" p. 176.

41. Marx and Engels, *The German Ideology*, in *The Marx-Engels Reader*, Tucker, ed., p. 201.

42. Heidi I. Hartmann, "The Family as the Locus of Gender, Class, and Political Struggle: The Example of Housework," *Signs: Journal of Women in Culture and Society* 6, no. 3 (1981): 371.

43. Engels, *The Origin of the Family, Private Property and the State*, pp. 71–72.

44. Hilda Scott, *Working Your Way to the Bottom* (London: Pandora Press, 1984), p. 142.

45. Ellen Malos, "Introduction," in *The Politics of Housework*, Ellen Malos, ed. (London: Allison & Busby, 1980), p. 17.

46. Ibid., p. 20.

47. Margaret Benston, "The Political Economy of Women's Liberation," *Monthly Review* 21, no. 4 (September 1969): 16.

48. Ibid., p. 21.

49. Mariarosa Dalla Costa and Selma James, "Women and the Subversion of the Community," in Mariarosa Dalla Costa and Selma James, *The Power of Women and the Subversion of Community* (Bristol, England: Falling Wall Press, 1972), p. 34.

50. In the final analysis, Dalla Costa and James viewed men as the dupes of capital rather than as the wily oppressors of women. Men, they said, appear to be

the sole recipients of domestic services, but in fact "the figure of the boss is concealed behind that of the husband" (ibid., pp. 35–36).

51. Wendy Edmond and Suzie Fleming expressed the same conviction in even more forceful terms: "Housewives keep their families in the cheapest way; they nurse the children under the worst circumstances and all the toiling of thousands of housewives enables the possessing classes to increase their riches, and to get the labour-power of men and children in the most profitable way" (Wendy Edmond and Suzie Fleming, "If Women Were Paid for All They Do," in *All Work and No Pay*, Wendy Edmond and Suzie Fleming, eds. [London: Power of Women Collective and Falling Wall Press, 1975], p. 8).

52. Ibid., p. 9.

53. In 1972 the Chase Manhattan Bank estimated that for her average 100-hour workweek, the housewife should be paid $257.53. In that same year white males in the workforce had average incomes of $172 a week; white females had average incomes of $108 a week. See A. C. Scott, "The Value of Housework for Love or Money?" *Ms.*, June 1972, pp. 56–58.

54. Unless a woman's salary is quite high, it may cost more for her to work outside the home than simply to work within the home. Many women report that their paychecks go to childcare expenses, commuter expenses, and new wardrobes. See Barbara Bergmann, *The Economic Emergence of Women* (New York: Basic Books, 1986), p. 212.

55. Carol Lopate, "Pay for Housework?" *Social Policy* 5, no. 3 (September-October 1974): 28.

56. Ibid., pp. 29–31.

57. Nancy Holmstrom, "'Women's Work,' the Family and Capitalism," *Science and Society* 45, no. 1 (Spring 1981): 208.

58. Johanna Brenner and Nancy Holmstrom, "Women's Self-Organization: Theory and Strategy," *Monthly Review* 34, no. 11 (April 1983): 40.

59. Johanna Brenner and Maria Ramas, "Rethinking Women's Oppression," *New Left Review* 144 (March-April 1984): 71.

60. Ibid., pp. 49–53.

61. Roslyn L. Feldberg, "Comparable Worth: Toward Theory and Practice in the United States," *Signs: Journal of Women in Culture and Society* 10, no. 2 (Winter 1984): 311–313.

62. "Paying Women What They're Worth," *QQ Report from the Center for Philosophy and Public Policy* 3, no. 2 (Spring 1983): 1.

63. Helen Remick, "Major Issues in A Priori Applications," in *Comparable Worth and Wage Discrimination: Technical Possibilities and Political Realities*, Helen Remick, ed. (Philadelphia: Temple University Press, 1984), p. 102.

64. Ibid., p. 103.

65. Jake Lamar, "A Worthy but Knotty Question," *Time*, February 6, 1984, p. 30.

66. Teresa Amott and Julie Matthaei, "Comparable Worth, Incomparable Pay," *Radical America* 18, no. 5 (September-October 1984): 25.

67. Ibid.

68. Ibid., pp. 26–27.

69. Paradoxically, Elshtain discovered precisely these sentiments in the work of Marxist feminist Sheila Rowbotham. See Sheila Rowbotham, *Woman's Consciousness, Man's World* (Baltimore, Md.: Penguin Books, 1973).

70. Jean Bethke Elshtain, *Public Man, Private Woman* (Princeton, N.J.: Princeton University Press, 1981), pp. 254–286.

71. Ibid.

72. Engels, *The Origin of the Family, Private Property and the State*, p. 145.

73. Alison M. Jaggar, *Feminist Politics and Human Nature* (Totowa, N.J.: Rowman & Allanheld, 1983), p. 221.

74. Engels, *The Origin of the Family, Private Property and the State*, p. 79.

75. Alison Jaggar, "Prostitution," in *Women and Values*, Marilyn Pearsall, ed. (Belmont, Calif.: Wadsworth, 1986), p. 112.

76. Karl Marx, *Economic and Philosophical Manuscripts of 1844* (New York: International Publishers, 1964), p. 133.

77. In fact, many of the men who use prostitutes are members of the working class. Some Marxists even argue that the more alienated and exploited a man is, the more likely he is to seek out the services of a prostitute.

78. V. I. Lenin, *The Emancipation of Women: From the Writings of V. I. Lenin* (New York: International Publishers, 1934), p. 101.

79. The line between contemporary Marxist feminists and socialist feminists is most difficult to draw. Despite my best efforts to assign thinkers to their correct category, I know that not everyone would agree with my classifications. Readers should be aware of this problem.

80. Heidi I. Hartmann, "The Unhappy Marriage of Marxism and Feminism: Towards a More Progressive Union," in *Women and Revolution: A Discussion of the Unhappy Marriage of Marxism and Feminism*, Lydia Sargent, ed. (Boston: South End Press, 1981), pp. 1–41.

81. In order not to complicate matters here, I have not attempted to explain the ways in which dual-systems theorists attempt to link their twofold analysis of patriarchy and capitalism with Marx and Engels's twofold analysis of reproduction and production. In order to justify the attention they pay to gender as well as class, socialist feminists frequently quote the following lines from *The German Ideology*: "According to the materialistic conception, the determining factor in history is, in the final instance, the production and reproduction of immediate life. This, again, is of a two-fold character: on the one side, the production of the means of existence, of food, clothing and shelter and the tools necessary for that production; on the other side, the production of human beings themselves, the propagation of the species. The social organization under which the people of a particular historical epoch and a particular country live is determined by both kinds of production; by the stage of development on the one hand and of the family on the other."

82. Iris Young, "Socialist Feminism and the Limits of Dual Systems Theory," *Socialist Review* 10, nos. 2–3 (March-June 1980): 174.

83. Juliet Mitchell, *Psychoanalysis and Feminism* (New York: Vintage Books, 1974), p. 412.

84. Juliet Mitchell, *Woman's Estate* (New York: Pantheon Books, 1971), pp. 100–101.

85. Although Mitchell's analysis is dated, women still have not come as long a way as they should have by now.

86. Mitchell was convinced that women's limited role in production cannot be explained solely or even primarily by their supposed physical weakness. In the first place, men have forced women to do "women's work," and "women's work" in all its varieties requires much physical strength. Second, even if women are not

as physically strong as men, and even if their original, limited role in production can be attributed to their gap in strength, this same gap cannot explain women's current, limited role in production" (Mitchell, *Woman's Estate*, p. 104).

87. Ibid., p. 107.

88. Ibid., pp. 114–115.

89. Mitchell, *Psychoanalysis and Feminism*, p. 408.

90. Ibid., pp. 415–416.

91. Ibid., p. 412.

92. Ibid., p. 415.

93. Iris Young, "Beyond the Unhappy Marriage: A Critique of the Dual Systems Theory," in *Women and Revolution*, Sargent, ed., p. 58.

94. Heidi Hartmann, "Capitalism, Patriarchy and Job Segregation by Sex," in *Capitalist Patriarchy and the Case for Socialist Feminism*, Zillah Eisenstein, ed. (New York: Monthly Review Press, 1979), p. 207.

95. Esther Boserup, *Women's Role in Economic Development* (London: George Allen and Unwin, 1970).

96. Young, "Beyond the Unhappy Marriage," pp. 59–61.

97. Jaggar, *Feminist Politics and Human Nature*, p. 353.

98. Ibid., p. 308.

99. Ibid., pp. 309–310.

100. Ibid., pp. 310–311.

101. Although Jaggar did not make specific points about in vitro fertilization, the points I raise here seem to fit her analysis.

102. Jaggar, *Feminist Politics and Human Nature*, p. 315.

103. Ibid.

104. Ibid., p. 316.

105. Ibid., p. 317.

106. Nancy Fraser, "What's Critical About Critical Theory? The Case of Habermas and Gender," in *Feminism and Philosophy: Essential Readings*, Nancy Tuana and Rosemarie Tong, eds. (Boulder, Colo.: Westview Press, 1995), p. 288.

107. Ibid., p. 288.

108. Jaggar, *Feminist Politics and Human Nature*, p. 371.

109. Ibid., p. 386.

Chapter Four

1. Cultural feminists and radical-cultural feminists are not to be conflated with each other. Although cultural feminists (whom I term "gender feminists") and radical-cultural feminists agree "women are 'essentially connected,' not 'essentially separate,' from the rest of human life," as legal theorist Robin West has pointed out, cultural and radical-cultural feminists disagree about whether women's connectedness is a blessing or a curse.

Valorizing the traits and behaviors traditionally associated with women, cultural feminists praise women's capacities for sharing, nurturing, giving, sympathizing, empathizing, and especially, connection. They believe the fact women menstruate, gestate, and lactate gives women a unique perspective on the meaning of human connection. For them, connection is not about women literally using their bodies to link one generation to the other. In cultural feminists' estimation, relationships with family members and friends are so important to women that they view separation from others as the quintessential harm.

Radical-cultural feminists point to a darker side of the connection thesis. They agree with cultural feminists that connection is women's fundamental reality, but they lament this state of affairs. They assert women's connections set women up for exploitation and misery: "Invasion and intrusion, rather than intimacy, nurturance and care, is the unofficial story of women's subjective experience of connection." Women are connected to others, most especially through the experience of heterosexual intercourse and pregnancy. But when the sugarcoating is licked off, those connecting experiences taste of women's violation. This harm is unique to women; men cannot understand it. Whereas men fear annihilation, isolation, disintegration of their fragile, artificially constructed communities, women fear occupation: "Both intercourse and pregnancy are literal, physical, material invasions and occupations of the body. The fetus, like the penis, literally occupies the body." According to radical-cultural feminists, women actually crave individuation—the freedom to reject their connectedness at both the ontological and political levels so they can pursue their own separate lives. But they dare not express this desire either to men or to those women who stress the positive dimensions of the connection thesis. Men might punish them for their self-assertions through violent retribution (rape) or emotional revenge (divorce or spinsterhood). And many women, including cultural feminists, might accuse them of rejecting the difference that for all its riskiness is also the source of women's special power: the female body.

See Robin West, "Jurisprudence and Gender," *University of Chicago Law Review* 55, no. 1 (Winter 1988).

2. This list of psychological traits is found in Mary Vetterling-Braggin, ed., *"Femininity," "Masculinity," and "Androgyny"* (Totowa, N.J.: Littlefield, Adams, 1982), pp. 5–6.

3. Sigmund Freud, *Sexuality and the Psychology of Love* (New York: Collier Books, 1968).

4. Sigmund Freud, "Some Psychical Consequences of the Anatomical Distinction Between the Sexes," in ibid., p. 192.

5. Ibid., pp. 187–188.

6. Sigmund Freud, "Femininity," in Sigmund Freud, *The Complete Introductory Lectures on Psychoanalysis*, James Strachey, trans. and ed. (New York: W. W. Norton, 1966), p. 542.

7. Ibid., pp. 593–596.

8. Some of Freud's arguments seem to run counter to the case for a shift in female erotogenic zones. Freud claimed that male and female sexual organs develop out of the same embryonic structures and that vestiges of the male reproductive structures are found in the female, and vice versa. Thus, human anatomy would seem to be bisexual. Moreover, Freud observed that although femininity is ordinarily associated with passivity and masculinity with activity, this association is misleading because women can be active and men passive in some directions. It is more precise to say that although feminine persons prefer passive aims and masculine persons active aims, considerable activity is required to achieve any aim whatsoever. When it comes to a sexual aim—switching one's erotogenic zone

, the clitoris to the vagina, for example—it takes incredible sexual energy or ᴧvity (libido) to accomplish the transition. See ibid., p. 580.

9. Ibid., p. 596.

10. Freud, "Some Psychical Consequences of the Anatomical Distinction Between the Sexes," p. 191.

11. Ibid., p. 193.

12. Freud, "The Passing of the Oedipus Complex," in Freud, *Sexuality and the Psychology of Love*, p. 181.

13. Betty Friedan, *The Feminine Mystique* (New York: Dell, 1974), pp. 93–94.

14. Ibid., p. 119.

15. Shulamith Firestone, *The Dialectic of Sex* (New York: Bantam Books, 1970), pp. 48–49.

16. Ibid., p. 69.

17. Ibid., pp. 68–69.

18. Ibid., p. 47.

19. Viola Klein, *The Feminine Character* (London: Routledge & Kegan Paul, 1971), p. 77.

20. Kate Millett, *Sexual Politics* (Garden City, N.Y.: Doubleday, 1970), p. 109.

21. Ibid., p. 185.

22. Sigmund Freud, *Dora: An Analysis of a Case of Hysteria*, Philip Rieff, ed. (New York: Collier Books, 1963), p. 142.

23. Ibid., p. 50.

24. Helene Deutsch, *The Psychology of Women: A Psychoanalytic Interpretation* (New York: Grune & Stratten, 1944), vol. 1, p. 327. For Deutsch, the feminine character has three components: passivity, masochism, and narcissism. Passivity is central and is modeled on both women's role in sexual intercourse and on their "attitude of receptive waiting and expectancy." This passivity is closely linked with women's masochism, which Deutsch defined not as the enjoyment of pain but as an attraction to experiences, such as sexual intercourse and childbirth, which mix pain and pleasure. Both of these characteristics are contrasted with narcissism, which in women can exceed its own bounds and thereby become an immature and unhealthy (but not unfeminine) demand for attention in order to make up for feelings of insecurity and inferiority.

The normal woman, then, is stretched atop a tightrope, balancing her passive masochistic existence for others with her narcissistic concern for herself. If she is too assertive, too aggressive, or too intellectual, she must be resisting her feminine role. Deutsch claimed this is harmful and unnatural, creating "inner conflict." Should a woman lose her balance by erring in the direction of narcissism, she will be plunged into another abyss of abnormality.

Deutsch claimed that the best way for the normal woman to maintain her feminine balance is to weigh herself down with a biological child who will discipline her selfish desires. For Deutsch, women's sexuality is "continuous with its natural consequences, pregnancy and childbirth," and any demand for recreational sex will compromise the procreative function of women's biology. Deutsch's notion was thus based on the idea that women are made, always and essentially, to be mothers, and therefore the normal woman orients herself and her sexuality toward men and procreation. The normal woman is feminine, and she is a mother—

and she is happy and healthy that way. For more on Deutsch, see Juanita Williams, *Psychology of Women: Behavior in a Biosocial Context* (New York: W. W. Norton, 1977), pp. 36–49.

25. Erik Erikson, "The Inner and Outer Space: Reflections on Womanhood," *Daedalus* 93, no. 2 (1964): 582–606. For Erik Erikson, not the psychology of women in particular but the ego formation of everyone in general is of central concern. Although Erikson paid close attention to the way in which environment shapes our biology, his emphasis on nurture failed to disabuse him of the idea there are innate psychological differences between men and women that originate in the "ground-plan of the body." In a study of children's play constructions, he noted that girls created stable interior scenes with an occasional male intruder, whereas boys created towers and buildings decorated with protrusions and subject to destruction. Erikson believed that these differences in spatial organization were analogous to the differences in male and female anatomies. Because of their biology, women are concerned with inner space and with procreation. Pregnancy means fulfillment, whereas childlessness means emptiness and despair. In Erikson's eyes, because the penis is so apparently present, the vagina and womb must by contrast be absent, representing some essential lack in women. In light of his discussion of inner and outer space, Erikson's protestations that social training matters tremendously and that he does not mean to "doom" every woman to "perpetual motherhood" fade considerably. In the final analysis, Erikson, like Deutsch, thought women are unable to escape their female biological destiny, "since woman is never not-a-woman." For more on Erik Erikson, see Williams, *Psychology of Women*, pp. 48–62.

26. Alfred Adler, *Understanding Human Nature* (New York: Greenberg, 1927).

27. Ibid., p. 123.

28. Karen Horney, "The Flight from Womanhood," in Karen Horney, *Feminine Psychology* (New York: W. W. Norton, 1973), pp. 54–70.

29. There has been much debate among feminists in regard to the theories of Karen Horney. In the past, feminists claimed she was more interested in the whole person's sexual development than in woman's sexual development. However, recent analyses have penetrated deeper into Horney's ideas and have shown them to have some very positive contributions to feminism. Very simply, Horney's theory of character development revolves around the idea there is a deep, true self within everyone. To allow that inner self free expression involves a resolution among three different pulls in character formation, which she calls the self-effacing, the expansive, and the resigned. When this triangle is not balanced, when too much weight is given to one need and not enough to the others, then the inner self is covered up and muffled by false, neurotic, or idealized conceptions of self. However, if a balance is achieved among the three, the inner self is allowed to be expressed. Many feminists now see this kind of inner liberation from unnatural, unhealthy pulls of any one of the three characteristics is a necessary step to any kind of further, external liberation for women within a society. See Susan Rudnick Jacobsohn, "An Ambiguous Legacy," *Women's Review of Books* 5, no. 4 (January 1988): 22.

30. Clara Thompson, "Problems of Womanhood," in *Interpersonal Psychoanalysis: The Selected Papers of Clara Thompson*, M. P. Green, ed. (New York: Basic Books, 1964).

31. For a more complete discussion of Adler, Horney, and Thompson, see Williams, *Psychology of Women*, pp. 65–73.

32. Dorothy Dinnerstein, *The Mermaid and the Minotaur: Sexual Arrangements and Human Malaise* (New York: Harper Colophon Books, 1977), p. 5.

33. Ibid., pp. 40–54.

34. Ibid., pp. 59–66.

35. Ibid., p. 66.

36. Given that a man cannot enter a symbiotic relationship with a woman without reinvoking painful memories of his total helplessness before the infinite power of the mother, Dinnerstein theorized that he will use his power to fulfill his basic needs for security, love, and self-esteem. This bid for omnipotence extends to control over both nature and women, two forces that must be kept in check lest their presumably uncontrollable powers be unleashed. In contrast to a man, a woman can safely seek symbiosis with a man as a means to attain the ends of security, love, and self-esteem. She can do this because, for her, symbiosis with a man does not conjure up the specter of the omnipotent mother. However, the *idea* of herself being or becoming an omnipotent mother does terrify her, and this specter may explain woman's discomfort with female power (ibid., p. 61).

37. Ibid., pp. 124–134.

38. Ibid.

39. Nancy Chodorow, *The Reproduction of Mothering: Psychoanalysis and the Sociology of Gender* (Berkeley: University of California Press, 1978), p. 32.

40. Ibid., p. 107.

41. Ibid., p. 126.

42. Ibid., p. 200.

43. Ibid., pp. 135, 187.

44. Ibid., p. 218.

45. Judith Lorber, "On *The Reproduction of Mothering:* A Methodological Debate," *Signs: Journal of Women in Culture and Society* 6, no. 3 (Spring 1981): 482–486.

46. After a while this whole debate becomes very frustrating. In Chodorow's defense, it must be pointed out that she espoused less of a one-way causality thesis (family→society) and more of an interactive thesis (family↔society) than many of her critics admitted.

47. Jean Bethke Elshtain, *Public Man, Private Woman* (Princeton, N.J.: Princeton University Press, 1981), p. 288.

48. Ibid., p. 290.

49. Alice Rossi, "On *The Reproduction of Mothering:* A Methodological Debate," *Signs: Journal of Women in Culture and Society* 6, no. 3 (Spring 1981): 497–500.

50. Of course this is a *traditional* caricature. Films and television series are currently celebrating a new kind of father who initially has a difficult time taking care of his infant or child but soon becomes better at the job than his wife or lover.

51. Critics of Chodorow who did not share Rossi's *biological* concerns argued that although dual parenting is an improvement over women's monopoly on mothering, "parenting . . . not just by biological parents but by communities of interested adults" is to be preferred to dual parenting. These critics insist although men and women have much to gain by engaging equally in parenting, everyone—particularly children—will be better off if we stop viewing children as the possessions and responsibilities of their biological parents and start viewing them

instead as people for whom society as a whole is responsible. Lorber, "On *The Reproduction of Mothering:* A Methodological Debate," 486.

52. Janice Raymond, "Female Friendship: Contra Chodorow and Dinnerstein," *Hypatia* 1, no. 2 (Fall 1986): 44–45.

53. Ibid., p. 37.

54. Juliet Mitchell, *Women's Estate* (New York: Pantheon Books, 1971), pp. 164–165.

55. Ibid.

56. Ibid., p. 170.

57. Juliet Mitchell, *Psychoanalysis and Feminism* (New York: Vintage Books, 1974), p. 370.

58. Ibid., p. 373.

59. Ibid., p. 375.

60. Ibid., p. 378.

61. Ibid., pp. 409–414.

62. Sigmund Freud, "Totem and Taboo," in *The Standard Edition of the Complete Psychological Works of Sigmund Freud,* James Strachey, trans. and ed. (New York: W. W. Norton, 1966), p. 144.

63. Jacques Lacan, *The Language of the Self* (Baltimore, Md.: Johns Hopkins University Press, 1968), p. 271.

64. Mitchell, *Psychoanalysis and Feminism,* p. 415.

65. Sherry B. Ortner, "Oedipal Father, Mother's Brother, and the Penis: A Review of Juliet Mitchell's *Psychoanalysis and Feminism,*" *Feminist Studies* 2, nos. 2–3 (1975): 179.

66. Ibid.

67. Carol Gilligan, *In a Different Voice,* (Cambridge: Harvard University Press, 1982), pp. 2–23.

68. Lawrence Kohlberg, "From Is to Ought: How to Commit the Naturalistic Fallacy and Get Away with It in the Study of Moral Development," in *Cognitive Development and Epistemology,* T. Mischel, ed. (New York: Academic Press, 1971), pp. 164–165.

69. Gilligan, *In a Different Voice,* pp. 74–75.

70. Ibid., p. 76.

71. Ibid., p. 77.

72. Ibid., p. 18.

73. Ibid.

74. Ibid., p. 81.

75. Ibid., p. 92.

76. Carol Gilligan, "Adolescent Development Reconsidered," in Carol Gilligan, Janie Victoria Ward, and Jill McLean Taylor, eds., *Mapping the Moral Domain* (Cambridge: Harvard University Press, 1988), p. xxii.

77. Nel Noddings, *Caring: A Feminine Approach to Ethics and Moral Education* (Berkeley: University of California Press, 1984), p. 3.

78. Ibid.

79. Ibid., pp. 3–4.

80. Ibid., p. 83.

81. Ibid., p. 5.

82. Ibid., p. 79.

83. Ibid., p. 80.

84. Ibid.

85. Ibid., p. 83.

86. Nel Noddings, *Women and Evil* (Berkeley: University of California Press, 1989), p. 91.

87. Ibid., p. 96.

88. Ibid.

89. Ibid., p. 167.

90. Ibid., pp. 167–168.

91. Ibid., p. 179.

92. Ibid., p. 181.

93. Ibid., p. 182.

94. Ibid., p. 206.

95. Ibid., p. 211.

96. Ibid., p. 213.

97. Ibid.

98. Ibid., pp. 221–222.

99. Ibid., p. 222.

100. A related debate emphasizes that Gilligan's readers are frequently left with the impression a female ethic of care is *better* than a male ethic of justice. Many radical feminists would gladly applaud Gilligan were she indeed arguing women's moral values are not only different from men's but also better. But Gilligan insisted she was claiming only a difference, not a superiority. Her aim, she stressed, was to ensure woman's moral voice be taken as seriously as man's. But if Gilligan was not making any superiority claims, then her book may not be normative enough. Critics probe: "So which is it better to be: just or caring? Should we be like Abraham, who was willing to sacrifice his beloved son Isaac so as to fulfill God's will? Or should we be like the mother whose baby Solomon threatens to cut in half?" (We will recall that in this biblical story, two women claim to be the same child's mother. When King Solomon threatened to divide the baby in two, he prompted the true mother to forsake her claim in order to secure her child's survival.) Gilligan resisted answering these questions, although she certainly led many of her readers to view Abraham as a religious fanatic and to view the real mother in the Solomon story as a person who has her values properly ordered.

As Gilligan saw it, the question of which is better—an ethics of care or an ethics of justice—is an apples-and-oranges question. Both an ethics of care and an ethics of justice are good. But to insist one kind of morality is the better is to manifest a nearly pathological need for a unitary, absolute, and universal moral standard that can erase our very real moral tensions as with a magic wand. If we are able to achieve moral maturity, Gilligan implied, we must be willing to vacillate between an ethics of care and an ethics of justice. But even if her critics were willing to concede ethical vacillation is indeed morally acceptable, they are not willing to let Gilligan simply describe an ethics of care on the one hand and an ethics of justice on the other without at least attempting to translate between these two systems. Such attempts at translation would, believe her critics, do much to reinforce Gilligan's later claim that the ethics of care and of justice are ultimately compatible. For more details, see Gilligan, *In a Different Voice*, pp. 151–174.

101. In a study of northern blacks migrating back to the rural South, sociologist Carol Stack discovered the men and women in her study valued equally the ethic

of care. Stack inferred from her data that "under conditions of economic deprivation there is a convergence between women and men in their construction of themselves in relationship to others" and that "these conditions produce a convergence also in women's and men's vocabulary of rights, morality, and the social good." Carol Stack, "The Culture of Gender: Women and Men of Color," *Signs: Journal of Women in Culture and Society* 11, no. 2 (Winter 1986): 322–323.

102. Sandra L. Bartky, *Femininity and Domination* (New York: Routledge, 1990), p. 105.

103. Ibid., p. 104.

104. Ibid., p. 109.

105. Ibid.

106. Ibid., p. 113.

107. Ibid., p. 118.

108. Bill Puka, "The Liberation of Caring: A Different Voice for Gilligan's 'Different Voice,'" *Hypatia* 5, no. 1 (Spring 1990): 59.

109. Ibid., p. 60.

110. Ibid.

111. Ibid.

112. Ibid., p. 62.

113. Sarah Lucia Hoagland, "Some Thoughts About *Caring*," in *Feminist Ethics*, Claudia Card, ed. (Lawrence: University Press of Kansas, 1991), p. 250.

114. Ibid., p. 251.

115. Ibid.

116. Ibid., pp. 252–253.

117. Claudia Card, "Caring and Evil," *Hypatia* 5, no. 1 (Spring 1990): 106.

118. Hoagland, "Some Thoughts About *Caring*," p. 254.

119. Ibid.

120. Noddings, *Caring*, p. 73.

121. Hoagland, "Some Thoughts About *Caring*," p. 255.

122. Sarah Lucia Hoagland, "Some Concerns About Nel Noddings' *Caring*," *Hypatia* 5, no. 1 (Spring 1990): 114.

123. Hoagland, "Some Thoughts About *Caring*," p. 256.

124. Ibid.

125. Elizabeth Cady Stanton, *The Woman's Bible*, 2 vols. (New York: Arno, 1972; originally published 1895 and 1899).

126. Barbara Houston, "Rescuing Womanly Virtues," in *Science, Morality, and Feminist Theory*, Marsha Hanen and Kai Nielsen, eds. (Calgary: University of Calgary Press, 1987), p. 131.

127. Sheila Mullett, "Shifting Perspectives: A New Approach to Ethics," in *Feminist Perspectives*, Lorraine Code, Sheila Mullett, and Christine Overall, eds. (Toronto: University of Toronto Press, 1989), p. 119.

128. Ibid.

Chapter Five

1. Margaret A. Simons and Jessica Benjamin, "Simone de Beauvoir: An Interview," *Feminist Studies* 5, no. 2 (Summer 1979): 336.

2. Terry Keefe, *Simone de Beauvoir* (Totowa, N.J.: Barnes & Noble, 1983).

3. G.W.F. Hegel, *The Phenomenology of Mind*, J. B. Baille, trans. (New York: Harper & Row, 1967).

4. Jean-Paul Sartre, *Being and Nothingness*, Hazel E. Barnes, trans. (New York: Philosophical Library, 1956).

5. Jean-Paul Sartre, *Existentialism*, Bernard Frechtman, trans. (New York: Philosophical Library, 1947), p. 115.

6. Sartre, *Being and Nothingness*, p. 364.

7. I owe this reminder to Michael Weber.

8. Sartre, *Being and Nothingness*, pp. 59–60.

9. Ibid., pp. 55–56.

10. Ibid., p. 56.

11. Jean-Paul Sartre, *The Emotions: Outline of a Theory*, Bernard Frechtman, trans. (New York: Philosophical Library, 1948).

12. Sartre, *Being and Nothingness*, pp. 252–302.

13. Ibid., pp. 378–379.

14. Ibid., p. 380.

15. Ibid., p. 381.

16. Ibid., p. 393.

17. Ibid., p. 412.

18. Dorothy Kaufmann McCall, "Simone de Beauvoir, *The Second Sex*, and Jean-Paul Sartre," *Signs: Journal of Women in Culture and Society* 5, no. 2 (1979): 210.

19. Simone de Beauvoir, *The Second Sex*, H. M. Parshley, trans. and ed. (New York: Vintage Books, 1974), p. 24.

20. Ibid., p. 41.

21. Ibid., p. 51.

22. Ibid., p. 55.

23. Ibid., p. 64.

24. Ibid., p. 72.

25. Ibid., pp. 89–90.

26. Ibid., p. 284.

27. De Beauvoir reserved special criticism for Montherlant and Lawrence. Unlike Claudel, Breton, and Stendhal, who believed the ideal woman freely chooses to sacrifice herself for man not because she is required to do so but because she wants to, Montherlant and Lawrence made of female self-sacrifice a nearly sacred duty (ibid., pp. 280–285).

28. Ibid., pp. 180–181.

29. Ibid., p. 256n.

30. Ibid., p. 500.

31. Ibid., pp. 502–503.

32. It is no secret that de Beauvoir was not enamored of motherhood as we know it. The following quotation is fairly representative of her view: "As motherhood is today, maternity-slavery, as some feminists call it, does indeed turn today's women into slaves. And I think that motherhood is the most dangerous snare for all those women who want to be free and independent, for those who want to earn their living, for those who want to think for themselves, and for those who want to have a life of their own" (Simons and Benjamin, "Simone de Beauvoir," p. 241).

33. De Beauvoir, *The Second Sex*, p. 571.

34. Ibid., pp. 761–763.

35. Ibid., p. 630.

36. De Beauvoir's view of the prostitute as an exceptional woman who dares to challenge the sexual mores of her society was rooted in several studies, especially those of ancient Greece describing the *hetaerae*. In these studies, Athens is described as a center for prostitution, where the prostitutes were divided into at least three classes. Lowest on the status ladder were the *pornai*, who were checked over before their services were bought. Of slightly higher status were the *ayletrides*, or players, who entertained guests with their music as well as their bodies. Occupying the highest position were the *hetaerae*. In some ways these intellectually gifted as well as physically endowed women were more privileged than were respectable Athenian wives and mothers who, unlike the *hetaerae*, were largely uneducated and somewhat confined to domestic affairs. Indeed, some *hetaerae* amassed great wealth and exerted considerable power in the public domain through the men they entertained—this at a time when these men's wives and mothers were without real economic and political power. See Will Durant, *The Life of Greece* (New York: Simon & Schuster, 1939).

Nevertheless, according to several scholars of antiquity, the *hetaerae* were not necessarily the most blessed of women. Sarah B. Pomeroy, for example, noted although the hetaira had access to the intellectual life of Athens and although she had freedom to be with whomever pleased her, her life had definite shortcomings. "That we know of some courtesans who attempted to live as respectable wives, while we know of no citizen wives who wished to be courtesans, should make us reconsider the question of which was the preferable role in Classical Athens—companion or wife" (Sarah B. Pomeroy, *Goddesses, Whores, Wives, and Slaves* [New York: Schocken Books, 1975], p. 92).

In short, the price the hetaira paid for sexual freedom and intellectual stimulation was not only status within the Athenian community but also some of the less glamorous, although meaningful, comforts of the home. According to de Beauvoir, however, this may not have been too high a price to pay for the privilege of living in the active rather than the passive voice and achieving a measure of independence from men. See de Beauvoir, *The Second Sex*, pp. 631–636.

37. De Beauvoir, *The Second Sex*, p. 700.

38. Ibid., pp. 710–711.

39. Ibid., p. 748.

40. Ibid., p. 795.

41. Simone de Beauvoir, *The Prime of Life*, Peter Green, trans. (Harmondsworth, England: Penguin Books, 1965), pp. 291–292.

42. De Beauvoir, *The Second Sex*, p. 791.

43. Sartre, *Being and Nothingness*, p. 412.

44. Josephine Donovan, *Feminist Theory: The Intellectual Traditions of American Feminism* (New York: Frederick Ungar, 1985), p. 136.

45. Ibid., p. 137.

46. Meredith Tax, "Woman and Her Mind: The Story of an Everyday Life," in *Notes from the Second Year: Women's Liberation—Major Writings of the Radical Feminists* (April 1970), p. 12.

47. Sandra Bartky, "Narcissism, Femininity and Alienation," *Social Theory and Practice* 8, no. 2 (Summer 1982): 137.

48. De Beauvoir, *The Second Sex*, p. 147.

49. Jean Bethke Elshtain, *Public Man, Private Woman* (Princeton, N.J.: Princeton University Press, 1981), p. 306.

50. Simone de Beauvoir, *Memoirs of a Dutiful Daughter*, James Kirkup, trans. (Harmondsworth, England: Penguin Books, 1963), p. 131.

51. De Beauvoir, *The Second Sex*, p. 553.

52. For an interesting analysis of de Beauvoir's "linguistic ambivalence" about the terms *brotherhood* and *sisterhood*, see Eléanor Kuykendall, "Linguistic Ambivalence in Simone de Beauvoir's Feminist Theory," in *The Thinking Muse*, Iris Young and Jeffner Allen, eds. (Bloomington: Indiana University Press, 1989).

53. Genevieve Lloyd, *The Man of Reason: "Male" and "Female" in Western Philosophy* (Minneapolis: University of Minnesota Press, 1984), p. 101.

54. Ibid.

55. Anne Whitmarsh, *Simone de Beauvoir and the Limits of Commitment* (Cambridge: Cambridge University Press, 1981), p. 151.

56. Ibid.

57. Ibid.

58. De Beauvoir, *The Second Sex*, p. 34.

59. De Beauvoir, *The Prime of Life*, p. 109.

60. Simons and Benjamin, "Simone de Beauvoir," p. 342.

61. Ibid.

62. Carol Ascher, *Simone de Beauvoir: A Life of Freedom* (Boston: Beacon Press, 1981), p. 146.

Chapter Six

1. Cited in Hélène Vivienne Wenzel, "The Text as Body/Politics: An Appreciation of Monique Wittig's Writings in Context," *Feminist Studies* 7, no. 2 (Summer 1981): 270–271.

2. For their part, directors of women's studies programs in France complain that U.S. academics have a very narrow conception of who counts as a French feminist or as a postmodern feminist. In a review of Claire Duchen's book, *Feminism in France: From May '68 to Mitterrand* (London: Routledge & Kegan Paul, 1986), Elaine Viennot wrote, "To taste the full flavor of these distortions, it is necessary to know that the French feminist movement is, in certain American universities, an object of study (I assure you right away, you would not recognize it . . .), and that this book has every possibility of being bought by every American library; it is also necessary to know that certain of our compatriots (J. Kristeva, J. Derrida . . .) reign over there as masters of the university enclave" (Eléanor Kuykendall, trans., *Etudes féministes: bulletin national d'information* 1 [Fall 1987]: 40). Whether the sentiments of this review, published by the Association pour les études féministes and the Centre lyonnais d'études féministes/Association femmes, féminisme et recherches Rhône Alpes and brought to my attention by Eléanor Kuykendall, are widely shared by French academics is a question for debate. In any event, Viennot's criticisms are not idiosyncratic and merit a careful reading.

3. John Sturrock, "Introduction," in *Structuralism and Since: From Lévi-Strauss to Derrida*, John Sturrock, ed. (New York: Oxford University Press, 1979), p. 14.

4. If any one of these women can be accused of discipleship, it is Kristeva, who usually writes within a Lacanian framework. Nevertheless, her writings depart from Lacan in significant ways.

5. Danièle Steward, "The Women's Movement in France," *Signs: Journal of Women in Culture and Society* 6, no. 2 (Winter 1980): 353.

6. Jacques Lacan, *Écrits: A Selection*, Alan Sheridan, trans. (New York: W. W. Norton, 1977), pp. 64–66.

7. Duchen, *Feminism in France*, p. 78.

8. Lacan, *Écrits: A Selection*, p. 2.

9. According to Lacan, the original mother-child unity is in some way a metaphor for truth—for an isomorphic relationship between word and object. Ideally, both mother and child, and word and object, would remain united; but society will not stand for such unity. As a result of the castration complex brought on by the arrival of the father, who represents social power symbolized by the phallus, not only mother and child but also word and object must be split.

10. Lacan, *Écrits: A Selection*, pp. 1–7.

11. Jacques Lacan, "The Meaning of the Phallus," in *Feminine Sexuality*, J. Mitchell and J. Rose, eds. (New York: W. W. Norton, 1982), p. 84.

12. I owe this point to Eléanor Kuykendall, who reminded me that Jacques Derrida often challenges feminist norms. See Jacques Derrida, *Spurs: Nietzsche's Styles*, Barbara Harlow, trans. (Chicago: University of Chicago Press, 1978); and Jacques Derrida, *The Post Card: From Socrates to Freud and Beyond*, Alan Bass, trans. (Chicago: University of Chicago Press, 1987).

13. Jacques Derrida, *Writing and Difference*, Alan Bass, trans. (Chicago: University of Chicago Press, 1978).

14. Toril Moi, *Sexual/Textual Politics: Feminist Literary Theory* (New York: Methuen, 1985), pp. 130–131.

15. Ann Rosalind Jones, "Writing the Body: Toward an Understanding of l'Ecriture Féminine," *Feminist Studies* 7, no. 1 (Summer 1981): 248.

16. Hélène Cixous and Catherine Clement, "Sorties," in *The Newly Born Woman*, Betsy Wing, trans. (Minneapolis: University of Minnesota Press, 1986), pp. 63, 65.

17. Ibid., p. 65.

18. Hélène Cixous, "The Laugh of the Medusa," in *New French Feminisms*, Elaine Marks and Isabelle de Courtivron, eds. (New York: Schocken Books, 1981), p. 249.

19. Ibid., p. 245.

20. Ibid., p. 262.

21. Elaine Marks and Isabelle de Courtivron, "Introduction III," in *New French Feminisms*, Marks and Courtivron, eds., p. 36.

22. Cixous, "The Laugh of the Medusa," p. 256.

23. Ibid., p. 251.

24. Ibid., pp. 259–260.

25. Ibid., p. 256.

26. Ibid., pp. 259–260.

27. Luce Irigaray has been critical of both Derrida and Lacan. In 1974 she challenged Lacan in her book *Speculum* and was fired from her academic position at the

University of Paris VIII (Vincennes) because of it. In order fully to appreciate Irigaray's differences from Lacan, readers should refer to Luce Irigaray, *Speculum of the Other Woman,* Gillian C. Gill, trans. (Ithaca, N.Y.: Cornell University Press, 1985).

28. Luce Irigaray, *This Sex Which Is Not One,* Catherine Porter, trans. (Ithaca, N.Y.: Cornell University Press, 1985), p. 28.

29. According to Claire Duchen, Irigaray believed "that before a 'feminine feminine,' a non-phallic feminine, can even be *thought,* women need to examine the male philosophical and psychoanalytical texts which have contributed to the construction of the 'masculine feminine,' the phallic feminine, in order to locate and identify it" (Duchen, *Feminism in France,* pp. 87–88).

30. Irigaray, *This Sex Which Is Not One,* p. 32.

31. Moi, *Sexual/Textual Politics,* p. 132.

32. Irigaray, *This Sex Which Is Not One,* p. 74.

33. Ibid.

34. Luce Irigaray, "Is the Subject of Science Sexed?" Carol Mastrangelo Bové, trans., *Hypatia* 2, no. 3 (Fall 1987): 66.

35. Irigaray, *This Sex Which Is Not One,* p. 32.

36. Moi, *Sexual/Textual Politics,* p. 140.

37. In an interview Irigaray stated that there is nothing other than masculine discourse. When the interviewer said, "I don't understand what 'masculine discourse' means," Irigaray retorted, "Of course not, since there is no other" (Irigaray, *This Sex Which Is Not One,* p. 140).

38. Ibid., p. 29.

39. Kelly Oliver, "Julia Kristeva's Feminist Revolutions," *Hypatia* 8, no. 3 (Summer 1993): 94.

40. Julia Kristeva, *Desire in Language,* Leon Roudiez, trans. (New York: Columbia University Press, 1982), pp. 205–206.

41. Oliver, "Julia Kristeva's Feminist Revolutions," p. 101.

42. Julia Kristeva, "The Novel as Polylogue," in *Desire in Language,* pp. 159–209.

43. Oliver, "Julia Kristeva's Feminist Revolutions," p. 98.

44. Julia Kristeva, *Powers of Horror,* Leon Roudiez, trans. (New York: Columbia University Press, 1982), pp. 205–206.

45. Julia Kristeva, from an interview with *Tel Quel,* in *New French Feminisms,* Marks and Courtivron, eds., p. 157.

46. Oliver, "Julia Kristeva's Feminist Revolutions," p. 98.

47. Ibid., pp. 98–99.

48. Duchen, *Feminism in France,* p. 102.

49. Elizabeth Grosz, "Sexual Difference and the Problem of Essentialism," in *The Essential Difference,* Naomi Schor and Elizabeth Weed, eds. (Bloomington: Indiana University Press, 1994), p. 88.

50. Ibid., p. 89.

51. Ibid.

52. Ibid., p. 91.

53. Ibid., pp. 91–92.

54. Ibid., p. 91.

55. Naomi Schor, "Introduction," in *The Essential Difference,* Schor and Weed, eds., p. vii.

56. Margaret Whitford, "Luce Irigaray and the Female Imaginary: Speaking as a Woman," *Radical Philosophy* 43 (Summer 1986): 7.

57. Teresa de Lauretis, "The Essence of the Triangle or, Taking the Risks of Essentialism Seriously," in *The Essential Difference,* Schor and Weed, eds., p. 3.

58. Ibid., p. 4.

59. Linda Alcoff, "Cultural Feminism Versus Post-Structuralism: The Identity Crisis in Feminist Theory," *Signs: A Journal of Women in Culture and Society* 13, no. 3 (1988): 434–435.

60. De Lauretis, "The Essence of the Triangle," p. 10.

61. Teresa de Lauretis, *Technologies of Gender* (Bloomington: Indiana University Press, 1987), p. x.

62. Ibid., p. 48.

63. Genesis 2:19.

64. Lao-tzu, "The Tao-te-Ching," in *The Texts of Taoism,* James Legge, ed. (New York: Dover, 1962).

65. Christine di Stefano, "Dilemmas of Difference," in *Feminism/Postmodernism,* Linda J. Nicholson, ed. (New York: Routledge, 1990), p. 75.

66. Ibid., p. 78.

Chapter Seven

1. Arthur M. Schlesinger Jr., *The Disuniting of America* (Knoxville, Tenn.: Whittle Books, 1991), p. 2.

2. Jung Young Lee, *Marginality: The Key to Multicultural Theology* (Minneapolis: Fortress Press, 1995), p. 35. Lee is citing Israel Zangwill, *The Melting Pot: A Drama in Four Acts.*

3. Schlesinger, *The Disuniting of America,* p. 2.

4. See, for example, Angela Y. Davis, "Gender, Class, and Multiculturalism: Rethinking 'Race' Politics," in *Mapping Multiculturalism,* Avery R. Gordon and Christopher Newfield, eds. (Minneapolis: University of Minnesota Press, 1996), pp. 40–48.

5. Blaine J. Fowers and Frank C. Richardson, "Why Is Multiculturalism Good?" *American Psychologist* 51, no. 6 (June 1996): 609.

6. Joseph Raz, "Multiculturalism: A Liberal Perspective," *Dissent* (Winter 1994): 74.

7. Ibid., p. 78.

8. Ibid., p. 77.

9. Elizabeth V. Spelman, *Inessential Woman: Problems of Exclusion in Feminist Thought* (Boston: Beacon Press, 1988), p. 11.

10. Ibid., pp. 11–12.

11. Ibid., p. 12.

12. Ibid., p. 13.

13. Spelman, *Inessential Woman: Problems of Exclusion in Feminist Thought,* p. 158.

14. Deborah King, "Multiple Jeopardy: The Context of a Black Feminist Ideology," in *Feminist Frameworks,* 3d edition, Alison M. Jaggar and Paula S. Rothenberg, eds. (New York: McGraw-Hill, 1993), p. 220.

15. bell hooks, *Yearning: Race, Gender, and Cultural Politics* (Boston: South End Press, 1990), p. 59.

16. Audre Lorde, "Age, Race, Class, and Sex: Women Redefining Difference," in *Race, Class, and Gender*, 2d edition, Margaret L. Andersen and Patricia Hill Collins, eds. (Belmont, Calif.: Wadsworth, 1995), p. 532.

17. Ibid., p. 539.

18. Audre Lorde, *The Cancer Journals* (San Francisco: Spinster/Aunt Lute, 1980).

19. Lorde, "Age, Race, Class, and Sex: Women Redefining Difference," p. 539.

20. Ibid.

21. Patricia Hill Collins, *Black Feminist Thought: Knowledge, Consciousness, and the Politics of Empowerment* (Boston: Unwin Hyman, 1990), p. 6.

22. Ibid.

23. Ibid., p. 7.

24. Ibid., p. 67.

25. Jill Lewis, "Sexual Division of Power: Motivations of the Women's Liberation Movement," in Gloria I. Joseph and Jill Lewis, *Common Differences: Conflicts in Black and White Feminist Perspectives* (Garden City, N.Y.: Anchor/Doubleday, 1981), pp. 44–45.

26. hooks, *Yearning: Race, Gender, and Cultural Politics*, pp. 58–59.

27. Tracey Gardner, "Racism in Pornography and the Women's Movement," in *Take Back the Night*, Laura Lederer, ed. (New York: William Morrow, 1986), p. 112.

28. Collins, *Black Feminist Thought: Knowledge, Consciousness, and the Politics of Empowerment*, p. 168.

29. Ibid.

30. Alice Walker, "Coming Apart," in *Take Back the Night*, Lederer, ed., p. 103.

31. Raymond M. Lane, "A Man's World: An Update on Sexual Harassment," *Village Voice*, December 16–22, 1981, pp. 1, 15, 16.

32. Karen Lindsey, "Sexual Harassment on the Job," *Ms.*, November 1977, p. 48.

33. Catharine A. MacKinnon, *Sexual Harassment of Working Women* (New Haven, Conn.: Yale University Press, 1979), p. 31.

34. Jack E. Hill, "The Stereotypes of Race," *Time*, October 21, 1991, p. 66.

35. Ibid.

36. Ibid.

37. Priscilla Painton, "Woman Power," *Time*, October 28, 1991, p. 24.

38. Ibid.

39. Angela Y. Davis, *Women, Race and Class* (New York: Random House, 1981), p. 196.

40. Jean MacKellar, *Rape: The Bait and the Trap* (New York: Crown Publishers, 1975), p. 72.

41. Diana Russell, *The Politics of Rape: The Victim's Perspective* (New York: Stein & Day, 1975), p. 163.

42. Davis, *Women, Race and Class*, p. 197.

43. Frederick Douglass, "The Lesson of the Hour," pamphlet published in 1894; reprinted under the title "Why Is the Negro Lynched?" in Philip S. Foner, *The Life and Writings of Frederick Douglass* (New York: International Publishers, 1950), vol. 4, p. 501.

44. Jesse Daniel Ames, *The Changing Character of Lynching, 1931–1941* (New York: AMS Press, 1973).

45. Marvin E. Wolfgang and Marc Riedel, "Rape, Race, and the Death Penalty in Georgia," *American Journal of Orthopsychiatry* 45 (July 1975): 658–668.

46. Barbara Omolade, *The Rising Song of African American Women* (New York: Routledge, 1994), p. 183.

47. Ibid., p. 184.

48. Ibid.

49. Ibid., p. 189.

50. Charlotte Bunch, "Prospects for Global Feminism," in *Feminist Frameworks*, Jaggar and Rothenberg, eds., p. 249.

51. Alice Walker, *In Search of Our Mothers' Gardens*. (New York: Harcourt Brace Jovanovich, 1983), p. xi.

52. Ann Russo, "'We Cannot Live Without Our Lives': White Women, Anti-Racism, and Feminism," in *Third World Women and the Politics of Feminism*, Chandra Talpads Mohanty, Ann Russo, and Lourde Torres, eds. (Bloomington: Indiana University Press, 1991), pp. 304–305.

53. Bunch, "Prospects for Global Feminism," p. 250.

54. Quoted in Nellie Wong, "Socialist Feminism: Our Bridge to Freedom," in *Third World Women and the Politics of Feminism*, Mohanty, Russo, and Torres, eds., p. 293.

55. Bunch, "Prospects for Global Feminism," p. 251.

56. Audre Lorde, *Sister Outsider* (Trumansburg, N.Y.: Crossing Press, 1984), p. 111.

57. Robin Morgan, *Sisterhood Is Global* (Garden City, N.Y.: Anchor, 1984), p. 35.

58. Eschel M. Rhoodie, *Discrimination Against Women: A Global Survey of the Economic, Educational, Social and Political Status of Women* (London: McFarland, 1989), p. 19.

59. Ibid.

60. Ibid., p. 20.

61. Angela Gillian, "Women's Equality and National Liberation," in *Third World Women and the Politics of Feminism*, Mohanty, Russo, and Torres, eds., p. 218.

62. Ibid., p. 224.

63. Ibid., p. 229.

64. Ibid.

65. Ibid.

66. Charlotte Bunch, "U.N. World Conference in Nairobi," *Ms.*, June 1985, p. 82.

67. Adele Clark, "Subtle Forms of Sterilization Abuse: A Reproductive Rights Analysis," in *Test-Tube Women: What Future for Motherhood?* Rita Arditti, Renate Duelli Klein, and Shelley Minden, eds. (London: Pandora Press, 1985), p. 198.

68. Helen Rodriguez-Treas, "Sterilization Abuse," in *Biological Woman: The Convenient Myth*, Ruth Hubbard, Mary Sue Henifin, and Barbara Fried, eds. (Cambridge, Mass.: Schenkman, 1982), p. 150.

69. "Contraceptive Raises Ethical Concerns," *Medical Ethics Advisor* 9, no. 2 (February 1991): 17.

70. Alison Jaggar, "Abortion and a Woman's Right to Decide," in *Woman and Philosophy: Toward a Theory of Liberation*, Carol C. Gould and Max W. Wartofsky, eds. (New York: Putnam's, 1976), p. 357.

71. Morgan, *Sisterhood Is Global*.

72. Nicholas D. Kristof, "China's Birth Rate on Rise Again as Official Sanctions Are Ignored," *New York Times*, April 21, 1987, p. 1.

73. Patrick E. Tyler, "Population Control in China Falls to Coercion and Evasion," *New York Times*, June 25, 1995, pp. 1, 6.

74. Maria Mies, "New Reproductive Technologies: Sexist and Racist Implications," in Maria Mies and Vandana Shiva, *Ecofeminism* (London: Zed, 1993), p. 194 (emphasis mine).

75. Morgan, *Sisterhood Is Global*, p. 5.

76. Ibid., p. 765.

77. Ibid., p. 16.

78. Ibid.

79. Maria Mies, "The Myths of Catching-up Development," in Mies and Shiva, *Ecofeminism*, p. 58.

80. Ibid., p. 60.

81. Ibid., p. 59.

82. Ibid., p. 66.

83. Ibid., p. 67.

84. Maria Mies, "The Need for a New Vision," in Mies and Shiva, *Ecofeminism*, p. 305.

85. Mies and Shiva, "Introduction: Why We Wrote This Book Together," in Mies and Shiva, *Ecofeminism*, pp. 10–11.

86. Ibid., p. 11.

87. Ibid., pp. 11–12.

88. Susan Sherwin, *No Longer Patient: Feminist Ethics and Health Care* (Philadelphia: Temple University Press, 1992), p. 62.

89. Ibid., p. 65.

90. Ibid., p. 67.

91. Ibid., p. 69.

92. Leonard J. Kouba and Judith Muasher, "Female Circumcision in Africa: An Overview," *African Studies Review* 28, no. 1 (March 1988): 105–109.

93. Sherwin, *No Longer Patient: Feminist Ethics and Health Care*, p. 71.

94. Ibid.

95. Ibid.

96. Ibid., p. 75.

97. Mies and Shiva, "Introduction: Why We Wrote This Book Together," p. 13.

98. Morgan, *Sisterhood Is Global*, p. 36.

99. Spelman, *Inessential Woman: Problems of Exclusion in Feminist Thought*, p. 178.

100. Ibid.

101. Ibid., pp. 178–179.

102. Ibid., p. 181.

103. Maria Lugones and Elizabeth Spelman, "Have We Got a Theory for You! Feminist Theory, Cultural Imperialism, and the Demand for 'the Woman's Voice,'" in *Feminist Philosophies*, Janet A. Kourany, James P. Sterba, and Rosemarie Tong, eds. (Englewood Cliffs, N.J.: Prentice-Hall, 1992), p. 388.

104. Ibid., p. 389.

105. bell hooks, *Feminist Theory: From Margin to Center* (Boston: South End Press, 1984), p. 404.

106. Ibid.

107. Lorde, *Sister Outsider*, p. 113.

108. Iris Marion Young, "The Ideal of Community and the Politics of Difference," *Feminism/Postmodernism*, Linda J. Nicholson, ed. (New York: Routledge, 1990), p. 308.

109. Nancie Caraway, *Segregated Sisterhood: Racism and the Politics of American Feminism* (Knoxville: University of Tennessee Press, 1991).

110. Young, "The Ideal of Community and the Politics of American Feminism," p. 311.

111. Caraway, *Segregated Sisterhood: Racism and the Politics of American Feminism*, p. 206.

112. Aristotle, *Nichomachean Ethics*, in *The Works of Aristotle Translated into English*, W. D. Ross, ed. (London: Oxford University Press, 1963).

Chapter Eight

1. Karen J. Warren, "The Power and the Promise of Ecological Feminism," in *Ecological Feminist Philosophies*, Karen J. Warren, ed. (Bloomington: Indiana University Press, 1996), p. 20.

2. Karen J. Warren, "Feminism and the Environment: An Overview of the Issues," *APA Newsletter on Feminism and Philosophy* 90, no. 3 (Fall 1991): 110–111.

3. Karen J. Warren, "Feminism and Ecology: Making Connections," in *Readings in Ecology and Feminist Theology*, Mary Heather MacKinnon and Marie McIntyre, eds. (Kansas City, Kans.: Sheed and Ward, 1995), p. 114.

4. Janet Biehl, *Rethinking Feminist Politics* (Boston: South End Press, 1991), p. 11.

5. Ibid., p. 17.

6. Rosemary Radford Ruether, *New Woman/New Earth: Sexist Ideologies and Human Liberation* (New York: Seabury Press, 1975), p. 204.

7. Rachel Carson, *Silent Spring* (Boston: Houghton Mifflin, 1962), pp. 16–23.

8. Robert Alter, trans. and comm., *Genesis* (New York: W. W. Norton, 1996).

9. Aldo Leopold, "The Land Ethic," in Aldo Leopold, *Sand County Almanac* (New York: Oxford University Press, 1987).

10. See John Hospers, *Understanding the Arts* (Englewood Cliffs, N.J.: Prentice-Hall, 1982).

11. Arne Naess, "The Deep Ecological Movement: Some Philosophical Aspects," *Philosophical Inquiry* 8 (1986): 10–13.

12. Peter S. Wenz, "Ecology and Morality," in *Ethics and Animals*, Harlan B. Miller and William H. Williams, eds. (Clifton, N.J.: Humana Press, 1983), pp. 185–191.

13. The optimum human population would be about 500 million, according to James Lovelock; 100 million according to Arne Naess. See Luc Ferry, *The New Ecological Order*, Carol Volk, trans. (Chicago: University of Chicago Press, 1992), p. 75.

14. William Aiken, "Non-Anthropocentric Ethical Challenges" in *Earthbound: New Introductory Essays in Environmental Ethics*, Tom Regan, ed. (New York: Random House, 1984), p. 269.

15. See George Sessions, "The Deep Ecology Movement: A Review," *Environmental Review* 9 (1987): 115.

16. Karen J. Warren, "Feminism and Ecology," *Environmental Review* 9, no. 1 (Spring 1987): 3–20.

17. Ariel Kay Salleh, "Deeper Than Deep Ecology: The Ecofeminist Connection," *Environmental Ethics* 6, no. 1 (1984): 339.

18. Ibid.

19. Ferry, *The New Ecological Order*, p. 118.

20. Ynestra King, "The Ecology of Feminism and the Feminism of Ecology," in *Healing the Wounds: The Promise of Ecofeminism*, Judith Plant, ed. (Philadelphia: New Society Publishers, 1989), pp. 22–23.

21. Ibid., p. 23.

22. Simone de Beauvoir, *The Second Sex*, H. M. Parshley, trans. and ed. (New York: Vintage Books, 1952), pp. 19–29.

23. Ibid., p. xxi.

24. Val Plumwood, "Ecofeminism: An Overview and Discussion of Positions and Arguments," *Australian Journal of Philosophy* 64, supplement (June 1986): 135.

25. Sherry B. Ortner, "Is Female to Male as Nature Is to Culture?" in *Readings in Ecology and Feminist Theory*, MacKinnon and McIntyre, eds., pp. 40–41.

26. Ibid., p. 51.

27. Ibid.

28. Ibid., pp. 52–53.

29. Ibid., p. 54.

30. Ibid., pp. 54–55.

31. Ibid., p. 55 (emphasis mine).

32. Mary Daly, *Pure Lust* (Boston: Beacon Press, 1984), p. 25.

33. Mary Daly, *Gyn/Ecology* (Boston: Beacon Press, 1978), pp. 63–64.

34. Ibid., pp. 10–11 (emphasis mine).

35. Ibid.

36. Ibid., pp. 12–13.

37. Ibid., p. 21.

38. See David Maccauley, "On Women, Animals and Nature: An Interview with Eco-feminist Susan Griffin," *APA Newsletter on Feminism* 90, no. 3 (Fall 1991): 118.

39. Susan Griffin, *Woman and Nature: The Roaring Inside Her* (New York: Harper & Row, 1978), p. 226.

40. Ibid., p. 1.

41. Griffin, *Woman and Nature: The Roaring Inside Her*, pp. 83–90.

42. Ibid., p. 67.

43. Maccauley, "On Women, Animals and Nature: An Interview with Eco-feminist Susan Griffin," p. 117.

44. Griffin, *Woman and Nature: The Roaring Inside Her*, p. 1.

45. Ibid., pp. 117–118.

46. Susan Griffin, *Pornography and Silence: Culture's Revenge Against Nature* (New York: Harper & Row, 1981), p. 2.

47. Maccauley, "On Women, Animals and Nature: An Interview with Eco-feminist Susan Griffin," p. 117.

48. Deena Metzger, Gloria Orenstein, Dale Colleen Hamilton, Paula Gum Alleo, Margot Adler, Dolores LaChapelle, A. K. Salleh, and Radha Bratt are also considered to be spiritual ecofeminists.

49. Riane Eisler, "The Gaia Tradition and the Partnership Future: An Ecofeminist Manifesto," in *Reweaving the World: The Emergence of Ecofeminism*, Irene Diamond and Gloria Feman Orenstein, eds. (San Francisco: Sierra Club Books, 1990), p. 23.

50. Starhawk, "Power, Authority, and Mystery: Ecofeminism and Earth-based Spirituality," in *Reweaving the World*, Diamond and Orenstein, eds., p. 86.

51. Starhawk, "Feminist, Earth-based Spirituality and Ecofeminism," in *Healing the Wounds: The Promise of Ecofeminism*, Plant, ed., p. 176.

52. Ibid., p. 177.

53. Ibid., p. 178.

54. Ibid.

55. Ibid.

56. Ibid., p. 179.

57. Ibid.

58. Ibid., p. 180.

59. Starhawk, "A Story of Beginnings," in *Healing the Wounds: The Promise of Ecofeminism*, Plant, ed., p. 115.

60. Dorothy Dinnerstein, "Survival on Earth: The Meaning of Feminism," in *Healing the Wounds: The Promise of Ecofeminism*, Plant, ed., p. 193.

61. Ibid.

62. Ibid., p. 174.

63. Marge Piercy, *Woman on the Edge of Time* (New York: Fawcett Crest, 1976).

64. Ibid., p. 105.

65. Warren, "The Power and the Promise of Ecological Feminism," p. 178.

66. Ibid., pp. 186–187.

67. Ibid., pp. 179–188.

68. Ibid., pp. 189–190.

69. Warren, "Feminism and Ecology: Making Connections," pp. 109–111.

70. Ibid., p. 113.

71. Ibid., pp. 112–114.

72. Ibid., pp. 114–115.

73. Ibid., p. 116, quoting Alison Jaggar.

74. Ibid., p. 118.

75. Ibid.

76. Maria Mies, "White Man's Dilemma: His Search for What He Has Destroyed," in Maria Mies and Vandana Shiva, *Ecofeminism* (London: Zed, 1993), pp. 132–163.

77. Ibid., p. 132.

78. Ibid.

79. Ibid., p. 133.

80. Ibid., pp. 137–138.

81. Karen J. Warren also presented a discussion similar to Shiva's in "Taking Empirical Data Seriously: An Ecofeminist Philosophy Perspective," in *Living with Contradictions: Controversies in Feminist Social Ethics*, Alison M. Jaggar, ed. (Boulder, Colo.: Westview Press, 1994), pp. 642–643.

82. Vandana Shiva, "The Chipko-Women's Concept of Freedom," in Mies and Shiva, *Ecofeminism*, p. 247.

83. Maria Mies, "The Need for a New Vision: The Subsistence Perspective," in Mies and Shiva, *Ecofeminism*, p. 319.

84. Ibid.

85. Ibid., p. 320.

86. Ibid., p. 321.

87. Ibid., p. 322.

88. Ibid.

89. Biehl, *Rethinking Feminist Politics*, p. 14.

90. Ibid., p. 16 (quoting from Simone de Beauvoir).

91. Ibid.

92. Maria Mies and Vandana Shiva, "Introduction," in Mies and Shiva, *Ecofeminism*, p. 19.

93. Ynestra King, "Engendering a Peaceful Planet: Ecology, Economy, and Ecofeminism in Contemporary Context," *Women's Studies Quarterly* 23 (Fall/Winter 1995): 19.

94. Mies and Shiva, "Introduction," p. 18.

95. Ibid.

96. Carolyn Merchant, *Radical Ecology: The Search for a Livable World* (New York: Routledge, 1992).

97. Biehl, *Rethinking Feminist Politics*, p. 19.

98. Sara Ruddick, *Maternal Thinking: Toward a Politics of Peace* (Boston: Beacon Press, 1989), p. 229.

99. King, "Engendering a Peaceful Planet: Ecology, Economy, and Ecofeminism in Contemporary Context," pp. 16–17.

100. Quoted in Judith Auerbach, "The Intersection of Feminism and the Environmental Movement, or What Is Feminist About the Feminist Perspective on the Environment?" *American Behavioral Scientist* 37, no. 8 (August 1994): 1095.

Conclusion

1. Aristotle, *Nichomachean Ethics*, in *The Works of Aristotle Translated into English*, W. D. Ross, ed. (London: Oxford University Press, 1963).

2. Audre Lorde, "Poetry Is Not a Luxury," in *The Future of Difference*, Alice Jardine and Hester Eisenstein, eds. (New Brunswick, N.J.: Rutgers University Press, 1985), p. 126.

Bibliography

Chapter One

The Eighteenth- and Nineteenth-Century Roots of Liberal Feminism

Bentham, Jeremy. *The Principles of Morals and Legislation*. New York: Hafner, 1965.

Berlin, Isaiah. *Two Concepts of Liberty*. Oxford: Clarendon Press, 1961.

Butler, Melissa A. "Early Liberal Roots of Feminism: John Locke and the Attack on Patriarchy." *American Political Science Review* 72(1), 1978, pp. 135–150.

Dworkin, Ronald. "Liberalism." In Stuart Hampshire, ed., *Public and Private Morality*. Cambridge: Cambridge University Press, 1978.

_____. *Taking Rights Seriously*. Cambridge: Harvard University Press, 1977.

Fuller, M. *Woman in the Nineteenth Century*. New York: W. W. Norton, 1971.

Gutmann, Amy. *Liberal Equality*. New York: Cambridge University Press, 1980.

Hobbes, Thomas. *Leviathan*. New York: E. P. Dutton, 1950.

Jaggar, Alison M. *Feminist Politics and Human Nature*. Totowa, NJ: Rowman & Allanheld, 1983.

Mill, John Stuart. *Utilitarianism, Liberty, and Representative Government*. New York: E. P. Dutton, 1910.

Pateman, Carole. *The Problem of Political Obligation: A Critique of Liberal Theory*. Berkeley: University of California Press, 1979.

Rawls, John. *A Theory of Justice*. Cambridge: Harvard University Press, 1971.

Sandel, Michael J. *Liberalism and Its Critics*. New York: New York University Press, 1984.

_____. *Liberalism and the Limits of Justice*. New York: Cambridge University Press, 1982.

Strauss, Leo. *Liberalism: Ancient and Modern*. New York: Basic Books, 1968.

Historical Development of Liberal-Feminist Thought

Berg, Barbara. *The Remembered Gate: Origins of American Feminism*. New York: Oxford University Press, 1979.

Bloom, Allan. *The Closing of the American Mind*. New York: Simon & Schuster, 1987.

Bridenthal, Renate and Claudia Koonz, eds. *Becoming Visible: Women in European History*. Boston: Houghton Mifflin, 1977.

Brockett, L. P. *Woman: Her Rights, Wrongs, Privileges, and Responsibilities.* Freeport, NY: Books for Libraries Press, 1970.

Carroll, Bernice A., ed. *Liberating Women's History: Theoretical and Critical Essays.* Urbana: University of Illinois Press, 1976.

Dahlberg, Frances, ed. *Woman the Gatherer.* New Haven, CT: Yale University Press, 1981.

DuBois, Ellen Carol, ed. *Elizabeth Cady Stanton, Susan B. Anthony: Correspondence, Writings, Speeches.* New York: Schocken Books, 1981.

Eisenstein, Zillah. *The Radical Future of Liberal Feminism.* Boston: Northeastern University Press, 1986.

Fuller, Margaret. *Woman in the Nineteenth Century.* New York: W. W. Norton, 1971.

Gilman, Charlotte Perkins. *Women and Economics.* New York: Harper & Row, 1966.

Godwin, William. *Memoirs of Mary Wollstonecraft.* W. Clark Durant, ed. New York: Bordon Press, 1972.

Grimke, Sarah. *Letters on "The Equality of the Sexes" and "The Condition of Woman."* New York: Burt Franklin, 1970.

Kant, Immanuel. *Groundwork of the Metaphysic of Morals.* H. J. Paton, trans. New York: Harper Torchbooks, 1958.

Korsmeyer, Carolyn W. "Reasons and Morals in the Early Feminist Movement: Mary Wollstonecraft." *Philosophical Forum* 5(1-2), Fall-Winter 1973, pp. 97–111.

Krouse, Richard. "Mill and Marx on Marriage, Divorce, and the Family." *Social Concept* 1(2), September 1983, pp. 36–75.

_____. "Patriarchal Liberalism and Beyond: From John Stuart Mill to Harriet Taylor." In Jean Bethke Elshtain, ed., *The Family in Political Thought.* Amherst: University of Massachusetts Press, 1981.

Martin, Jane Roland. *Reclaiming a Conversation: The Ideal of the Educated Woman.* New Haven, CT: Yale University Press, 1985.

Mill, John Stuart. *Autobiography.* London: Oxford University Press, 1924.

_____. "Periodical Literature 'Edinburgh Review.'" *Westminster Review* 1(2), April 1824.

_____. "The Subjection of Women." In Alice S. Rossi, ed., *Essays on Sex Equality.* Chicago: University of Chicago Press, 1970.

Rossi, Alice S. *The Feminist Papers: From Adams to De Beauvoir.* New York: Columbia University Press, 1973.

_____. "Sentiment and Intellect: The Story of John Stuart Mill and Harriet Taylor Mill." In John Stuart Mill and Harriet Taylor Mill, *Essays on Sex Equality,* Alice S. Rossi, ed. Chicago: University of Chicago Press, 1970.

Rousseau, Jean-Jacques. *Emile.* Allan Bloom, trans. New York: Basic Books, 1979.

Sabrosky, Judith A. *From Rationality to Liberation.* Westport, CT: Greenwood Press, 1979.

Wollstonecraft, Mary. *A Vindication of the Rights of Woman.* Carol H. Poston, ed. New York: W. W. Norton, 1975.

Nineteenth-Century Liberal Feminist Action

Davis, Angela Y. *Women, Race and Class.* New York: Random House, 1981.

Hole, Judith and Ellen Levine. *Rebirth of Feminism.* New York: Quadrangle, 1971.

"Seneca Falls Declaration of Sentiments and Resolutions (1848)." In Miriam Schneir, ed., *Feminism: The Essential Historical Writings*. New York: Random House, 1972.

Stanton, Anthony Gage. *History of Woman Suffrage*. New York: Arno Press, 1969.

Stanton, Elizabeth Cady, Susan B. Anthony, and Matilda Joslyn Gage. *History of Woman Suffrage*. Vol. 1 (1848–1861). New York: Fowler and Wells, 1881.

Wright, Frances. *Life, Letters and Lectures, 1834/44*. New York: Arno Press, 1972.

Twentieth-Century Liberal Feminist Action

Amnesty International. *Human Rights Are Women's Right*. New York: Amnesty International Publications, 1995.

_____. *Women in the Front Line*. New York: Amnesty International Publications, 1991.

Bird, Caroline. *Born Female*. New York: David McKay Company, 1968.

Carden, Maren Lockwood. *The New Feminist Movement*. New York: Russell Sage Foundation, 1974.

Friedan, Betty. "Betty Friedan Critiques Feminism and Calls for New Directions." *New York Times Magazine*, July 5, 1981, pp. 13–15, 32–33, 35.

_____. "Feminism Takes a New Turn." *New York Times Magazine*, November 18, 1979, pp. 40, 92ff.

_____. "N.O.W.—How It Began," *Women Speaking*, April 1967.

Ireland, Patricia. "The State of NOW." *Ms.*, July/August 1992.

NOW Bill of Rights. In Robin Morgan, ed., *Sisterhood Is Powerful*. New York: Random House, 1970.

Peters, Julia and Andrea Wolper, eds. *Women's Rights, Human Rights: International Feminist Perspectives*. New York: Routledge, 1995.

Richards, Janet Radcliffe. *The Skeptical Feminist*. London: Routledge & Kegan Paul, 1980.

Steinem, Gloria. "Now That It's Reagan." *Ms.*, January 1981, pp. 28–33.

Twentieth-Century Liberal Feminist Thought: Treating Women and Men the Same or Differently?

Ackerman, Bruce. "Political Liberalisms." *Journal of Philosophy* 91(7), 1994, pp. 364–386.

Friedan, Betty. *The Feminine Mystique*. New York: Dell, 1974.

_____. *The Fountain of Age*. New York: Simon & Schuster, 1993.

_____. *The Second Stage*. New York: Summit Books, 1981.

Kanowitz, Lee. *Women and the Law: The Unfinished Revolution*. Albuquerque: University of New Mexico Press, 1969.

Leo, John. "Are Women 'Male Clones'?" *Time*, August 18, 1986.

Rossi, Alice. "Equality Between the Sexes: An Immodest Proposal." *Daedalus* 93(2), 1964, pp. 607–652.

Stacey, Judith. *Brave New Families: Stories of Domestic Upheaval in Late Twentieth Century America*. New York: Basic Books, 1990.

_____. "The New Conservative Feminism." *Feminist Studies* 9(3), Fall 1983.

Contemporary Directions in Liberal Feminism

Baehr, Amy R. "Toward a New Feminist Liberalism: Okin, Rawls, and Habermas." *Hypatia* 11(1), Winter 1996, pp. 49–66.

Bem, Sandra L. "Probing the Promise of Androgyny." In Alexandra G. Kaplan and Joan P. Bean, eds., *Beyond Sex-Role Stereotypes: Reading Toward a Psychology of Androgyny*. Boston: Little, Brown, 1976.

Code, Lorraine. *What Can She Know? Feminist Theory and the Construction of Knowledge*. Ithaca, NY: Cornell University Press, 1991.

English, Jane. "Sex Roles and Gender: Introduction." In Mary Vetterling-Braggin, Frederick A. Elliston, and Jane English, eds., *Feminism and Philosophy*. Totowa, NJ: Rowman & Littlefield, 1977.

Galston, William A. *Liberal Purposes: Goods, Virtues, and Diversity in the Liberal State*. Cambridge: Cambridge University Press, 1991.

Heilbrun, Carolyn G. *Toward the Promise of Androgyny*. New York: Alfred A. Knopf, 1973.

Hunter College Women's Studies Collective. *Women's Realities, Women's Choices: An Introduction to Women's Studies*. New York: Oxford University Press, 1983.

Okin, Susan Moller. *Women in Western Political Thought*. Princeton, NJ: Princeton University Press, 1979.

Person, Ethel Spector. "Sexuality as the Mainstay of Identity: Psychoanalytic Perspectives." *Signs: Journal of Women in Culture and Society* 5(4), Summer 1980, p. 606.

Stack, Carol. *All Our Kin*. New York: Harper & Row, 1974.

Steinem, Gloria. *Outrageous Acts and Everyday Rebellions*. New York: Holt, Rinehart and Winston, 1983.

Trebilcot, Joyce. "Two Forms of Androgynism." In Mary Vetterling-Braggin, ed., *"Femininity," "Masculinity," and "Androgyny."* Totowa, NJ: Rowman & Littlefield, 1982.

Critiques of Liberal Feminism

Bolotin, Susan. "Voices from the Post-Feminist Generation." *New York Times Magazine*, October 17, 1982, p. 28.

Brennan, Teresa and Carole Pateman. "'Mere Auxiliaries to the Commonwealth': Women and the Origins of Liberalism." *Political Studies* 27(2), June 1979, pp. 183–200.

Clark, Lorenne M.B. "Women and Locke: Who Owns the Apples in the Garden of Eden?" In Lorenne M.B. Clark and Lydia Lange, eds., *The Sexism of Social and Political Theory*. Toronto: University of Toronto Press, 1979.

Davis, Angela Y. "Reflections on the Black Woman's Role in the Community of Slaves." *Black Scholar* 3, 1971, p. 7.

Dowling, Colette. *The Cinderella Syndrome: Women's Hidden Fear of Independence*. New York: Summit Books, 1981.

Elshtain, Jean Bethke. "Feminism, Family and Community." *Dissent* 29, Fall 1982, p. 442.

_____. *Meditations on Modern Political Thought: Masculine/Feminine Themes from Luther to Prendt*. New York: Praeger, 1986.

_____. *Public Man, Private Woman*. Princeton, NJ: Princeton University Press, 1981.

Evans, Sara. "The Origins of the Women's Liberation Movement." *Radical America* 9(2), 1975, pp. 3–4.

Ferguson, Kathy E. "Liberalism and Oppression: Emma Goldman and the Anarchist Feminist Alternative." In Michael C.G. McGrath, ed., *Liberalism and the Modern Polity*. New York: Marcel Dekker, 1978.

_____. *Self, Society and Womankind: The Dialectic of Liberation*. Westport, CT: Greenwood Press, 1980.

Flammang, Janet Angela. "Feminist Theory: The Question of Power." *Current Perspectives on Social Theory* 4, 1983, pp. 37–83.

_____. "The Political Consciousness of American Women: A Critical Analysis of Liberal Feminism in America." Ph.D. diss., University of California, Los Angeles, 1980.

Gibson, Mary. "Rationality." *Philosophy and Public Affairs* 6(3), Spring 1977, pp. 193–225.

Harper, Ida Husted, ed. *History of Woman Suffrage*. Vol. 5. New York: National American Woman Suffrage Association, 1922.

Hewlett, Sylvia Ann. *A Lesser Life: The Myth of Women's Liberation in America*. New York: William Morrow, 1986.

MacLean, Douglas and Claudia Mills, eds. *Liberalism Reconsidered*. Totowa, NJ: Rowman & Allanheld, 1983.

Pearsall, Marilyn, ed. *Women and Values: Readings in Recent Feminist Philosophy*. Belmont, CA: Wadsworth, 1986.

Richards, Janet Radcliffe. *The Skeptical Feminist*. London: Routledge & Kegan Paul, 1980.

Scheman, Naomi. "Individualism and the Objects of Psychology." In Sandra Harding and Merrill B. Hintikka, eds., *Discovering Reality: Feminist Perspectives on Epistemology, Metaphysics, Methodology, and the Philosophy of Science*. Dordrecht, Netherlands: D. Reidel, 1983.

Thorne, Barrie and Marilyn Yalom, eds. *Rethinking the Family: Some Feminist Questions*. Boston: Northeastern University Press, 1989.

Wendell, Susan. "A (Qualified) Defense of Liberal Feminism." *Hypatia* 2(2), Summer 1987, pp. 65–94.

Willis, Ellen. "The Conservatism of *Ms.*" In Redstockings, ed., *Feminist Revolution*. New York: Random House, 1975.

Chapter Two

The Distinction Between Radical-Libertarian and Radical-Cultural Feminists

Alcoff, Linda. "Cultural Feminism Versus Poststructuralism: The Identity Crisis in Feminist Theory." *Signs: Journal of Women in Culture and Society* 13(3), 1988, p. 408.

Echols, Alice. "The New Feminism of Yin and Yang," In Ann Snitow, Christine Stansell, and Sharon Thompson, eds., *Powers of Desire: The Politics of Sexuality*. New York: Monthly Review Press, 1983.

Hole, Judith and Ellen Levine. *Rebirth of Feminism*. New York: Quadrangle, 1971.
Jaggar, Alison M. and Paula S. Rothenberg, eds. *Feminist Frameworks*. New York: McGraw-Hill, 1984.
Koedt, Anne, Ellen Levine, and Anita Rapone, eds. *Radical Feminism*. New York: Quadrangle, 1973.
Stanton, Elizabeth Cady. *The Woman's Bible*. 2 vols. New York: Arno Press, 1972; originally published 1895 and 1899.

Radical-Libertarian and Radical-Cultural Feminists: Interpreting the Sex/Gender System

Analyzing the Oppressive Features of Gender ("Masculinity" and "Femininity")

Allen, Jeffner. "Motherhood: The Annihilation of Women." In Marilyn Pearsall, ed., *Women and Values: Readings in Recent Feminist Philosophy*. Belmont, CA: Wadsworth, 1986.
Alpert, Jane. "Mother Right: A New Feminist Theory." *Ms.*, August 1973.
Barry, Herbert, III, Margaret K. Bacon, and Irwin L. Child. "A Cross-Cultural Survey of Some Sex Differences in Socialization." In Robert F. Winch, Robert McGinnis, and Herbert R. Barringer, eds., *Selected Studies in Marriage and the Family*. 2d ed. New York: Holt, Rinehart and Winston, 1962.
Cahill, Susan, ed. *Motherhood*. New York: Avon Books, 1982.
Daly, Mary. *Beyond God the Father: Toward a Philosophy of Women's Liberation*. Boston: Beacon Press, 1973.
_____. *Gyn/Ecology: The Metaethics of Radical Feminism*. Boston: Beacon Press, 1978.
_____. *Pure Lust: Elemental Feminist Philosophy*. Boston: Beacon Press, 1984.
Dinnerstein, Dorothy. *The Mermaid and the Minotaur: Sexual Arrangements and Human Malaise*. New York: Harper Colophon Books, 1977.
Eisenstein, Hester. *Contemporary Feminist Thought*. Boston: G. K. Hall, 1983.
Ferguson, Ann. "Motherhood and Sexuality: Some Feminist Questions." *Hypatia* 1(2), Fall 1986, pp. 3–22.
Firestone, Shulamith. *The Dialectic of Sex*. New York: Bantam Books, 1970.
French, Marilyn. *Beyond Power: On Women, Men and Morals*. New York: Summit Books, 1985.
Friedan, Betty. *The Feminine Mystique*. New York: Dell, 1974.
Giovanni, Nikki. *My House*. New York: William Morrow, 1972.
Grahn, Judy. *The Work of a Common Woman*. New York: St. Martin's Press, 1979.
Jaggar, Alison M. *Feminist Politics and Human Nature*. Totowa, NJ: Rowman & Allanheld, 1983.
Miller, Henry. *Sexus*. New York: Grove Press, 1965.
Millett, Kate. *Sexual Politics*. Garden City, NY: Doubleday, 1970.
Morey-Gaines, Ann-Janine. "Metaphor and Radical Feminism: Some Cautionary Comments on Mary Daly's *Gyn/Ecology*." *Soundings* 65(3), Fall 1982, pp. 347–348.
Nietzsche, Friedrich. *On the Genealogy of Morals*. Walter Kaufmann and R. Hollingdale, trans. New York: Vintage Books, 1969.

Rossi, Alice. "Sex Equality: The Beginning of Ideology." In Betty Roszak and Theodore Roszak, eds., *Masculine/Feminine*. New York: Harper & Row, 1969.

Rubin, Gayle. "The Traffic in Women." In Rayna R. Reiter, ed., *Toward an Anthropology of Women*. New York: Monthly Review Press, 1975.

Trebilcot, Joyce. "Conceiving Wisdom: Notes on the Logic of Feminism." *Sinister Wisdom* 3, Fall 1979.

_____, ed. *Mothering: Essays in Feminist Theory*. Totowa, NJ: Rowman & Allanheld, 1984.

Analyzing the Oppressive Features of Sexuality
("Male Domination" and "Female Subordination")

Blumstein, Philip and Pepper Schwartz. *American Couples*. New York: William Morrow, 1983.

Cornelisen, Ann. *Women of the Shadows*. Boston: Little, Brown, 1976.

Dworkin, Andrea. *Our Blood: Prophecies and Discourses on Sexual Politics*. New York: G. P. Putnam, 1981.

_____. *Right-Wing Women*. New York: Coward-McCann, 1983.

_____. *Woman Hating: A Radical Look at Sexuality*. New York: E. P. Dutton, 1974.

Echols, Alice. "The Taming of the Id." In Carole S. Vance, ed., *Pleasure and Danger: Exploring Female Sexuality*. Boston: Routledge & Kegan Paul, 1984.

English, Deirdre, Amber Hollibaugh, and Gayle Rubin. "Talking Sex: A Conversation on Sexuality and Feminism." *Socialist Review* 11(4), July/August 1981, pp. 43–62.

Fairchilds, Cissie. "Female Sexual Attitudes and the Rise of Illegitimacy: A Case Study." *Journal of Interdisciplinary History* 8(4), Spring 1978, pp. 627–667.

Ferguson, Ann. "Sex War: The Debate Between Radical and Liberation Feminists." *Signs: Journal of Women in Culture and Society* 10(1), Autumn 1984, pp. 106–135.

Frye, Marilyn. *The Politics of Reality: Essays in Feminist Theory*. Trumansburg, NY: Crossing Press, 1983.

Koedt, Anne, Ellen Levine, and Anita Rapone, eds. *Radical Feminism*. New York: Quadrangle, 1973.

Lee, Patrick C. and Robert Sussman Stewart, eds. *Sex Differences: Cultural and Developmental Dimensions*. New York: Urizen, 1976.

Linden, Robin Ruth, Darlene R. Pagano, Diana E.H. Russell, and Susan Leigh Star, eds. *Against Sadomasochism: A Radical Feminist Analysis*. East Palo Alto, CA: Frog in the Well Press, 1982.

Maccoby, Eleanor, ed. *The Development of Sex Differences*. Stanford, CA: Stanford University Press, 1966.

Martin, Del. *Battered Wives*. New York: Pocket Books, 1976.

Off Our Backs 12(6), June 1982.

Parker, Katy and Lisa Leghorn. *Woman's Worth: Sexual Economics and the World of Women*. London: Routledge & Kegan Paul, 1981.

Redstockings, ed. *Feminist Revolution*. New York: Random House, 1975.

Rubin, Gayle. "Thinking Sex: Notes for a Radical Theory of the Politics of Sexuality." In Carole S. Vance, ed., *Pleasure and Danger: Exploring Female Sexuality*. Boston: Routledge & Kegan Paul, 1984.

Schechter, Susan. *Women and Male Violence*. Boston: South End Press, 1982.

Schulman, Alix Kates. "Sex and Power: Sexual Bases of Radical Feminism." *Signs: Journal of Women in Culture and Society* 5(4), Summer 1980, pp. 590–604.

Shafer, Carolyn M. and Marilyn Frye. "Rape and Respect." In Marilyn Pearsall, ed., *Women and Values: Readings in Recent Feminist Philosophy*. Belmont, CA: Wadsworth, 1986.

Spender, Dale. *Man Made Language*. Boston: Routledge & Kegan Paul, 1980.

Vance, Carole S., ed. *Pleasure and Danger: Exploring Female Sexuality*. Boston: Routledge & Kegan Paul, 1984.

Wakoski, Diane. *The Motorcycle Betrayal Poems*. New York: Simon & Schuster, 1971.

Women, Gender, and Philosophy. Special issue of *Radical Philosophy* 34, Summer 1983.

Pornography: Symptom and Symbol of Male-Controlled Female Sexuality or Opportunity for Female-Controlled Female Sexuality?

Blakely, Mary Kay. "Is One Woman's Sexuality Another Woman's Pornography?" *Ms.*, April 1985, pp. 37–47.

Dworkin, Andrea. "'Pornography's Exquisite Volunteers.'" *Ms.*, March 1981, pp. 65–66, 94–96.

English, Deirdre. "The Politics of Porn: Can Feminists Walk the Line?" *Mother Jones*, April 1980, pp. 20–23, 44–50.

English, Deirdre, Amber Hollibaugh, and Gayle Rubin. "Talking Sex: A Conversation on Sexuality and Feminism." *Socialist Review* 11(4), July/August 1981, pp. 43–62.

Griffin, Susan. *Pornography and Silence*. New York: Harper & Row, 1981.

_____. *Rape: The Power of Consciousness*. San Francisco: Harper & Row, 1979.

Lederer, Laura, ed. *Take Back the Night: Women on Pornography*. New York: William Morrow, 1980.

MacKinnon, Catharine A. "Feminism, Marxism, Method, and the State: An Agenda for Theory." *Signs: Journal of Women in Culture and Society* 7(3), Spring 1982, p. 533.

_____. "Francis Biddle's Sister: Pornography, Civil Rights, and Speech." In Catharine A. MacKinnon, *Feminism Unmodified: Disclosures on Life and Law*. Cambridge: Harvard University Press, 1987.

McCarthy, Sarah J. "Pornography, Rape, and the Cult of Macho." *Humanist* 40(5), September-October 1980, pp. 11–20.

Soble, Alan. *Pornography: Marxism, Feminism, and the Future of Sexuality*. New Haven, CT: Yale University Press, 1986.

Taylor, Stuart, Jr. "Pornography Foes Lose New Weapons in Supreme Court." *New York Times*, February 25, 1986, p. 1.

Lesbianism: A Mere Sexual Preference or the Paradigm for Female-Controlled Female Sexuality?

Allen, Jeffner. *Lesbian Philosophy: Explorations*. Palo Alto, CA: Institute of Lesbian Studies, 1986.

Atkinson, Ti Grace. *Amazon Odyssey*. New York: Links, 1974.

_____. "Lesbianism and Feminism." In Phyllis Birkby, Bertha Harris, Jill Johnston, Esther Newton, and Jane O'Wyatt, eds., *Amazon Expedition: A Lesbian-Feminist Anthology*. Washington, NJ: Times Change Press, 1973.

_____. "Radical Feminism: A Declaration of War." In Marilyn Pearsall, ed., *Women and Values: Readings in Recent Feminist Philosophy*. Belmont, CA: Wadsworth, 1986.

Beck, Evelyn Torton, ed. *Nice Jewish Girls: A Lesbian Anthology*. Watertown, MA: Persephone Press, 1982.

Bulkin, Elly, Minnie Bruce Pratt, and Barbara Smith. *Yours in Struggle: Three Feminist Perspectives on Anti-Semitism and Racism*. New York: Long Haul Press, 1984.

Califia, Pat. "Feminism and Sadomasochism." *Co-evolution Quarterly* 33, Spring 1981.

_____. *Sapphistry: The Book of Lesbian Sexuality*. Tallahassee, FL: Naiad Press, 1983.

Goodman, Gerre, George Lakey, Judy Lahof, and Erika Thorne. *No Turning Back: Lesbian and Gay Liberation for the '80's*. Philadelphia: New Society Publishers, 1983.

Grier, Barbara and Colette Reid, eds. *The Lavender Herring: Lesbian Essays from "The Ladder."* Baltimore, MD: Diana Press, 1976.

Johnston, Jill. *Lesbian Nation: The Feminist Solution*. New York: Simon & Schuster, 1974.

Koedt, Ann. "The Myth of the Vaginal Orgasm." *Notes from the Second Year: Women's Liberation—Major Writings of the Radical Feminists*, April 1970.

Laner, M. R. and R. H. Laner. "Sexual Preference or Personal Style? Why Lesbians Are Disliked." *Journal of Homosexuality* 5(4), 1980, pp. 339–356.

Law, Sylvia. "Homosexuality and the Social Meaning of Gender." *Wisconsin Law Review* 2, 1988, pp. 187–235.

McCandlish, Barbara M. "Against All Odds: Lesbian Mother Family Dynamics." In Frederick W. Bozert, ed., *Gay and Lesbian Parents*. New York: Praeger, 1987.

Redstockings Manifesto. In Robin Morgan, ed., *Sisterhood Is Powerful*. New York: Random House, 1970.

Rich, Adrienne. "Compulsory Heterosexuality and Lesbian Existence." In Alison M. Jaggar, ed., *Living with Contradictions: Controversies in Feminist Social Ethics*. Boulder, CO: Westview Press, 1994.

Rule, Jane. *Lesbian Images*. Trumansburg, NY: Crossing Press, 1982.

Samois. *Coming to Power: Writings and Graphics on Lesbian S/M*. Palo Alto, CA: Up Press, 1981.

Radical-Libertarian and Radical-Cultural Feminists: On Reproduction and Mothering

Atwood, Margaret. *The Handmaid's Tale*. New York: Fawcett Crest Books, 1985.

Blank, Robert H. *Mother and Fetus: Changing Notions of Maternal Responsibility*. New York: Greenwood Press, 1992.

Chesler, Phyllis. *Sacred Bond: The Legacy of Baby M*. New York: Times Books, 1988.

Chodorow, Nancy. *The Reproduction of Mothering*. Berkeley: University of California Press, 1978.

Corea, Genea. "Egg Snatchers." In Rita Arditti, Renate Duelli Klein, and Shelley Minden, eds., *Test-Tube Women: What Future for Motherhood?* London: Pandora Press, 1984.

_____. *The Mother Machine: Reproduction Technologies from Artificial Insemination to Artificial Wombs*. New York: Harper & Row, 1985.

Donchin, Anne. "The Future of Mothering: Reproductive Technology and Feminist Theory." *Hypatia* 1(2), Fall 1986, p. 131.

Dworkin, Andrea. *Right-Wing Women*. New York: Coward-McCann, 1983.

Ehrenreich, Barbara and Deirdre English. *For Her Own Good*. New York: Anchor/Doubleday, 1979.

Gilder, George. *Sexual Suicide*. New York: Quadrangle, 1973.

al-Hibri, Azizah. *Research in Philosophy and Technology*. Paul T. Durbin, ed. London: JAL Press, 1984, vol. 7, p. 266.

Jaggar, Alison M. *Feminist Politics and Human Nature*. Totowa, NJ: Rowman & Allanheld, 1983.

Ketchum, Sara Ann. "Selling Babies and Selling Bodies." In Helen Holmes and Laura M. Purdy, eds., *Feminist Perspectives in Medical Ethics*. Bloomington: Indiana University Press, 1992.

Mahowald, Mary Briody. *Women and Children in Health Care: An Unequal Majority*. New York: Oxford University Press, 1993.

Mellown, Mary Ruth. "An Incomplete Picture: The Debate About Surrogate Motherhood." *Harvard Women's Law Journal* 8, Spring 1985, pp. 231–246.

Mendell, Betty Reid. *Where Are the Children? A Close Analysis of Foster Care and Adoption*. Lexington, MA: Lexington Books, 1973.

Oakley, Ann. *Woman's Work: The Housewife, Past and Present*. New York: Pantheon Books, 1974.

O'Brien, Mary. *The Politics of Reproduction*. Boston: Routledge & Kegan Paul, 1981.

Overall, Christine. *Ethics and Human Reproduction: A Feminist Analysis*. Boston: Allen & Unwin, 1987.

_____. *Feminist Perspectives: Philosophical Essays on Method and Morals*. Toronto: University of Toronto Press, 1988.

_____. *Human Reproduction: Principles, Practices, Policies*. New York: Oxford University Press, 1993.

"The Pathogenic Commune." *Science News* 122, 76, July 3, 1982, p. 76.

Piercy, Marge. *Woman on the Edge of Time*. New York: Fawcett Crest Books, 1976.

Purdy, Laura. *In Their Best Interest? The Case Against Equal Rights for Children*. Ithaca, NY: Cornell University Press, 1992.

_____. *Reproducing Persons: Issues in Feminist Bioethics*. Ithaca, NY: Cornell University Press, 1996.

Raymond, Janice. *Women as Wombs: Reproductive Technologies and the Battle over Women's Freedom*. San Francisco: Harper & Row, 1993.

Rich, Adrienne. *Of Woman Born*. New York: W. W. Norton, 1979.

Rowland, Robyn. "Reproductive Technologies: The Final Solution to the Woman Question." In Rita Arditti, Renate Duelli Klein, and Shelley Minden, eds., *Test-Tube Women: What Future for Motherhood*? London: Pandora Press, 1984.

Ruddick, Sara. "Maternal Thinking." In Joyce Trebilcot, ed., *Mothering*. Totowa, NJ: Rowman & Allanheld, 1984.

Sherwin, Susan. *No Longer Patient: Feminist Ethics and Health Care*. Philadelphia: Temple University Press, 1992.

"A Surrogate's Story of Loving and Losing." *U.S. News & World Report*, June 6, 1983, p. 12.

Tiger, Lionel. *Men in Groups*. New York: Random House, 1969.

Tong, Rosemarie. *Feminist Approaches to Bioethics*. Boulder, CO: Westview Press, 1997.

Vetterling-Braggin, Mary, ed., *"Femininity," "Masculinity," and "Androgyny."* Totowa, NJ: Rowman & Littlefield, 1982.

Wolf, Susan, ed. *Feminism and Bioethics: Beyond Reproduction*. Oxford: Oxford University Press, 1996.

Critiques of Radical-Libertarian and Radical-Cultural Feminism

Beard, Mary R. *Woman as Force in History*. New York: Collier Books, 1972.

Cocks, Joan. "Wordless Emotions: Some Critical Reflections on Radical Feminism." *Politics and Society* 13(1), 1984, pp. 27–58.

Elshtain, Jean Bethke. *Public Man, Private Woman*. Princeton, NJ: Princeton University Press, 1981.

Ferguson, Ann. "The Sex Debate in the Women's Movement: A Socialist-Feminist View." *Against the Current,* September/October 1983.

_____. "Sex War: The Debate Between Radical and Libertarian Feminists." *Signs: Journal of Women in Culture and Society* 10(1), Autumn 1984, pp. 106–112.

Jaggar, Alison M. *Feminist Politics and Human Nature*. Totowa, NJ: Rowman & Allanheld, 1983.

Lorde, Audre. "An Open Letter to Mary Daly." In Cherríe Moraga and Gloria Anzaldúa, eds., *This Bridge Called My Back*. Watertown, MA: Persephone Press, 1981.

Rowbotham, Sheila. *Women, Resistance and Revolution*. New York: Vintage Books, 1972.

Chapter Three

Some Marxist Concepts and Theories: Their Feminist Implications

The Marxist Concept of Human Nature

Buchanan, Allen. *Marx and Justice: The Radical Critique of Liberalism*. Totowa, NJ: Littlefield, Adams, 1972.

Holmstrom, Nancy. "A Marxist Theory of Women's Nature." *Ethics* 94(1), April 1984, p. 464.

Marx, Karl. *A Contribution to the Critique of Political Economy*. New York: International Publishers, 1972.

Schmitt, Richard. *Introduction to Marx and Engels*. Boulder, CO: Westview Press, 1987.

Slaughter, Cliff. *Marx and Marxism: An Introduction*. New York: Longman, 1985.

Vogel, Lise. *Marxism and the Oppression of Women: Towards a Unitary Theory*. New Brunswick, NJ: Rutgers University Press, 1983.

The Marxist Theory of Economics

Acton, Henry Burrows. *What Marx Really Said*. London: MacDonald, 1967.

Benston, Margaret. "The Political Economy of Women's Liberation." *Monthly Review* 21(4), September 1969, pp. 13–27.

Heilbroner, Robert L. *Marxism: For and Against*. New York: W. W. Norton, 1980.

Kuhn, Annette and Ann Marie Wolpe, eds. *Feminism and Materialism: Women and Modes of Production*. Boston: Routledge & Kegan Paul, 1978.

Mandel, Ernest. *An Introduction to Marxist Economic Theory*. New York: Pathfinder Press, 1970.

Marx, Karl. *Grundrisse: Foundations of the Critique of Political Economy*. T. B. Bottomore, trans. and ed. New York: Vintage Books, 1973.

Suchting, Wallis Arthur. *Marx: An Introduction*. New York: New York University Press, 1983.

The Marxist Theory of Society

Foreman, Ann. *Femininity as Alienation: Women and the Family in Marxism and Psychoanalysis*. London: Pluto Press, 1977.

Marx, Karl. "Economic and Philosophic Manuscripts." In T. B. Bottomore, trans. and ed., *Early Writings*. New York: McGraw-Hill, 1964.

_____. *The 18th Brumaire of Louis Bonaparte*. New York: International Publishers, 1968.

Quick, Paddy. "The Class Nature of Women's Oppression." *Review of Radical Political Economics* 9(3), Winter 1977, pp. 42–53.

Saffiote, Heleieth I.B. *Women in Class Society*. Michael Vale, trans. New York: Monthly Review Press, 1978.

Wood, Allen W. *Karl Marx*. London: Routledge & Kegan Paul, 1981.

The Marxist Theory of Politics

Marx, Karl and Friedrich Engels. *The German Ideology*. In Robert C. Tucker, trans. and ed., *The Marx-Engels Reader*. New York: W. W. Norton, 1978.

McLellan, David. *Karl Marx*. New York: Penguin Books, 1975.

Friedrich Engels: The Origin of the Family, Private Property, and the State

Engels, Friedrich. *The Origin of the Family, Private Property and the State*. New York: International Publishers, 1972.

Flax, Jane. "Do Feminists Need Marxism?" In *Building Feminist Theory: Essays from "Quest," a Feminist Quarterly*. New York: Longman, 1981.

Kruks, Sonia. *Situation and Human Existence: Freedom, Subjectivity and Society*. New York: Routledge, 1990.

Lane, Ann J. "Woman in Society: A Critique of Friedrich Engels." In Bernice A. Carroll, ed., *Liberating Women's History*. Champaign: University of Illinois Press, 1976.

Millett, Kate. *Sexual Politics*. New York: Ballantine Books, 1969.

Oakley, Ann. *Sex, Gender, and Society*. London: Temple Smith, 1972.

Reed, Evelyn. *Problems of Woman's Liberation*. New York: Pathfinder Press, 1970.

Sacks, Karen. "Engels Revisited: Women, the Organization of Production and Private Property." In Rayna R. Reiter, ed., *Toward an Anthropology of Women*. New York: Monthly Review Press, 1975.

Contemporary Marxist Feminism

The Family, or Household, Under Capitalism

Braudel, Fernand. *Capitalism and Material Life 1400–1800.* Miriam Kochan, trans. New York: Harper & Row, 1973.

Bridenthal, Renate. "The Dialectics of Production and Reproduction in History." *Radical America* 10(2), March-April 1976, pp. 3–11.

Chao, Paul. *Woman Under Communism: Family in Russia and China.* Bayside, NY: General Hall, 1977.

Coulson, Margaret, Branka Magas, and Hilary Wainwright. "'The Housewife and Her Labour Under Capitalism': A Critique." *New Left Review* 89, January-February 1975, pp. 59–71.

Hartmann, Heidi I. "The Family as the Locus of Gender, Class, and Political Struggle: The Example of Housework." *Signs: Journal of Women in Culture and Society* 6(3), 1981, pp. 366–394.

_____. "The Unhappy Marriage of Marxism and Feminism: Towards a More Progressive Union." In Lydia Sargent, ed., *Women and Revolution: A Discussion of the Unhappy Marriage of Marxism and Feminism.* Boston: South End Press, 1981.

Malos, Ellen, ed. *The Politics of Housework.* London: Allison & Busby, 1980.

Mitterauer, Michael and Reinhard Sieder. *The European Family: Patriarchy to Partnership from the Middle Ages to the Present.* Karla Oosterveen and Manfred Horzinger, trans. Oxford: Blackwell, 1982.

Molyneux, Maxine. "Beyond the Domestic Labour Debate." *New Left Review* 116, July-August 1979, pp. 3–27.

Rosenberg, Charles E., ed. *The Family in History.* Philadelphia: University of Pennsylvania Press, 1975.

Scott, Hilda. *Working Your Way to the Bottom.* London: Pandora Press, 1984.

Secombe, Wally. "The Housewife and Her Labour Under Capitalism." *New Left Review* 83, January-February 1973, pp. 3–24.

Tilly, Louise A. and Joan W. Scott. *Women, Work, and Family.* New York: Holt, Rinehart and Winston, 1978.

The Socialization of Domestic Labor

Benston, Margaret. "The Political Economy of Women's Liberation." *Monthly Review* 21(4), September 1969, p. 16.

Cowan, Ruth Schwartz. "The 'Industrial Revolution' in the Home: Household Technology and Social Change in the Twentieth Century." *Technology and Culture* 17(1), 1976, pp. 1–23.

Ferguson, Ann. "The Che-Lumumba School: Creating a Revolutionary Family-Community." *Quest* 5(3), February-March 1980.

Guettel, Charnie. *Marxism and Feminism.* Toronto: Women's Education Press, 1974.

Humphries, Jane. "The Working Class Family, Women's Liberation and Class Struggle: The Case of Nineteenth Century British History." *Review of Radical Political Economics* 9(3), Fall 1977, pp. 25–41.

Landes, Joan B. "Women, Labor and Family Life: A Theoretical Perspective." *Science and Society* 41(1), Spring 1977, pp. 386–409.

MacKinnon, Catharine A. "Feminism, Marxism, Method and the State: An Agenda for Theory." *Signs: Journal of Women in Culture and Society* 7(3), Spring 1982, pp. 515–544.

Zarestsky, Eli. "Capitalism, the Family, and Personal Life." *Socialist Revolution* 3(1-2), January-April 1973, pp. 69–125.

The Wages-for-Housework Campaign

Beechey, Veronica. "Some Notes on Female Wage Labour in Capitalist Production." *Capital and Class*, Autumn 1977, pp. 45–66.

Bergmann, Barbara. *The Economic Emergence of Women.* New York: Basic Books, 1986.

Brenner, Johanna and Nancy Holmstrom. "Women's Self-Organization: Theory and Strategy." *Monthly Review* 34(11), April 1983, p. 40.

Brenner, Johanna and Maria Ramas. "Rethinking Women's Oppression." *New Left Review* 144, March-April 1984, p. 71.

Dalla Costa, Mariarosa. "A General Strike." In Wendy Edmond and Suzie Fleming, eds., *All Work and No Pay.* London: Power of Women Collective and Falling Wall Press, 1975.

Dalla Costa, Mariarosa and Selma James. *The Power of Women and the Subversion of Community.* Bristol, England: Falling Wall Press, 1972.

Davin, Delia. *Woman-Work: Women and the Party in Revolutionary China.* Oxford: Clarendon Press, 1976.

Edmond, Wendy and Suzie Fleming. "If Women Were Paid for All They Do." In Wendy Edmond and Suzie Fleming, eds., *All Work and No Pay.* London: Power of Women Collective and Falling Wall Press, 1975.

Gardiner, Susan. "Women's Domestic Labour." *New Left Review* 89, January-February 1975, pp. 47–58.

Garson, Barbara. *All the Livelong Day: The Meaning and Demeaning of Routine Work.* New York: Penguin Books, 1975.

Gerstein, Ira. "Domestic Work and Capitalism." *Radical America* 7(4-5), July-October 1973, pp. 101–128.

Glazer-Malbin, Nona. "Housework." *Signs: Journal of Women in Culture and Society* 1(4), 1976, pp. 905–922.

Gordon, David M., Richard Edwards, and Michael Reich. *Segmented Work, Divided Workers.* New York: Cambridge University Press, 1982.

Holmstrom, Nancy. "'Women's Work,' the Family and Capitalism." *Science and Society* 45(1), Spring 1981, p. 208.

Lopate, Carol. "Pay for Housework?" *Social Policy* 5(3), September-October 1974, p. 28.

Nicholson, Linda J. *Gender and History: The Limits of Social Theory in the Age of the Family.* New York: Columbia University Press, 1986.

Scott, A. C. "The Value of Housework for Love or Money?" *Ms.*, June 1972, pp. 56–58.

Comparable Worth

Amott, Teresa and Julie Matthaei. "Comparable Worth, Incomparable Pay." *Radical America* 18(5), September-October 1984, p. 25.

Feldberg, Roslyn L. "Comparable Worth: Toward Theory and Practice in the United States." *Signs: Journal of Women in Culture and Society*, 10(2), Winter 1984, pp. 311–313.

Lamar, Jake. "A Worthy but Knotty Question." *Time*, February 6, 1984, p. 30.

"Paying Women What They're Worth." *QQ Report from the Center for Philosophy and Public Policy* 3(2), Spring 1983, p. 1.

Remick, Helen. "Major Issues in A Priori Applications." In Helen Remick, ed., *Comparable Worth and Wage Discrimination: Technical Possibilities and Political Realities.* Philadelphia: Temple University Press, 1984.

Critiques of Marxist Feminism

Barrett, Michele. *Women's Oppression Today: Problems in Marxist Feminist Analysis.* London: Verso and New Left Books, 1980.

Berch, Bettina. *The Endless Day: The Political Economy of Women and Work.* New York: Harcourt Brace Jovanovich, 1982.

Elshtain, Jean Bethke. *Public Man, Private Woman.* Princeton: NJ: Princeton University Press, 1981.

Hartmann, Heidi and Ann R. Markusen. "Contemporary Marxist Theory and Practice: A Feminist Critique." *Review of Radical Political Economics* 12(2), Summer 1980, pp. 87–93.

Jaggar, Alison. "Prostitution." In Marilyn Pearsall, ed., *Women and Values: Readings in Recent Feminist Philosophy.* Belmont, CA: Wadsworth, 1986.

Martin, Gloria. *Socialist Feminism: The First Decade, 1966–1976.* Seattle: Freedom Socialist Publications, 1978.

Rowbotham, Sheila. *Woman's Consciousness, Man's World.* Baltimore, MD: Penguin Books, 1973.

Sargent, Lydia, ed. *Women and Revolution: A Discussion of the Unhappy Marriage of Marxism and Feminism.* Boston: South End Press, 1981.

Contemporary Socialist Feminism

Bartky, Sandra L. *Femininity and Domination.* New York: Routledge, 1990.

_____. "Narcissism, Femininity and Alienation." *Social Theory and Practice* 8(2) Summer 1982, pp. 127–144.

_____. "On Psychological Oppression." In Sharon Bishop and Marjorie Weinzweig, eds., *Philosophy and Women.* Belmont, CA: Wadsworth, 1979.

Boserup, Esther. *Women's Role in Economic Development.* London: George Allen and Unwin, 1970.

Caulfield, Mina Davis. "Imperialism, the Family, and Cultures of Resistance." *Socialist Revolution* 20(4), October 1974, pp. 67–85.

Delphy, Christine. *Close to Home: A Materialist Analysis of Women's Oppression.* Diana Leonard, trans. and ed. Amherst: University of Massachusetts Press, 1984.

Durkheim, Emile. *The Rules of Sociological Method.* New York: Free Press, 1964.

Easton, Barbara. "Socialism and Feminism I: Toward a Unified Movement." *Socialist Revolution* 4(1), January-March 1974, pp. 59–67.

Ehrenreich, Barbara. "Life Without Father: Reconsidering Socialist-Feminist Theory." *Socialist Review* 14(1), January–March 1974, pp. 59–67.

_____. "What Is Socialist Feminism?" *Win*, June 3, 1976, pp. 4–7.

Eisenstein, Zillah, ed. *Capitalist Patriarchy and the Case for Socialist Feminism*. New York: Monthly Review Press, 1979.

Fraser, Nancy and Linda J. Nicholson. "Social Criticism Without Philosophy: An Encounter Between Feminism and Postmodernism." In Linda J. Nicholson, ed., *Feminism/Postmodernism*. New York: Routledge, 1990.

Harding, Sandra. "The Instability of the Analytical Categories of Feminist Theory." *Signs: Journal of Women and Culture and Society* 11(4), 1987, pp. 645–665.

Hartmann, Heidi. "Capitalism, Patriarchy, and Job Segregation by Sex." In Zillah Eisenstein, ed., *Capitalist Patriarchy and the Case for Socialist Feminism*. New York: Monthly Review Press, 1979.

_____. "The Unhappy Marriage of Marxism and Feminism: Towards a More Progressive Union." In Lydia Sargent, ed., *Women and Revolution: A Discussion of the Unhappy Marriage of Marxism and Feminism*. Boston: South End Press, 1981.

Jaggar, Alison. "Feminist Ethics." In Lawrence Becker with Charlotte Becker, eds., *Encyclopedia of Ethics*. New York: Garland, 1992.

_____. "Feminist Ethics: Projects, Problems, Prospects." In Claudia Card, ed., *Feminist Ethics*. Lawrence: University of Kansas Press, 1991.

_____. *Feminist Politics and Human Nature*. Totowa, NJ: Rowman & Allanheld, 1983.

_____. "Prostitution." In Marilyn Pearsall, ed., *Women and Values: Readings in Recent Feminist Philosophy*. Belmont, CA: Wadsworth, 1986.

Lenin, V. I. *The Emancipation of Women: From the Writings of V. I. Lenin*. New York: International Publishers, 1934.

MacKinnon, Catharine A. "Feminism, Marxism, Method, and the State: An Agenda for Theory." *Signs: Journal of Women in Culture and Society* 7(3), Spring 1982, pp. 515–545.

Mitchell, Juliet. *Psychoanalysis and Feminism*. New York: Vintage Books, 1974.

_____. *Woman's Estate*. New York: Pantheon Books, 1971.

_____. "Women: The Longest Revolution." *New Left Review* 40, November–December 1966, pp. 11–37.

Nicholson, Linda J. *Gender and History: The Limits of Social Theory in the Age of the Family*. New York: Columbia University Press, 1986.

Nussbaum, Karen. "Women Clerical Workers." *Socialist Review* 10(1), January–February 1980, pp. 151–159.

Page, Margaret. "Socialist Feminism—A Political Alternative." *m/f* 2, 1978.

Phelps, Linda. "Patriarchy and Capitalism." *Quest* 2(2), Fall 1975, pp. 35–48.

Rosaldo, Marilyn. "Women, Culture, and Society: A Theoretical Overview." In Marilyn Rosaldo and Louise Lamphere, eds., *Women, Culture, and Society*. Stanford, CA: Stanford University Press, 1974.

Rowbotham, Sheila, Lynne Segal, and Hilary Wainwright. *Beyond the Fragments: Feminism and the Making of Socialism*. London: Merlin Press, 1979.

Weinbaum, Batya. *The Curious Courtship of Women's Liberation and Socialism*. Boston: South End Press, 1978.

Weinbaum, Batya and Amy Bridges. "The Other Side of the Paycheck: Monopoly Capital and the Structure of Conscription." *Monthly Review* 28(3), July–August 1976, pp. 88–103.

Young, Iris. "The Ideal of Community and the Politics of Difference." In Linda J. Nicholson, ed., *Feminism/Postmodernism*. New York: Routledge, 1990.

_____. "Socialist Feminism and the Limits of Dual Systems Theory." *Socialist Review* 10(2-3), March-June 1980, p. 174.

_____. *Throwing Like a Girl and Other Essays in Feminist Philosophy and Social Theory*. Bloomington: Indiana University Press, 1990.

Chapter Four

The Roots of Psychoanalytic Feminism: Sigmund Freud

Bernstein, Anne E. and Gloria Marmar Warna. *An Introduction to Contemporary Psychoanalysis*. New York: J. Aronson, 1981.

Cohen, Ira H. *Ideology and Unconscious: Reich, Freud, and Marx*. New York: New York University Press, 1982.

Erdelyi, Matthew Hugh. *Psychoanalysis: Freud's Cognitive Psychology*. New York: W. H. Freeman, 1984.

Freud, Sigmund. *Civilization and Its Discontents*. James Strachey, trans. New York: W. W. Norton, 1962.

_____. "Femininity." In Sigmund Freud, *The Complete Introductory Lectures on Psychoanalysis*. James Strachey, trans. and ed. New York: W. W. Norton, 1966.

_____. *Sexuality and the Psychology of Love*. New York: Collier Books, 1968.

Hall, Calvin Springer. *A Primer of Freudian Psychology*. New York: New American Library, 1954.

Joes, Ernest. *The Life and Work of Sigmund Freud*. New York: Basic Books, 1961.

Laplanche, Jean. *The Language of Psychoanalysis*. New York: W. W. Norton, 1973.

Lichtman, Richard. *The Production of Desire: The Integration of Psychoanalysis into Marxist Theory*. New York: Free Press, 1982.

Reppen, Joseph, ed. *Beyond Freud: A Study of Modern Psychoanalytic Theorists*. Hillsdale, NJ: Analytic Press, 1985.

Roazen, Paul. *Freud: Political and Social Thought*. New York: Alfred A. Knopf, 1968.

Standard Feminist Critiques of Freud

Adler, Alfred. *Understanding Human Nature*. New York: Greenberg, 1927.

Beauvoir, Simone de. *The Second Sex*. H. M. Parshley, trans. and ed. New York: Vintage Books, 1974.

Firestone, Shulamith. *The Dialectic of Sex*. New York: Bantam Books, 1970, pp. 48–49.

Friedan, Betty. *The Feminine Mystique*. New York: Dell, 1974.

Izenberg, Gerald N. *The Existentialist Critique of Freud: The Crisis of Autonomy*. Princeton, NJ:. Princeton University Press, 1976.

Klein, Viola. *The Feminine Character*. London: Routledge & Kegan Paul, 1971.

Millett, Kate. *Sexual Politics*. New York: Ballantine Books, 1969.

Van Herik, Judith. *Freud on Femininity and Faith*. Berkeley: University of California Press, 1982.

Voloshinov, V. N. *Freudianism: A Marxist Critique*. New York: Academic Press, 1976.

Pursuing Psychoanalysis in Feminist Directions

Chesler, Phyllis. *Women and Madness*. Garden City, NY: Doubleday, 1972.

Cockburn, David. *Other Human Beings*. New York: St. Martin's Press, 1992.

Cott, Nancy. *The Grounding of Modern Feminism*. New Haven, CT: Yale University Press, 1987.

Derrida, Jacques. "The Ends of Man." In Jacques Derrida, *Margins of Philosophy*. Alan Bass, trans. Sussex, England: Harvester, 1982.

Deutsch, Helene. *The Psychology of Women: A Psychoanalytic Interpretation*. New York: Grune & Stratten, 1944.

Engel, Stephanie. "Femininity as Tragedy: Re-examining the 'New Narcissism.'" *Socialist Review* 10(5), September-October 1980, pp. 77–104.

Erikson, Erik. *Childhood and Society*. New York: W. W. Norton, 1963.

Ferguson, Ann. "Motherhood and Sexuality: Some Feminist Questions." *Hypatia* 1(2), Fall 1986, pp. 3–22.

Gallop, Jane. *The Daughter's Seduction: Feminism and Psychoanalysis*. Ithaca, NY: Cornell University Press, 1982.

Gatens, Moira. *Feminism and Philosophy: Perspectives of Difference and Equality*. Cambridge: Polity, 1991.

Gould, Carol, ed. *Beyond Domination: New Perspectives on Women and Philosophy*. Totowa, NJ: Rowman & Allanheld, 1983.

Grimshaw, Jean. *Philosophy and Feminist Thinking*. Minneapolis: University of Minnesota Press, 1986.

Nagel, Thomas. *The View from Nowhere*. Oxford: Oxford University Press, 1986.

Rorty, Richard. *Philosophy and the Mirror of Nature*. Princeton, NJ: Princeton University Press, 1979.

The Feminist Rejection of Freud's Biological Determinism

Adler, Alfred. *Understanding Human Nature*. New York: Greenberg, 1927.

Garrison, Dee. "Karen Horney and Feminism." *Signs: Journal of Women in Culture and Society* 6(4), 1981, pp. 672–691.

Horney, Karen. "The Flight from Womanhood." In Karen Horney, *Feminine Psychology*. New York: W. W. Norton, 1973.

Irigaray, Luce. *Speculum of the Other Woman*. Gillian C. Gill, trans. Ithaca, NY: Cornell University Press, 1985.

Kofman, Sarah. *The Enigma of Woman: Woman in Freud's Writings*. Ithaca, NY: Cornell University Press, 1985.

Miller, Jean Baker, ed. *Psychoanalysis and Women*. Baltimore, MD: Penguin Books, 1974.

Rudnick Jacobsohn, Susan. "An Ambiguous Legacy." *Women's Review of Books* 5(4), January 1988, p. 22.

Thompson, Clara. "Problems of Womanhood." In M. P. Green, ed., *Interpersonal Psychoanalysis: The Selected Papers of Clara Thompson*. New York: Basic Books, 1964.

Vetterling-Braggin, Mary, ed. *"Femininity," "Masculinity," and "Androgyny."* Totowa, NJ: Rowman & Littlefield, 1982.

Williams, Juanita. *Psychology of Women: Behavior in a Biosocial Context*. New York: W. W. Norton, 1977.

Toward a Feminist Reinterpretation of the Oedipus Complex

Chodorow, Nancy. *The Reproduction of Mothering: Psychoanalysis and the Sociology of Gender*. Berkeley: University of California Press, 1978.

Dinnerstein, Dorothy. *The Mermaid and the Minotaur: Sexual Arrangements and Human Malaise*. New York: Harper Colophon Books, 1977.

Eisenstein, Hester. *Contemporary Feminist Thought*. Boston: G. K. Hall, 1983.

Elshtain, Jean Bethke. *Public Man, Private Woman*. Princeton, NJ: Princeton University Press, 1981.

Freud, Sigmund. "Totem and Taboo." In Sigmund Freud, *The Standard Edition of the Complete Psychological Works of Sigmund Freud*. James Strachey, trans. and ed. New York: W. W. Norton, 1966.

Friedman, Marilyn. "Feminism and Modern Friendship: Dislocation in the Community." In Neera Kapur Badhwar, ed., *Friendship: A Philosophical Reader*. Ithaca, NY: Cornell University Press, 1991.

Lacan, Jacques. *The Language of the Self*. Baltimore, MD: Johns Hopkins University Press, 1968.

Lorber, Judith. "On *The Reproduction of Mothering:* A Methodological Debate." *Signs: Journal of Women in Culture and Society* 6(3), Spring 1981, pp. 482–486.

Mitchell, Juliet. *Psychoanalysis and Feminism*. New York: Vintage Books, 1974.

_____. *Women's Estate*. New York: Pantheon Books, 1971.

Ortner, Sherry B. "Oedipal Father, Mother's Brother, and the Penis: A Review of Juliet Mitchell's *Psychoanalysis and Feminism*." *Feminist Studies* 2 (2-3), 1975, p. 179.

Raymond, Janice. "Female Friendship: Contra Chodorow and Dinnerstein." *Hypatia* 1(2), Fall 1986, pp. 44–45.

Rossi, Alice. "On *The Reproduction of Mothering:* A Methodological Debate." *Signs: Journal of Women in Culture and Society* 6(3), Spring 1981, pp. 497–500.

Gender Feminism

Baier, Annette. *Postures of the Mind*. Minneapolis: University of Minnesota Press, 1985.

_____. "What Do Women Want in a Moral Theory?" In Annette Baier, *Moral Prejudices*. Cambridge: Harvard University Press, 1985.

Benhabib, Seyla and Drucilla Cornell. "Introduction: Beyond the Politics of Gender." In Seyla Benhabib and Drucilla Cornell, eds., *Feminism as Critique*. Minneapolis: University of Minnesota Press, 1987.

Bordo, Susan. "Feminism, Postmodernism, and Gender-Scepticism." In Linda J. Nicholson, ed., *Feminism/Postmodernism*. New York: Routledge, 1990.

Card, Claudia. "Caring and Evil." *Hypatia* 5(1), Spring 1990, p. 106.

Gilligan, Carol. "Adolescent Development Reconsidered." In Carol Gilligan, Janie Victoria Ward, and Jill McLean Taylor, eds., *Mapping the Moral Domain*. Cambridge: Harvard University Press, 1988.

_____. *In a Different Voice*. Cambridge: Harvard University Press, 1982.

Held, Virginia. *Feminist Morality: Transforming Culture, Society, and Politics*. Chicago: University of Chicago Press, 1993.

Hoagland, Sarah Lucia. "Some Thoughts About *Caring*." In Claudia Card, ed., *Feminist Ethics*. Lawrence: University Press of Kansas, 1991.

Houston, Barbara. "Rescuing Womanly Virtues: Some Company." In Marsha Hanen and Kai Nielsen, eds., *Science, Morality, and Feminist Theory*. Calgary: University of Calgary Press, 1987.

Kohlberg, Lawrence. "From Is to Ought: How to Commit the Naturalistic Fallacy and Get Away with It in the Study of Moral Development." In T. Mischel, ed., *Cognitive Development and Epistemology*. New York: Academic Press, 1971.

Moody-Adams, Michele M. "On the Alleged Methodological Infirmity of Ethics." *American Philosophical Quarterly* 27(3) 1991, pp. 225–236.

Moon, J. Donald. *Constructing Community: Moral Pluralism and Tragic Conflicts*. Princeton, NJ: Princeton University Press, 1994.

Mullett, Sheila. "Shifting Perspectives: A New Approach to Ethics." In Lorraine Code, Sheila Mullett, and Christine Overall, eds., *Feminist Perspectives*. Toronto: University of Toronto Press, 1989.

Nicholson, Linda J. *Gender and History: The Limits of Social Theory in the Age of the Family*. New York: Columbia University Press, 1986.

Nietzsche, Friedrich. *On the Genealogy of Morals*. Walter Kaufmann and R. Hollingdale, trans. New York: Vintage, 1969.

Noddings, Nel. *Caring: A Feminine Approach to Ethics and Moral Education*. Berkeley: University of California Press, 1984.

_____. "A Response." *Hypatia* 5(1), Spring 1990, p. 122.

_____. *Women and Evil*. Berkeley: University of California Press, 1989.

Puka, Bill. "The Liberation of Caring: A Different Voice for Gilligan's 'Different Voice.'" *Hypatia* 5(1), Spring 1990, p. 59.

Stack, Carol. "The Culture of Gender: Women and Men of Color." *Signs: Journal of Women in Culture and Society* 11(2), Winter 1986, pp. 322–323.

Tong, Rosemarie. *Feminine and Feminist Ethics*. Belmont, CA: Wadsworth, 1993.

Tronto, Joan. *Moral Boundaries: A Political Argument for an Ethic of Care*. New York: Routledge, 1993.

Chapter Five

Sartre's Being and Nothingness: *A Backdrop to* The Second Sex

Aron, Raymond. *Marxism and the Existentialists*. New York: Harper & Row, 1969.

Bartky, Sandra. "Narcissism, Femininity and Alienation." *Social Theory and Practice* 8(2), Summer 1982, p. 137.

Caws, Peter. *Sartre*. Boston: Routledge & Kegan Paul, 1979.

Chiodi, Pietro. *Sartre and Marxism*. Atlantic Highlands, NJ: Humanities Press, 1976.

Donovan, Josephine. *Feminist Theory: The Intellectual Traditions of American Feminism*. New York: Frederick Ungar, 1985.

Grene, Marjorie. *Dreadful Freedom : A Critique of Existentialism*. Chicago: University of Chicago Press, 1948.

_____. *Sartre*. New York: New Viewpoints, 1973.

Kaufmann, Walter Arnold, ed. *Existentialism from Dostoevsky to Sartre*. New York: New American Library, 1975.

Novak, George, ed. *Existentialism vs. Marxism: Conflicting Views of Humanism*. New York: Dell, 1966.

Pomeroy, Sarah B. *Goddesses, Whores, Wives, and Slaves*. New York: Schocken Books, 1975.

Sartre, Jean-Paul. *Being and Nothingness*. Hazel E. Barnes, trans. New York: Philosophical Library, 1956.

_____. *The Emotions: Outline of a Theory*. Bernard Frechtman, trans. New York: Philosophical Library, 1948.

_____. *Existentialism*. Bernard Frechtman, trans. New York: Philosophical Library, 1947.

Sullivan, Shannon. "Domination and Dialogue in Merleau-Ponty's Phenomenology of Perception." *Hypatia* 12(1), Winter 1997, p. 1.

Tax, Meredith. "Woman and Her Mind: The Story of an Everyday Life." In *Notes from the Second Year: Women's Liberation—Major Writings of the Radical Feminists*, April 1970.

Simone de Beauvoir: Existentialism for Women

Beauvoir, Simone de. *Adieux: A Farewell to Sartre*. New York: Pantheon Books, 1984.

_____. *The Ethics of Ambiguity*. New York: Citadel Press, 1967.

_____. *Memoirs of a Dutiful Daughter*. James Kirkup, trans. Harmondsworth, England: Penguin Books, 1963.

_____. *The Prime of Life*. Peter Green, trans. Harmondsworth, England: Penguin Books, 1965.

_____. *The Second Sex*. H. M. Parshley, trans. and ed. New York: Vintage Books, 1974.

Hegel, G.W.F. *The Phenomenology of Mind*. J. B. Baille, trans. New York: Harper & Row, 1967.

Jardine, Alice. "Interview with Simone de Beauvoir." *Signs: Journal of Women in Culture and Society* 5(2), 1979, pp. 224–236.

Keefe, Terry. *Simone de Beauvoir*. Totowa, NJ: Barnes & Noble, 1983.

Kruks, Sonia. "Simone de Beauvoir: Teaching Sartre About Freedom." In Margaret A. Simons, ed., *Feminist Interpretations of Simone de Beauvoir*. University Park: Pennsylvania State University Press, 1995.

La Caze, Marguerite. "Simone de Beauvoir and Female Bodies." *Australian Feminist Studies* 20, 1995, pp. 91–105.

McCall, Dorothy Kaufmann. "Simone de Beauvoir, *The Second Sex*, and Jean Paul Sartre." *Signs: Journal of Women in Culture and Society* 5(2), 1979, p. 210.

Moi, Toril. *Simone de Beauvoir: The Making of an Intellectual Woman*. Oxford: Blackwell, 1994.

Simons, Margaret A. and Jessica Benjamin. "Simone de Beauvoir: An Interview." *Feminist Studies* 5(2), Summer 1979, pp. 330–345.

Critiques of Existentialist Feminism

Ascher, Carol. *Simone de Beauvoir: A Life of Freedom*. Boston: Beacon Press, 1981.

Beauvoir, Simone de. *Memoirs of a Dutiful Daughter*. James Kirkup, trans. Harmondsworth, England: Penguin Books, 1963.

Dietz, Mary G. "Introduction: Debating Simone de Beauvoir." *Signs: Journal of Women in Culture and Society* 18(1), 1983, pp. 74–88.

Elshtain, Jean Bethke. *Public Man, Private Woman.* Princeton, NJ: Princeton University Press, 1981.

Kuykendall, Eléanor H. "Linguistic Ambivalence in Simone de Beauvoir's Feminist Theory." In Iris Young and Jeffner Allen, eds., *The Thinking Muse.* Bloomington: Indiana University Press, 1989.

Lloyd, Genevieve. *The Man of Reason: "Male" and "Female" in Western Philosophy.* Minneapolis: University of Minnesota Press, 1984.

Schutte, Ofelia. "A Critique of Normative Heterosexuality: Identity, Embodiment, and Sexual Difference in Beauvoir and Irigaray." *Hypatia* 12(1), Winter 1997, p. 40.

Whitmarsh, Anne. *Simone de Beauvoir and the Limits of Commitment.* Cambridge: Cambridge University Press, 1981.

Chapter Six

Some Major Influences on Postmodern Feminist Thought

Derrida, Jacques. *The Post Card: From Socrates to Freud and Beyond.* Alan Bass, trans. Chicago: University of Chicago Press, 1987.

_____. *Writing and Difference.* Alan Bass, trans. Chicago: University of Chicago Press, 1978.

Duchen, Claire. *Feminism in France: From May '68 to Mitterrand.* London: Routledge & Kegan Paul, 1986.

Flax, Jane. *Thinking Fragments: Psychoanalysis, Feminism, and Postmodernism in the Contemporary West.* Berkeley: University of California Press, 1989.

Lacan, Jacques. *Écrits: A Selection.* Alan Sheridan, trans. New York: W. W. Norton, 1977.

Moi, Toril, ed. *French Feminist Thought: A Reader.* New York: Blackwell, 1987.

Steward, Danièle. "The Women's Movement in France." *Signs: Journal of Women in Culture and Society* 6(2), Winter 1980, p. 353.

Sturrock, John. "Introduction." In John Sturrock, ed., *Structuralism and Since: From Lévi-Strauss to Derrida.* New York: Oxford University Press, 1979.

Wenzel, Hélène Vivienne. "The Text as Body/Politics: An Appreciation of Monique Wittig's Writings in Context." *Feminist Studies* 7(2), Summer 1981, pp. 270–271.

Postmodern Feminism and Deconstruction

Alcoff, Linda. "Cultural Feminism Versus Post-Structuralism: The Identity Crisis in Feminist Theory." In Nancy Tuana and Rosemarie Tong, eds., *Feminism and Philosophy: Essential Readings.* Boulder, CO: Westview Press, 1995.

Connolly, William. "Taylor, Foucault, and Otherness." *Political Theory* 13(3), 1985, pp. 365–376.

Cornell, Drucilla. *Beyond Accommodation: Ethical Feminism, Deconstruction, and the Law.* New York: Routledge, 1991.

Derrida, Jacques. *The Post Card: From Socrates to Freud and Beyond.* Alan Bass, trans. Chicago: University of Chicago Press, 1987.

_____. *Spurs: Nietzsche's Styles*. Barbara Harlow, trans. Chicago: University of Chicago Press, 1978.

_____. *Writing and Difference*. Alan Bass, trans. Chicago: University of Chicago Press, 1978.

Grosz, Elizabeth. *Jacques Lacan: A Feminist Introduction*. New York: Routledge, 1990.

Lacan, Jacques. *Écrits: A Selection*. Alan Sheridan, trans. New York: W. W. Norton, 1977.

_____. "The Meaning of the Phallus." In J. Mitchell and J. Rose, eds., *Feminine Sexuality*. New York: W. W. Norton, 1982.

Weedon, Chris. *Feminist Practice and Poststructuralist Theory*. Cambridge: Blackwell, 1987.

Postmodern Feminism: Three Perspectives

Bree, Germaine. *Women Writers in France*. New Brunswick, NJ: Rutgers University Press, 1973.

Burke, Carolyn Greenstein. "Report from Paris: Women's Writing and the Women's Movement." *Signs: Journal of Women in Culture and Society* 4(4), Summer 1978, pp. 843–854.

Butler, Judith. "The Body Politics of Julia Kristeva." *Hypatia* 3(3), Winter 1989, pp. 104–118.

Chanter, Tina. *Ethics of Eros: Irigaray's Rewriting of the Philosophers*. New York: Routledge, 1995.

Cixous, Hélène. "Castration or Decapitation?" *Signs: Journal of Women in Culture and Society* 7(1), Summer 1981, pp. 41–55.

_____. "The Laugh of the Medusa." In Elaine Marks and Isabelle de Courtivron, eds., *New French Feminisms*. New York: Schocken Books, 1981.

Cixous, Hélène and Catherine Clement. "Sorties." In Betsy Wing, trans. *The Newly Born Woman*. Minneapolis: University of Minnesota Press, 1986.

Clement, Catherine. *The Lives and Legends of Jacques Lacan*. New York: Columbia University Press, 1983.

Conley, Verena. "Missexual Mystery." *Diacritics* 7(2), Summer 1977, pp. 70–82.

Duchen, Claire. *Feminism in France: From May '68 to Mitterrand*. London: Routledge & Kegan Paul, 1986.

Faure, Christine. "Absent from History." *Signs: Journal of Women in Culture and Society* 7(1), 1981, pp. 71–80.

Fraser, Nancy and Linda J. Nicholson. "Social Criticism Without Philosophy: An Encounter Between Feminism and Postmodernism." In Linda J. Nicholson, ed., *Feminism/Postmodernism*. New York: Routledge, 1990.

Gallop, Jane. "The 'Ladies' Man." *Diacritics* 5(4), Winter 1976, pp. 28–34.

Irigaray, Luce. "Is the Subject of Science Sexed?" Carol Mastrangelo Bové, trans. *Hypatia* 2(3), Fall 1987, p. 66.

_____. *Speculum of the Other Woman*. Gillian C. Gill, trans. Ithaca, NY: Cornell University Press, 1985.

_____. *This Sex Which Is Not One*. Catherine Porter, trans. Ithaca, NY: Cornell University Press, 1985.

Jardine, Alice and Hester Eisenstein, eds. *The Future of Difference*. New Brunswick, NJ: Rutgers University, Press, 1985.

Jones, Ann Rosalind. "Writing the Body: Toward an Understanding of *l'Écriture Féminine*." *Feminist Studies* 7(1), Summer 1981, p. 248.

Kristeva, Julia. *Desire in Language*. Leon Roudiez, trans. New York: Columbia University Press, 1982.

_____. *Powers of Horror*. Leon Roudiez, trans. New York: Columbia University Press, 1982.

_____. "Women's Time." *Signs: Journal of Women in Culture and Society* 7(1), Summer 1981, pp. 13–35.

Kuykendall, Eléanor H. "Toward an Ethic of Nurturance: Luce Irigaray on Mothering and Power." In Joyce Trebilcot, ed., *Mothering: Essays in Feminist Theory*. Totowa, NJ: Rowman & Allanheld, 1984.

Lyotard, Jean-François. *The Postmodern Condition: A Report on Knowledge*. Minneapolis: University of Minnesota Press, 1984.

Marks, Elaine. "Review Essay: Women and Literature in France." *Signs: Journal of Women in Culture and Society* 3(4), Summer 1978, pp. 832–842.

Miller, Jean. *Toward a New Psychology of Women*. Boston: Beacon Press, 1976.

Mitchell, Juliet and Jacqueline Rose, eds. *Feminine Sexuality: Jacques Lacan and the Ecole Freudienne*. Jacqueline Rose, trans. New York: W. W. Norton, 1982.

Moi, Toril. *Sexual/Textual Politics: Feminist Literary Theory*. New York: Methuen, 1985.

Oliver, Kelly. "Julia Kristeva's Feminist Revolutions." *Hypatia* 8(3), Summer 1993.

Whitford, Margaret. *Luce Irigaray: Philosophy in the Feminine*. New York: Routledge, 1991.

_____. "Rereading Irigaray." In Teresa Brennan, ed. *Between Feminism and Psychoanalysis*. New York: Routledge, 1989.

_____, ed. *The Irigaray Reader*. Cambridge: Blackwell, 1991.

Wittig, Monique. *Les Guérillères*. New York: Viking, 1971.

Wolin, Sheldon. "Modernism vs. Postmodernism." *Telos* 62, 1984–85, pp. 9–29.

Zerilli, Linda M.G. "A Process Without a Subject: Simone de Beauvoir and Julia Kristeva on Maternity." *Signs: Journal of Women in Culture and Society* 8(1), 1982, pp. 111–135.

Critiques of Postmodern Feminism

Belenky, Mary Field, Blythe McVicker Clinchy, Nancy Rule Goldberger, and Jill Mattuck Tarule. *Women's Ways of Knowing: The Development of Self, Voice, and Mind*. New York: Basic Books, 1986.

Di Stefano, Christine. "Dilemmas of Difference." In Linda J. Nicholson, ed., *Feminism/Postmodernism*. New York: Routledge, 1990.

Fausto-Sterling, Anne. *Myths of Gender: Biological Theories About Women and Men*. New York: Basic Books, 1985.

Flax, Jane. "Postmodernism and Gender Relations in Feminist Theory." In Linda J. Nicholson, ed., *Feminism/Postmodernism*. New York: Routledge, 1990.

_____. *Thinking Fragments: Psychoanalysis, Feminism, and Postmodernism in the Contemporary West*. Berkeley: University of California Press, 1990.

Foucault, Michel. *Power/Knowledge*. Colin Gordon, ed. New York: Random House, 1981.

Whitford, Margaret. "Luce Irigaray and the Female Imaginary: Speaking as a Woman." *Radical Philosophy* 43, Summer 1986, p. 7.

Chapter Seven

Multicultural Feminism

Ames, Jesse Daniel. *The Changing Character of Lynching, 1931–1941*. New York: AMS Press, 1973.

Barry, Kathleen. *Female Sexual Slavery*. Englewood Cliffs, NJ: Prentice-Hall, 1979.

Berger, Gilda. *Women, Work and Wages*. New York: Franklin Watts, 1986.

Bernard, Jessie. *The Female World from a Global Perspective*. Bloomington: Indiana University Press, 1987.

Bunch, Charlotte. "Prospects for Global Feminism." In Alison M. Jaggar and Paula S. Rothenberg, eds., *Feminist Frameworks*. 3d edition. New York: McGraw-Hill, 1993.

Cohen, Marcia. *The Sisterhood*. New York: Simon & Schuster, 1988.

Collins, Patricia Hill. *Black Feminist Thought: Knowledge, Consciousness, and the Politics of Empowerment*. Boston: Unwin Hyman, 1990.

Davis, Angela Y. "Gender, Class, and Multiculturalism: Rethinking 'Race' Politics." In Avery R. Gordon and Christopher Newfield, eds., *Mapping Multiculturalism*. Minneapolis: University of Minnesota Press, 1996.

Douglass, Frederick. "The Lesson of the Hour." Pamphlet published in 1894. Reprinted under the title "Why Is the Negro Lynched?" In Philip S. Foner, *The Life and Writings of Frederick Douglass*. Vol. 4. New York: International Publishers, 1950.

Fowers, Blaine J. and Frank C. Richardson. "Why Is Multiculturalism Good?" *American Psychologist* 51(6), June 1996, p. 609.

Gardner, Tracey. "Racism in Pornography and the Women's Movement." In Laura Lederer, ed., *Take Back the Night*. New York: William Morrow, 1986.

Hill, Jack E. "The Stereotypes of Race." *Time*, October 21, 1991, p. 66.

hooks, bell. *Yearning: Race, Gender, and Cultural Politics*. Boston: South End Press, 1990.

Kry, Deborah. "Multiple Jeopardy: The Context of a Black Feminist Ideology." In Alison M. Jaggar and Paula S. Rothenberg, eds., *Feminist Frameworks*. 3d edition. New York: McGraw-Hill, 1993.

Lane, Raymond M. "A Man's World: An Update on Sexual Harassment." *Village Voice*, December 16–22, 1981.

Lee, Jung Young. *Marginality: The Key to Multicultural Theology*. Minneapolis: Fortress Press, 1995.

Lewis, Jill. "Sexual Division of Power: Motivations of the Women's Liberation Movement." In Gloria I. Joseph and Jill Lewis, *Common Differences: Conflicts in Black and White Feminist Perspectives*. Garden City, NY: Anchor/Doubleday, 1981.

Lorde, Audre. "Age, Race, Class, and Sex: Women Redefining Difference." In Margaret L. Andersen and Patricia Hill Collins, eds., *Race, Class, and Gender*. 2d edition. Belmont, CA: Wadsworth, 1995.

_____. *The Cancer Journals*. San Francisco: Spinster/Aunt Lute, 1980.

MacKellar, Jean. *Rape: The Bait and the Trap*. New York: Crown Publishers, 1975.

MacKinnon, Catharine A. *Sexual Harassment of Working Women*. New Haven, CT: Yale University Press, 1979.

Omolade, Barbara. *The Rising Song of African American Women*. New York: Routledge, 1994.

Painton, Priscilla. "Woman Power." *Time*, October 28, 1991, p. 24.

Raz, Joseph. "Multiculturalism: A Liberal Perspective." *Dissent*, Winter 1994, p. 74.

Rothman, Sheila. *Woman's Proper Place*. New York: Basic Books, 1978.

Rubin, Lillian Breslow. *Worlds of Pain*. New York: Basic Books, 1976.

Russell, Diana. *The Politics of Rape: The Victim's Perspective*. New York: Stein & Day, 1975.

Schlesinger, Arthur M., Jr. *The Disuniting of America*. Knoxville, TN: Whittle Books, 1991.

Sivard, Ruth. *Women: A World Survey*. Washington, DC: World Priority, 1986.

Spelman, Elizabeth V. *Inessential Women: Problems of Exclusion in Feminist Thought*. Boston: Beacon Press, 1988.

Walker, Alice. "Coming Apart." In Laura Lederer, ed., *Take Back the Night*. New York: William Morrow, 1986.

Wolfgang, Marvin E. and Marc Riedel. "Rape, Race, and the Death Penalty in Georgia." *American Journal of Orthopsychiatry* 45, July 1975, pp. 658–668.

Global Feminism

Angelou, Maya. *I Know Why the Caged Bird Sings*. New York: Bantam, 1969.

Anzaldúa, Gloria. "Tlitlli, Tlapalli: The Path of the Red and Black Ink." In Rick Simonson and Scott Walker, eds., *The Graywolf Annual Five: Multi-Cultural Literacy*. St. Paul, MN: Graywolf Press, 1988.

Aptheker, Bettina. *Tapestries of Life: Women's Work, Women's Consciousness and the Meaning of Daily Experience*. Amherst: University of Massachusetts Press, 1989.

_____. *Woman's Legacy: Essays on Race, Sex, and Class*. Amherst: University of Massachusetts Press, 1982.

Belenky, Mary Field, Blythe McVicker Clinchy, Nancy Rule Goldberger, and Jill Mattuck Tarule. *Women's Ways of Knowing : The Development of Self, Voice, and Mind*. New York: Basic Books, 1986.

Bennett, Lerone, Jr. *Before the Mayflower: A History of Black America*. 5th ed. New York: Penguin, 1982.

Berg, Barbara. *The Remembered Gate: Origins of American Feminism*. Oxford: Oxford University Press, 1978.

Bordo, Susan. "Feminism, Postmodernism, and Gender-Skepticism." In Linda J. Nicholson, ed., *Feminism/Postmodernism*. New York: Routledge, 1990.

Boserup, Esther. *Women's Role in Economic Development*. London: George Allen and Unwin, 1970.

Brownmiller, Susan. *Against Our Will: Men, Women, and Rape*. New York: Bantam Books, 1976.

Bulkin, Elly, Minnie Bruce Pratt, and Barbara Smith. *Yours in Struggle: Three Feminist Perspectives on Anti-Semitism and Racism*. New York: Long Haul Press, 1984.

Bunch, Charlotte. "U.N. World Conference in Nairobi." *Ms.*, June 1985, p. 82.

Burnham, Linda. "Has Poverty Been Feminized in Black America?" *Black Scholar* 16(2), March-April 1985, pp. 14–24.

Cade, Toni, ed. *The Black Woman*. New York: New American Library, 1970.

Caraway, Nancie. *Segregated Sisterhood: Racism and the Politics of American Feminism*. Knoxville: University of Tennessee Press, 1991.

Carby, Hazil V. "It Just Be's Dat Way Sometime: The Sexual Politics of Women's Blues." In Ellen Carol DuBois and Vicki L. Ruiz, eds., *Unequal Sisters*. New York: Routledge, 1990.

_____. "'On the Threshold of Woman's Era': Lynching, Empire, and Sexuality in Black Feminist Theory." *Critical Inquiry* 12, Autumn 1985, pp. 262–277.

Cash, W. J. *The Mind of the South*. New York: Alfred A. Knopf, 1941.

Clark, Adele. "Subtle Forms of Sterilization Abuse: A Reproductive Rights Analysis." In Rita Ardetti, Renate Duelli Klein, and Shelley Minden, eds., *Test-Tube Women: What Future for Motherhood?* London: Pandora Press, 1985.

Cott, Nancy. *The Bonds of Womanhood*. New Haven, CT: Yale University Press, 1977.

Curtin, Leslie B. *Status of Women: A Comprehensive Analysis of Twenty Developing Countries*. Reports on the World Fertility Survey, no. 5. Washington, DC: Population Reference Bureau, 1982.

Davis, Elizabeth Gould. *The First Sex*. New York: Putnam, 1971.

Delphy, Christine. *The Main Enemy: A Materialist Analysis of Women's Oppression*. London: Women's Research and Resources Centre Publications, 1977.

Diner, Helen. *Mothers and Amazons*. John Philip Lundin, ed. and trans. Garden City, NY: Anchor/Doubleday, 1973.

Dworkin, Andrea. *Woman Hating*. New York: E. P. Dutton, 1974.

Eichelberger, Brenda. "Voices on Black Feminism." *Quest* 3(4), 1977, pp. 16–28.

Ellmann, Mary. *Thinking About Women*. New York: Harcourt Brace Jovanovich, 1968.

Enloe, Cynthia. *Bananas, Beaches, and Bases: Making Feminist Sense of International Politics*. Berkeley: University of California Press, 1990.

Esposito, John L. *Women in Muslim Family Law*. Syracuse, NY: Syracuse University Press, 1982.

Freeman, Jo. *The Politics of Women's Liberation*. New York: Longman, 1977.

Gillian, Angela. "Women's Equality and National Liberation." In Chandra Talpads Mohanty, Ann Russo, and Lourde Torres, eds., *Third World Women and the Politics of Feminism*. Bloomington: Indiana University Press, 1991.

al-Hibri, Azizah, ed. *Women and Islam*. Oxford: Pergamon Press, 1982.

hooks, bell. *Feminist Theory: From Margin to Center*. Boston: South End Press, 1984.

Howe, Florence, ed. *Women and the Power to Change*. New York: McGraw-Hill, 1975.

Jaggar, Alison. "Abortion and a Woman's Right to Decide." In Carol C. Gould and Max W. Wartofsky, eds., *Woman and Philosophy: Toward a Theory of Liberation*. New York: Putnam's, 1976.

Kouba, Leonard J. and Judith Muasher. "Female Circumcision in Africa: An Overview." In *African Studies Review* 28(1), March 1988, pp. 105–109.

Kristof, Nicholas D. "China's Birth Rate on Rise Again as Official Sanctions Are Ignored." *New York Times*, April 21, 1987.

Larson, Ann. *Fertility and the Status of Women*. Washington, DC: Population Reference Bureau, 1981.

Lerner, Gerda. *Black Women in White America*. New York: Random House, 1973.

_____. *The Female Experience: An American Documentary*. Indianapolis: Bobbs-Merrill, 1977.

Linday, Beverly. *Comparative Perspectives of Third World Women: The Impact of Race, Sex, and Class*. New York: Praeger, 1980.

Lugones, Maria and Elizabeth Spelman. "Have We Got a Theory for You! Feminist Theory, Cultural Imperialism, and the Demand for 'the Woman's Voice.'" In Janet A. Kourany, James P. Sterba, and Rosemarie Tong, eds., *Feminist Philosophies*. Englewood Cliffs, NJ: Prentice-Hall, 1992.

Morgan, Robin. *Sisterhood Is Global*. Garden City, NY: Anchor, 1984.

Newland, Kathleen. *The Sisterhood of Man*. New York: W. W. Norton, 1979.

Rhoodie, Eschel M. *Discrimination Against Women: A Global Survey of the Economic, Educational, Social and Political Status of Women*. London: McFarland, 1989.

Rodriguez-Treas, Helen. "Sterilization Abuse." In Ruth Hubbard, Mary Sue Henifin, and Barbara Fried, eds., *Biological Woman: The Convenient Myth*. Cambridge, MA: Schenkman, 1982.

Russo, Ann. "'We Cannot Live Without Our Lives': White Women, Anti-Racism, and Feminism." In Chandra Talpads Mohanty, Ann Russo, and Lourde Torres, eds., *Third World Women and the Politics of Feminism*. Bloomington: Indiana University Press, 1991.

Sherwin, Susan. *No Longer Patient: Feminist Ethics and Health Care*. Philadelphia: Temple University Press, 1992.

Steady, Filomina Chioma, ed. *The Black Woman Cross-Culturally*. Cambridge, MA: Schenkman, 1981.

Stone, Merlin. *Ancient Mirrors of Womanhood*. 2 vols. New York: New Sibylline Books, 1979.

_____. *When God Was a Woman*. New York: Dial Press, 1976.

Thompson, Mary L., ed. *Voices of the New Feminism*. Boston: Beacon Press, 1970.

Tyler, Patrick E. "Population Control in China Falls to Coercion and Evasion." *New York Times*, June 25, 1995.

Wong, Nellie. "Socialist Feminism: Our Bridge to Freedom." In Chandra Talpads Mohanty, Ann Russo, and Lourde Torres, eds., *Third World Women and the Politics of Feminism*. Bloomington: Indiana University Press, 1991.

Chapter Eight

The Roots of Ecofeminism

Adorno, Theodor W. *Minima Moralia: Reflections from Damaged Life*. E.F.M. Jephcott, trans. London: New Left Books, 1974.

Caldecott, Leonie and Stephanie Leland, eds. *Reclaim the Earth*. London: Women's Press, 1983.

Carson, Rachel. *Silent Spring*. Boston: Houghton Mifflin, 1962.

Cheney, Jim. "Ecofeminism and Deep Ecology." *Environmental Ethics* 9(2), 1987, pp. 115–145.

_____. "The Neo-Stoicism of Radical Environmentalism." *Environmental Ethics* 11(4), 1989, pp. 293–326.

_____. "Postmodern Environmental Ethics: Ethics as Bioregional Narrative." *Environmental Ethics* 11(2), 1989, pp. 117–134.

Code, Lorraine. *Epistemic Responsibility*. Hanover, NH: University Press of New England, 1987.

Collard, Andree with Joyce Contrucci. *Rape of the Wild: Man's Violence Against Animals and the Earth*. Bloomington: Indiana University Press, 1988.

Devall, Bill and George Sessions. *Deep Ecology: Living as If Nature Mattered*. Salt Lake City: Peregrine Smith Books, 1985.

Eisler, Riane. "The Gaia Tradition and the Partnership Future: An Ecofeminist Manifesto." In Irene Diamond and Gloria Feman Orenstein, eds., *Reweaving the World: The Emergence of Ecofeminism*. San Francisco: Sierra Club Books, 1990.

Ferry, Luc. *The New Ecological Order*. Carol Volk, trans. Chicago: University of Chicago Press, 1992.

Harding, Sandra. *The Science Question in Feminism*. Ithaca, NY: Cornell University Press, 1986.

Leopold, Aldo. "The Land Ethic." In *Sand County Almanac*. New York: Oxford University Press, 1987.

McDaniel, Jay B. *Earth, Sky, God, and Mortals: Developing an Ecological Spirituality*. Mystic, CT: Twenty-Third Publications, 1990.

Naess, Arne. "The Deep Ecological Movement: Some Philosophical Aspects." *Philosophical Inquiry* 8, 1986, pp. 10–13.

_____. "The Shallow and the Deep, Long-range Ecology Movement: A Summary." *Inquiry* 16, 1973, pp. 95–100.

Wenz, Peter S. "Ecology and Morality." In Harlan B. Miller and William H. Williams, eds., *Ethics and Animals*. Clifton, NJ: Humana Press, 1983.

Ecofeminism: New Philosophy or Ancient Wisdom?

Aiken, William. "Non-Anthropocentric Ethical Challenges." In Tom Regan, ed., *Earthbound: New Introductory Essays in Environmental Ethics*. New York: Random House, 1984.

Allen, Paula Gunn. "The Woman I Love Is a Planet; the Planet I Love Is a Tree." In Irene Diamond and Gloria Feman Orenstein, eds., *Reweaving the World: The Emergence of Ecofeminism*. San Francisco: Sierra Club Books, 1990.

Beauvoir, Simone de. *The Second Sex*. H. M. Parshley, trans. and ed. New York: Vintage Books, 1952.

Biehl, Janet. *Rethinking Feminist Politics*. Boston: South End Press, 1991.

Corrigan, Theresa. *And a Deer's Ear, Eagle's Song, and Bear's Graces: Relationships Between Animals and Women*. Pittsburgh: Cleis Press, 1990.

Corrigan, Theresa and Stephanie T. Hoppe. *With a Fly's Eye, Whale's Wit, and Woman's Heart: Animals and Women*. Pittsburgh: Cleis Press, 1989.

Daly, Mary. *Gyn/Ecology*. Boston: Beacon Press, 1978.

_____. *Pure Lust*. Boston: Beacon Press, 1984.

Diamond, Irene and Gloria Feman Orenstein, eds. *Reweaving the World: The Emergence of Ecofeminism*. San Francisco: Sierra Club Books, 1990.

Dinnerstein, Dorothy. "Survival on Earth: The Meaning of Feminism." In Judith Plant, ed., *Healing the Wounds: The Promise of Ecofeminism*. Santa Cruz, CA: New Society Publishers, 1989.

Easlea, Brian. *Science and Sexual Oppression: Patriarchy's Confrontation with Women and Nature*. London: Weidenfeld & Nicolson, 1981.

Fox, Warwick. "The Deep Ecology-Ecofeminism Debate and Its Parallels." *Environmental Ethics* 11(1), 1989, pp. 5–25.

Garry, Ann and Marilyn Pearsall, eds. *Women, Knowledge, and Reality*. Boston: Unwin Hyman, 1989.

Gray, Elizabeth Dodson. *Green Paradise Lost*. Wellesley, MA: Roundtable Press, 1981.

_____. *Sacred Dimensions of Women's Experience*. Wellesley, MA: Roundtable Press, 1988.

Griffin, Susan. *Pornography and Silence: Culture's Revenge Against Nature*. New York: Harper & Row, 1981.

_____. *Woman and Nature: The Roaring Inside Her*. New York: Harper & Row, 1978.

Kheel, Marti. "The Liberation of Nature: A Circular Affair." *Environmental Ethics* 7(2), 1985, pp. 135–149.

King, Ynestra. "The Ecology of Feminism and the Feminism of Ecology." In Judith Plant, ed., *Healing the Wounds: The Promise of Ecofeminism*. Santa Cruz, CA: New Society Publishers, 1989.

LaChapelle, Dolores. *Earth Wisdom*. Silverton, CO: Way of the Mountain Learning Center and International College, 1978.

Maccauley, David. "On Women, Animals and Nature: An Interview with Ecofeminist Susan Griffin." *APA Newsletter on Feminism and Philosophy* 90(3), Fall 1991, p. 118.

McDaniel, Jay B. *Of God and Pelicans: A Theology of Reverence for Life*. Louisville, KY: Westminster/John Knox Press, 1989.

Merchant, Carolyn. *The Death of Nature: Women, Ecology, and the Scientific Revolution*. San Francisco: Harper & Row, 1980.

Mies, Maria and Vandana Shiva. *Ecofeminism*. London: Zed, 1993.

Mills, Patricia Jagentowicz. *Woman, Nature, and Psyche*. New Haven, CT: Yale University Press, 1987.

Nordquist, Joan. "Ecofeminist Theory: A Bibliography." In *Social Theory: A Bibliographic Series* 36. Santa Cruz, CA: Reference and Research Services, 1994.

Ortner, Sherry B. "Is Female to Male as Nature Is to Culture?" In Mary Heather MacKinnon and Marie McIntyre, eds., *Readings in Ecology and Feminist Theory*. Kansas City, KA: Sheed and Ward, 1995.

Piercy, Marge. *Woman on the Edge of Time*. New York: Fawcett Crest Books, 1976.

Plant, Judith, ed. *Healing the Wounds: The Promise of Ecofeminism*. Santa Cruz, CA: New Society Publishers, 1989.

Ruether, Rosemary Radford. *New Woman/New Earth: Sexist Ideologies and Human Liberation*. New York: Seabury Press, 1975.

Salleh, Ariel Kay. "Deeper Than Deep Ecology: The Ecofeminist Connection." *Environmental Ethics* 6(1), 1984, p. 339.

Sessions, George. "The Deep Ecology Movement: A Review." *Environmental Review* 9(1), Spring 1987, p. 115.

Spretnak, Charlene. "Toward an Ecofeminist Spirituality." In Judith Plant, ed., *Healing the Wounds: The Promise of Ecofeminism*. Philadelphia, PA: New Society Publishers, 1989.

_____, ed. *The Politics of Women's Spirituality*. Garden City, NY: Anchor, 1982.

Starhawk. "Feminist, Earth-based Spirituality and Ecofeminism." In Judith Plant, ed., *Healing the Wounds: The Promise of Ecofeminism*. Philadelphia: New Society Publishers, 1989.

_____. "Power, Authority, and Mystery: Ecofeminism and Earth-based Spirituality." In Irene Diamond and Gloria Orenstein, eds., *Reweaving the World: The Emergence of Ecofeminism*. San Francisco: Sierra Club Books, 1990.

Warren, Karen J. "Feminism and Ecology." *Environmental Review* 9(1), Spring 1987, pp. 3–20.

_____. "Feminism and Ecology: Making Connections." In Mary Heather MacKinnon and Marie McIntyre, eds., *Readings in Ecology and Feminist Theology*. Kansas City, KA: Sheed and Ward, 1995.

_____. "Feminism and the Environment: An Overview of the Issues." *APA Newsletter on Feminism and Philosophy* 90(3), Fall 1991, pp. 110–111.

_____. "The Power and the Promise of Ecological Feminism." In Karen J. Warren, ed., *Ecological Feminist Philosophies*. Bloomington: Indiana University Press, 1996.

_____. "Taking Empirical Data Seriously: An Ecofeminist Philosophy Perspective." In Alison M. Jaggar, ed., *Living with Contradictions: Controversies in Feminist Social Ethics*. Boulder, CO: Westview Press, 1994.

Critiques of Ecofeminism

Auerbach, Judith. "The Intersection of Feminism and the Environmental Movement, or What Is Feminist About the Feminist Perspective on the Environment?" *American Behavioral Scientist* 37(8), August 1994, p. 1095.

Biehl, Janet, *Rethinking Feminist Politics*. Boston: South End Press, 1991.

King, Ynestra. "Engendering a Peaceful Planet: Ecology, Economy, and Ecofeminism in Contemporary Context." *Women's Studies Quarterly* 23, Fall/Winter 1995, p. 19.

Merchant, Carolyn. *Radical Ecology: The Search for a Livable World*. New York: Routledge, 1992.

Plumwood, Val. "Ecofeminism: An Overview and Discussion of Positions and Arguments." *Australian Journal of Philosophy* 64, supplement, June 1986, p. 135.

Ruddick, Sara. *Maternal Thinking: Toward a Politics of Peace*. Boston: Beacon Press, 1989.

Index

Abolitionist movement, 20–22
Absolutism, 238–239, 241–242
Adler, Alfred, 138
Advertising, 50–51
African American women. *See* Black
    women
Against Our Will: Men, Women, and
    Rape (Brownmiller), 223
Alcoff, Linda, 48
al-Hibri, Azizah, 75
Alienation, 5, 98–100, 124–126
    from body, 125, 252–253
    from nature, 54, 99, 269–270
American Woman Suffrage
    Association, 22
Ames, Jessie Daniel, 224
Amott, Teresa, 113–114
Androgyny, 31–35
    desirable traits, 51–52
    monoandrogyny, 34–35
    moral, 158
    radical feminist view of, 3, 47,
        53–61
    rejection of, 58–61
    self as integrated whole, 40
Anthony, Susan B., 21, 22
Ascher, Carol, 192
Association of Southern Women
    for the Prevention of Lynching,
    224
Atwood, Margaret, 78, 85
Autonomy, 14–15, 38–40

Balzac, Honoré de, 183
Barnard College sexuality conference,
    68–69
Bartky, Sandra Lee, 166–167, 188
Bartmann, Sarah, 220

Beard, Mary, 88
Beauvoir, Simone de, 6, 173–174, 195,
    252–254, 273, 304(nn 27, 32),
    305(n36)
Being and Nothingness (Sartre), 173–179,
    187
Bem, Sandra, 34
Benjamin, Jessica, 173
Benston, Margaret, 107–108, 110
Bergmann, Barbara, 109
Beyond God the Father: Toward a
    Philosophy of Women's Liberation
    (Daly), 56–58
Beyond Power (French), 54–56
"Beyond the Unhappy Marriage"
    (Young), 123–124
Bhasin, Kamla, 272–273
Biehl, Janet, 273
Biological differences, 35–38
    as destiny, 135, 138–140, 151,
        298–299(nn 24, 25)
    existential feminist view of, 179–180
    normative dualism and, 38–40
    See also Motherhood; Reproduction
Black women
    feminists, 216–218
    multiple jeopardy and, 217
    pornography and, 219–220
    rape and, 223–225
    sexism in black community and,
        218–219, 225
    sexual harassment and, 220–221
    See also Multicultural feminism
Body
    alienation from, 125, 252–253
    existential feminist view of, 179–180,
        184, 189–192
Boserup, Esther, 124